In the Shadow of the State

DA

D1109265

Critical Studies in Latin American and Iberian Cultures

SERIES EDITORS
James Dunkerley
John King

This major series – the first of its kind to appear in English – is designed to map the field of contemporary Latin American and Iberian cultures, which have enjoyed increasing popularity in Britain and the United States in recent years.

The series aims to broaden the scope of criticism of Latin American and Iberian cultures, which tend still to extol the virtues of a few established 'master' works, and to examine cultural production within the context of twentieth-century history. These clear, accessible studies are aimed at those who wish to know more about some of the most important and influential cultural works and movements of our time.

Other titles in the series

DRAWING THE LINE: ART AND CULTURAL IDENTITY IN CONTEMPORARY LATIN AMERICA by Oriana Baddeley and Valerie Fraser

PLOTTING WOMEN: GENDER AND REPRESENTATION IN MEXICO by Jean Franco

JOURNEYS THROUGH THE LABYRINTH: LATIN AMERICAN FICTION IN THE TWENTIETH CENTURY by Gerald Martin

MAGICAL REELS: A HISTORY OF CINEMA IN LATIN AMERICA by John King

MEMORY AND MODERNITY: POPULAR CULTURE IN LATIN AMERICA by William Rowe and Vivian Schelling

MISPLACED IDEAS: ESSAYS ON BRAZILIAN CULTURE by Roberto Schwarz

THE GATHERING OF VOICES: THE TWENTIETH-CENTURY POETRY OF LATIN AMERICA by Mike Gonzalez and David Treece

DESIRE UNLIMITED: THE CINEMA OF PEDRO ALMODÓVAR by Paul Julian Smith

JORGE LUIS BORGES: A WRITER ON THE EDGE by Beatriz Sarlo

THE MOTORCYCLE DIARIES: A JOURNEY AROUND SOUTH AMERICA by Ernesto Che Guevara

PASSION OF THE PEOPLE? FOOTBALL IN SOUTH AMERICA by Tony Mason

VISION MACHINES: CINEMA, LITERATURE AND SEXUALITY IN SPAIN AND CUBA, 1983–1993 by Paul Julian Smith

In the Shadow of the State

Intellectuals and the Quest for National Identity in Twentieth-century Spanish America

NICOLA MILLER

V

VERSO

London • New York

First published by Verso 1999
© Nicola Miller 1999
All rights reserved

The moral rights of the author have been asserted

Verso
UK: 6 Meard Street, London W1V 3HR
US: 180 Varick Street, New York, NY 10014–4606

Verso is the imprint of New Left Books

ISBN 1–85984–738–2
ISBN 1–85984–205–4 (pbk)

British Library Cataloguing in Publication Data
A catalogue record for this book is available from the British Library

Library of Congress Cataloging-in-Publication Data
A catalog record for this book is available from the Library of Congress

Typeset by SetSystems Ltd, Saffron Walden, Essex
Printed by Biddles Ltd, Guildford and King's Lynn

For Jeremy M.

Contents

Acknowledgements

Most of the research for this book was carried out with the help of a generous Personal Research Grant from the British Academy, which enabled me to make several extended visits to Spanish America. Additional funding for these trips came from University College London Graduate School, UCL Faculty of Social and Historical Sciences' Dean's Travel Fund, and UCL History Department's Hale Bellot Fund. I am grateful to all of them.

I would also like to thank my colleagues Christopher Abel, Mary Turner and Jason Wilson for their helpful comments upon earlier drafts of this book, and I am especially indebted to Jeremy Morgan for the care and attention with which he read the whole manuscript through more than once. His many valuable suggestions did much to improve the final text.

Unless stated otherwise, the translations in this book were done by the author and Caroline Williams. For Caroline's linguistic skills and her patience beyond the call of friendship, I would like to express my affectionate thanks. For repeatedly rescuing me from the vagaries of my computer, I shall be eternally obliged to Rachel Aucott and Simon Renton. I would also like to express my appreciation to Professors John North and David French, successively heads of the history department at UCL, for allowing me to take the time I needed to finish this book, and not subjecting me to the managerial performance targets that are becoming all too common in universities nowadays.

My thanks also go to staff at Verso, especially Jane Hindle and Felicity Rawlings. Last, but not least, I am very grateful to the academic editors of this series, James Dunkerley and John King, for their guidance, insight and encouragement through several drafts, without which this book would never have reached its final form.

Introduction

[T]he fate and independence of a people cannot be separated from the fate and independence of its intellectual 'elites'.[1]

Since the 1960s, when the Cuban Revolution and the novels of the literary 'boom' brought Spanish American politics and culture to the West's attention, two different interpretations of the role of Spanish American intellectuals in the formation of popular national identities have emerged. First, many of the 'boom' writers themselves, echoed by some Western literary critics, began to emphasize the distinctive contribution of intellectuals as 'keepers of the national consciousness'.[2] Implicit in this image of the intellectuals was the idea that they had played a leading role in the politics of their nations. This, too, is a claim that has primarily gained ground in the West since the 1960s: it is worth recalling that in an early sociological study, based on a symposium held in 1967, several of the contributors devoted much of their energy to refuting what was then the standard US stereotype of twentieth-century Spanish American intellectuals as effete aristocrats of the spirit who had made little if any contribution to the process of nation-building.[3] In contrast, the cosmopolitan novelists of the literary 'boom' publicly lamented the Spanish American 'tradition of the president–poet' which obliged them to become politically active to the detriment of their creative potential.[4] In the 1970s, the high profile of many Spanish American intellectuals in protesting against the unprecedently widespread human rights abuses perpetrated by military dictatorships strengthened the impression that the region's intellectuals had acted, by default, as substitutes for the structures of civil society.[5] This position was encapsulated by Carlos Fuentes when he suggested that, in the absence of a well-developed civil society, the Spanish American intellectual had 'foisted upon him' the responsibilities of acting as 'a tribune, a member of parliament, a labor leader, a journalist, a redeemer of his society'.[6]

Expressing an alternative view, several Spanish American intellectuals (and a few Western commentators) have argued that the promotion of a search for national identity was a self-legitimating device for the intellectuals themselves. César Graña, for example, attributed the idea that intellectuals were the 'bearers' of the spiritual, moral and symbolic repertory of society to 'the metaphysics of cultural frustration',[7] caused by a loss of elite status in the process of modernization. Arguing that '"historical destiny", "cultural integrity" and "national soul" [were] symbolic creations invented by intellectuals as a means of invoking a collective greatness of which they could become the oracles and mentors', he sought to illustrate that the construct of national identity was an 'endlessly tautological system'.[8] With its elaboration of inert popular stereotypes such as the stoic Indian and the heroic *gaucho* (River Plate cowboy/plainsman), he contended, the pursuit of cultural identity in an 'anguished language of anxiety and melancholy' constituted a strategy of infinite postponement which enabled Spanish American intellectuals to sustain an otherwise untenable position as mediators between the state and the masses.[9] As a result, he implied, vital questions of economic and political power were subsumed into existential speculation: 'we must not speak of what can be seen, heard or known, of what definitely *exists*. That's against the rules of the game. We must talk about what Latin America will be when it comes into being.'[10] From this perspective, intellectuals – far from fulfilling a representative role as 'the voice of the voiceless' – served to perpetuate a social order in which popular demands were ignored or repressed.

This book explores the role of intellectuals in the creation of popular national identities in twentieth-century Spanish America, seeking to isolate the factors that might lie behind two such contrasting evaluations of their contribution. My starting point was a hunch that the most probable scenario was that, in Eduardo Galeano's words, intellectuals were 'neither such gods nor such insects'.[11] One of the main issues at stake is the character of modernity in Spanish America.[12] The complexities of this debate are exemplified by the tension between Spanish American intellectuals' perception of themselves as 'ultra-modernizers' and their elaboration of national cultures drawing on pre-modern archetypes.[13] The conventional account of modernization in Spanish America hinges on the apparent paradox that while the region had a flourishing literary 'modernist' movement in the avant-garde of the 1920s, its 'modernity' was at that stage far behind Europe's. In consequence, the Spanish American *vanguardista* movements are deemed to be primarily derivative of European experience rather than a product of socio-economic change within the region itself. José Joaquín Brunner, for example, sees the intellectual developments of the 1920s as aberrations and argues that modernity arrived with the growth of the international media industry in the 1950s, effectively 'behind the backs of our intellectuals'.[14] Alternatively, the Spanish American avant-gardes have been reinterpreted as a distinctive response to incipient modernization on the periphery, with all its particular opportunities and constraints – influenced by European developments, but by no means wholly determined by them.[15] Beatriz Sarlo's term 'peripheral modernity' captures the uneven and dependent character of a historical process that is best thought of as one of modernity,[16] rather than predominantly of pre-modernity (as US modernization theorists and some Spanish American intellectuals used to suggest) or 'a sort of postmodernism *avant la lettre*', as some critics now hold.[17] In comparative terms, Spanish America was hardly unique in undergoing a historically fractured process of modernization: the region's history is distinctive because of its early decolonization, resulting in a lengthy experience of formal political sovereignty being compromised by economic dependence. The main hypothesis of this book is that intellectual life in Spanish America and, correspondingly, the role of the intellectual were both subject to the same 'peripheral modernization' as other sectors of Spanish American society.

Modernization brought about a fundamental realignment of power and knowledge in Spanish America, where for most of the nineteenth century no clear division had existed between intellectual and political spheres. The exclusivity of higher education had enabled a privileged minority (the *letrados*, or educated) from the socio-economic elite to combine intellectual and political authority. When, from the 1870s onwards, the process of modernization began to introduce a degree of professionalization into intellectual activity, opening up opportunities for people from outside the elites to earn a living (at least potentially) from intellectual work,[18] the changes involved were not solely economic, but also entailed an increasing separation of politics and culture. Traditions from the early to the mid-nineteenth century of hybrid roles such as the *caudillo–pensador* (leader – usually military – and thinker) and the *licenciado–político* (scholar–politician) may have helped to inform late-nineteenth-century formulations of a role that was specifically *intellectual*, but there was a crucial difference in that the newly self-identified 'intellectuals' were by definition marginal figures who, in contrast to their predecessors, felt excluded from state power. In Spanish America, those who aspired to fulfil the modern role of 'intellectual' found themselves confronting a market offering only highly restricted opportunities while at the same time being displaced from political office in a newly emerging type of state committed to modernization.

Throughout the region, the early twentieth century brought a transition from what Laurence Whitehead calls the 'oligarchic' state to the 'modernizing' state.[19] This terminology serves as a useful adaptation to the Spanish American context of Gramsci's distinction, drawn from European history, between an 'aristocratic' state governed by a 'closed caste' and a 'bourgeois' state which saw itself as 'capable of absorbing the entire society, assimilating it to its own cultural and economic level'.[20] In schematic terms, the main differences are as follows: the Spanish American oligarchic state was identified with the landed colonial families, export-led growth, European-dominated culture and exclusionary, primarily political nationalisms; the modernizing state came to be associated with the middle sectors, urban industrial interests (some of which were not so much a new bourgeoisie as the result of diversification by the oligarchy), import-substitution industrialization, and inclusionary nationalisms with a high economic, cultural and popular content. The important distinction between the European and the Spanish American experiences of modernity is that, while in Europe modernization was carried out by states closely identified with the interests of a secure, dominant bourgeoisie, in Spanish America modernization was attempted by states that came under conflicting pressures from comparatively weak and divided middle classes, from oligarchies that retained substantial economic power, and from the military. This absence of an established consensus on nation-building between the state and a strong, self-conscious bourgeoisie had marked consequences for Spanish American intellectuals.

As implied above, for the purposes of this analysis the noun 'intellectual' will be treated as a word with its own history rather than as a generic term. A fuller discussion of theoretical issues relating to the definition of 'intellectuals', particularly in a Spanish American context, can be found in Chapter 1, but a brief outline helps to elucidate the argument here. The first point concerns the importance of taking into account the circumstances in which the idea of 'an intellectual' initially became current in Spanish America during the early twentieth century, soon after the Dreyfus Manifesto of 1898 had popularized the term in France. Although Spanish Americans were certainly influenced by French usage, the comparison with France elicits an important distinction between these two contexts in which the concept of 'an intellectual' arose. In France, those who claimed to be 'intellectuals' did so in order to break out of the ghetto of increasingly specialized knowledge and reclaim the universal moral and critical authority of the *philosophes*. The term was new, but the function was not: in France, the role of the modern intellectual dated back to the Enlightenment, and the coining of the term served precisely as a reminder and a reassertion of a universalist position that was perceived to be under threat. In Spanish America, by contrast, adoption of the word was symptomatic of the fact that the conditions for professional intellectual life were only incipient; in other words, the resonance of the idea was dependent on a nascent modernity. A complex set of structural and ideological factors lay behind the gradual replacement of the nineteenth-century term *pensador* with the twentieth-century concept of an intellectual. The *pensadores* of the nineteenth century are not, therefore, considered here as intellectuals because they were operating in distinct socio-economic conditions that gave them a correspondingly differing conception of the relationship between power and knowledge. The *pensadores*, who were 'at once men of thought and men of action ... fighting men and nation-builders',[21] sought to have influence on specific issues because they were generally learned men; intellectuals, on the other hand, who sought to dedicate themselves to culture, had first to establish their distinction in a speciality in order to justify a bid for wider social influence. Far from recalling former glories, as in France, in Spanish America the use of the term 'intellectual' marked out a new role that had not previously existed.[22]

In the following chapters, the term 'intellectual' will be employed narrowly, as it is most commonly used in Spanish America, and not to refer, in the inclusive sense of a sociological category, to virtually anybody who has received higher education (lawyers, doctors, academics, teachers, engineers, and so forth). Instead, it will be used to identify those people Enrique Krauze epitomized as 'cultural *caudillos*' – people who have won recognition as intellectual leaders of their society.[23] The idea of a cultural *caudillo* captures the particularly close interrelationship between knowledge and power in Spanish America; it also hints at the persistence of a high degree of authoritarianism and personalism in the region's intellectual life. Above all, it invokes the element of charisma associated with being an intellectual, which is perhaps common to all less developed nations where education has remained a privilege rather than a right, but has been especially powerful in Spanish America because of the influence of liberalism and Romanticism. In any society, the processes of legitimation that determine that one person is deemed to be 'an intellectual' while another is not are complex and often elusive. As a starting point, we can identify three main constituencies involved: other intellectuals, the intelligentsia, and the masses, the respective importance of which varies with time and place, as do the criteria by which each grants recognition of intellectuality. Most of the people discussed in this book are creative writers, but 'intellectual' is not necessarily synonymous with 'writer'. Until the Second World War, it was in practice almost exclusively writers who were acknowledged as intellectuals in Spanish America, but in the 1950s some social scientists, particularly economists, began to be granted that status. Analysis of such shifts in the criteria for being deemed 'an intellectual' is, perhaps, more revealing about the relationship between power and knowledge in a particular society than any attempt to operate within a fixed definition of the term.

That said, this book does not adopt a position of complete relativism: the following criteria determined the selection of representative intellectuals for the purposes of this study. First, they had to have been national rather than local figures (and, by implication, urban rather than rural). Second, although the distinctions are admittedly fine, they were people who sought professional recognition for their intellectual work and whose texts were based on intellectual rather than political criteria – to be judged as examples of reasoned critical enquiry or creative mastery, not in terms of their success as polemic or propaganda. Figures like Fidel Castro or Che Guevara, who were primarily interested in achieving political rather than intellectual authority, and employed their writing to that end, were therefore excluded from this survey. Third, those included had all contributed to public debates on general social affairs (as distinct from confining themselves to their field of expertise) and used their established intellectual authority to make a successful bid for national influence. Those who restricted themselves to their specialisms and refrained from public comment on topical issues are not counted here as 'intellectuals': instead, they are classified as doctors, lawyers, economists, university lecturers, poets or novelists, as they would have been regarded in Spanish America during the period under discussion, and referred to collectively as 'the intelligentsia'. While it was possible to become an intellectual from any of these positions in the cultural hierarchy, merely occupying such a place did not in itself make someone an intellectual. Finally, those included as 'intellectuals' had to have maintained their independence (at least as an aim) from both church and state. Thus, leading Catholic theologians will not be discussed. The term 'intellectual' will be used below in the sense of an independent social critic.

It proved to be difficult for intellectuals to achieve independence from the state in twentieth-century Spanish America, partly because the market for their work was so limited, and partly because intellectuals who sought such independence were quickly identified as a threat – both by military officers (who in the early twentieth century developed their own institutions of professionalization) and by civilian politicians from the emerging middle sectors (whose claim to social status was largely founded upon their own educational achievements). The fate of Spanish American intellectuals remained bound up with the interventionist state, even when they defined themselves in opposition to it – not only because they were often dependent upon it for employment, but also because it offered the only route to the realization of their visions. Thus, the tradition of the Spanish American intellectual as national redeemer was sustained alongside the belief in the efficacy of state-led development. It lasted, therefore, well into the 1960s (when it was reinvented for the benefit of Western audiences during the literary 'boom'), but from then onwards became increasingly less plausible as the process of bureaucratic state expansion begun nearly half a century earlier collapsed into authoritarianism and debt crisis.

The decades from 1920 until 1970 can, therefore, legitimately be seen as a distinctive period in the cultural history of Spanish America,[24] and are the focus of this book. The discussion draws on five case studies: Argentina,

Chile, Cuba, Mexico and Peru. These countries were selected partly because all of them, at varying times, have been important centres of intellectual activity in the region, and partly because their diversity of historical experience, political formation and ethnic composition provides a broad basis for comparison.[25] The argument is comparative throughout – not least because, despite the varying intellectual traditions of each of the five countries, Spanish American intellectuals themselves repeatedly invoked the concept of a regional cultural community. Brazil is not included, on the grounds that it has a different intellectual and cultural tradition from the Spanish American countries, an argument to be explored more fully in the Conclusion. This book touches on the contribution of novelists or poets to national identity at a metaphorical level in their works of literature, but these issues have already been extensively analysed elsewhere,[26] and the main concern in what follows is with intellectuals' ideological and political roles. Part I of the book aims to illustrate how the condition of peripheral modernity affected the locales of intellectual life, focusing on the question of the relationship between the intellectuals and the state. Part II analyses the contributions made by intellectuals to three major subjects in the discourses of popular national identity: bi-culturalism, anti-imperialism and history. In conclusion, it will be suggested that the experiences of Spanish America require us to rethink in general some of our ideas about intellectuals and national identity. The theoretical background to these issues is the subject of Chapter 1.

Part I

Peripheral Modernity and Its Discontents

1

Intellectuals and National Identity:
Theoretical Perspectives

The nations of Spanish America have usually been relegated to the foot-
notes of comparative studies on nationalism. In contributions to the main
theoretical debates about the relative importance of ethnicity versus state-
building in nation formation, they are mentioned only as potential exceptions to the main line of an argument. This is the case with both Anthony
Smith's emphasis on ethnicity ('we should note the possibility of forming
nations without immediate antecedent *ethnie* ... [as in Latin America]')[1]
and Ernest Gellner's on statehood ('it is arguable that the political strength
of ... Latin Americans ... did suffer from the fragmentation of their
political [roof]').[2] Conventional periodization also sets Spanish America to
one side: historians have tended to distinguish between the older nations of
Europe which 'evolved' into national self-consciousness from the late eighteenth century onwards, and those nations that were more self-consciously
'created' after the Second World War in order to repudiate colonial rule in
Africa, Asia and the Caribbean. Spanish American experiences of nationhood, for all their interest as some of the world's earliest attempts to 'found'
nations, clearly do not conform to this pattern of two 'waves' of nationalism,
and have rarely been considered in their own right. The first comparative
work to devote more than a few pages to the region, indeed, to any part of
the Americas, saw their nationalism largely in terms of a by-product of
European experience, transferred from the Old World to the New.[3] Subsequent references to Spanish America were mainly confined to Mexico,
the components of whose national identity are more comparable to European experience than are those of the other Spanish American nations.
Mexico can call upon a pre-Columbian civilization as the ethnic basis for a
modern sense of nationality; the post-revolutionary Mexican state, with its
strong secularizing and educational drive to convert peasants into citizens
(or, at least, a skilled industrial labour force) is comparable with modern
France or Germany; so, arguably, is the role played by intellectuals, backed

by the state, in creating the cultural and ideological resources of national identity. Mexico aside, Spanish American examples were introduced by historians to support generalizations about other post-colonial nations.[4] While there are valid comparisons to be drawn about the ways that nation-alism has been used as a political tool by governments of less-developed countries seeking to resist the impositions of the more developed world, it is to do less than justice to the history of Spanish American nationalisms to treat them as merely confirmatory of other post-colonial experiences. Nation formation was a markedly different historical project in the early nineteenth century than in the ever more interdependent world created after 1945.[5] In general, the nations of Spanish America fit uneasily, if at all, into existing typologies of nationalism. Anthony Smith distinguishes three types of national identity, based on (1) ethnic heritage (for example, Greece); (2) civic rights (England, France); and (3) pluralism (the USA, Canada, Australia).[6] When we look at twentieth-century Spanish America, we might place Mexico, Bolivia and, stretching the point, Peru under the first heading.[7] In contrast, Argentina has neither a pre-colonial ethnic heritage nor a sustained tradition of civic rights, nor has it developed a 'pluralist' national identity, despite a history of immigration comparable in some respects with the USA, Canada and Australia. And where in any of the three categories identified by Smith would we place Chile, Cuba, Venezuela or Colombia?

Historians of nationalism typically adopt a comprehensive definition of intellectuals, including teachers, journalists and members of the liberal professions, who are perhaps more likely than the creative writers and philosophers traditionally identified as intellectuals to have acquired the skills necessary to the promotion of nationalism.[8] Such a collectivity is closer to the idea of an intelligentsia. It is widely accepted that intelligentsias played a prominent part in founding nationalist movements in countries that were decolonized after the Second World War. In nineteenth-century Russia and Germany, where the intelligentsia ascribed to themselves a specific role in nation creation, their involvement was equally evident. More recently, there has been extensive analysis of the role of intellectuals in creating the identities of the older nations. For almost everywhere, includ-ing the United States, the contribution of intellectuals has been found to be significant.[9] With respect to Spanish America, however, it has been customary to attribute the spread of a sense of nationality in these countries primarily to the state (the spread of popular education, greater administra-tive capacity to counter local power bases, the use of military conscription to instil patriotism) during the first half of the twentieth century and, since then, to the expansion of mass electronic media throughout most of the territories during the 1960s and 1970s. Are we to conclude, then, that the state was largely if not entirely responsible for nation-building in the region, and that Spanish American intellectuals played a negligible role in the development of national identities?

Who are 'the Intellectuals'?

To define 'an intellectual' is notoriously problematic. Broadly speaking, until the 1970s, theories about the function of intellectuals in society tackled the problem from two perspectives. On the one hand, sociologists, drawing on Weber's ideas, defined intellectuals primarily in terms of their relationship to knowledge.[10] According to this approach, intellectuals were, by the nature of their commitment to the pursuit of truth and their shared discourse of critical reason, distanced if not altogether divorced from society ('free-floating'), and not only could, but should, maintain a critical perspective on power. On the other hand, political theorists influenced by Marx and Lenin saw the position of intellectuals as determined mainly by their relationship to power; the most influential exponent of such an approach in the twentieth century was Gramsci.[11] In the 1970s, however, it increasingly came to be accepted that emphasizing either power or knowledge to the virtual exclusion of the other was inadequate, and that the role of intellectuals in society could be understood only in terms of the relationship between power and knowledge. This argument was made, with differing emphases, from within the Marxist tradition (Raymond Williams's development of cultural history), the sociological tradition (Pierre Bourdieu's work on cultural and political 'fields') and French post-structuralism (most notably by Michel Foucault).[12] The first part of this chapter assesses the strengths and weaknesses of Weberian, Gramscian and post-structuralist approaches as applied to Spanish America. It aims to illustrate the extent to which all of them are ultimately based upon analyses of European socio-economic and political structures and therefore make assumptions that are historically accurate only with respect to Europe. This by no means renders such theories irrelevant to Spanish America, given that European formations and traditions were historically a constitutive part of the region's societies, but it does imply that they cannot be transposed without careful qualification.

Regarding intellectuals and power, there are two main issues: their relationship to the state and their relationship to class. Gramsci's work, which is the most comprehensive attempt to address both those questions, was not widely known in Spanish America until the 1970s. It had first been introduced in Argentina, where comparisons with Italy were deemed particularly appropriate; a series of translated excerpts from the *Prison Notebooks* was published in Buenos Aires from 1958 to 1962. During the 1960s, Gramsci's ideas filtered through to Spanish American university communities, partly as a by-product of enthusiasm for Althusser's writings. But it was not until the 1970s that Spanish-language editions of Gramsci's work were readily available throughout the region. During the 1970s and 1980s, Gramscian terms such as 'hegemony', 'civil society', 'political society' and 'national–popular' came to dominate the discourse of the Spanish American Left, extending beyond intellectual circles (and even, at least in Mexico, becoming fashionable in government ranks).[13] Most important for the argument here, many Spanish American analyses since the 1970s of the role of intellectuals in the region have been influenced by Gramsci's ideas.[14]

According to the Argentine Marxist José Aricó, Gramsci's ideas initially excited interest among the region's intellectuals because he alleviated their sense of guilt for being privileged possessors of culture, and analysed how intellectuals could make best use of their cultural attributes in political struggle.[15] While this might seem, at first sight, to be yet another instance of the oft-noted tendency towards self-preoccupation among intellectuals, it does touch upon a crucial point concerning the conditions under which Spanish American intellectuals worked. They lacked not only the institutional and cultural resources enjoyed by their colleagues in Western Europe, but also the opportunities for direct political power open to their counterparts in the more recently decolonized nations. The welcome Gramsci's work received in Spanish America during the 1970s was largely attributable to the resonance of his main theoretical contribution: in Aricó's words, that the failure of intellectual models to reflect social reality should not be attributed, as it so often was, 'solely to the blindness [to reality] of the intellectuals, to their condition as a free-floating *intelligentsia*'.[16] In contrast to the liberal view of intellectuals as somehow 'above' or 'outside' society, Gramsci's position was that the condition of being an intellectual was *in itself* 'an integral part of the concrete materiality of those processes that constitute . . . societies'.[17] This is not to claim that socio-economic conditions mechanically determine consciousness, but rather that material circumstances can operate either to facilitate or to constrain the development of consciousness, while at the same time themselves being subject to modification by it. Gramsci argued that the complexity of this interaction was particularly acute in the case of intellectuals:

> The relationship between the intellectuals and the world of production is not as direct as it is with the fundamental social groups but is, in varying degrees, 'mediated' by the whole fabric of society and by the complex of superstructures, of which the intellectuals are, precisely, the 'functionaries'.[18]

This insight of Gramsci's lies at the heart of my own analysis of intellectuals and national identity in Spanish America. Expositions of Spanish American cultural history that over-emphasize the autonomy of ideas are not completely convincing,[19] not least because they neglect what has proved to be a major preoccupation of many intellectuals, namely political power. Equally, while the socio-economic conditions of intellectual life are important in shaping the opportunities – both cultural and political – available to intellectuals, it does not follow that they are all-determining. It would not be possible to explain the views of twentieth-century Spanish American intellectuals without taking into account that many of their ideas evolved in reaction to negative images of Spanish America propagated in Europe or the United States. This, in turn, was related to Spanish American intellectuals' need to win recognition within their own societies, but cannot entirely be reduced to it. Ideas in themselves carry weight, perhaps especially in situations of cultural dependency. What Gramsci identified as the 'necessary reciprocity' between ideas and social conditions is the most fruitful area of analysis.[20]

By the mid-1970s, the main appeal of Gramsci's ideas in Spanish America lay in the perception that they offered a route back to the study of *national* reality, a perspective that had been rejected or abandoned by orthodox Marxism-Leninism. The failure of guerrilla movements throughout the region in the 1960s and early 1970s prompted left-wing Spanish American intellectuals to re-evaluate many of their previous convictions about according priority to armed struggle and internationalism. Whereas classical Marxist theory had privileged class over all other historical actors, including the state, which the orthodox view deemed to be merely the agent of the ruling class, Gramsci dwelt on the importance of the state as a key variable in capitalist development, particularly in the late-industrializing countries. Many Spanish American intellectuals saw fruitful grounds for comparison between their own countries and conditions in what Gramsci referred to as 'peripheral capitalist States' (Italy, Poland, Spain and Portugal), which were classified with the West in Gramsci's famous distinction between Western and Eastern states.[21] In 'peripheral States', Gramsci argued, national unification had been late and incomplete, and constitution of a liberal state had resulted from a revolution from above rather than a revolutionary or reformist movement from below. Because these nations depended heavily upon foreign capital, he concluded, the 'peripheral' state never achieved the degree of autonomy enjoyed in advanced capitalist countries; for the same reason, the absence of a dominant, autonomous national class meant that the state operated in a social vacuum, protected by the military, thereby exacerbating the economic conditions favourable to the further penetration of foreign capital. It is not difficult to appreciate why Gramsci's thoughts on how to bring about social transformation under such conditions were welcomed by the Spanish American Left during the 1970s and 1980s.

Gramsci's conception of 'civil society' also appealed strongly to left-wing Spanish American intellectuals contending with the authoritarian military regimes that dominated the region during those decades. The term 'civil society' requires brief discussion here. It became the subject of sharp political contestation during the 1980s,[22] when the neo-liberal Right achieved ideological ascendancy in the United States, Britain and elsewhere. Thinkers of the New Right attached a highly positive value to 'civil society', arguing that it existed in absolute opposition to the state, and was the ultimate political benefit to be derived from stimulating free market forces. Exponents of such a view tended to emphasize the early-nineteenth-century liberal sense of civil society as 'atomized productive individualism based on private property'.[23] This economic understanding of the term originally arose from the separation between structures of production and institutions of power that took place in the early modern period, as Europe made the transition from feudal to industrializing societies. The concept of civil society as an economic sphere separate from and in opposition to the state was attacked by Marx as fundamentally fraudulent – in Gellner's exposition, as 'a facade for a hidden and maleficent domination' of the state by the owners of the means of production.[24] The idea of civil society later acquired primarily political connotations as it came to refer to private associations, in which participation was voluntary and periodically subject to reaffirmation (such as trade unions or political parties open to membership), and which as a matter of course made representations to the state but maintained themselves separately from its apparatus. In this sense, the term 'civil society' denoted 'a plurality of institutions – both opposing and balancing the state, and in turn controlled and protected by the state'.[25] The liberal view was that civil society should coexist in productive tension with the state rather than seek to erode it to a minimum, as the neo-liberals would wish. Largely because of the New Right's appropriation of the term and consequent attempts to restrict its application to purely private interests (Margaret Thatcher's famous claim, 'There is no such thing as society; there are only individual men and women and their families', was dependent on a neo-liberal conception of civil society, even if she took it to extremes in rejecting any notion of the collective), many on the Left remained suspicious of the idea of civil society into the 1980s. In Latin America, however, under the military dictatorships, the idea of civil society, introduced mainly through Gramsci, acquired emphatically positive connotations, implying possibilities for debate and participation which had been ferociously repressed by military regimes and long denied to ordinary citizens even by elected governments. From a comparative perspective, the social movements that emerged in Latin America during the 1980s and 'played an important political and social role in most of the transitions from authoritarian rule' have been highlighted as offering a potentially far more active model of civil society than has yet developed in the former socialist economies, where the notion of ' "building civil society" ' has been 'in effect reduced to a simple notion of ending state interference, state funding and state control'.[26]

Gramsci's use of the term 'civil society' was not completely clear or consistent (as was the case with several of his concepts, which is perhaps not altogether surprising given the conditions of hardship under which he developed them). At one point in the *Prison Notebooks*, he seemed to separate civil society from the state: 'What we can do, for the moment, is to fix two major superstructural "levels": the one that can be called "civil society", that is the ensemble of organisms commonly called "private", and that of "political society" or "the State".'[27] Such a separation was in line with the usual approach of both the liberal and the Marxist traditions, which simply attached different values (positive in the case of liberals, negative in the case of Marxists) to this historical separation of military and civil activities. Elsewhere, in contrast, Gramsci emphasized that civil society could function as part of the state, rather than, as in the liberal conception, in opposition to it. His best-known formulation of this idea was: 'the general notion of State includes elements which need to be referred back to the notion of civil society (in the sense that one might say that State = political society + civil society, in other words hegemony protected by the armour of coercion)'.[28] This theoretical inconsistency at least has the merit of drawing attention to the extent to which variations can occur in how far the state is prepared to cede ground to civil society. Gramsci shared Marx's basic conception of civil society as spurious. But more than his predecessors, and in response to later historical developments, especially in Europe, he argued for the need to recognize the importance of this alleged fiction in sustaining the rule of the bourgeoisie. The key area of scrutiny lay, Gramsci maintained, in 'the organic relations between State or political society and "civil society"'.[29] Moreover, he also implied that it was not necessarily the power or independence of the state that was a façade in relation to civil society, but that in some historical situations this relationship could be reversed, with civil society existing in a nominal form without any real independence from the state. The crucial sentence was: 'In Russia the State was everything, civil society was primordial and gelatinous; in the West, there was a proper relation between State and civil society, and when the State trembled a sturdy structure of civil society was at once revealed.'[30]

Gramsci's suggestion about the extent to which civil society could be absorbed by the state seems particularly apposite to Spanish American societies, and helps to avoid many of the problems inherent in trying to analyse the region in terms of a liberal concept of civil society which emerged in Europe. Ernest Gellner has suggested that the survival of civil society is crucially dependent upon certain historical developments (to name only a few: perpetual economic growth based on scientific innovation; the privatization of virtue after the Reformation; and the creation of a culture in which, despite specialization of labour, education facilitated a range of employment prospects and therefore social mobility).[31] Such conditions, to date, have been fully realized only in some European nations, the United States and a relatively small number of other 'developed' countries. In Spanish America, the economic decentralization upon which the development of civil society is held to depend never fully took place; in the absence of a unified and self-conscious bourgeoisie, the state assumed the role of entrepreneur. While Spanish American countries have certainly experienced, to varying degrees, the political centralization that is deemed to be a precondition for civil society, Gellner's associated criteria of account-ability, rotation of governance and not disproportionate rewards for politi-cians have been met only intermittently, and fallibly at that. Yet the strong liberal tradition meant that some idea of civil society was constantly present in twentieth-century Spanish America, even if the term itself was not necessarily used, and even if it functioned in practice only for limited periods. Gramsci's flexible conception of the relationship between state and civil society is helpful here. It enables us to bridge the long gap between the early twentieth century, when it was realistic to talk of an incipient, albeit precarious, civil society in at least some Spanish American countries, and the region's generalized return to elected rule in the 1980s, when the idea of civil society acquired unprecedented value. The intervening period saw the region's governments demonstrate an increasing willingness and capacity first to pursue populist policies – which by their nature were aimed at eliminating civil society by bringing about an identification of the people with the state – and later to use force to preclude the emergence of political pluralism. But neither populism nor repression succeeded in eliminating completely the (liberal) ideal of civil society as a countervailing force to the state. Gramsci's formula of an overlapping relationship between the state and civil society provides a means of understanding how these complex processes operated in societies where the gap between an abstract ideal of mutual exclusion and concrete practices of incorporation was especially wide. His idea of civil society as the result of human will and struggle in the battle of ideas, distinct from the liberal representation of it as a 'natural' state of affairs, is also useful to thinking about Spanish America.

However, the ways in which Gramsci's ideas about intellectuals and class have been applied to Spanish America highlight several problems inherent in adopting his approach completely in any analysis of the region's cultural history. As is well known, Gramsci questioned the assumption that intellec-tuals could be defined by any reference to the allegedly 'intrinsic nature of intellectual activities', arguing that 'there is no human activity from which every form of intellectual participation can be excluded: *homo faber* cannot be separated from *homo sapiens*'.[32] Besides, he added, outside of working life, everyone 'carries on some form of intellectual activity, that is, . . . is a "philosopher", an artist, a [person] of taste'.[33] The factor that decided whether someone was to be categorized as an intellectual or a manual worker was social function: in his famous formulation, 'All men are intellectuals, one could therefore say: but not all men have in society the function of intellectuals.'[34] The key question, for Gramsci, then became to ascertain how those who fulfilled an intellectual function were related to the class structure. All intellectuals could be divided into two main categories, he suggested: those who were ready to acknowledge their class position ('organic' intellectuals) and those who were not ('traditional' intellectuals). By claiming that their activities were autonomous from society, Gramsci argued, 'traditional' intellectuals unavoidably acted as accomplices of the ruling group in the battle for hegemony: 'The intellectuals are the dominant group's "deputies" exercising the subaltern functions of social hegemony and political government.'[35] Even when they were critical of the status quo, Gramsci implied, 'traditional' intellectuals ultimately allowed the dominant value system to shape the terms of their debates. The 'whole of idealist philosophy [could] . . . be defined as the expression of that social utopia by which the intellectuals think of themselves as "independent", autonomous, endowed with a character of their own'.[36] By further implication, the ruling class could then congratulate itself on its capacity to tolerate dissent while remaining in power unthreatened by any serious challenge to its values. One of Gramsci's major theoretical contributions was to oblige historians interested in cultural and ideological change to extend the category of 'the intellectuals' beyond what he called 'the traditional and vulgarized type of the intellectual . . . given by the man of letters, the philosopher, the artist'.[37] Under the rubric of 'traditional' intellectuals he included not only philosophers, literati, scientists and other academics, but also lawyers, doctors, teachers, clerics and military leaders.[38]

Gramsci's argument that far more people than those classically thought of as intellectuals play a part in cultural processes is undeniably valid in general terms. But Spanish America's historical experience raises two problems concerning his very broad category of 'traditional' intellectuals who allegedly uphold the hegemony of the ruling class. First, Gramsci's theory depends upon the Marxist interpretation of Europe's historical experience, according to which feudalism and aristocratic rule were replaced by capitalism and bourgeois rule. These processes were partially but not fully replicated in Spanish America. Second, his theory subsumes questions of status to class interests. Spanish American examples suggest that, as Weber argued, status cannot satisfactorily be reduced to class; this may especially be the case in those countries where class formation was far less clearcut or consolidated than in Europe.

Spanish America's experience of 'peripheral modernity' complicates Gramsci's distinction between the 'traditional' intellectuals who act as unwitting accomplices of the ruling group and the 'organic' intellectuals who acknowledge their position within the class structure. In Spanish America, the early twentieth century saw the onset of a power struggle between the oligarchy and a rising bourgeoisie which, with the exception of Mexico, is still not fully resolved. The term 'bourgeoisie' in itself implies more class coherence and self-consciousness than was present anywhere in the region at that time. As Spanish American economies made the uneasy transition from exportation of raw materials and otherwise largely subsistence agrarian production to industrialization and modern commercial agriculture, the old oligarchic families often simply diversified into the new sectors of the economy. Whereas in Europe and the United States, intellectuals could position themselves at a distance both from a clearly differentiated consumerist middle class and from a state geared to bourgeois interests, in most Spanish American countries the situation has been more complex. Throughout the region, the entrepreneurial dynamic customarily associated with a 'bourgeoisie' has been located either in the state or outside the national territory. At times, twentieth-century Spanish American intellectuals found themselves allying with the state precisely because they opposed the socio-economic dominance of the oligarchy and/or foreign corporations.

The issue of Spanish American intellectuals' relationship to class has been further clouded by their own tendency, from the 1960s onwards, to use Gramsci's idea of an 'organic' intellectual to refer to any intellectual who expressed support for social revolution. This was perhaps not surprising given that many Spanish Americans came to Gramsci through their reading of Althusser.[39] In *For Marx*, Althusser mentions Gramsci several times, but does not pursue any extended exposition of his ideas. On intellectuals, he confines himself to the following imprecise observation: 'it should be realized that Gramsci's concept of the *intellectual* is infinitely wider than ours, that is, it is not defined by the idea intellectuals have of themselves, but by their social *role* as *organizers* and (more or less subordinate) *leaders*'. To illustrate this, Althusser quotes one of Gramsci's own loosest formulations: 'all the members of a political party should be regarded as intellectuals . . . what [matters] is their function, which is to direct and organize, that is, it is educational, which means intellectual'.[40] In similar vein, Oscar Terán drew a generic distinction between an '*intelectual comprometido*' (politically committed intellectual) who addressed himself to his peers and an 'organic intellectual' who directed himself to the people or the working class 'in order to draw support from them and to fight their cause'.[41] In a discussion of Argentina, Oscar Landi equated the organic intellectual with the party militant of the 1970s.[42] Likewise, Gabriel García Márquez, looking back from the late 1980s, claimed: 'Only now can we see how organic we really were, and how useful this whole intellectual support for the Cuban Revolution actually was.'[43]

Gramsci does not spell out the distinction, but a careful reading of the *Prison Notebooks* suggests that, for him, 'organic' intellectuals were *not* equivalent to 'traditional' intellectuals recruited to the ranks of the rising class. He argued that all social groups that played a historically significant economic role created their own intellectuals to justify that role:

> Every social group, coming into existence on the original terrain of an essential function in the world of economic production, creates together with itself, organically, one or more strata of intellectuals which give it homogeneity and an awareness of its own function not only in the economic but also in the social and political fields.[44]

Such people, according to Gramsci, made no claim to be 'apart' from society; they directed their intellectual activity entirely towards furthering the interests of their own class. So, for example, the 'organic' intellectuals of the entrepreneurial bourgeoisie were 'the industrial technician, the specialist in political economy, the organizers of a new culture, of a new legal system, etcetera'.[45] The organic intellectuals of the proletariat, by analogy, would be people of working-class origin who had educated themselves in order to use the language of their bourgeois rulers to express the interests of the working class and advance their fortunes in the struggle for hegemony. During the 1960s and 1970s, some Spanish American intellectuals of petty-bourgeois or bourgeois social origins claimed to be organic in the sense that they had identified with the plight of the masses, but this was not at all what Gramsci had meant by 'organic' intellectuals. He distinguished between the organic intellectuals of any rising class (including presumably, the working class) and those traditional intellectuals who had been recruited to its cause:

> One of the most important characteristics of any group that is developing towards dominance is its struggle to assimilate and to conquer 'ideologically' the traditional intellectuals, but this assimilation and conquest is made quicker and more efficacious the more the group in question succeeds in simultaneously elaborating its own organic intellectuals.[46]

In his writings on education, also from 1932 (which are separated from the section on intellectuals in the most commonly used English translation of the *Prison Notebooks* but published together in the standard Italian version),[47] Gramsci made it clear that his main concern was with the question of how to create intellectuals of the working class. Without a change in the schooling system, Gramsci argued, the battle for hegemony was already lost, because 'school is the instrument through which intellectuals of various levels are elaborated', and 'each social group has its own type of school, intended to perpetuate a specific traditional function, ruling or subordinate'.[48] In order to overcome the respective advantages and disadvantages that children from prosperous, urban backgrounds enjoyed over those living in rural poverty, Gramsci proposed a system of fully comprehensive state education (the 'common school'), which he envisaged as 'organized like a college, with a collective life by day and by night', so that '[t]he entire function of educating ... the new generations ceases to be private and becomes public; for only thus can it involve them in their entirety, without divisions of group or caste'.[49] While he did not underestimate the problems involved – 'If our aim is to produce a new stratum of intellectuals, including those capable of the highest degree of specialization, from a social group which has not traditionally developed the appropriate attitudes, then we have unprecedented difficulties to overcome' – Gramsci concluded that these issues were 'extremely acute'.[50] He maintained that, '[i]n the modern world, technical education, closely bound to industrial labour even at the most primitive and unqualified level, must form the basis of the new type of intellectual'.[51]

The idea of 'organic intellectuals' of the proletariat was founded, then, on the premiss that workers had access to formal education. Such opportunities were extremely rare in Spanish America until after the Second World War, and ever since have remained very limited beyond secondary level. In addition, given that Spanish American income differentials have remained large, it was not always easy for a student from a poor background to resist the process of embourgeoisement that becoming educated implies in most modern societies. If such a person then no longer wished to identify with the working class of his origin, he would cease to meet the criteria for being considered an organic intellectual of the proletariat. The key factor that made it possible for members of the working class to remain intellectuals *of* their class was, according to Gramsci, the existence of a revolutionary party. Thus, there was no such thing as an organic intellectual of the peasantry:

> ... the mass of the peasantry, although it performs an essential function in the world of production, does not elaborate its own 'organic' intellectuals, nor does it 'assimilate' any stratum of 'traditional' intellectuals, although it is from the peasantry that other social groups draw many of their intellectuals and a high proportion of traditional intellectuals are of peasant origin.[52]

From this perspective, very few Spanish American intellectuals actually conformed to Gramsci's definition of an organic intellectual of the working class. One exception was the founder of the Chilean Socialist Workers' Party (POS) (later the Communist Party), Luis Recabarren (1876–1924), a printing worker who wrote plays and poetry, and contended that 'True Socialism [would] always be revealed by its exquisitely cultured ways'.[53] But the overwhelming majority of the intellectuals who operated at a national level in twentieth-century Spanish America were bourgeois or petty-bourgeois both by birth and by chosen lifestyle, whatever their political sympathies. As the left-wing Uruguayan writer Mario Benedetti observed in 1971: 'we have all been brought up in a social and pedagogic context wholly dominated by the bourgeoisie'.[54] The situation may have been different at local level, although all too often it is assumed that 'organic' is equivalent to 'local' or 'rural', whereas there is no indication that this was what Gramsci intended either. On the contrary: Gramsci's view was that '[i]ntellectuals of the rural type [were] for the most part "traditional"'.[55] Whether or not one accepts this contention that provincial intellectuals tended to be 'traditional' (the rather scanty evidence that we have suggests that they were often active in revolutionary or reformist movements), it remains the case that locale should not be confused with class position. A schoolteacher or priest who acted as an ideologue in a rural community might have been just as bourgeois or petty-bourgeois in background as a famous novelist who achieved international recognition: the difference lay in their respective spheres of operations – local versus national or international – not in their class differences. Overall, while Gramsci suggests that the organic intellectuals of one historical period could form the basis of the traditional intellectuals of subsequent eras, nowhere does he imply (despite his overall emphasis on voluntarism) that traditional intellectuals could make themselves organic. His view was that those traditional intellectuals who wished to support the cause of the proletariat should join the revolutionary political party, which he saw as 'responsible for welding together the organic intellectuals of a given group . . . and the traditional intellectuals'.[56]

This leads us to a final difficulty in applying Gramsci's categories of intellectuals to Spanish America. How are we to account for those bourgeois or petty-bourgeois writers, philosophers and academics who identified themselves not necessarily specifically with the proletariat but, more broadly, with the cause of 'the people'? When Gramsci looked at Latin America in the early 1930s, he saw only a comparatively small sector of traditional intellectuals: members of the clergy and the military, both tied to the oligarchy. By that time, however, Spanish America had already produced José Martí, Juan B. Justo, Julio Antonio Mella, José Carlos Mariátegui, César Vallejo, Víctor Raúl Haya de la Torre, and so forth, all of whom had committed themselves to political struggle against the oligarchy. Since all of these intellectuals joined or, indeed, founded political parties intended to develop a mass base, they could be described in Gramscian terms as 'traditional' intellectuals recruited to the party of the revolution. This was a category of intellectuals that Gramsci mentioned in passing, but did not discuss in any detail. It still leaves open the question of how to account for the status of figures like José Vasconcelos, a Hispanophile and in many ways a conservative thinker who nevertheless worked for the post-revolutionary Mexican government in the cause of popular education, or Emilio Roig de Leuchsenring, who did not join the Cuban Communist Party founded by his contemporaries but whose work on anti-imperialism made a major contribution to the cause of Cuban popular nationalism. Nevertheless, it might be argued that during the period that Gramsci was analysing, there were few Spanish American cases that could not be accounted for by his basic framework of traditional intellectuals, organic intellectuals, and traditional intellectuals who joined the party of revolution.

The picture changed from the 1930s onwards. Among at least one sector of 'traditional' intellectuals, namely writers, and, increasingly after the Second World War, academics, identification with the people became a common political position. Only in Argentina did an important group of intellectuals continue to sustain into the 1950s the idea of the apolitical intellectual, and, in response, many other Argentine intellectuals who did become politicized chose to reject the label of 'intellectual'.[57] The espousal of the cause of the people by an admittedly numerically small (but archetypal) group of Spanish American intellectuals arose partly out of their preoccupation with national identity. As Jorge Castañeda has pointed out, it was glaringly obvious in the Spanish America of the 1920s that the mass of the people (poor, ill-educated and perceived by the elites to be ethnically distinct and inferior) were excluded from the nations in which they were theoretically sovereign.[58] It followed that: 'Anyone who [was] socially minded [had to] be nationalistic, since focusing on the "social" inevitably [implied] emphasizing the recapture of the confiscated nationality, the nation sequestered' by foreign-oriented elites.[59] During the 1940s, 1950s and 1960s, to link the causes of national identity and social justice became standard practice among this sector of 'traditional' intellectuals throughout the region. Most of them did not join political parties, perhaps mainly because the parties to which intellectuals were sympathetic offered no route to real influence in an era dominated by populism. Instead, they tried to enlist the prestige attached to their very status as intellectuals in support of the causes of social justice and popular nationalism. This was true of all the leading novelists of the 1960s literary 'boom': Carlos Fuentes, Julio Cortázar, Gabriel García Márquez and others were all champions of the Cuban revolution, while none of them belonged to political parties in his own country. They were not 'organic', at least not in Gramsci's sense of the term; they were members of the educated bourgeoisie – and hence 'traditional' intellectuals – who adopted the cause of the masses without going so far as to be fully recruited to political militancy. Indeed, it could be argued that the assumption of the role of 'organic' intellectual by Spanish American intellectuals who were actually 'traditional' in Gramsci's sense helped to perpetuate myths of national identity that obscured class divisions.

Does this necessarily imply, then, that they should all be thought of as 'traditional' intellectuals who, unwittingly or not, furthered the interests of the ruling class?

Many observers would say that it does. Spanish American intellectuals have often been reproached for alleged complicity with their class of origin (whether the oligarchy or the bourgeoisie). In a particularly scathing attack, Victor Alba argued that the nationalism of these intellectuals was 'a simple diversionary tactic – first, as regards the uneconomic and inhuman in the social structure and, also, with regard to their own mediocrity'.[60] They have also been accused of pretension in claiming to speak for the masses 'without fully mobilizing them, naturally, either in reality or in literature, and often enough without the masses even hearing them'.[61] Both these arguments to some extent strike a responsive chord, but neither is wholly convincing. Castañeda has observed that one of the major impediments to nation-building in Spanish America was that it required a popular constituency, which in turn entailed recognition by nationalists of that constituency's social demands, and therefore at least an implicit challenge to the elites.[62] This dynamic set up a complex series of shifting relationships between the state, the elites, the intellectuals and the masses in the development of national identities in twentieth-century Spanish America. The question of Spanish American intellectuals' class position has been complicated by the region's economic dependency and its peripheral modernity. The consequences of these historical conditions (recalling Gramsci's own central insight that intellectuals themselves are not above socio-economic processes but part of them) are obscured by a typology such as Gramsci's that is founded on the premiss that intellectual allegiances will ultimately be determined by class origin.

This in turn raises the question of the status of intellectuals, and brings us to consider the relevance to Spanish America of Weberian theories which sought to define intellectuals in terms of their relationship to knowledge. Gramsci's main critique of this approach remains convincing: it is highly problematic to identify intellectuals as people with certain allegedly innate special qualities. In the first place, it is impossible to define with any precision attributes such as 'an unusual sensitivity to the sacred [or] an uncommon reflectiveness about the nature of their universe';[63] and, second, it is hard to see why they should not be present in a person who had received little or no formal education. As Gramsci argued, all people use their intellects to some extent: the difference is one of degree, not of kind. Although, at least in modern times, many intellectuals have claimed a universal dimension to their activities, attempts to identify absolutist constituents of intellectuality are always likely to encounter exceptions. Theories of intellectuals based on their relationship to knowledge tend to lead to very broad definitions of 'an intellectual' or even the abandonment of a definition altogether for a taxonomy of different types of intellectual. Writing on Mexico, for example, James Cockcroft defines intellectuals as 'persons who possess, and continually make use of, an advanced education and relatively high standards of logic, criticism, and sustained ideological or technical conversation, acquired through either university instruction, professional training, or self-education'.[64] This leads him to include Francisco Madero (1873–1913), the wealthy landowner and leader of the campaign (at first political, later military) that launched the Mexican revolution in 1910–11. Despite the publication of one book cautiously criticizing the Porfiriato (dictatorship of Porfirio Díaz),[65] Madero certainly did not consider himself an intellectual and he was not generally regarded as such by his contemporaries.

With the failure to be definitive about intellectuality, however, there has perhaps been too much of a tendency to neglect the cultural sources of an intellectual's legitimation, and to accept the Gramscian view of them all as ideologues. The acquisition of knowledge is invariably one component of being an intellectual, even if the type of knowledge that acquires social prestige may vary widely in different cultural contexts. The Argentine critic Beatriz Sarlo has defined an intellectual as someone who combines a vocation for politics with 'the desire to know',[66] a formulation that captures the non-academic hue of intellectuality in Spanish America, where universities have traditionally been associated with the colonial legacies of scholasticism and obscurantism. In his inaugural speech as a member of the Peruvian Academy of Language in 1977, Mario Vargas Llosa observed, 'The words "academy" and "academic" . . . still seem to me to be closely related to Spanish purism, conservatism and Catholicism.'[67] Not coincidentally, one key element in securing recognition as an intellectual in Spanish America – especially during the early part of the twentieth century – was creativity. Those who had published a written text of literary merit were granted a public platform that an average lawyer, medical practitioner or teacher was not. The potential of their social function as intellectuals was thereby greatly enhanced. This emphasis on creative writing was a result both of the historical power of the written word in Spanish America, and of the legacy of late Romanticism, with its emphasis on prophetic genius. Pierre Bourdieu has argued persuasively that the Romantic idea of individual creativity was a myth, but it was a none the less powerful one. Chapter 3 discusses its influence on the development of archetypes of the intellectual in Spanish America.

A second criterion of intellectuality in Spanish America for most of the twentieth century was universality. Being a member of the liberal professions (a specialism) has tended to rule out a Spanish American for consideration as an intellectual: in Daniel Cosío Villegas's words, 'the doctor, the lawyer, the economist, the engineer, the agronomist etcetera . . . are not intellectuals'.[68] The claim to universalism has been a particularly marked aspect of

Spanish American intellectuals' own definitions of their role. The controversy provoked by many of Octavio Paz's pronouncements on Mexican society can partly be explained by the fact that he staked his claim to authority on being a universal intellectual, not a specialist, and therefore sparked off 'fiery polemics generated by sociologists, political scientists or historians, all guardians of their highly specialised fields'.[69] The distinction upheld in Spanish America between professionals and intellectuals was nowhere revealed more clearly than after what became known as the 'Padilla affair'. In 1971, from 20 March to 25 April, the Cuban government imprisoned the poet Heberto Padilla, who subsequently publicly denounced himself and close associates for counterrevolutionary activities. To many among the literati of both Europe and Spanish America, this was too close for comfort to Stalinist practice, and they publicly called upon Castro to moderate his position and respect cultural freedom. When this plea met with no response, some of them (although by no means all) chose to withdraw their support for the Cuban revolution.[70] The important point for my argument here is that, in a major speech shortly afterwards, Castro inveighed against the idea that the term 'intellectual' should apply only to a small group of 'sorcerers' which had 'monopolized the title of intellectual', disregarding 'the teachers, the engineers, the technical experts, the researchers'.[71] In other words, he expanded the category of intellectuals to include the professionals who would normally be excluded in Spanish America, in a specific attempt to shatter the aura surrounding those literary luminaries who had turned against Cuba.

To make the term 'intellectual' synonymous with 'ideologue' – as Gramsci does – neglects crucial issues concerning the processes of self-identification and recognition of 'intellectuals' within different societies. It also results in a confusion of intellectual and political authority. Many Spanish American political leaders have functioned as ideologues, in the sense that they have communicated their own distinctive visions of society, but few would consider that they all commanded sufficient cultural capital to qualify as 'an intellectual', although the majority possessed an academic title as a result of being university graduates (Fidel Castro, for example, could use the title 'Dr' because of his law degree). In Spanish America, such titles confer social rather than intellectual distinction; as Carlos Fuentes recalled being advised by Alfonso Reyes, 'A title is like the handle on a cup; without it, no-one will pick you up.'[72] In any case, Octavio Paz's distinction between intellectuals and ideologues suggests that cultural capital can be lost as well as gained:

> Intellectuals in government cease to be intellectuals; although they may continue to be cultured, intelligent and even honourable, in accepting the privileges and responsibilities of office they substitute ideology for criticism. It is one thing to

be an ideologue for a regime . . . and quite another to be an intellectual in the modern sense of the word.[73]

Gramsci's work had a great value in reminding us that cultural functions in society are carried out by a far broader range of people than are usually thought of as 'intellectuals'. But it still remains the case that in twentieth-century Spanish America, few of the people recognized as 'intellectuals' have qualified for the label of 'organic', and few of Gramsci's 'traditional intellectuals' (from the clergy or the military) have been regarded in their own societies as 'intellectuals'. Sociological studies concentrating on the issues of knowledge and status, and political analyses emphasizing power relationships, both yield insights about the social position of Spanish American intellectuals, but neither approach is in itself adequate to stand alone as a theoretical framework for analysing the role of intellectuals in the region.

During the 1970s, especially in France, the theoretical emphasis in debates about the role of intellectuals shifted to the idea that the category of 'the intellectuals' was historically and culturally conditioned. Bourdieu, for example, argued that the behaviour of intellectuals was influenced by both class *and* status considerations, some of which were complementary and others of which were in conflict, at least for part of the time. His findings, based on a broad sample of bourgeois intellectuals in France, were that in a potentially revolutionary situation such as the late 1960s, intellectuals (by which he primarily meant university academics) tended to behave according to class interests.[74] But the difficulty in applying this kind of approach to Spanish America is that what Bourdieu referred to as the 'intellectual field' was clearly defined and highly institutionalized in France, whereas in Spanish America it was not. In France, the route to cultural distinction traversed 'membership of the Académie Française and mention in the *Larousse*, publication in a paperback series (Gallimard's 'Idées' or Seuil's 'Points') [which conferred] a kind of classic status, membership of the editorial committee of intellectual reviews, and finally connections with the popular media, television and widely read weeklies (*Le Nouvel Observateur*)'.[75] Apart from the periodicals, there was no real equivalent of this anywhere in Spanish America. While French intellectuals had too much at stake, both in class and professional terms, to make it worth their while to join the revolutionary struggle, the choice was weighted rather differently in Spanish America. Mario Vargas Llosa drew exactly this contrast when he argued that Latin American intellectuals had nothing to lose by fighting for national liberation because although a French intellectual might well have cause to lament the consequent loss of the cultural achievements of bourgeois society, Latin American ruling classes had been responsible for creating only 'illiterate countries, lacking in culture, with a literary or artistic life which is [at best] embryonic and [at worst] alienating, without writers, without publishers'.[76] In Spanish America during the 1960s, some middle-class intellectuals became ardent proponents of, and in some cases active participants in, revolutionary militancy – although it was primarily students rather than intellectuals who actually followed Régis Debray's injunction to take up arms. In societies where the 'intellectual field' was relatively precariously defined and maintained, the potential for conflict between defending a class loyalty and safeguarding a position as an intellectual (which might in itself be buttressed by a degree of political commitment at odds with class origin) was exacerbated. It is noteworthy that the two decades in which Spanish American intellectuals were most active in revolutionary politics, the 1920s and the 1960s, were the same decades in which significant socio-economic changes offered them new but tantalizingly restricted opportunities. The 1920s were a time of emerging but by no means assured intellectual autonomy; in the 1960s, an expansion of the universities gave intellectuals a mass base for the first time, although their influence was by then already being undercut by the growth of the mass electronic media. Beatriz Sarlo contends that Bourdieu's distinction between political and intellectual 'fields' is dependent upon a separation of power and knowledge that simply did not happen within Spanish American societies to the extent that it did in Western Europe. Moreover, Bourdieu's ideas also assume integrated national societies, and cannot take into account the phenomenon of cultural dependency, whereby the source of ultimate cultural validation in Spanish America lies outside the domain of the nation, and instead in the more developed world. This phenomenon was especially acute not – as might have been expected – in those countries where modernization was least advanced, but precisely 'in those countries of the subcontinent where the levels of modernization and cultural secularization were highest',[77] which made them more disposed to nurture a 'European superego'.[78]

   Some European intellectuals have suggested that intellectuals in developing nations enjoy a high degree of autonomy from society and an enviable scope for clarity of response to the status quo. In 1985, Jean Baudrillard encapsulated this view when he argued, 'Intellectuals of the Third World have the privilege of holding a clear critical position and of having the possibility of struggle, which is also totally clear. Confusion, in their case, is not possible.'[79] By implication, they somehow enjoyed greater room for political or, at least, ideological, manoeuvre than their counterparts in Western Europe. In the case of Spanish America, this proposition was and remains highly misleading. There is a valid analytical point underlying it, namely that those Spanish American intellectuals who dissented from the status quo tended to operate in a social vacuum, confronting very real difficulties in disseminating their ideas among the largely illiterate and fragmented masses. As a result, Alain Touraine has argued, Spanish American intellectuals have shown 'a great capacity to create interpretative systems which do not serve any specific social actor'.[80] This point about social and ideological isolation highlights the inappropriateness when applied to Spanish America of any theory of intellectuals wholly based on class determinism. Touraine suggested that, as soon as the conditions under which intellectuals produced their work were taken into account, the idea that Spanish American intellectuals were linked to the oligarchy evaporated. This was partly because the oligarchy (and, later, the bourgeoisie) looked to Europe for its culture; and partly because intellectuals '[appeared] instead in the spaces left empty between an oligarchy in decline and the rising power of the state'.[81] European assumptions about the value to the intellectual of independence and critical distance may have to be reconsidered in the Spanish American context. The Peruvian historian Pablo Macera put the case somewhat wryly when he remarked that it could so easily be the case in underdeveloped countries that 'independence is the name that we intellectuals give to our marginalization'.[82] It is not necessary to succumb to all the mythology about 'the agony of the intellectual' to take the view that intellectual activity in any society involves, to some degree, a perverse relationship to reality. Baudrillard himself noted:

> It's very difficult to measure the efficacy, even the silent efficacy, of certain ideas. . . . Intellectual activity is a kind of wager, a defiance. It is a bet on the real situation. An intellectual would be nothing if he didn't lay his bets, if he didn't defy something, at least at the level of discourse.[83]

But that crucial qualifying clause, 'at least at the level of discourse', assumes the existence of an arena in which ideas enjoy common currency, whereas in Spanish America, as José Aricó has argued, 'the real significance of the social struggle has always been extraneous to discourse'.[84]

Under such conditions, where the institutional basis of intellectual life was weak, one important means of self-identification by Spanish American intellectuals has been the idea of the 'generation', a term that in itself raises issues that cannot satisfactorily be reduced to either class or status. The theoretical drawbacks to the model of intellectual 'generations' are numerous and well-known.[85] In brief, they are that people may well have other sources of self-identification – for example, political, ideological or institutional – that outweigh the mere fact of being one of a peer group. Almost invariably, the use of the term 'generation' is a *post hoc* rationalization, involving retrospective judgements about who was important and who had something in common, especially given that the implication is that the people in such a group have all been marked by one particular major historical experience (such as war or revolution). The term often comes to characterize only one particular, often quite small, coterie of intellectuals.

There are always leading intellectual figures who do not fit into a cultural history based on generations. The theory of generations does have the advantages that it focuses discussion on change over time, and helps to account for the breaks and discontinuities of intellectual life. But these, too, have their negative corollary: a tendency to emphasize historical ruptures at the expense of exploring continuities. However, despite all these problems, the term 'generation' has been so prevalent among Spanish American intellectuals themselves, especially since the 1920s, when Ortega y Gasset was influential in reinforcing the idea, that it is difficult to dismiss it altogether. Cultural histories of most Spanish American nations have been written in terms of the landmarks of 'generations', starting from the wars of independence. This becomes especially important in countries where institutional continuity has been lacking, and where the means of passing on intellectual traditions were usually *ad hoc*, revolving around café society. In the context of a conflict-ridden university system, a weak press and a severely constrained book publishing industry, the main medium for exchange of ideas in Spanish America has been the periodical. It is no coincidence that many of the intellectual generations in Spanish America were identified with a particular *revista* (review), the offices of which provided a focus for intellectual meetings and discussion. In societies where national intellectual life throughout most of this century consisted of a few hundred people who knew each other ('a genealogical tree of culture', as Enrique Krauze described it),[86] the idea of intellectual 'generations' acquired undeniable significance.

In the light of all the above, then, there is a valid case with respect to the cultural history of Spanish America for adopting a restricted definition of 'intellectuals', as outlined in the introduction. Self-evidently, this definition of 'intellectuals' excludes various types of cultural producers who may well have contributed significantly to processes of ideological and political change. First, the role of, say, all those who have received a higher education (referred to here as the intelligentsia), particularly in developing countries, is an important historical question.[87] Second, if one wishes to examine the contribution of creators and disseminators of ideology to any particular historical process, then a narrow definition based on 'cultural *caudillos*' is likely to prove inadequate. Alan Knight has argued in the case of the Mexican revolution that whereas 'intellectuals of the classic type . . . exercised only a feeble and limited influence during the decade of armed conflict', local intellectuals, whom he refers to as 'organic' intellectuals, 'performed an important . . . role in the development of popular rural revolution, and . . . their ideological contribution was a vital component to class, regional, and clientelist mobilization'.[88] Knight is right to comment that 'the noisy, "great" intellectuals may not be the important intellectuals' and 'it is often the stolid, silent ruminants who count'.[89] In her comparative study of the evolution of national consciousness among the peasantry in Mexico and Peru, Florencia Mallon supports the same idea:

> The people who led the process of discursive transformation were local intellectuals. In the villages, local intellectuals were those who labored to reproduce and rearticulate local history and memory, to connect community discourses about local identity to constantly shifting patterns of power, solidarity, and consensus. Political officials, teachers, elders, and healers – these were the ones who 'knew'.[90]

Cumulatively, across Spanish America, the ideological impact of people such as local priests and schoolteachers may well have outweighed the contribution of the 'cultural *caudillos*'. Almost certainly, the combined force for conservatism of those whom Gramsci identified as 'traditional' intellectuals in Spanish America, notably the clergy and the military, was greater than either Knight's local 'ruminants' or the grand 'cultural *caudillos*'. The processes of creating political cultures throughout a national territory are still something about which historians of Spanish America know relatively little, especially for the early decades of the twentieth century (a lot of recent work concentrates on the emergence of popular movements, some of which are anti-national, since the 1970s). We can identify what was coming down from the top, but understand far less about how it was received and mediated. Mallon's work on the development of popular nationhood illustrates how both state and intellectual projects of national identity were at least partially disseminated at village level in Mexico and Peru during the 1920s. This evidence, along with that offered by Alan Knight and Mary Vaughan on Mexico before 1940, leads one to conjecture – at this stage, it is not possible to do more – that local, rather than national, intellectuals might prove to have been the most important mediators between the state and the masses.[91] Nevertheless, it was the 'cultural *caudillos*' who claimed for themselves, and were granted, the status of intellectual, and who assumed the specific social role of creating national identities. In the 1990s, now that the concepts of the universal intellectual and of national identity have both been subject to critical scrutiny for two decades, it is an apposite time to examine the historical validity of Spanish American intellectuals' claims to having been national redeemers.

Nationalism and National Identity

The main debate among scholars of nationalism is between those who emphasize the 'historical embeddedness' of nations in ethnic communities (perennialists), and those who prefer to stress the relationship of nations to modernity and their consequent created or 'invented' character (modernists).[92] Perennialists argue that only a deeply felt sense of ethnicity rooted in common historical experience can account for the persistence, the irrationality and the strength of nationalism. Modernists, on the other hand, focus on the role of the bureaucratic state in nation-building. They see nations as the product of modern conditions: capitalism, industrialization, secularization, and the extension of mass communications; they argue, too, that national identities were deliberately created and not in any sense 'natural' or historically given. For modernists, national identity served as 'a means of bridging the gap between state and civil society opened up in Europe since the Reformation'.[93] In other words, the unifying 'traditions' associated with national identity were invented by the elites to control the masses and to secure their acquiescence in socio-economic transitions that were potentially damaging and divisive. In this view, the dissemination of national identities was not only the means by which the European bourgeoisies imposed their class mores and beliefs on the rest of their societies but also the mark of their success in so doing: national identity replaced religion as the 'opium of the people'.

While issues related to nation formation and national identity are inescapably touched upon in virtually any history written about Spanish America, relatively few studies have focused specifically on the question of nationalism in the region. There is a debate about the extent to which the independence movements can be characterized as 'national', but this controversy, for all its intrinsic interest, has little bearing on the development of twentieth-century national identities. The existence of a restricted idea of 'nation' among a small creole minority 'should not be confused with nationalism which possesses or develops a mass basis among the people in the form of national consciousness . . . although there may be historical links between the two'.[94] The first book-length treatments covering twentieth-century Spanish American nationalism were published in the 1960s, largely in response to what one US professor of Latin American history, John J. Johnson, identified as a 'nationalist ferment' in the region.[95] The comparison with far more recent post-colonial experience was again invoked: in a pioneering series of lectures on the topic, Arthur Whitaker noted the spread of 'an ambiguous popular-authoritarian nationalism among the underdeveloped peoples of Asia, Africa and Latin America'.[96] Whitaker offered a periodization of the development of Latin American nationalism which remains a useful starting point despite betraying a Cold War perspective. According to him, Latin American nationalism had passed through five stages: (1) from independence to the late nineteenth century, when it was 'political, introspective and liberal', and when cultural nationalism 'hardly existed save for a vague literary Americanism', and economic nationalism was 'rudimentary'; (2) the 1890s, which saw 'an injection of an economic content, partly under socialist influence', for example, Juan B. Justo in Argentina, but also José Batlle y Ordóñez's attempts to regulate foreign investment in Uruguay, along with the launch of cultural nationalism, catalysed by Rodó's *Ariel* (1900); (3) the centennial celebrations of 1910 onwards, which acted as a further stimulus to nationalism, making it 'cultural and economic as well as political and military, and outward-looking rather than introspective', especially in countries where middle sectors were expanding, and governments were beginning to assume an international role, for example, the diplomatic 'ABC' alliance between Argentina, Brazil and Chile; (4) the 1930s, when Communists allegedly 'used Latin American intellectuals as their cat's-paws in propagating divisive ideas' and induced them '[to foment] a narrow nationalism by playing up the glories of each national culture in Latin America'; and (5) the 1960s, which supposedly saw a return to the more moderate nationalism of before the 1930s.[97] The last two stages of this schema are less than convincing, and the key change from nineteenth- to twentieth-century nationalisms in the region was surely the shift from exclusion to inclusion of the masses rather than any movement from being 'inward-looking' to 'outward-looking', but Whitaker's emphasis on the introduction of economic and cultural components into Latin American nationalisms around the turn of the century remains valid. Furthermore, he identified the military, the middle classes, intellectuals and labour as the main actors in Latin American nationalisms,[98] although he came to few conclusions about their relative significance. Largely descriptive in approach, the works on nationalism of the 1960s concentrated mainly on trying to assess to what extent the 'new type' of Latin American nationalism posed a threat to US interests. Whitaker concluded that, although it could act as 'a bar to trade and investment; . . . and . . . to communication', on balance it was 'an asset to the United States and the free world at large, for it [was] the most effective of all barriers against the penetration of the area by the Sino-Soviet bloc'.[99] Gerhard Masur agreed that nationalism in Latin America could be 'a constructive and positive' unifying force, although he also argued that it could lead to revolutionary ferment, exploitation by Communist interests, and the rekindling of the 'tendency toward strong paternalistic government, so deeply rooted in the Spanish tradition'.[100] From a celebratory rather than a critical perspective, Claudio Veliz saw nationalism as creating the potential for a strong state, 'firmly rooted in an autocthonous centralist tradition', with the capacity to overcome the region's economic and cultural dependency.[101]

Scholars who have examined the Spanish American cases nearly all argue, implicitly or explicitly, that the historical experience of these countries overwhelmingly supports the modernist position. It would be difficult to deny the importance of the state to nation-building throughout the region, or to dispute the common wisdom that in most cases state preceded nation in this part of the world.[102] Others who have commented in passing on the subsequent development of these nationalisms have also emphasized the role of the state. John Lynch, for example, has argued that a sense of nationality was fostered in Spanish America primarily by 'federal justice and the national army'.[103] Richard Morse sees nationalism as one component of state-building in the post-independence period, together with legitimacy, constitutionalism and personalism.[104] Perhaps the most explicit example of the application of the modernist perspective on nationalism to Spanish America is to be found in a brief essay by Eric Hobsbawm.[105] Hobsbawm identified three phases of nationalism in the region. During the first stage, from independence until the mid-nineteenth century, 'the nation' was thought of in Enlightenment terms, as equivalent to 'the people', defined in no more limited way than as a union of individuals, living together within a shared territory, under a common legal and political system. Soon ideas about the specificity of certain peoples emerged within the German Romantic movement (itself partly a reaction against the claim to universalism of French 'national' values), particularly Johann Gottfried von Herder's concept of the Volk, but until then, ' "[t]he nation" was an open invitation to join it'.[106] During this period, those primarily concerned with 'the nation' were the educated and the military. Hobsbawm's second phase coincided with the establishment of central government under liberal rule in the mid-late nineteenth century, when 'the nation' became identified with progress, defined in terms of modernization through economic development and the extension of state power over the national territory. In this reformulation of the idea of nation, a greater degree of exclusion was practised: 'Only those committed to progress, or who at least accepted it, could be seen as true members of the nation.'[107] The third phase, which Hobsbawm dates from the Mexican revolution, brought the rise of popular nationalism: 'the recognition, among intellectuals and politicians, that the nation consisted of the people – all the people'.[108] The university reform movement of 1918 'inspired new populist-democratic and nationalist movements', he argued, 'like the future APRA, and perhaps the future PRI, MNR, Acción Democrática and others'.[109] Hobsbawm characterized this type of nationalism, which he identified as dominant in the region since the 1930s, as primarily political: ' "developmentalist", anti-imperialist, . . . popular and concerned with the condition of the mass of the people, and politically leaning to the left'.[110] He argued that Spanish America 'has remained largely immune to modern ethnic-cultural nationalism to this day'.[111] Although he saw populist leaders as important in advancing the process of mass identification with the nation, his conclusion was that 'the most decisive force for creating national consciousness was undoubtedly the development of modern mass culture, especially as reinforced by technology'.[112]

The perennialists' main contention – namely that ' "the myth of the modern nation" fails to grasp the continuing relevance and power of pre-modern ethnic ties and sentiments in providing a firm base for the nation-to-be'[113] – seems to have little explanatory power for a region in which the only basis for a nation on such a criterion was the united republic

of Spanish America envisaged by Simón Bolívar. The perennialist argument
could most plausibly be applied to Mexico or Peru, where established ethnic
communities existed before the arrival of the Spanish, and where nationalist
ideology and iconography have drawn substantially on the pre-Columbian
civilizations, especially in Mexico. It remains the case, however, that most of
the other nationalities in Spanish America were formed by states that
anteceded a sense of nationality.[114] The perennialist interpretation of
nationalism posits ethnicity as a major *causative* factor in the emergence of
nation-states but has so far failed to account for the fact that, by 1825,
independence leaders in the former American colonies of Spain and
Portugal (and, indeed, Britain and France) had founded new political
communities on the basis of (at least aspirant) nationhood, notwithstanding
the lack of ethnic or linguistic distinctions between either themselves and
their colonial rulers or between each other. That the Spanish American
nations sought, once they had actually come into existence, to distinguish
themselves from each other along ethnic lines demonstrates no more than
that ethnicity is a factor that can reinforce nationalism; it does not prove it
to be either a causative or even a constitutive factor.

Analogous points can be made about the role of language in nation-
building: evidence from Spanish America suggests that the promotion of
distinctive languages was used as a means of reinforcing rather than creating
national consciousness. The first stage was differentiation from the former
colonial power: early in the life of the newly independent Spanish American
republics, educated liberals began to criticize the Castilian language for
being an instrument of empire. Indeed, in its cumulative effects, it had
functioned as such, although two caveats should be made. First, early in the
period of colonization, language policy had been the cause of some dispute
between the Crown (which wanted the Indians to learn Spanish) and
missionaries (who discovered that the Indians were brought more rapidly to
God via their own languages). The extent to which American Spanish was
influenced by indigenous languages throughout the colonial period is
becoming increasingly evident. Second, the Catholic Church, unlike the
Reformed Church, remained opposed to any extensive use of the vernacu-
lar. Latin was the sole language used to teach theology, the arts and law at
the region's two major universities of Mexico City and San Marcos in Lima.
It was not until the late eighteenth century, when Spain belatedly underwent
its own (partial) Enlightenment, and Bourbons on the Spanish throne
began to be more forceful about language policy, that Spanish began to be
used as a teaching language, and then mainly only in the more modern
science of medicine. At the time of Spanish American independence,
Castilian – now so often represented as the language of conquest and
domination over the indigenous languages and peoples – was accorded a
lesser status than Latin in educated circles.[115] After Independence, as the

influence of the liberals and their preference for English and French culture gave way to the increasingly Americanist mood of the late nineteenth and early twentieth centuries, one means of asserting Hispanic American identity was to insist on the validity of American Spanish, in defiance of the Royal Academy's continued dismissal of it as an inferior variant.[116] When the Peruvian writer and lexicographer Ricardo Palma (1833–1919) visited Spain as a delegate to the 1892 celebrations, he submitted a list of 350 carefully collected Spanish-American words and idioms to the Spanish academicians, only to return highly disillusioned by their chauvinist response.[117] Nearly half a century later, Borges famously defended the Spanish of the River Plate against an attack on it by a Spanish intellectual – Américo Castro (himself born in Brazil) – as plebeianized speech.[118] Among the literati of the 1940s onwards, defence of American varieties of Spanish shifted to celebration of their idiomatic richness in what came to be known as the 'recolonization' of the language. The language issue also acquired a distinctly national dimension: studies in linguistics multiplied from the end of the nineteenth century onwards, and dedicated work went into compendia of Peruvianisms, Chileanisms and so on, all designed to substantiate the claim that these nations were different not only from Spain but also from each other.[119] But again, as with ethnicity, although linguistic distinctiveness was used as a means of stimulating a sense of national identity in existing nation-states, it had not been a motivation for their founding. The experience of the Americas as a whole obliges us to reconsider the salience of both ethnicity and language in the emergence of nations. The existence of a previous community differentiated by language or ethnicity might make it easier to forge nationhood, but it is clearly not a necessary precondition.

Although the modernists' case appears to be strong in relation to Spanish America, some of the general criticisms of modernist arguments made by perennialists are still pertinent. Their most telling point is that it is risky to assume that the state is all-powerful:

> ... state-building, though it may foster a strong nationalism (whether loyal or resistant to the state in question), is not to be confused with the forging of a national cultural and political identity among often culturally heterogeneous populations. The establishment of incorporating state institutions is no guarantee of a population's cultural identification with the state, or of acceptance of the 'national myth' of the dominant [ethnic community]; indeed, the invention of a broader, national mythology by the elite to bolster the state's legitimacy may leave significant segments of the population untouched or alienated.[120]

Anthony Smith's caveat is particularly relevant to a region where, for much of the twentieth century, the state still exerted only a tenuous hold over large areas of many national territories. In all cases, there may be significant limitations on the capacity of either the state or intellectuals to forge national identities in their own image. In this regard, the modernists' concentration on elite actions begins to seem increasingly unsatisfactory, if only because it fails to explain why nationalism becomes important to ordinary people. Richard Morse has argued, in a discussion of Spanish America, that popular identities are complex and not always subject to imposition from above, despite the tendency for intellectuals and academics to see identity – in the Enlightenment tradition – 'as manipulable by technological and institutional innovation'.[121] Morse's analysis is not specifically devoted to national identity (it ranges more broadly to encompass sub-national and supra-national identities), but nevertheless his words of caution command attention. In the absence of literacy, he suggested, identities would be shaped by oral tradition: 'For literati and universities, one might venture, identity is not their invention but their belated recognition of social circumstance.'[122] The idea that national identity can be fashioned at will by political leaders or intellectuals is at best only a half-truth.

In departing from the modernist emphasis on public policy-making in nation-building, Benedict Anderson was also the first comparative historian to devote sustained attention to the question of nationalism in Spanish America. He not only emphasized the importance of these early attempts to found nations, but took this argument a step further to claim that modal nations originated not from Europe, but from the Americas. Here his position is largely based on evidence from the United States, and is less convincing for any of the Latin American republics. Nevertheless, his focus on the American experiences acted as a useful corrective to the previous tendency among historians of nationalism to neglect them. Working from within the modernist tradition, but not wholly convinced by it, Anderson argued that a nation was best thought of as the representation of an idea – an 'imagined community' – rather than as an actually existent political entity.[123] Lending a new dimension to debates about the relationship between intellectuals and nationalism, Anderson reasoned from this that nationalism was not readily susceptible of definition by the categories conventionally employed (for example, ethnicity, language, territorial sovereignty, constitutional statehood and so on). He offered two main general explanations for the evolution of national consciousness: first, the development of what he referred to as 'print-capitalism' (the industrialization of printing to enable the sale of printed goods – books and newspapers – on a mass scale); second, changing cultural representations of time. In the second edition of his book, he also noted the importance of changing perceptions of space. He argued that the growth of the press, particularly, was vital to the capacity of the educated elites to begin imagining a community on the scale of the nation. He also linked the emergence of the novel as a genre with the stirrings of national consciousness. Anderson's approach has been subjected to some criticism, in terms both of its generalities and of its specifics. It has been argued that although he succeeded in establishing the importance of newspapers, periodicals and literary productions both as a precondition for the development of national consciousness and as a reinforcing element once it had taken hold, he failed to convince the reader that print capitalism was a causative factor in the formation of the national idea.[124]

With respect to Spanish America, his claim that the independence movements were national in character went further than most historians would accept.[125] While, as Simon Collier has argued, '[w]ithout recourse to some such principle [of at least potential nationality], the very demand for independence is a logical absurdity', it is also the case that 'few would claim that it was dominant or in any sense universal at the outset', and that the 'ideal of separate nationhood spread . . . as the struggle unfolded'.[126] Most historians of independence would also agree that, in John Lynch's words, 'in so far as there was a [potential] nation, it was a creole nation'.[127] Even among creoles, only a minority sought independence in 1810, and their conceptions of a nation were based primarily on the idea of territory. Bolívar's sense of nationalism, for example, was 'not tied to closely defined ethnic, cultural, linguistic, or religious moorings'; his 'standard metaphor . . . for the nation-as-collection-of-people was the family' and his 'ultimate criterion of nationality . . . was political in nature': 'nationality . . . was open to all who accepted certain political principles'.[128] A nation seems to have been conceived by Bolívar and other independence leaders largely as a vehicle for realizing the liberal ideals of liberty and progress; at this stage, the idea had little more content than that. The main agents of nationalism in Spanish America, according to Anderson, were 'pilgrim creole function-aries and provincial creole printmen'.[129] He explained this in terms of print capitalism, especially newspapers, and the fact that the Spanish Crown tended to confine creoles to bureaucratic positions within the territories of individual vice-royalties; the highest possible positions to which they might aspire were likely to be in the capital, so that their sense of socio-economic opportunities became bounded by the territorial units that were to become nations. Although he did discuss the first novel to be published in Spanish America, *El periquillo sarniento* [*The Itching Parrot*],[130] by José Joaquín Fernán-dez de Lizardi (known as *el pensador mexicano*), which appeared in 1816 in New Spain, Anderson's overall view was that the Spanish American intelli-gentsia at that time was too small to be of historical significance in the imagining of the new communities. In reaching this conclusion, he seems to have neglected the contribution made by creole Jesuits, who were expelled from Spanish dominions in 1767 and wrote from exile about the distinctive features of the New World societies they had come to identify as their homelands. These writers certainly had their part to play in creating an incipient national consciousness.[131] Recent work also suggests, intriguingly, that the works of late-colonial scientists, particularly naturalists, may have made an important contribution by delimiting distinct and unified physical spaces.[132] Anderson's account of the emergence of nations in Spanish America is not completely convincing in itself. Neither does his thesis that the novel was a major vehicle for forging national consciousness work very well for subsequent periods: Rowe and Schelling argue that this idea 'corresponds more to the desires of the bourgeoisie than to the works that were actually produced' and that 'what the major works of literature display are the fundamental divisions of culture, language and territory that make the formation of modern nation-states difficult'.[133]

Despite all the problems, however, it is difficult to escape a sense that the kernel of Anderson's idea retains a powerful explanatory value. His emphasis on the 'imagined' qualities of the nation helped to modify the modernist position away from overly structural explanations of the emergence of nationalism as the inevitable consequence of capitalism, industrialization and the concentration of power in a centralized state, and towards consideration of the more intangible features of national consciousness, which had previously been largely the preserve of the perennialists. This is particularly apposite in the case of the Spanish American nations, which were not based on distinctive ethnicity and underwent a late and incomplete process of modernization. Anderson usefully reminds us of Collier's point that: 'Nationalism . . . was not . . . a "natural" development in Spanish America in the way it may have been in Europe; it had to be induced, nurtured, fostered.'[134] This statement remained applicable to the popular nationalism of the twentieth century just as much as to the more elitist versions of the nineteenth century.

Perhaps the most fruitful approach to the question of national identity is to see it as founded *both* on a state political project *and* on a shared culture (in Louis Panabière's terms, *l'institution politique* and *l'institution imaginaire*). With the latter concept Panabière seeks to evoke more than is conventionally thought of as ideology: 'the concrete expression (in art, literature, music and theatre) of a whole set of cultural codes for endowing the world with meaning', which, given the tendency of intellectuals to dissent, may well be opposed to – or, at least, in tension with – the official ideology.[135] Any approach to the development of national consciousness in Spanish America that emphasizes either the political or the cultural components of nation-building to the exclusion of the other will provide only a partial explanation, missing the valid points of the other. The perennialists' emphasis on ethnicity and the modernists' emphasis on the state has meant that the relationship between the two has not always been sufficiently recognized.[136]

Concerning the nature of the state in Spanish America, my starting point is Alfred Stepan's view that:

> ... the state must be considered as something more than the 'government'. It is the continuous administrative, legal, bureaucratic and coercive systems that attempt not only to structure relations *between* civil society and public authority in a polity but also to structure many crucial relationships *within* civil society as well.[137]

In general, but particularly in the case of Spanish America, both the liberal-pluralist representation of the state as an arbiter and the classic Marxist view of the state as the servant of particular class interests are incomplete in that both underemphasize the state's potential for autonomous action. Some dubious arguments in the historiography about the supposed persistence of a 'centralizing tradition' in Spanish America can be passed over, primarily on the grounds that state-building in the region has been complicated precisely by the variety of intellectual and ideological currents that were influential: Aristotelian and Thomistic conceptions of the organic state with a moral purpose coexisted alongside liberalism and, later, Marxism and dependency theory. But it is not necessary to embrace the views of cultural determinists to accept that, by the early twentieth century, nearly all contenders for political power in Spanish America regarded the state as 'directly responsible for service to the body politic' and expected it to act as the leading force for modernization. This was 'a turning away from the more individualistic notions of society and the traditional evolutionary concept of the state implicit in much of the nineteenth-century literature'.[138] Most of the region's intellectuals subscribed to the consensus about the potential benefits of state interventionism.

The importance of the relationship between twentieth-century intellectuals and the state in Spanish America has often been noted in previous studies, but the focus of these works has usually been on the restrictions imposed by one particular type of state, the argument – or, at least, the implication – being that a different type of state, perhaps one more politically acceptable to the author, would adopt a different attitude towards intellectuals. For example, the Peronist supporter Juan José Hernández Arregui identified the variety of means, both direct and indirect, by which the Argentine state had undermined intellectuals before 1916, when it was still controlled by the oligarchy, but said nothing about the not dissimilar methods employed against intellectuals by Juan Domingo Perón.[139] In what follows, the term 'state' is used precisely in order to emphasize the contention that the desire to limit the power of intellectuals has not been restricted to any one type of regime in twentieth-century Spanish America, but has been a goal continually pursued by authoritarian, democratic, populist and revolutionary governments alike. In order to explore this idea, the discussion draws upon Guillermo O'Donnell's view of what he calls the 'embeddedness' of the state:

> It is a mistake to conflate the state with the state apparatus, the public sector, or the aggregation of public bureaucracies. These, unquestionably, are part of the state, but are not all of it. The state is also, and no less primarily, a set of social relations that establishes a certain order, and ultimately backs it with a centralized coercive guarantee, over a given territory.[140]

In that sense, O'Donnell suggests, not only regimes can be categorized as authoritarian or democratic (or, indeed, as anti-intellectual), but states too. If the legal system, which he defines as 'a constitutive element of the state', 'does not have real effectiveness, or can be annulled *ad hoc*, or is subordinate to secret rules and/or to the whim of the rulers', then the social order regulated by that state is predominantly authoritarian. If, conversely, 'there exist public powers which are capable and willing to enforce – according to properly established procedures – . . . rights and guarantees even against other public powers, that state and the order it helps to implant are democratic'.[141] Rather than thinking about the state only or primarily as 'an actor', this approach enables historians to appreciate that 'states matter because their organizational configurations, along with their overall patterns of activity, affect political culture, encourage some kinds of group formation and collective political actions (but not others), and make possible the raising of certain political issues (but not others)'.[142]

It is important, however, not to overemphasize the strength of the state in Spanish America, especially during the first half of the twentieth century. The state's varying scope for independence from socio-economic forces needs to be taken into account, 'because the very *structural potentials* for autonomous state actions change over time, as the organizations of coercion and administration undergo transformations, both internally and in their relations to societal groups and to respective parts of government'.[143] State capacities for independent action vary in relation to sovereign integrity, military and administrative control over territory, financial resources and quality of personnel, and can be markedly different across the range of policy areas. Across Spanish America, state capacities for independent action were often severely compromised by foreign interventionism and the lack of legitimacy attached to those occupying power, and were generally on the low side, although experiences varied widely.[144] However, most national governments in early-twentieth-century Spanish America were committed to an extension of bureaucratic control, even if only to defeat alternative power bases within the territory, for example, regional administrations or the Catholic Church. The aim of Chapter 2 is to illustrate how these state policies affected intellectuals.

Intellectuals and the Modernizing State
in Spanish America

The State and the powers-that-be both need [intellectuals] and fear us. They need us because we give them prestige they lack; they fear us because our sentiments and views can damage them. In the history of power in Latin America, there are only military dictatorships or intellectuals. No wonder then ... that there was so much coddling of the intellectuals by the State.

(Gabriel García Márquez)[1]

The intellectual has not taken a seat at the table of power because, with rare exceptions, he has not been accepted at it.

(Mario Vargas Llosa)[2]

The above two statements capture the tension at the heart of the relationship between Spanish American intellectuals and the state. Have the region's intellectuals been courted and cosseted by the wielders of state power, as García Márquez argues, or despised and ignored, as Vargas Llosa alleges? Both men have themselves been offered high political office on the strength of their prestige as writers, so their contradictory views cannot be explained by different personal experiences. Vargas Llosa was virtually invited to take his pick of government posts by Peruvian president Fernando Belaúnde Terry during the early 1980s,[3] and, moreover, took Alberto Fujimori to a second round in the presidential elections of 1990; García Márquez has refused not only several ambassadorships but also the opportunity to stand as a Colombian presidential candidate. My hypothesis is that these two writers' apparently contradictory views both contain partial truths, and both are symptomatic of the underlying reality that, in comparatively underdeveloped Spanish America, the main source of status for intellectuals has been the state, rather than any particular class or social sector, because, until at least the 1960s, there was no mass reading public to provide an audience and a market for their work.

García Márquez is stretching a point to suggest that Latin American countries have been governed only by military men or intellectuals. Such an interpretation carries conviction only if the term 'intellectuals' is understood in the broad sense of the intelligentsia, but García Márquez's own reference to the capacity of 'intellectuals' to enhance or undermine a state's legitimacy implies that, for him too, 'intellectuals' subscribe to a degree of critical distance from power that is consonant only with a narrower definition of the term. In that case, his generalization does not stand up. There have been many twentieth-century Spanish American civilian politicians who could be called 'intellectuals' only in the sense that they were university graduates. What García Márquez does capture here, however, is the Spanish American tradition of the statesman–intellectual, which, for much of the twentieth century, has coexisted alongside the intellectuals' own sense, conveyed by Vargas Llosa's grim remark, that nobody listens to them and that they enjoy very little influence on public policy. In what follows, my analysis attempts to unravel this contradiction between intellectuals' wildly diverging claims to both political omnipotence and impotence.

Mexico

Mexico, where the revolution of 1910–20 effected the earliest comprehensive transfer of power from oligarchy to bourgeoisie in Spanish America,[4] is often held up as the classic case of a Spanish American state that 'coddles' its intellectuals. The Mexican state has only relatively rarely tried to coerce the intellectual community (the main instances were in the 1930s, the late 1950s and the late 1960s). Since the 1930s, Mexican intellectuals have not suffered the involuntary exile that has been the fate of their counterparts in so many other Spanish American countries. Mexico does, indeed, register the highest overall level of co-option among the five countries discussed in this book, but the most zealous policies of co-option were not pursued until the 1970s, after the breakdown of a relationship hitherto primarily sustained by containment at institutional level. The term 'containment' will be used to refer to a network of state controls, both direct and indirect, over the institutions of intellectual life, the most important of these being the universities, but also including intellectual honours (prizes, scholarships and fellowships), prestigious appointments (for example, to the directorship of a national library), publishing and the press. States came to monopolize the routes by which Spanish American intellectuals were able to acquire what Pierre Bourdieu has called 'cultural capital'.[5]

The response of post-revolutionary Mexican leaders to independent bids by intellectuals for political power has to be understood in the light of two factors: the salient role that educated men had played in nineteenth-century Mexican politics, and the equally conspicuous lack of participation by intellectuals in the revolution. The height of intellectual influence on Mexican political life had been during the Restored Republic (1867–76), when a generation of liberal men of letters were drafted in by President Benito Juárez to promote a national culture and a national history.[6] Porfirio Díaz, who was quite simply 'allergic to anything intellectual',[7] skilfully managed to subordinate intellectual influence to military power by promoting a select group, the positivist *científicos*, as advisers to his dictatorship (1884–1911). Other pretenders to intellectual influence were marginalized: emerging middle-class intellectuals found it difficult to make their way under the Porfirian state.[8] For example, Luis Cabrera (1876–1954), a lawyer who turned to journalism in frustration at the lack of political opportunities available to him, ruefully observed: 'There is not one *científico* who is poor. Their luck in business is proverbial. The best franchises are theirs, the best-paid jobs are theirs. The positions of responsibility are theirs.'[9] Díaz bestowed public office upon these favoured intellectuals, but at the same time he encouraged them to enrich themselves to the extent that they had become the objects of intense popular loathing by the end of his rule. By these means, he both contained and ultimately undermined intellectuals' claims to public influence, while preserving the appearance – and, to a limited extent, the substance – of state patronage of cultural life. There were government subsidies to the press, and in addition the leading positivist, Justo Sierra (1848–1912), who was appointed as Education Minister in 1905, helped several of the young intellectuals who went on to found the Ateneo de la Juventud (Athenaeum of Youth) in 1909 by sponsoring their studies in Europe, patronizing many of their events, and instigating a 'program of bringing European musicians and artists to Mexico which contributed to the flourishing of a cultural milieu in which Ateneo youth matured and thrived'.[10] The Ateneo's cult of the individual heroic genius (drawing on Romanticism, Spanish American idealism, Nietzsche, Schopenhauer's aesthetic of the will, and Bergson's celebration of intuitionism as a route to knowledge) constituted no political challenge and, despite its proclaimed revolt against positivism, did not fundamentally dissent from the liberal-positivist idea that art's primary function was to act as a civilizing influence.

Although James Cockcroft argues that intellectuals were 'critically important' to the revolution,[11] there is little convincing evidence to support this contention, and it has been disputed by several leading historians of Mexico.[12] Many intellectuals from what became known as the *ateneista* generation backed the reformist democrat Francisco Madero with varying degrees of enthusiasm, but once mass uprising had broken out they adopted various modes of retreat: self-imposed exile,[13] support for the repressive policies of Huerta, romanticism about Villa (for example, the novelist Martín Luis Guzmán), or apoliticism.[14] Few intellectuals supported Carranza,[15] who, far from being anti-intellectual (like most of the revolutionary *caudillos*), 'read the classics on campaign' and indeed believed that the 'intellectual element' and not the illiterate masses should govern Mexico.[16] It was symptomatic of the declining role for intellectuals in the post-revolutionary order that they played very little part in drafting the new constitution in 1917.[17] The Constitutional Congress at Querétaro was primarily made up of middle-class professionals, most of whom were keen to recite the litany of the *licenciado* (university graduate), displaying their knowledge of 'the American Constitution, the French Revolution, Rousseau and Spencer, Hugo and Zola', but few of whom were identified with the new generation of 'intellectuals'. The leading contribution from anyone who could possibly have claimed to be considered an intellectual was made by the sociologist Andrés Molina Enríquez, an old-style liberal-positivist famous for his celebration of *mestizaje* (racial mixing) as Mexico's salvation. He wrote the first draft of Article 27, the notorious clause stipulating Mexican national ownership of all its natural resources, including land, water and subsoil minerals, but 'his arid theories appalled his listeners' and, in any case, he was more often thought of by contemporaries as a 'professional politician'.[18] In his memoirs, Vasconcelos owned that Mexican intellectuals had been 'belittled' by the inadequacy of their response to revolution;[19] for this reason alone, those generals who prevailed in the revolutionary struggle were hardly likely to hold the intellectuals in high regard.

Nevertheless, the new leaders of the post-revolutionary government established in 1920 were aware that intellectuals had been influential in the events leading up to the removal of Díaz. What also soon transpired was that the Sonoran state (1920–34)[20] saw itself as the sole arbiter of competing interests and 'could not allow any criticism, any protest, any power apart from itself'.[21] Intellectuals were identified as potential rivals, although President Álvaro Obregón (1920–24) also recognized that they could be useful in cultivating legitimacy for his initially beleaguered government both at home and abroad.[22] He sought to win the cultural elite's backing through the limited expedient of granting just one of their leading members a prominent role in the post-revolutionary order: José Vasconcelos, who was unusual among intellectuals in that he had been a participant in the revolution, at least until 1915. A *maderista* since 1909, Vasconcelos had been imprisoned by Huerta in 1913. After being released, he flirted with *villismo* in 1914–15, a fact that was 'carefully played down in his autobiography'.[23] Carranza, who had been recognized as 'First Chief of the Revolution' late in 1913, appointed him Director of the National Preparatory School (ENP), but Vasconcelos lasted only two weeks in this post because of his refusal to swear a formal oath of allegiance to Carranza. He attended the Convention of Villistas and Zapatistas held at Aguascalientes in October 1914, where he helped to draft the statement that proclaimed that the only legal authority in Mexico was the convention, thereby challenging Carranza. In the provisional government nominated by the convention, Vasconcelos was appointed Secretary of Public Instruction and Fine Arts, but shortly afterwards he left for exile in Washington,[24] disenchanted with his erstwhile allies both politically (as a result of the collapse of Eulalio Gutiérrez's government in January 1915) and personally (after a *zapatista* leader had apparently threatened to kill him during a drunken incident).[25] In the United States, Vasconcelos made one last attempt to secure diplomatic recognition for Gutiérrez, but when that failed he withdrew altogether from Mexican politics and departed for Peru to work for an educational company.[26]

In 1920, however, Obregón decided that Vasconcelos was one of the few intellectuals who should not 'retire to private life'[27] and installed him as Rector of the National University. The new President (himself a former schoolteacher) was persuaded that Vasconcelos had the drive and the commitment to launch a post-revolutionary project of social engineering in education, which was one of the few policies upon which the divided revolutionary coalition could agree. In effect, Vasconcelos presented Obregón with a *fait accompli*, having taken full advantage of his position as Rector to campaign in local state legislatures for a national public educational system.[28] By the time Obregón formalized his appointment as Secretary of Public Education in October 1921, Vasconcelos had been issuing edicts on general education matters for well over a year. Obregón allowed Vasconcelos to exercise a degree of autonomy as minister ('he had practically a free hand') which was to prove rare in the increasingly presidential Mexican system.[29] But it was the comparatively generous budget granted to education by the Obregón government (up from 15 million pesos in 1921 to 35 million in 1923)[30] that enabled Vasconcelos's policies to make a major impact.

Vasconcelos proved adept at establishing a comprehensive bureaucratic apparatus for the state administration of culture; under his aegis a ministry of education (known as the Secretariat of Public Education or SEP) was re-established and organized into three departments incorporating all aspects of high culture: schools, libraries and fine arts. He resisted pressures both to import US teachers and to act on the advice of those who claimed to be educational experts, whom he dismissed as 'a dangerous breed'.[31] According to his own account, having despatched them to the countryside to write their reports, Vasconcelos – in a classic instance of the creative intellectual's contempt for the technocrat – then proceeded to pour scorn on the results:

> For heaven's sake, don't give me ideas; I can make up ideas myself or buy them in fifty-cent pamphlets; give me creative activity. Don't tell me about the condition of the Indians, I already know their condition: hungry in body and soul; don't tell me what life is like in the poor districts; I don't live closeted in the cabinet office; I go to visit the poor, I don't need your reports.[32]

He founded public printing presses to produce cheap editions of the classics, and, although he has been harshly mocked for his apparent conviction that the peasant masses would benefit from reading Homer and Virgil, it is often forgotten that Vasconcelos was also responsible for some perhaps more realistic attempts to disseminate culture. One of his most influential initiatives was a magazine for teachers, *El Maestro* (1921–23), which was 'designed as a small manual of general culture, with distinct sections: national and international information, world history, literature, children's pages, practical tips, poetry and "diverse subjects" (all sorts of essays)'.[33]

For a man often characterized as preoccupied mainly with spiritual and philosophical matters, Vasconcelos was surprisingly politically astute, incorporating representatives of most of the revolutionary factions 'from the original *maderistas* to former *zapatistas*' into his staff at SEP.[34] He also succeeded in persuading the leading intellectuals of both his own and the following generations to join his cultural crusade. His inaugural speech on becoming, briefly, Rector of the National University in 1920 laid the foundations of all subsequent relations between Mexican intellectuals and post-revolutionary governments. Describing himself as 'a delegate of the Revolution', Vasconcelos declared:

> The post I occupy makes it my duty to become an interpreter of popular aspirations, and in the name of that people ... I ask you, and ... all the intellectuals of Mexico, to abandon your ivory towers and seal a pact of allegiance to the Revolution.[35]

His claim that 'the Revolution is now in search of the learned', was all the more convincing because, as a leading intellectual himself, his use of the familiar form of the second person (*vosotros*) instead of the more formal *usted* did not strike a dissonant note with his university audience.[36] Vasconcelos's skilful use of rhetorical devices enabled him to build up a complex series of identifications culminating in the idea that the route to freedom for intellectuals lay in adopting the cause of the people. First, he distinguished the people from himself and, by implication, all other intellectuals, by claiming, 'The type of art the people reveres [third person] is the free and magnificent art of the great and the noble who were neither servile nor lowly.' But in giving examples he moved quickly to identify himself with the popular will: 'I recall Dante banished and brave, and Beethoven lofty and profound.' He then moved on to close the gap between himself and the people, at the same time enlarging the distance between 'good' and 'bad' intellectuals: 'The others, the courtesans, do not interest us, the sons of the people.' This prepared the ground for his final manoeuvre bringing together himself, as representative of the revolutionary state, the intellectuals and the masses: 'We free men who do not want to see on the face of the earth either masters or slaves, victors or vanquished, must join forces to work and prosper. Let us initiate a crusade for public education.'[37] But despite the international attention attracted by Vasconcelos's ambitious literacy campaigns, Obregón disbanded his ministry in 1924 and sent him into exile as a condition of resolving the presidential succession crisis of 1923–24.[38] By that stage, the Obregón government had already secured the support of a generation of intellectuals for its nation-building project, at a time when the National University, as an institution, was a site of opposition. In Octavio Paz's words, 'The intellectual vocation of [that] generation was indistinguishable from its will for social, political and moral reform. . . . they all conceived their activity not as in contrast or opposition to the State, but as part of it.'[39] Appointing Vasconcelos minister had served its purpose.

Two more decades were to pass, however, before the Mexican state was in a sufficiently strong position to establish institutional mechanisms to contain the intellectual community by means of the universities. In the interim, governments pursued a policy of divide-and-rule towards intellectuals. One technique adopted was to marginalize the traditionally central figure of the writer in favour of anthropologists and artists. It is likely that no works of art have been so closely identified with a political process as the murals came to be with the Mexican revolution, but the way in which the murals initially won recognition in itself said much about the interactions of the Mexican state and the cultural community during the 1920s. The murals were originally Vasconcelos's idea; as Secretary of Education, he summoned his old colleague from the Ateneo, Diego Rivera, back from Europe to decorate the walls of the National Preparatory School (ENP) with what the Education Minister had envisaged as the secular equivalent of devotional paintings, intended to diffuse a sense of spirituality and classical harmony (civilization) among the (barbarous) illiterate. Vasconcelos, the self-styled *Ulises criollo*,[40] was not very different from his predecessor Justo Sierra in that he too 'advocated the use of art as a method of social control'.[41] Rivera, who was influenced by socialist realism, had very different ideas about the purposes and potential of mural art, seeing it as a means of introducing the illiterate to their own history. The result was that whereas Vasconcelos 'asked him for racial and cosmogonic allegories . . . Diego painted the sickle and the machete'.[42] Apparently, when Vasconcelos first saw the murals at the new SEP building, he lamented, 'Oh, Dieguito, Indians, more Indians!'[43] although he did nothing to interfere with this travesty of his own designs. Many of the bourgeois cultural elite were horrified by the murals (indeed, so were the students at the ENP),[44] but foreign artists and intellectuals were so fascinated that finally the Mexican regime came to recognize that these bold images of landowners as tyrants and Indians as martyrs could lend credence to their claim that the revolution had transformed Mexican culture. It was primarily because of the interest of foreigners that the murals became a symbol of Mexico.[45] Once the muralists had established international artistic reputations, Mexican leaders perceived the added advantages of permitting them to play the part of flamboyant bohemian which in Spanish America had more often been assumed by writers. Diego Rivera in particular both appalled and fascinated the Mexican establishment with his rumbustious love life, radical politics and stormy relationship with the Communist movement – from being on the central committee of the Mexican Communist Party (PCM), he was expelled by Stalinists in 1929 and was instrumental in securing Mexican asylum for Trotsky, but he subsequently renounced the Fourth International and finally, in 1952, begged to be readmitted to the PCM. Rivera's notoriety became all the greater after a consumerist bourgeoisie had begun to consolidate itself in the 1940s ('Have you heard about the scandal surrounding Diego Rivera's mural in the Prado Hotel? They say that he painted "God does not exist".')[46] Rivera and the Mexican state played a game of political cat-and-mouse until his death in 1957, both parties enhancing their legitimacy through the ritual confrontations. It was at the very least convenient for Mexican governments to have the figure of the adversarial, Communist intellectual incarnated in someone who was painting internationally acclaimed murals (quite a few of them in the United States) which gave pictorial prominence to the role of workers and peasants in Mexican history.

During the 1930s, Mexican governments succeeded in pitting the socialist realist commitment of the muralists against those intellectuals who, in trying to preserve their intellectual independence, adopted political positions that could be presented as right-wing.[47] Especially during the presidency (1934–40) of Lázaro Cárdenas, the state was able to reduce intellectual dissent almost to the point of elimination (most intellectuals were anti-Cárdenas at the time, although he was to become a hero among the intelligentsia in the late 1970s).[48] Plutarco Elías Calles's speech at the foundation of the National Revolutionary Party (PNR) in 1930 set the tone for the decade: he stated that he wanted the party to unite 'workers from the countryside and the city, [workers] from the middle classes and the lower middle classes, and intellectuals *of good faith*'.[49] Those deemed to be of bad faith – that is, those who rejected the state's project of national integration around the ideal of *mexicanidad* – rapidly found themselves marginalized. For example, the poets and philosophers associated with the journal *Contemporáneos*, who maintained that Mexican culture was inescapably shaped by European culture, were accused of being homosexual and reactionary.[50] By this stage, government policies precluded any middle way between participation in state endeavours and the isolation of individual expression. President Cárdenas himself made it only too clear what options the intellectuals faced when, in 1935, he informed the members of the university that, 'We government officials have no prejudices against high culture, on the contrary, it is our duty [to ensure] that all its representatives add their efforts to ours, in order to carry out the programme for economic improvement and to put an end to the superstition and vice which affect our people.'[51] Cárdenas's clamp-down on dissent from the apostles of high culture may have been related to the situation at the local level, where the central state increasingly found itself obliged to make concessions on cultural policy as communities, often led by teachers, 'accepted, discarded, and altered aspects of the state's project, [appropriating] the school and [forging] new identities and linkages'.[52] But in the main it was a logical outcome of the readiness of the post-revolutionary generation of intellectuals (led by Vasconcelos) to accept a state monopoly on culture. The sting in the tail had been there to detect in Vasconcelos's initial rallying cry at the National University, when his assurance that 'contemporary revolutions want experts and they want artists' was immediately qualified by 'but on condition that knowledge and art serve to improve the human condition'.[53] Vasconcelos established the blueprint for a model of state-run culture that marginalized independent intellectuals like himself.[54]

Post-revolutionary Mexican governments had a particular incentive for paying attention to middle-class demands for higher education, given that the revolution itself had destroyed most of the pre-revolutionary routes to bourgeois enrichment. The National University had been founded in 1910 by the positivist Minister of Education Justo Sierra, with statutes stipulating ultimate state control.[55] From the outset, it had been envisaged less as an institution of higher learning than as an instrument of nation-building. After the revolution, relations between the Mexican state and the National University evolved through four stages: (1) 1920–29 – state control and outright opposition from the university; (2) 1929–44 – partial autonomy, conflict and state attempts to undermine the university; (3) 1944–68 – full autonomy in a collaborative relationship; and (4) 1968 to the present – state initiatives to recover that level of collaboration, after it had been badly shaken by the Massacre of Tlatelolco in 1968, when the government sent troops to fire on demonstrating students, academics and workers, killing over two hundred people.

It was not until late in the Second World War, when the Mexican government took the decision to embark upon a post-war development strategy of full industrialization, that relations between the federal state and the National University began to assume a co-operative rather than a coercive form. Historians of Mexico increasingly concur that when autonomy was granted to the National University in 1929, this was done at the instigation of the state rather than of the academic community, and was designed primarily to undermine student support for Vasconcelos's independent presidential candidacy.[56] At that stage, autonomy was not absolute: the President still appointed the Rector. In 1933, Vicente Lombardo Toledano and Antonio Caso conducted their famous debate about the place of Marxism in university teaching practice, with Lombardo advocating the comprehensive implementation of materialist methodology, and Caso arguing the case for intellectual freedom. After the liberals had triumphed, the government of President Abelardo Rodríguez (1932–34) promulgated a new Organic Law for the University which conferred full autonomy, but simultaneously removed the word 'National' from its title and cancelled its annual grant, with the aim of compelling it to become a private institution. The university was thereby warned that if it wanted to be fully independent from the state, it would have to sacrifice public financial support. State funding was not restored until the leftists regained control of the university in 1935. Cárdenas spelt out the terms:

> The Revolution has granted the University its autonomy, so that it may stand apart from the contingencies of politics. ... I am reluctant to believe that the University of Mexico would misuse its autonomy by sponsoring currents contrary to the tenets of the Revolution.[57]

His administration did not only suppress dissent from the intellectual community: it also took steps to consolidate the institutional basis for ensuring that most routes to intellectual recognition ultimately led back to the state. An early initiative was the launch in 1934 of a state publishing house, the Fondo de Cultura Económica, which continued to be the main imprint for academic works until heavy-handed intervention by the Díaz Ordaz government in 1965 prompted an Argentine exile, Arnaldo Orfila, to establish Siglo XXI in Mexico City. The prestigious Colegio de México was founded under Cárdenas, who overrode Congress to ensure its minimum annual grant.[58] Moreover, Cárdenas seized the ideological initiative by funding the pro-Republican League of Revolutionary Writers and Artists during the Spanish Civil War, thereby appropriating the Republican cause for the Party of the Mexican Revolution (PRM, later the Institutional Revolutionary Party, or PRI), and undermining the intellectuals' claims to be the revolutionary conscience of the nation.[59]

During the late 1940s, as the PRI's commitment to full industrialization created a demand for professionals, the National University was restored to a central role in Mexico's development. Another Organic Law in 1944 reaffirmed full autonomy; Alfonso Caso, the last presidential appointee, stepped down as Rector in 1945, and the institution was henceforth known as UNAM (National Autonomous University of Mexico). President Miguel

Alemán (1946–52), whose statement on education policy in 1947 empha-sized the need for 'men of science . . . who can place their knowledge and their expertise at the service of the nation',[60] went on to consolidate an alliance between the National University and the state, since when all of Mexico's presidents have been alumni of UNAM.[61] The PRI's strategy for maintaining indirect state control over the intellectual community was to establish UNAM as the institution through which all young Mexicans aspiring to political power had to pass. This completed the centralization of Mexican cultural life in the capital, further ensuring that provincial univer-sities would not become centres of dissidence. Such was the level of what Gabriel Zaid has dubbed 'UNA Megalomania' that in the post 1945 period, the word *universitario* came to refer only to students at UNAM.[62] A degree from UNAM became an essential rite of passage for anyone seeking public office in Mexico. By this means, the state was able to attract generations of educated men who preferred the prestige and perks of political office to the meagre rewards and recognition available to the independent intellec-tual. Such men were trained not as generalists but as the specialists required for state-led industrialization. This institutional mechanism for precluding the emergence of independent intellectuals meant that from the mid-1940s onwards, the ruling party had little need to offer any of them executive posts and very rarely did so.

Once the post-revolutionary Mexican state had consolidated its power during the 1940s, direct repression of intellectuals occurred far more rarely than hitherto; instead, politicians preferred to nurture what they saw as a mutually beneficial relationship. In its role as 'cultural entrepreneur', the one-party state sponsored the institutions that supported intellectuals,[63] thereby maintaining a situation in which intellectuals saw sufficient advan-tages in co-operating with the state to ensure that the tacit alliance between the two proved remarkably durable. Intellectuals from what Enrique Krauze refers to as the mid-century generation could all get jobs at UNAM, and both UNAM and the Colegio de México began to fund much-coveted research trips to Paris.[64] This generation was known for 'criticism and cosmopolitanism': for a couple of decades, government policy was flexible enough for intellectuals to play a critical role, albeit with certain tacit limitations. When the PRI did finally resort to severe repression during the Díaz Ordaz presidency (1964–70), that relationship came under strain, but even then it did not break down completely. After the Massacre of Tlate-lolco, tension heightened around the hitherto uncontroversial option of critical support for the regime. The most famous example of this occurred in June 1971, when Carlos Fuentes continued to back President Luis Echeverría (in office 1970–76) following repression of the first student demonstration since 1968, on the grounds that Echeverría merited defend-ing against the truly guilty, whom the novelist identified as the invisible forces of the Right. For this stance, Fuentes was attacked as an *entreguista* (someone who has sold out) who had surrendered 'the power of the pen to the power of the sword'.[65] In a public letter, Gabriel Zaid denounced him, saying: 'By using your international prestige to bolster the presidency . . . you have made [intellectual] independence more difficult.'[66] Fuentes's response was to dismiss independence as a bourgeois value, but Zaid's point was ultimately more telling. The events of 1968 obliged intellectuals to examine more critically the idea that by serving the state they were serving the people.

Nevertheless, Krauze suggests, the repression against the independent daily newspaper *Excélsior* in 1976 was probably more important than the events of 1968 in provoking a more lasting parting of the ways between the intellectual Left and the state. It was in the wake of 1976, rather than 1968, that intellectuals founded a number of newspapers and journals (including *Proceso*, *Vuelta*, *Nexos*, *Unomásuno* and *La Jornada*) designed to stimulate public debate on politics and culture. Krauze notes that when guerrillas embarked on armed revolution in the mountains of Guerrero in late 1968, they failed to gain even rhetorical support from intellectuals, who allowed themselves to be wooed by the incoming President, Echeverría. It was only when the government made the mistake of interfering directly in intellectual life by attacking *Excélsior* that intellectuals began to take serious steps to enhance their independence from the state.[67] Even so, a few years later most of these journals were receiving an indirect state subsidy in the form of public sector advertising.

The Mexican revolution resulted in the consolidation of a state that was fundamentally anti-intellectual but nevertheless acquired sufficient strength and flexibility to reach an accommodation with intellectuals that proved to be in its own best interests. Ironically enough, given that socio-economic frustration had been a contributory factor to many intellectuals' support for Madero in 1910, the outcome of the revolution was ultimately to consolidate the hegemony of commercial values. Far from accommodating the universal intellectual, the post-revolutionary state replicated the Porfirian tradition of specialists – administrators and technicians. Once revolutionary power was institutionalized in Mexico, intellectuals either had to accept full-time political positions, or remain on the margins of political power with little more than ritual obeisance made to them by the government for their creative achievements. In consequence, contrary to the common perception of Mexico as the Spanish American country where intellectuals have enjoyed the most influence in politics, one of the most dominant ideas in Mexican cultural life since the 1930s has been that 'those who are genuine intellectuals must know how to keep their distance from power'.[68] In other words, influence was to be obtained only at the price of renouncing the role of universal 'intellectual' and occupying a bureaucratic niche as a specialist

'expert'. The post-revolutionary Mexican state has repeatedly proved resistant to the views of intellectuals who aspired to an independent, universal
role. Even the public statements of a figure as prestigious as Paz have been
disregarded by officialdom: his calls for the election results of 1985 and
1991 to be respected fell on deaf ears.[69] A few intellectuals of international
renown have been flattered and honoured individually by Mexican governments, but Roderic Camp's research lends support to the argument that
'any influence of the [twentieth-century Mexican] intellectual on public
policy has been the exception rather than the rule'.[70] Mexico is a clear
example of a modernizing state that declined to accord the same degree of
political authority to its twentieth-century intellectuals as its oligarchic
predecessor had conceded to the nineteenth-century *licenciado–políticos*.

Argentina

Argentine intellectuals maintain that their relationships with both the state
and civil society have consistently been more conflictual than in other major
Spanish American republics. By the 1960s, their sense of exclusion had
become acute. They contrasted their experience of 'a definite mistrust . . .
regarding the function of intellectuals in politics' unfavourably with the
position of Mexican or Brazilian intellectuals, whom they saw as enjoying
not only a relatively stable institutional base but also access to state power.[71]
Indeed, it is the case that, since 1930, the Argentine state has attacked the
heart of intellectual life, the universities, more persistently than virtually any
other major state in the region. It was in Córdoba, Argentina, that the
university reform movement – aimed at eliminating corrupt practices and
outdated curricula from the region's universities – first began. But having
initiated reform, Argentina's universities – subject to intervention by military
regimes in 1930, 1943, 1955, 1966 and 1976 – have spent most of the
subsequent years struggling to win it back from reactionary governments.
Argentina's academic community has been among the most politicized on
the continent: 'Rather than just the university, we refer to "the Peronist
university" of 1946 to 1955, "the reformist university" of 1955 to 1966, "the
Peronist university, version two" after 1973, "the university of the *Proceso*
[military rule]" of 1976 to 1983 and, after that, "the democratic university".'[72] Direct state censorship of published literary and academic work has
been in force for much of the twentieth century. The only Argentine
governments before the redemocratization process of the 1980s that did not
use a significant degree of coercion as a way of controlling the intellectual
community were those of Radicals Hipólito Yrigoyen (1916–22 and
1928–30), Arturo Frondizi (1958–62) and Arturo Illia (1963–66).[73] Yet,
policies of co-option have also played an important role at certain key

stages, above all during the first decade of the twentieth century. Moreover, both co-option and containment were more significant features of the first Peronist government's policies towards intellectuals than is generally recognized.

Argentina is a special case in that the oligarchy was successful in sustaining its nineteenth-century role as patron of the arts for far longer than its counterparts in other Spanish American countries. Many members of the first generation of professional intellectuals in Argentina were dependent to some degree on the liberal elite for the means to support their status, either through state funding of culture or through the oligarchs' ownership of the leading newspapers, which expanded their remit to become national rather than almost exclusively *porteño* (of Buenos Aires) during the first decade of the twentieth century.[74] Around the time of the Independence Centenary of 1910, the Argentine oligarchy, which directly controlled the state until 1916, was sufficiently confident of its position to tolerate and even sponsor a relatively broad range of intellectual activity, including the work on education, *La restauración nacionalista* (1909), by the then self-proclaimed Marxist Ricardo Rojas, whose research trip to Europe and publication costs were all paid by the government of José Figueroa Alcorta (1906–10).[75] An elementary law to protect intellectual copyright was introduced in 1910, and a system of relatively generous annual state prizes for literature and the sciences was instituted in 1913.[76] In these circumstances, middle-class intellectuals tended to adopt aristocratic values; in any case, few of them were enthused when the Radical Civic Union (UCR) representing middle-class interests was decisively elected in 1916. Fewer still anticipated that Yrigoyen's government would implement university reform only two years later.

A close analysis of the events of 1918 reveals both the extent to which the Argentine state retained the initiative in relation to the universities and the ultimately restricted nature of the concessions it granted. The University of Córdoba, where the reform movement began, was the most conservative of Argentine academic institutions, still dominated by the ecclesiastical orthodoxies of scholasticism. It had remained immune to the mild currents of reform that had permeated the University of Buenos Aires (UBA) in 1903–08, prompting some democratization of the process for selecting staff and a consequent updating, at least in part, of the curriculum. In 1918, the Córdoba students' main demand was that the system of staff appointments already in place at UBA and the relatively new Universidad Nacional de La Plata (founded in 1902) should also apply in their institution, namely, they wanted to end the practices both of the President appointing the Rector and of academics with life tenure choosing their own successors. Yrigoyen's official mediator, liberal oligarch José N. Matienzo, was installed on 11 April 1918, just over a month after the Reform Committee had published its first manifesto, and he quickly acceded to student demands that the Rector should be elected by academic staff. The main student disturbances were sparked off when it became clear that Corda Frates (an elite Catholic cabal which informally controlled the university) could orchestrate sufficient support for its own candidate to control the new democratic procedure. Student activism was thenceforth designed to provoke a second intervention from the Yrigoyen government, which was duly decreed on 2 August. Yrigoyen baited his Catholic opposition by initially calling in a liberal intellectual, Telemaco Susini, who had sympathized with the students from the outset. The President then bowed to the resulting pressure from the Right and nominated instead José Salinas, his Minister of Public Instruction. Salinas hesitated, the reformists occupied the university on 9 September, and Yrigoyen – having smoked out his enemies – made a further gesture to the Right by sending in two army units and police to arrest the eighty-three students. But within forty-eight hours the charges had been dropped and Salinas initiated an intervention that concluded with new university statutes conceding the principles of autonomy, significant student participation in university governance, and free tuition. The government thereby outmanoeuvred the Catholic Church, and subsequently used the umbrella of reform to bring the universities of Santa Fe and Tucumán under state control.[77]

The precariousness of the concessions won by the reform movement, and the extent to which it had been subject to manipulation, became evident during the more conservative Radical Party government of Marcelo T. de Alvear (1922–28). Alvear, who relied on the Right to strengthen his own political position against the charismatic and populist Yrigoyen, sent troops into the universities and rewrote the statutes to remove students from a direct role in university governance. At the same time, Alvear's government was careful not to engage in blanket repression on a national level: civil liberties were largely respected, which made it difficult for reformist intellectuals to adopt a wholly adversarial stance.[78] The state's combination of accommodation and repression ensured that the intellectual community oriented itself in relation to the state in a way that neither strategy alone could have achieved. Violent protests and defiant manifestos alternated in rapid succession with conciliatory petitions to the President.[79]

Private patronage continued to be an important source of income for intellectuals throughout the 1920s, with institutions such as the Institute of Public Lectures, founded in 1914 by the owners of *La Prensa*, the elitist Association for Friends of the Arts, launched in 1924, and even that men-only pinnacle of *porteño* social distinction, the Jockey Club, acting as leading centres of cultural activities. This situation persisted not least because the Radical governments of 1916–30, which sought to represent themselves as the forgers of a new Argentina, failed to introduce their own measures either to co-opt intellectuals or to sponsor their work. The rivalry between intellectuals and reformist politicians over popular national identity was nowhere revealed more clearly than in Yrigoyen's claim, made in 1923, that he had been the incarnation of *argentinidad* for more than thirty years.[80] Although a small group of intellectuals in 1928 campaigned for Yrigoyen's re-election (including Leopoldo Marechal and Jorge Luis Borges), few intellectuals expressed any public regrets over the military overthrow of the Radical government in 1930. A group of right-wing nationalists (among them Leopoldo Lugones and Carlos Ibarguren) actively supported General José Uriburu's coup. The attitude of most intellectuals was probably captured in a statement issued after the coup by the recently established Argentine branch of the PEN Club, which declared:

> Independently [of] any political opinion and remembering only our condition as writers, we want to note on the record that we were almost never paid any attention by the authorities of the previous government, which never showed the slightest interest in us, either as a collective entity or as individuals, or in our work.[81]

While lack of recognition is a not infrequent complaint of intellectuals the world over, the peculiarly bitter tone of this pronouncement suggests that the Radical governments had neglected the intellectual community to an extent that was counterproductive to the UCR's own self-interest.

During the *década infame* (infamous decade), Agustín Justo's government (1932–38) tried to re-establish a relationship between the state and intellectuals through a series of initiatives which included: reinstating the university teachers dismissed by Uriburu because of their Radical sympathies; resuming the annual award of national prizes, which had lapsed during the second Yrigoyen government; subsidizing cultural activities; updating the law on intellectual property rights (1933); and creating a National Commission of Culture (1935).[82] But these measures proved inadequate to persuade more than a small minority of the intellectual community to support a corrupt, conservative regime intent on preserving the role of the oligarchy. The reinstated *oficialista* tradition of oligarchic liberalism faced two new challenges: one from the authoritarian Right, many of whom identified with European Fascism; and the other from a group of disaffected young Radicals, who in 1935 formed a breakaway group called FORJA (Radical Force for the Guidance of Argentine Youth). These young intellectuals attacked the Argentine oligarchy and its supposed collaboration with imperialism; their programme was to elaborate a popular nationalism, elements of which were subsequently adopted by Perón *en route* from his stronghold as Labour Secretary in a military regime to popularly elected president in 1946.

Perón himself became notorious among the international intellectual community for the 'promotion' of Jorge Luis Borges from his job in a Buenos Aires library to poultry inspector in the local street market (whereupon Borges duly resigned from public employ). However, Peronist cultural policy was more complex than might be suggested by this crudely philistine gesture, or by slogans such as '*alpargatas* [cotton shoes for the workers] yes, books, no'. It is hardly surprising that the anti-oligarchic Peronist government chose to make an example of Borges – who could all too easily be represented as the epitome of an aristocratic intellectual – in order to pursue its populist agenda of marking intellectuals out as enemies of the people. (The subsequent military regime, which committed itself to extirpating Peronism from Argentine society, correspondingly moved quickly to reinstate Borges, making him Director of the National Library in 1955, and awarding him the National Prize for Literature the following year.) The anti-intellectualism inherent in all populist rhetoric became particularly virulent among Peronists, for whom the word 'intellectual' was always a term of abuse.[83] Evita, who played on her femininity to identify herself as 'the heart' of the Peronist movement, was central to this: for example, in a series of lectures on the history of Peronism, she declared, 'as a woman and a Peronist, I'm going to try to carry forward the history of Peronism with my heart' and claimed 'we don't need many intellects, but [we do need] many hearts, for justicialism is learnt with the heart rather than with the mind'.[84] But it would be a mistake to think that Perón did not believe culture to be important: on the contrary, he understood the significance of the battle for hegemony only too well, regarding culture not only as a 'moral preparation and a weapon for sustaining the position of each man in the daily struggle but also an indispensable means of ensuring that political life develops with tolerance, honesty and understanding' – in other words, a key determinant of social cohesion and political stability.[85] He may not have been prepared to grant recognition to intellectuals who had emphasized the relationship of culture to national identity, but he undoubtedly took their ideas on board, stating in 1948 that 'the wrecking of a people's culture is equivalent to the loss of its very national being'.[86]

It has been argued that Perón was content to leave culture in the hands of conservative Catholics, seeing this as a politically expedient way of keeping the church from moving into opposition against him. However, this was rather more true of the 1943–46 military government than of Perón's own regime. President Pedro Ramírez had quickly intervened in the universities to enforce the teaching programme of the right-wing Catholic bloc (Jordán Bruno Genta, appointed as *interventor* [inspector with extraordinary powers] at the Universidad del Litoral, wanted to bring back Aristotle); in early 1944 a decree insisting that Catholicism be taught in all educational institutions reversed secularization laws dating back to 1884.

Once elected, Perón himself had a far more ambitious cultural project than simply allowing a regression to scholasticism. He saw the reorientation of culture as an essential element of the overall transformation he intended to make in Argentine society: a 'national culture' was declared to be Peronism's fifth and final objective (after a mass social base, an economic base, a political base and reform of the justice system).[87] Revealingly, in her history of Peronism, Eva represented Perón himself as a cultural rather than a political leader, attributing to him all the qualities more commonly associated with intellectuals: 'Perón is not a politician; Perón is a leader, he is a genius, he is a teacher, he is a guide.'[88] Introducing a metaphor that was to recur in her lectures, Eva declared the 'New Argentina' promised by Peronism to be '*a work of art*', for which, in Perón, 'we have *the artist*'.[89] Above all, claimed Evita, Perón was '*a creator* who has no cause to envy [any of] the great creators in the history of humanity'.[90] Particularly after his political project of building national unity had begun to founder on economic crisis in the early 1950s, Perón devoted ever more attention to the creation of 'a national culture which [was] genuinely Argentine and within the reach of all Argentines'.[91] 'National culture' was described in his Second Five-year Plan as including not only traditional songs, legends, music, dances and crafts, but also 'the spiritual inheritance bequeathed to us by classical cultures, especially those of Greek and Latin origin . . . with the addition of all those manifestations of modern world culture which do not contradict the guiding principle of those [classical] forms'.[92] This statement suggested that Perón's vision of an ideal Argentine culture was much closer to Rodó's idea of Spanish America as the repository of the riches of the classical world than to the paraphernalia of folkloric gauchos and tango with which Perón is customarily associated in populist mythology. Eva's *Historia del peronismo* was also liberally sprinkled with classical references, including the claim that Lycurgus the lawgiver, to whom she attributed, almost certainly inaccurately, a redistribution of Spartan land, was the 'first Justicialist in human history'.[93] On being awarded an honorary doctorate by the University of Buenos Aires in 1947, Perón referred to Spain as 'our mother' (in repudiation of the nineteenth-century liberals' epithet of 'stepmother') and informed his audience that the motto 'The sun will never set on our Hispanic culture' would be emblazoned across the frontispiece of Argentine universities in order to compensate for 'the centuries of neglect and the hours of ingratitude'.[94] This emphasis on Spanish and creole culture enabled him both to appease the vocal minority group of *hispanista* (pro-Spanish) right-wing nationalists that had developed in the 1930s, and to reassert the legitimacy of the Spanish/creole inheritance, renouncing the cosmopolitan bias of liberals.

As he did with other potentially dissident groups, Perón managed his relationship with intellectuals through a combination of institutional infiltration, targeted repression during politically difficult periods,[95] social and economic marginalization, and an often underestimated degree of co-option. The instances of institutional control, repression and marginalization are well known and require only brief recapitulation to provide context, given that the main purpose here is to explore the often-neglected elements of containment and co-option inherent in Perón's policies.

Perón did not delay before intervening in the universities (which had been so bitterly opposed to Perón in the February 1946 elections that they had supported the US-backed Democratic Union). In May 1946, one month before his inauguration, government administrators were appointed to all universities. Later, student organizations were temporarily banned (to be replaced with the regime's own student organization, the Peronist University Youth, or JUP) and the universities were purged of 70 per cent of their staff in just one year between mid-1946 and mid-1947. The 1947 University Law formally reversed most of what had been achieved by the 1918 reform: it abolished university autonomy and democratic channels of administration, restoring nomination of rectors by the national president. In 1950, a General University Confederation (CGU) was established, which was specifically intended to replace the University Federation of Argentina (FUA) (a product of the reform movement). The purge continued: by 1953, 90 per cent of the university staff of 1945 had been ousted.[96] In so far as Perón had any project for the universities, it was that they should turn out skilled professionals dedicated to serving the nation as he envisaged it: enshrined in the 1949 constitution was a provision that the universities should offer compulsory courses dedicated to acquainting students with 'the essence of what it is to be Argentine'.[97] In practice, however, he left the running of the universities to Catholic conservatives.[98] It was not until Peronism was overthrown in 1955 that a government intervention at UBA, led by José Luis Romero, tried to do 'what Perón had never dared: to cut the university's links with the traditional oligarchy of the city and province and to open its doors to previously excluded groups'.[99]

A less noted aspect of Perón's cultural policy is the degree to which he extended state control and/or patronage over many areas of cultural life. In November 1946, he announced: 'The state has to concern itself with the culture of the people, because nations that lack a culture of their own are highly vulnerable to becoming semi-colonial countries.'[100] His intention to involve the state fully was signalled in an article on culture he published in 1948: in this, Perón argued that for culture to be worthwhile, it had to be an expression of national, rather than individual, genius. Recognizing that most creative people would be reluctant to shackle their talent to the national interest, Perón stipulated that such renunciations of individual genius would have to be encouraged by 'careful vigilance on the part of the highest and most educated ranks of the people's political organiz-ation'.[101] As with other areas of social policy, Perón established an extensive bureaucracy to administer culture, centred on a Secretariat of Education, which was separated from the Ministry of Justice in 1948, and appointed two sub-secretaries, one for education and one for culture.[102] In 1948 also, a National Board of Intellectuals was launched, which proposed to guarantee intellectuals a series of statutory benefits such as copyright protection, on condition that they signed up to a Register of Intellectual Workers.[103] This initiative foundered, but was followed in 1953 by a General Confederation of Professionals (the CGP, intended to be a parallel organization to the workers' CGT). To counter the anti-Peronist Argentine Society of Writers (SADE), the Peronist government encouraged a new organization, the Association of Argentine Writers (ADEA), led by Leopoldo Marechal, Hugo Wast and Manuel Gálvez, of which Perón and his wife were made honorary members.[104] In 1950, Perón introduced Awards for Merit in art, science and technology, medals which were to be awarded personally by the President. In his Second Five-year Plan, the Secretariat of Education was assigned responsibility for co-ordinating 'all the tasks carried out by cultural bodies, be they public or private' in order to ensure that 'all national manifestations of art and science should be at the service of the people'.[105] The plan also envisaged the establishment of a National Academy of Language to prepare a national dictionary (incorporating regional dialects), and of a state publisher to produce cheap editions of the leading works of Argentine and world literature. Perón evidently did not intend to repeat Yrigoyen's mistake of hoping that if he ignored intellectuals, they might all go away.

Perón dealt with the members of FORJA by simultaneously co-opting yet marginalizing them. Accommodatingly, they had dissolved their own organization in 1945 on the grounds that Perón embodied their aims. None was offered the prestigious intellectual posts (for example, Rector of UBA) that they may have coveted; most took jobs in public administration. Arturo Jauretche was made president of the Banco de la Provincia de Buenos Aires, despite not being renowned for his financial abilities.[106] The most interesting case concerned the mentor of the FORJA intellectuals, Raúl Scalabrini Ortiz, who hailed Perón as the new Yrigoyen,[107] and who wrote the book that was instrumental in providing an intellectual justification for Perón's nationalizations of the British-owned railways on 1 March 1948.[108] A few weeks later, Scalabrini Ortiz found himself in the Ministry of Public Works, confronted by an army general who informed him that Perón had decided that he, Scalabrini Ortiz, was the man to run the railways. Scalabrini Ortiz, who had already refused various posts in the state bureaucracy, found the prospect unenticing and declined on personal grounds. From that point on, the Peronist state turned against him, mysteriously dropping a proposal to name a railway station after him (when the newly nationalized railway lines had already been baptized Urquiza, Mitre, Sarmiento and Roca after the heroes of liberal nation-building),[109] withdrawing official support from publications that printed his work, and slighting him in a multitude of minor ways.[110] Comforting himself with the thought that this was the work of pro-imperialist infiltrators into the Peronist state, Scalabrini Ortiz apparently continued to believe that Peronism was progressive, although he prudently refrained from public political comment until after Perón's overthrow.[111]

It was not until the late 1950s that Perón and Scalabrini Ortiz conducted their now-famous correspondence, in which Perón, by then in exile, asked Scalabrini Ortiz to lead a movement of intellectuals in support of Peronism. This approach should be understood in the context of the increased political influence of intellectuals in Argentina during the late 1950s, particularly the group around the journal *Contorno*, who had declared their support for Arturo Frondizi's candidacy in the February 1958 presidential election. Frondizi, whose Intransigent Radical Civic Union (UCR-I) had broken away from the Radical Party in March 1957, had made a secret deal with Perón to secure Peronist votes. Perón was confident that the Peronist masses were disciplined, but feared that he was losing the battle for hegemony among the middle classes, whose support he needed to win in order to expand his core support base.[112] In this strategy, Perón was influenced by his close adviser, John William Cooke, who himself had claims to be an intellectual. (By the late 1960s, Peronism was to succeed in transforming itself from the almost exclusively working-class movement it was in 1955 to a far more broadly based coalition, including significant sectors of the middle classes.) In his letter of invitation, Perón rather grudgingly granted Scalabrini Ortiz a prophetic role in the transformation of Argentina: 'To you, the initiator of a development that fed the national revolution, we owe the honour due to precursors.' But, he hastily added, 'the credit for having popularized and realized the principles of economic independence and political sovereignty is exclusively due to Justicialism, which linked them closely with the social problem'.[113] That is, Perón was jealously guarding the historical significance of his own social philosophy; once again, we can detect the populist politician's apprehension about the intellectuals' potential hold over *lo popular*. Characteristically, Scalabrini Ortiz refused to place his reputation at Perón's service by leading the proposed group of intellectuals, but the General went ahead regardless and appropriated his work to the Peronist cause, responding, 'We always count you as one of us, and every line you write is a contribution to the Peronist movement.'[114]

Perón accorded a high profile to those few well-known intellectuals who were prepared to collaborate with him. The poet and novelist Leopoldo Marechal (1900–70) was the most prestigious of the Peronist literary intellectuals, even though his metaphysical, stream-of-consciousness stylistic experimentation (particularly in the Joycean *Adán Buenosayres*, published in

1948) hardly conformed to populist precepts. Having worked for the preceding military government as Director General of National Culture (1945–46), from 1947 to 1955 Marechal served the Peronist state as Director of Artistic Training, supervising schools of fine arts and crafts and the National Conservatory. The anti-imperialist and former socialist intellectual Manuel Ugarte maintained that Perón was no egalitarian, but Ugarte welcomed his election in the conviction that he would do everything possible 'to make the country independent'.[115] Ugarte initially made a favourable impression on Perón, who concluded after a meeting between the two in mid-1946, 'we must incorporate him and make good use of him in the revolution',[116] and despatched him to be ambassador to Mexico. By June 1948, however, tensions had begun to develop as Ugarte voiced his concerns about what he saw as increasing bureaucratization around Perón; after being shuffled around from Mexico to Nicaragua and then to Cuba, Ugarte was finally recalled to Buenos Aires, without explanation, at the end of 1949. He resigned in disgust, after which he received no official aid or state pension.[117]

It should be noted that, despite periodic confrontations (and Victoria Ocampo's notorious period of imprisonment),[118] Perón did not close down either the literary magazine *Sur*, or the literary supplement of *La Nación*, both of which were identified in the public eye with intellectuals of the old oligarchy. Perón's main concern was to prevent the emergence of any movement that could rival his own version of nationalism. In that respect, *Sur*'s translations of the debates between Camus and Sartre were not deemed to represent any threat. Moreover, as Juan José Sebreli argues, Peronist official culture was itself elitist, run by two members of the oligarchy, Ignacio Pirovano and his wife Lía Elizalde (daughter of Bebe Elizalde de Pirovano, who in 1924 had founded the influential literary society Friends of the Arts). As Secretary of Culture, Pirovano organized showings of all the latest avant-garde films, classical concerts and theatre. According to Sebreli, tango and folklore were not officially promoted until after Perón's fall, under Frondizi in the late 1950s.[119] By these means, Perón prevented the intelligentsia as a whole from moving into outright opposition.

The ultimate effect of Peronist policies was to close off all avenues for intellectuals apart from apoliticism (a philosophical commitment for a minority, a tactical retreat for most) or collaboration. Allowing *Sur* to continue publishing proved to be a shrewd policy in that it precluded intellectuals from claiming with any plausibility that Peronism prohibited high culture. Some discreet opposition did operate, mostly centred on the journals *Contorno* (1953–59) and *Imago mundi* (1953–56), with the latter functioning as an 'alternative university'.[120] This restriction of options was comparable to the experience of Mexican intellectuals during the 1930s and 1940s, but with the crucial difference that the Mexican state invested resources in creating an institutional base for its intellectuals and also offered far more attractive incentives for them to be co-opted. In the aftermath of Perón's overthrow in 1955, it was hardly surprising that intellectuals, especially from the *Contorno* group, leapt at the apparent chance of influencing public policy offered a few years later by Frondizi.[121] However, notwithstanding the policy differences that soon emerged, Frondizi explicitly stated that his *desarrollista* (developmentalist) strategy relied upon 'the experts required by the technological and social advances of modern industry',[122] and he preferred to listen to a man like Rogelio Frigerio, 'an entrepreneur linked with the industrial sectors' and an advocate of 'a state-planned economy',[123] rather than to generalist intellectuals, for whom the resulting disillusionment was bitter. Denied the opportunity to influence public policy, Argentine intellectuals found that, unlike their counterparts in Mexico, they also lacked the institutional conditions to enable them to concentrate on their intellectual pursuits. But, at root, it was the consistent refusal of Argentine governments throughout the twentieth century to allow any plausible role for intellectuals that created the structural conditions of an anti-intellectual state, and paved the way for the radicalization and militancy of many of them in the 1960s and 1970s.

Peru

While the Peruvian state has consistently practised a high level of coercion with respect to intellectuals, there has also been a significant measure of co-option and a notable degree of containment. The dictatorships of General Oscar Benavides (1933–39) and Manuel Odría (1948–56) did not hesitate to repress intellectuals; but most other governments, including those of José Bustamante y Rivero (1945–48) and Manuel Prado (1939–45 and 1956–62), preferred to try co-option, albeit to a limited extent. Their strategy was similar to that pioneered by the Obregón government in Mexico: appoint one leading intellectual to a prestigious post and hope that the rest will remain content to occupy more lowly positions in the public administration of culture, living in expectation of better things to come. For example, the historian Jorge Basadre served as Minister of Education briefly in 1945 in the government of his old friend Bustamante y Rivero, and again from 1956 to 1958 under Prado; the *indigenista* writer Luis Valcárcel (1893–1986), was Minister of Education for APRA [American Popular Revolutionary Alliance] (1945–47); and the literary critic and historian Raúl Porras Barrenechea (1897–1960), conservative in all but his anti-imperialism, was Prado's Minister of Foreign Affairs from 1958 until 1960. Both President Fernando Belaúnde Terry (1963–68), himself a professional architect, and the reformist military government (1968–80) favoured the co-option of intellectuals. The changeable fortunes of the *indigenista* novelist and ethnographer José María Arguedas (1911–69) are not atypical. Having been imprisoned by Benavides for taking part in a student demonstration against the visit of an Italian Fascist (an experience he recalled in *El sexto*),[124] Arguedas later held various posts in state institutes of folklore and ethnology, eventually under Belaúnde, becoming Director of the House of Culture and the National Museum of History.

The foundations of the modernizing Peruvian state's relationship with intellectuals were laid during the autocratic *oncenio* (eleven-year rule, from 1919 to 1930) of Augusto Leguía. Leguía was from an old family that had lost its fortune; he himself had become a successful businessman. Having been President from 1909 to 1912 with the support of the oligarchic Partido Civil (when he had taken the prudent step of appointing Peru's then leading radical intellectual, Manuel González Prada, as Director of the National Library), he defeated a *civilista* candidate in the 1918 elections, carried out a coup and declared himself dictator. At first, Leguía's second regime sought to rally the support of nascent middle sectors behind a reform programme that in some respects challenged the interests of the oligarchy. Within four years, however, he had adopted a more defensive line and sought more conservative allies. Historians differ as to whether Leguía is best understood as the champion of a rising middle class that reacted against the Aristocratic Republic (1895–1919), or as the head of a new faction that emerged from within an already fracturing oligarchy.[125] What is most important to the argument here, however, is that he was a modernizer who sought, at least initially, the support of the middle classes in order to undercut the political – if not the social – privileges of the *civilistas*. During his *oncenio*, the state was modernized, the middle sectors became far more diversified, and Lima was transformed: it was said of Leguía that his zeal for 'progress' was such that he would have been capable of paving the Andes.[126] By expanding the state, Leguía created a new basis for political patronage. But precisely because he did so little to challenge the economic or social status quo, the struggle for cultural hegemony became a central issue. Moreover, in contrast to its counterpart in Argentina, the Peruvian oligarchy had failed to leaven its self-declared monopoly of culture with measures to promote and pay for it.[127]

The intellectual sectors of Peruvian society had already proven themselves to have what Leguía must have regarded as a potentially dangerous tendency to express dissent and harbour political ambition. Many writers of the previous Generation of 1900 had become acutely preoccupied with 'the national question' in the aftermath of Peru's débâcle in the War of the Pacific (1879–1883), and had supported José de la Riva Agüero's National Democratic Party (PND), founded in 1915. The party ceased functioning in

1919, but by then had advocated a programme of moderate constitutional, political and social reform (including an attempt to address 'the Indian question', motivated by fear of descent into a state of chaos similar to that then engulfing Mexico). Members of this intellectual generation belonged to the oligarchy, but, contrary to the conventional view of them, the majority were not in fact *civilistas*.[128] Indeed, Jorge Cornejo Pilar has argued that although Peruvian intellectuals have since been involved in the founding of other parties, the foundation of Riva Agüero's PND was the first and last case in Peru of virtually an entire intellectual generation committing itself to party politics.[129] From Leguía's point of view, if the intellectual sectors of the oligarchy were capable of showing such determination to win political power on a reformist platform, then the emergence in the 1920s of the far more radical Centenary Generation presented a much greater potential threat. In their majority, the members of this new generation of intellectuals had been born not into the oligarchy but the middle classes, and their sense of exclusion was compounded by the fact that they hailed from the provinces rather than Lima.

In these circumstances, Leguía, whose government characterized itself as being 'of the Idea',[130] paid some attention to intellectuals, and tried – successfully with many – to incorporate them into his project. A few members of the Generation of 1900, notably Javier Prado y Ugarteche (1871–1921) and José Antonio Encinas (1888–1958), were influential in securing *indigenista* clauses in the 1919 constitution and acted as advisers on Leguía's early policies towards Indians. He was prepared to go to some lengths to protect and support those intellectuals whom he regarded as politically sympathetic. The most notorious example was the *modernista* poet José Santos Chocano (1875–1934), who is now generally considered a minor talent but was acclaimed during the early twentieth century as the 'poet of America'. Santos Chocano was fêted by Leguía's government when he returned to his native country in 1921 after a sixteen-year absence; he was crowned Poet Laureate of Peru the following year, and commissioned to write a poem to commemorate the centenary of the Battle of Ayacucho. After he was imprisoned for murder following the fatal wounding of his fellow bard Edwin Elmore Letts in a shooting incident in 1925, Leguía oversaw the passage of an amnesty law through Congress: Santos Chocano was freed at the end of 1927 (only to be murdered himself in Santiago seven years later).[131] The government also took some limited measures to subsidize cultural life, launching two official publications, *Mundial* and *Variedades*, which accepted contributions even from critics of the regime such as José Carlos Mariátegui and César Vallejo.[132] Leguía instituted a practice of low-level co-option of intellectuals, which has been continued by the ideologically diverse regimes that have since controlled the Peruvian state. Nevertheless, he excluded them from policy-making in education, preferring to appoint a US director of education and US advisers to oversee his projected expansion of public elementary schooling. Even Encinas, described by Cornejo Pilar as 'one of the great teachers of modern Peru and one of the founders of national pedagogy', was excluded from Leguía's Ministry of Education.[133]

Leguía's main tactic for dealing with those intellectuals whom he was unable to co-opt was to send them into exile. This was the fate of the three leading opposition intellectuals of these years. The most adroitly managed instance concerned the young Mariátegui, whose newspaper *La Razón* was the only one to give unequivocal and sustained backing both to the workers in their campaign for an eight-hour day and to the students in their bid for university reform. Mariátegui 'was soon highly revered among student and labor leaders alike', and when the workers were granted most of their demands by Leguía shortly after his coup in July 1919, the three thousand or so of them who were on their way to the presidential palace to meet Leguía descended first on Mariátegui's editorial office 'to show their gratitude' for his support.[134] It is safe to assume that the incoming president was none too pleased that 'it fell on Mariátegui, too, to step onto a balcony and address a multitude of people'.[135] *La Razón* then persisted with its anti-government campaign, threatening to unite militant workers and students under a charismatic intellectual leadership. Leguía, basking in widespread approval after his release of the political prisoners who had been detained by the Aristocratic Republic, wanted to thwart opposition journalists without resorting himself to direct repression. He therefore offered Mariátegui and two of his associates government grants to travel to Europe, tempering the bait by bestowing upon them the title 'Official Propagandists for Peru', which they all accepted.[136] Mariátegui never saw Leguía as his main political target, despite being arrested twice for his activism (in 1924 and again in 1927, when his journal *Amauta* and its associated publishing house were closed down by the government). He envisaged the transformation of Peru as a long-term task to which Leguía's anti-oligarchic measures and enthusiasm for capitalist development could contribute, both by undermining feudal structures and by highlighting the importance of socialism as an alternative.[137] Even after Leguía had abandoned most of his reform programme in 1923, Mariátegui apparently continued to identify 'some positive results from Leguía's policies', particularly his 'efforts to break up the large estates',[138] and he maintained a public stance of neutrality.

As the regime became more conservative, its methods for dealing with intellectual dissent became harsher. The avant-garde poet César Vallejo, who had offended the establishment with his erotic/religious imagery, was arrested and imprisoned on fabricated charges. He subsequently departed for Europe – without government sponsorship – in 1923. The student leader, Víctor Raúl Haya de la Torre, who, unlike Mariátegui, denounced the *oncenio* as a continuation of oligarchic rule, was arrested for organizing demonstrations against Leguía's attempt to retain the support of the church by consecrating Peru to the Sacred Heart of Jesus, and he was forced into exile in 1923.

At the institutional level, Leguía moved quickly to neutralize the Peruvian branch of the university reform movement, but he did so, at least initially, by accommodation rather than repression. Soon after taking power, his government, which was opposed by most academics, declared support for the students and conceded their demands almost before they had succeeded in formulating them. A decree issued on 20 September 1919 authorized academic freedom and student co-government; the following February, a second edict enabled students to participate in staff recruitment. In the early years of Leguía's regime, the student federation accorded him the title 'Mentor of Youth' (although this was denounced by a dissident group led by Haya de la Torre). As also happened in Argentina, a regime scorned by most intellectuals manipulated the reform movement to advance its own struggle for cultural hegemony; at the same time, Leguía snuffed out the incipient mobilization of the intellectual community by addressing most of their immediate concerns – significantly though, not autonomy, which was not granted until 1931, the year after Leguía had been deposed.[139] When he moved to the right in 1923, consolidating an alliance with his former enemies in the church, *civilista* groups tried to turn the university into an anti-government stronghold, and university reformists advanced openly into the political arena with the formation of APRA. After several years of squabbling between the Leguía regime and the university, the by then beleaguered government moved back on to the defensive in 1928 by issuing a new statute expressly designed to bring the university under the direct control of the state. According to Jorge Basadre, Leguía's then Minister of Education, Pedro Oliveira, presented the choice in stark terms: 'the university was either controlled by elite circles or controlled by the state'.[140] As was also to prove the case in Cuba, the Peruvian state's repressive reflex proved far more damaging to the status quo than the earlier policy of granting limited concessions which, had they been sustained, might well have succeeded in containing effective opposition from the intellectual community.

The received wisdom about Peruvian intellectuals is that they have been leading figures in national politics: Mariátegui, who launched the Peruvian Socialist Party (PSP) in 1928; Vargas Llosa, who came close to being elected President in 1990; and, perhaps the most frequently cited example, Haya de la Torre, who was the founder and long-standing leader of APRA. But each of these cases needs qualification. Mariátegui's activities were semi-tolerated by Leguía (perhaps partly because after Mariátegui's illness in 1924 it was evident that he was severely weakened and in all probability not long for this world); the PSP became far less radical after he died in 1930. In terms of direct political effect, Mariátegui's impact was not great (the influence of his ideas is analysed in Chapters 4 and 5). Vargas Llosa's presidential campaign, itself deemed 'unprecedented not only in Peru but also in Latin America',[141] became possible only because of a redefinition in relations between Spanish American intellectuals and the state that occurred in the 1980s. In earlier years, Vargas Llosa would simply not have been able to achieve the same degree of independence from the state (a result of the changed market conditions that had enabled him to become an international best-selling author) and hence lend a certain plausibility to his attempt to win power on the grounds of ideological innocence.[142] The late 1980s was also an exceptional historical moment in that public disillusionment with political actors across the party spectrum was unusually high, and created an opportunity for the moral authority of the intellectual to shine forth as an apparent beacon in a morass of widespread corruption. In the event, it was the other outsider, Fujimori, who won.

The case of Haya de la Torre and APRA deserves careful consideration. Among this book's five case studies, Peru stands alone in that it had a leading opposition party that was not only founded by an intellectual but was also one in which intellectuals continued to participate. Haya de la Torre would have become President after his narrow electoral victory in 1962 had not the military vetoed him. Another important example is the literary historian, Luis Alberto Sánchez, who served as an *aprista* deputy (1945–48 and 1963–68) and senator (1980–85), and eventually became Alán García's Vice-President (1985–90). Nevertheless, there is a strong case for accepting Geoffrey Bertram's argument that 'APRA's approach to state power was primarily instrumental, aimed at securing influence and patronage at lower levels of the state apparatus rather than at taking command of the system at the top'.[143] In that sense, participation in APRA was less of an expression of dissent against the status quo than the party's rhetoric may have implied. APRA in effect functioned more as a peripheral wing of the state than as a part of civil society, and the role of intellectuals in APRA should therefore be seen as an instance of indirect co-option by the state rather than as a case of independently based political influence.

Cuba

The attitude of Cuban politicians towards intellectuals during the early years of the republic has to be viewed in the light of the fact that, had it not been for a stray bullet in 1895, Cuba's first President might well have been the poet and journalist José Martí. Martí was referred to as 'El Presidente' during the few weeks he spent on military campaign; although he rejected the title, the peasants, undeterred, also gave him a white horse.[144] The independence struggle had stimulated an active press and a relatively wide-ranging public debate, particularly among Cuban exile communities in the United States, and Martí, who always maintained that 'the people . . . are the true leaders of revolutions',[145] had built up an extensive network of contacts with Cuban working people.[146] The first US military government (1898–1902) quickly adopted a policy of divide-and-rule intended to ensure that no successor to Martí emerged. The United States took direct charge of elementary education (indeed, public primary schooling in Cuba was virtually created by the United States). In deference to nationalist sensibilities, the US governor appointed one leading Cuban intellectual, Enrique José Varona, to supervise a reform of secondary and higher education which affected only a minority (in 1900–01, just 601 students were enrolled in Cuba's secondary schools). Varona was strongly opposed to Spanish scholasticism, and largely concurred with the US conception of education as vocational and scientific. He complied with the US policy of sending Cuban teachers to the United States for training, rather than investing in national institutions for teacher training.[147] The admiration felt by Varona and many subsequent intellectuals for US education policy was to compromise their position not only towards the Cuban state but also on the issue of neocolonialism. One key effect of the two US occupations of the island (1898–1902 and 1906–09) was that education became the main battleground for cultural hegemony between anti-imperialists and those who sought US tutelage in some form. Educational reform continued to be a persistent and passionate theme in the writings of Cuban intellectuals from the early years of the republic until the 1950s. But although – indeed, perhaps, because – intellectuals influenced the direction of debates on education, Cuban governments offered them remarkably few opportunities to implement their ideas: intellectuals were rarely given executive posts in the Secretariat (later Ministry) of Education. Gerardo Machado, whose government initially sought to appease the professional class by responding to their concerns about education, appointed the politically conservative historian, Ramiro Guerra y Sánchez, to the administrative post of Superintendent of Schools in the mid-1920s, but he achieved only minor reforms. Jorge Mañach, who had helped to draft the manifesto of the main organization of middle-class resistance to Machado, the 'ABC',[148] was politically despised by most of his fellow intellectuals for having served briefly in Carlos Mendieta's government as Minister of Education in 1934, and, even more, for having collaborated with Batista from 1940 to 1944.[149]

The university reform movement in Cuba, which began in 1923, is a further illustration of the extent to which the movement's capacity to achieve lasting gains depended heavily on a government that identified its own interests with a change in the cultural status quo. In Cuba, where this was only fleetingly the case, the movement won student representation in the governance of the university and the removal of inadequate teaching staff, but failed to gain either university autonomy or any significant improvements in facilities for students.[150] An initial concession, approving a new centre of power in the university, the University Assembly, which had a remit to modernize curricula, purge teaching staff and secure autonomy, was granted by President Alfredo Zayas's government (1920–24) in March 1923, just three months after the foundation of the Federation of Cuban Students. But thereafter, President Zayas simply bided his time, anticipating a reactionary backlash in the university, which did indeed culminate in the election of a conservative rector in May 1924. When Machado took office as President in 1925, he correctly calculated that the student body would fail to unite in support of the reform leader, Julio Antonio Mella, who was duly expelled from the University of Havana in October 1925 without majority protest. In 1926, Machado felt sufficiently confident of his position to dissolve the University Assembly; soon afterwards, the university awarded him an honorary doctorate. The state had made minimal concessions, divided the student movement, and effectively restored the status quo. If Machado had not opted for *continuísmo* (perpetuation of power) in 1927–28, enabling the campaign for university reform to become emblematic of a broader popular struggle, the movement might well have lost its momentum. As it was, the university community went on to play an important role in events leading to Machado's ousting in 1933 and the installation of a revolutionary government. The assassination of Mella in Mexico City in January 1929 by Machado's agents galvanized student militancy – which had already revived in protest against *continuísmo* – into a well-supported anti-Machado demonstration, during the course of which another student leader was killed. Machado, who had already abolished the reform committee and temporarily closed the university, then moved into full repressive gear, denouncing the university as a bastion of communism and closing it indefinitely, along with most of the high schools. In September 1930, the student leaders published a new programme, denouncing their lecturers as 'the intellectual props of the dictatorship' and calling for Machado's immediate resignation,[151] a manifesto that became the 'focal expression of militant anti-Machado Cuban nationalism'.[152]

Cuban intellectuals were prominent in the growing political resistance to the status quo which had been catalysed by the first major collapse in world sugar prices in 1920. The most famous incident was the 'Protest of the Thirteen' in March 1923, when writers led by the poet and lawyer Rubén Martínez Villena (1899–1934) walked out of a meeting of the Cuban Academy of Sciences attended by the Minister of Justice. Their denunciation of any 'person liable to the accusation of lack of patriotism or of civic decorum' was published the following day.[153] Fernando Ortiz established a National and Civic Renovation Committee that same year. But intellectuals' involvement later went far beyond public statements. The most significant example is Julio Antonio Mella's key role in the foundation of the Cuban Communist Party (PCC) in 1925. Martínez Villena, once he had joined the party in 1927, was also crucial to its survival and development, especially because of Mella's exile. As recalled by a fellow Communist, Fabio Grobart, Martínez Villena '[was] the only intellectual in the PCC, and he rapidly [stood out] as the comrade of greatest ability, culture and preparation'.[154] Outlawed in 1927, the PCC managed to persist so successfully during 1928–29 under Martínez Villena's leadership that by 1930 it had wrested control of the most powerful labour organization the Cuban National Workers' Confederation (CNOC), from anarchists, and rapidly developed a strong base especially among sugar workers.

The Cuban revolution of 1933 provided some important lessons for intellectuals. The removal of Machado resulted from the convergence of several different pressures on the status quo (not to mention backroom manoeuvring by Franklin Roosevelt's Ambassador Extraordinaire, Sumner Welles). In the context of the catastrophic impact on the Cuban economy of the 1929 Depression, and Machado's manifest incapacity to meet the situation with any policy other than repression, working-class unrest, much of which was organized albeit not completely controlled by the Communist Party, ultimately prompted a rebellion by army sergeants, students, and the more modernizing elements of a bourgeoisie suffering from financial collapse. Ramón Grau San Martín, a university professor of physiology, emerged as the leader of a new government headed by a 'Pentarchy' of professionals and intellectuals. But the initial alliance of students and sergeants gave way to a US-mediated coalition between the sergeants' leader, Fulgencio Batista, and the aspirant bourgeoisie. Batista proved willing to acquiesce in the US machinations which largely succeeded in neutralizing the revolution's initial reforms: in January 1934, he transferred the army's support from Grau San Martín's junta, which Washington refused to recognize, to the US-backed Nationalist Union leader, Carlos Mendieta, whose government was granted State Department recognition within five days.[155] This was the crucial moment of transition, in which intellectuals, who had played a key role in ridding Cuba of Machado, lost the political initiative. Henceforth, Batista was *de facto* in charge of Cuba, although he did not officially assume the presidency until elected in 1940. Immediately after the removal of Grau San Martín, Batista's new coalition set about introducing populist reformist measures to co-opt the workers and, by securing the abrogation of the much-resented Platt Amendment in 1934,[156] restructured the relationship with the United States, making it less overtly neo-colonial and therefore harder for radical nationalists to attack. The intellectual vanguard became marginalized for lack of a lasting political support base among the masses. What initially appeared to have been a victory for intellectual sectors rapidly turned into a defeat at the hands of the military allies whom they had been obliged to inveigle into their project in the first place: Batista soon sidelined intellectuals and cultivated allies more congenial to his own interests.

Given the salience of education policy as a touchstone for debate about Cuba's national future, it is not surprising that when Batista sought to consolidate power and promote political legitimacy in the aftermath of the derailed 1933 revolution, he opted for educational reform. In 1937, the University of Havana (occupied by troops after student involvement in a general strike two years previously) was reopened, as were the normal and secondary schools, which had functioned only intermittently since 1930. Batista extended bureaucratic control, authorizing the formation of a National Council of Education and Culture to oversee the technical aspects of educational reform. But much of this reforming zeal was inspired by the need to pacify the rural areas. Batista realized that he could kill two birds with one stone by promoting a programme of rural education: it would both provide a mechanism for controlling rural social unrest and, at the same time, counter intellectual and popular criticisms of the Cuban education system. In February 1936, he launched a programme of what became known as 'civic–military–rural education'. Under this scheme, army sergeants, who were answerable only to his command and not to the Secretary of Education, were sent out into the countryside as teachers. In short, education was militarized. Payment of military teachers was funded by a new sugar tax imposed in December 1936; in effect, Batista secured funds to expand the army under the guise of extending education.[157] He added insult to injury as far as intellectuals were concerned by introducing the Flor Martiana (a white artificial pansy flower awarded as a badge of merit) in a crude attempt to reappropriate the legacy of Martí and the tradition of *Cuba Libre*.[158]

Articles in Cuban literary journals published during the 1940s and 1950s were full of complaints by intellectuals about how they were neglected by a state which paid little attention to culture. José Rodríguez Feo's attack on the newly formed National Institute of Culture in 1955 is representative:

> In our country where culture has always been somewhat improvised and superficial, the artist has lived on the margins of society. Scorned and lacking in the least encouragement from the state and its official bodies, [the artist] is the true pariah of the nation.[159]

United in the belief that the 1933 revolution had been betrayed, the generation that reached maturity in the early 1930s rejected politics in favour of a retreat into aestheticism. According to one member, 'We opted for disdain. We thought that getting mixed up in political life would be tantamount to contaminating ourselves with its pestilence. So we placed our faith in realities such as Literature, Beauty, Nobility and Goodness.'[160] Direct censorship or government bankrolling of most publications in the 1940s and 1950s meant that no tradition of criticism in Cuba developed to build upon the liveliness of debate seen in the 1920s. It is important to remember this historical background when considering the role of intellectuals in post-revolutionary Cuba. Roberto González Echevarría has suggested: 'Many of the figures engaged in literary activity in the fifties are those in the Cuban cultural establishment today, and when they overreact to criticism they do so because they are not used to a critical atmosphere.'[161] Most of the leading Cuban intellectuals of the 1940s and 1950s spent very little time living freely in Cuba: they were either in prison or in exile, and thus had scant opportunity to acquaint themselves with conditions in their country.

It is in this context that we have to set not only the initial enthusiasm felt by intellectuals for the Cuban revolution, but also the continuing support of many of them even after clampdowns on cultural freedom were imposed in the late 1960s. Relations between Cuba's intellectuals and the state experienced a dramatic shift after the revolution in 1959, which at the time seemed to offer Cuban intellectuals the possibility to start anew. A 1959 article in *Lunes de Revolución* (a cultural supplement to the government's daily newspaper) expressed it thus:

> We, from *Lunes de Revolución*, think that it is high time for our generation . . . to find a means of self-expression. . . . Until now all the means of expression were too short-lived, too compromised, and too identified [with vested interests]. . . . Now the revolution has broken all the barriers and permitted the intellectual . . . to become integrated into national life.[162]

It was not surprising that in the 1960s many Cuban writers continued to believe that 'there has never existed in the history of our country a better time for intellectuals'.[163] Many were also prepared to embrace the idea that 'To teach how to read and write, to learn how to handle a gun, to cut cane, are component parts of our essential duties as intellectuals in an under-developed country in revolution.'[164]

Cuba's revolutionary government initially proved ready to invest in cultural institutions, Castro having been persuaded that, in the context of increasing economic and political isolation, promoting cultural contacts was a policy that might reap dividends.[165] But early hopes of state tolerance towards intellectual freedoms were undermined from the mid-1960s onwards as the Cuban state began to encroach ever further into cultural life. In 1968, the government closed down all private publishing and brought the industry entirely under state control (the main outlets being the Institute of the Book, the Casa de las Américas and the university). Henceforth, it was impossible for any author to be published in Cuba without the approval of the state. The Padilla affair of 1971 resolved any remaining doubts about the meaning of Castro's notorious 'Words to the Intellectuals' in 1961: 'within the Revolution, everything; against the Revolution, nothing'.[166] Afterwards, Cuban officials made it clear that intellectuals were expected to contribute to the collective endeavour, primarily by acting as propagandists against imperialism.[167] As part of a bureaucratic reorganization following the enactment of a USSR-influenced constitution in 1976, a Ministry of Culture was created. The government's responses to cultural works henceforth tended to be shaped by the perceived relationship of their creator to the revolutionary regime: those deemed to be loyal enjoyed some leeway, those suspected of dissidence did not. The Cuban revolutionary state – in contrast to the Mexican – proved unable to contain the political criticisms of its intellectuals.

Chile

Historians have habitually distinguished Chile from its neighbours by virtue of a history of institutional continuity (virtually unbroken elected rule from independence until 1973), and the vitality of its party political system, particularly its apparent capacity to accommodate the activities of Marxist parties. Chile's intellectual tradition also had some distinctive features that made it an apparent exception to the Spanish American rule in terms of relations between intellectuals and the state. In contrast to Mexico and Argentina, conservatism remained the dominant force in Chile from 1830 until the 1880s; therefore Chile did not establish the liberal tradition of men of letters occupying high state office. Even after liberalism had gained ascendancy in the 1880s, few such opportunities arose. A few scientists (many of whom were foreigners) were appointed to run the public works programmes instigated by President José Manuel Balmaceda (1886–91), but 'scientific politics' was applied far less extensively in Chile than in Mexico, and no group comparable to the *científicos* or the Generation of 1880 in Argentina ever emerged.

It has been argued that one of the main effects of the civil war of 1891 was a transformation of Chilean political culture.[168] This war had taken the form of a dispute between the executive and legislative branches of the state (although the extent to which this conflict actually *caused* the civil war is a matter of debate).[169] In the succeeding Parliamentary Republic (1891–1920), emphasis shifted from conservative ideas of the organic state towards a growing sense of 'society' as a complicated web of interests which might wish to define themselves in opposition to, or at least in distinction from, the state.[170] Negotiation was favoured over conflict; political freedoms and freedom of expression were largely respected; and civil society was given priority over militarism. Although the Parliamentary Republic retained a basically oligarchic mode of government, Bernardo Subercaseaux argues, 'it is no less evident that the prevailing liberal principles made way for the arrival of new social actors, allowing them expression at the level of civil society'.[171] However, intellectuals were offered few opportunities to participate formally in national affairs during these years.

The main explanation for this was that in Chile the university community had been ascribed a specific role in the process of modernization over half a century before this was proposed in other Spanish American countries. The University of Chile was founded in 1842 (compared with the foundation of the National University of Mexico in 1910 and the National University of La Plata in 1902), and was explicitly intended to be a national project. In his foundation speech, Andres Bello declared: 'The university's curriculum is wholly Chilean: if it borrows scientific conclusions from Europe, it does so in order to apply them to Chile. All the paths of research that its members propose to follow . . . converge on one centre: the *patria*.'[172] The university was expected both to create a modern scientific and academic tradition in Chile and to oversee the creation of the professionals it was believed Chile needed in order to modernize. To this end, the university was assigned the supervision of all public education. Although the university was fundamentally dependent upon the state, the need for a working degree of autonomy was recognized from the start, and it was significantly increased by an Act of 1879 which also instituted free tuition in higher education.[173] It was not until 1931 that supervision of public education was removed from the university and directly assumed by the state. One result of the university's early role in nation-building was that for most of the twentieth century, Chile was one of the few countries in the region where the word 'academic' did not become virtually a term of abuse. Among the Chilean intelligentsia, being defined as an academic did not necessarily disqualify someone from being granted recognition as an intellectual, unlike elsewhere in Spanish America, where academia was associated with fossilized irrelevancy at best and doctrinaire Catholic conservatism at worst. The figure of the *pensador* was never as dominant in Chile as in other parts of Spanish America; nor was the writer-as-intellectual, although neither was completely absent. Rather, as in twentieth-century Brazil, the social scientist became the prevalent ideal of an intellectual, although this development became fully evident in Chile only during the 1950s (whereas in Brazil it dates back to the 1930s). In other words, Chilean governments attempted to contain intellectual power within specialisms far earlier than did the state in other Spanish American countries. For all these reasons, at the beginning of the twentieth century any presumed link between knowledge and power was correspondingly weaker in Chile than in Argentina or Mexico.

Despite these distinctive features, when political consensus broke down during the 1960s, Chilean intellectuals proved as unable to sustain an independent role as had their counterparts in other Spanish American countries that lacked correspondingly democratic traditions. They too abandoned their intellectual authority in the quest for direct political power. The events of the 1960s and 1970s revealed the fragility of the division of power between the oligarchy and the middle sectors, upon which the most stable democracy in Latin America had hitherto rested. The upheaval of those years also demonstrated that the existence of active political parties and a tradition of respect for freedom of speech had obscured the fact that in Chile, as elsewhere in Spanish America, little separation between culture and politics had taken place. Alicia Barrios and José Joaquín Brunner have argued that, until the 1980s, Chile – like most of the region's republics – lacked a cultural tradition that maintained a distinction between scientific and political practice.[174] This suggests that, despite a different nineteenth-century experience, the state and intellectuals in twentieth-century Chile had a relationship comparable to that in the other countries under scrutiny here.

The modernizing state began to take shape in Chile in the wake of an economic crisis (1918–20) caused by the collapse of the nitrate industry compounded by the impact of the First World War. The election of Arturo Alessandri in 1920 appalled the oligarchy, to whom he seemed to be the incarnation of the *caudillo* populism they had worked so hard to exclude from the executive throughout the nineteenth century. As a young, provincial law student in Santiago, Alessandri had apparently preferred discussing literature to politics, and was a frequenter of the Friends of the Arts club and the Ateneo.[175] During his election campaign, Alessandri traded on his own bohemian links when addressing university audiences, and stated his support for the university reform movement, using it as a counterweight to the oligarchy. Student backing for Alessandri enabled him to mobilize electoral support through contacts with the Universidad Popular José Victorino Lastarria, which 'laid the bases of a powerful political groundswell that was skilfully exploited by the people's candidate'.[176] In an early presidential address, he reiterated his campaign pledges:

> My inclination . . . is to use all the means at my disposal to make our university match up to the high and elevated aims which it is called upon to pursue within . . . the state. It would be desirable for our university, endowed with autonomy and a character of its own, distancing itself a little from its current role as a school for training professionals, to convert itself into a true laboratory of scientific experimentation in all branches of human knowledge, so that, as in other countries, the day might arrive when it becomes a fertile source of intellectual light and life, able to radiate and project the definitive cultural precepts for genuine and lasting national progress.[177]

Later, however, Alessandri betrayed his promises to the students. He had no more interest than his predecessors in allowing the universities to establish any expanded role in nation-building beyond their existing assign-ment to produce professionals. His election campaign had been founded on the claim that he himself was 'the man charged, by a mysterious design, to transform the social conditions of Chileans',[178] and he held that 'the state, represented by the government, must command the necessary resources to defend the proletariat physically, morally and intellectually'.[179] Having proclaimed his own receptivity to 'the vibrations of the national soul',[180] Alessandri was reluctant to see intellectuals gain credibility as the voice of the people. As radicalism died down among the students them-selves, Alessandri allegedly sponsored a rival organization to the Federation of Chilean Students (FECh).[181] When the issue of university reform was revived in the early 1930s, a new generation of student militants, who ten years earlier had sought to be in the vanguard of national reform and inveighed against the idea that the university was no more than 'a produc-tion line for professionals', professed that their duty to the Chilean people was to struggle for university reform in its narrow definition (namely, reform of those matters directly affecting higher education) rather than pursuing a grand historical mission of national redemption.[182]

Like their counterparts in other Spanish American countries, Chilean regimes of the 1920s tried to ensure that an independent intellectual community was unable to cohere. The Chilean state assumed an entrepre-neurial role in the creation of a technocracy, so that the route to public office was perceived to be linked to expertise – that is, the opposite of the intellectual's claim to universal judgement. This was a policy continued by a series of governments of highly varied ideological complexions: the dictator Carlos Ibáñez (1927–31) promoted an engineering and administrative technocracy; the Popular Front government created CORFO, the Chilean Development Corporation, in 1939; Ibáñez, returned in populist guise (1952–58), passed a law channelling 0.5 per cent of all federal and export taxes into a University Construction and Research Fund, and established a Science and Technology Committee which attracted US public and private grants;[183] and the conservative, Jorge Alessandri (1958–64) launched what became known as 'the managerial revolution'.[184] From about 1960 onwards, the state began to sponsor the development of modern social science. In Chile, modernizing administrations were in a position to move earlier than any others in Spanish America (including the Mexican state, which did not consolidate its position until the 1940s) to create a technocracy which, by its very existence, undermined the role of the independent intellectual by making specialism rather than universalism the route to public influence. Containment became the main political strategy for curtailing the influence of intellectuals, with coercion and co-option playing only minimal roles until the *coup d'état* in 1973. Chile's comparatively successful history of institutional stability meant that governments could afford to be more tolerant in their policies towards intellectuals while ultimately pursuing the same political aims as in Mexico, Peru or Argentina. Eugenio Tironi suggests that it was not so much that the intellectuals in Chile were different from their colleagues in other Spanish American countries; rather, the politicians enjoyed a relatively secure base of their own in party electioneering from the 1930s onwards and therefore had fewer grounds to fear the charisma or the moral authority of the intellectuals.[185]

In consequence, the archetype of the politicized creative intellectual, which took hold from the 1920s onwards in Mexico, Cuba and Peru, did not appear in Chile until the 1940s. It is noteworthy that Chile's most famous example, the poet Pablo Neruda, was radicalized not by any events or experiences in his own country but rather by the impact of the Spanish Civil War, particularly the death of Federico García Lorca at the hands of fascists. Neruda's experience is telling about the constraints on the participation of intellectuals in Chilean politics. His career as an activist began with the Spanish Civil War; already an internationally renowned poet, he was made inaugural president of the Chilean branch of the international Alliance of Intellectuals for the Defence of Culture in 1937. The alliance declared full support for the presidential campaign of the Radical Party leader and former university teacher Pedro Aguirre Cerda, who led a Popular Front coalition including Socialists and Communists to victory in 1938. The alliance's periodical *Aurora de Chile* hailed him as the 'candidate of Culture',[186] and subsequently noted in an editorial that:

> The intellectual worker in Chile has invariably experienced the worst social and economic conditions. . . . But the present government represents a fundamental and profound change for the country, and one proof of this is the invitation issued by the President to the intellectual workers to serve not his government but the country, in a great movement to develop national culture, on the basis of a plan that the state will assume the responsibility of funding in fulfilment of a supreme obligation.[187]

Aguirre Cerda did a considerable amount to promote public education, and was himself a vigorous exponent of a *chilenidad* that functioned as 'a mirror in which his own image was reflected'.[188] But after his death in 1941, the government – by then struggling to survive – devoted few resources to cultural or economic nationalism. On the fall of the Spanish Republic, Neruda had persuaded his President to let him go to Paris to administer a scheme to help refugees to emigrate to Chile. Later, however, tensions developed between Neruda and the Popular Front government. As Consul to Mexico, the poet thrice transgressed in the eyes of the Chilean authorities. First, Neruda technically exceeded his authority by issuing a visa, at the request of Cárdenas's government, to David Alfaro Siquieros, so that he could go to Chile and paint a mural at a school in Chillán, which had been hit by an earthquake early in 1939. For this, Neruda was suspended for a month without pay.[189] His second mistake was to publish a magazine called *Araucanía*, with a picture of an Indian woman on its cover: 'Most heinous of sins! Another rap on the knuckles from the Ministry. People in Mexico would start to think that Chile was a country full of Indians.'[190] Lastly, in 1943, Neruda provoked a minor diplomatic incident with Brazil when he protested at President Getúlio Vargas's refusal to allow the Communist leader Luis Carlos Prestes out of jail to attend his mother's funeral.[191] Having resigned from the diplomatic service later that year, Neruda returned to Chile and was recruited as Gabriel González Videla's election campaign manager, despite the fact that, as ambassador to Paris, the presidential candidate had felt overshadowed by Neruda's celebrity.[192] Neruda was himself elected in 1945 as a senator representing a northern region rich in nitrates, and joined the Chilean Communist Party shortly afterwards. The immense popularity of Neruda's poetry readings among working people, not only in his own constituency but throughout Chile, began to alarm the Popular Front coalition, but it was only when Neruda tried to play the role of an independent social critic that the government's patience finally snapped. In early 1948, Neruda delivered a speech to the senate denouncing González Videla, in which he consciously adopted 'a Zola-like tone, titling it in his own handwriting, "I Accuse" . . . [having] read the *Dreyfus Case* many times'.[193] Shortly afterwards, with a warrant out for his arrest, Neruda went into exile, which was almost certainly what the government had intended. González Videla recorded in his memoirs: 'I told the police: "Look for him but don't find him" ';[194] the President had no wish to attract the international condemnation that would probably have ensued if Chile's most famous writer had been imprisoned. After this incident, Neruda took no further part in Chilean politics, although he remained a party member, until he was nominated as the Communists' stalking-horse candidate to lead the Popular Unity coalition in 1970. Even in Chile, which probably enjoyed the most active party political system in the region, the pattern of intellectuals actively participating in the legislature, but hardly at all in the executive, was repeated.

Until Pinochet's *coup d'état*, Chile was the least coercive of the five states in its policies towards intellectuals, but neither was co-option a significant feature. The first government to hold power in Chile in the twentieth century that seriously tried to co-opt intellectuals as distinct from hiring specialists was Popular Unity (1970–73). Again, the predominant strategy was one of containment, which was more generously and consistently funded in Chile than elsewhere in the region. Before 1973, Chilean intellectuals enjoyed a better institutional base in universities, political parties, the mass media and a network of non-university institutions than their colleagues in virtually any other Spanish American country. But

Brunner suggests that, even so, this comparatively strong institutional frame-work had defined the role of the intellectual not in terms of independent criticism but 'almost exclusively in relation to the production of ideolo-gies'.[195] During the 1960s, the emphasis on an ideological function for intellectuals made politics central to Chilean intellectual life, because it offered the shortest route to putting ideologies into practice. It also enhanced the importance to intellectuals of the state – as the ultimate arena and expression of politics. As in Mexico, the existence of a state-sanctioned support base for intellectual life acted less to promote critical independence than to draw intellectuals back into the orbit of the state.

A Comparative Perspective

Four general points stand out from the above survey of relations between intellectuals and the state in Spanish America: (1) intellectuals were system-atically excluded from participating in high-level public policy-making, but were co-opted into the lower levels of state bureaucracy; (2) exclusion and low-level co-option were masked by the granting of prestigious diplomatic appointments to a select minority of internationally renowned (or locally well-connected) intellectuals; (3) when co-option failed, rapid action was taken (usually successfully) to eliminate political challenges from charis-matic individual intellectuals; and (4) state leaders further undermined the position of intellectuals by appropriating cultural symbols to themselves. The remainder of this chapter explores each of these points in turn.

Contrary to the tradition of the 'president–poet', twentieth-century Span-ish American intellectuals have rarely occupied executive office, or indeed been appointed as advisers on public policy, even in areas where they might have been expected to play a significant role, such as education. In Europe, broadening access to education became one of the great nation-building crusades of what Gellner describes as the 'gardening' state,[196] and it dovetailed neatly with the ambitions of the *philosophes* and their counterparts to preach the gospel of Reason to the common man. Across Spanish America, by contrast, politicians saw intellectuals as competitors for the allegiance of the people and, with the exception of Mexico, marginalized them from policy-making in elementary education during the 1920s and 1930s. Even Mexico was only a partial exception. The crucial role played by Vasconcelos as Secretary of Education in Obregón's government proved unusual during both his own and subsequent generations. The lawyer Narciso Bassols (1897–1959) served as Secretary of Education from 1931 until 1934 and introduced the original 'socialist education' measures, but President Cárdenas, who preferred to credit Obregón rather than Vascon-celos with the educational achievements of the early 1920s,[197] chose to conduct his own literacy campaign without the participation of independent intellectuals. In general, whereas the liberal positivists of the late nineteenth-century Spanish American elites had played a leading role in advising the oligarchic state on its education policies,[198] their twentieth-century counterparts had little impact on basic education policy and were obliged to channel their reforming zeal into the universities.

There was one significant exception to this exclusion of intellectuals from state power. Curiously, given Venezuela's comparatively low standing as a centre of intellectual activity in the region, it is this nation that has so far produced the only undisputed example of a president–intellectual in twentieth-century Spanish America: Rómulo Gallegos (1884–1968), who served as the democratically elected leader of his country for just nine months before being overthrown by the military in 1948. It is worth pausing to consider the circumstances that enabled this exception to occur. Gallegos, who was from a modest middle-class background, had to interrupt his law degree at the University of Caracas for financial reasons and became a teacher. He remained in Venezuela for most of the dictatorship of Juan Vicente Gómez (1908–35), trying to propagate his ideas through teaching and writing. It was not until his novel of 1929 about the Venezuelan frontier, *Doña Bárbara*, met with acclaim both at home and abroad that Gallegos attracted the attention of his president. Summoned into the dictator's presence, awarded a prize and appointed as a senator, Gallegos soon afterwards took refuge in exile, from where he publicly resigned this nominal political position.[199]

Following the death of Gómez in 1935, the incoming indirectly elected government of President Eleázar López Contreras restored constitutional liberties and, anxious to secure a measure of legitimacy, invited Gallegos back from Spain to become Minister of Education. Gallegos had lengthy experience as a teacher and a consistent record of campaigning for reform of Venezuela's education system, but what most recommended him to the new government was that he had no association with the previous regime and, indeed, had openly refused its patronage. In an echo of the rejection of Mexico's *científicos* by the *ateneistas*, Gallegos symbolized the new liberal, middle-class intellectual who in post-Gómez Venezuela was to usurp the position of collaborators with the dictatorship such as Laureano Vallenilla Lanz.

Gallegos was soon dropped as Minister of Education when he made public his sympathy with student-led protests against the increasing repressiveness of the López Contreras regime, but he resumed a political career as a deputy for Caracas between 1937 and 1940. In 1941, he became Mayor of Caracas, and when the government announced that, once again, the next presidential elections would be indirect (a decision all too evidently designed to ensure the officially designated succession of the presidency to

General Isaias Medina Angarita), Gallegos was chosen to stand as a symbolic opposition candidate. The opposition movement formally constituted itself as a political party, Democratic Action (AD), a few months later, in September 1941. The reasons for selecting Gallegos, as explained by Rómulo Betancourt, who was subsequently to become leader of AD, were revealing: first, Gallegos had taught many of the young members of the opposition in the Liceo Caracas, including Betancourt himself, and most of them regarded him as a mentor; second, he had taken a principled stand against the Gómez dictatorship, and, as a congressman, had shown constant support for democracy; third, he was not a political militant and indeed was reluctant to pursue high public office; finally, and most important, 'he had written *Doña Bárbara* – the great national novel, he was loved by the people and his name enjoyed international prestige'.[200] It was no coincidence that his candidacy was launched from the state of Apure, which was the setting for *Doña Bárbara*.[201]

It was, however, the politician Betancourt who assumed the presidency when AD was brought to power in 1945 by the action of disaffected sectors of the military. But by the time this ill-fated government had decided to hold Venezuela's first direct presidential elections in 1947, Gallegos was the only person among them whose moderation, probity and integrity made him an acceptable candidate both to the Right and the radical Left of Democratic Action. He had deliberately been kept at a distance from AD's coup plotting in 1945, precisely in order to keep his reputation untarnished from any involvement with the military.[202] He was also distrusted by some officers to a lesser extent than Betancourt. Furthermore, Gallegos was manifestly not corrupt, whereas most other members of the AD government were at least under suspicion, notwithstanding Betancourt's controversial campaign for political probity. In a country where corruption had been an especially persistent feature of politics, the intellectual's claim to moral authority carried particular weight. Betancourt, whom several leading AD leaders preferred as their nominee, was himself reluctant to renege on the Revolutionary Junta's commitment that none of them would run for the presidency at the end of their provisional regime.[203] Betancourt, who felt great personal loyalty to his former teacher, also argued that Gallegos was entitled to the nomination after his symbolic candidacy.[204] Gallegos's over-whelming victory at the polls was accompanied by a widespread feeling that his triumph was a victory for the masses.[205]

Gallegos was that rare bird among Spanish American intellectuals of the 1920s to 1940s, a political moderate. In many ways he was anachronistic, retaining liberal-positivist beliefs in the efficacy of education, freedom of thought and expression, and democratic civilian politics. His ideas recall those of José Martí. While many of Gallegos's Spanish American counter-parts during those decades were calling upon intellectuals to establish themselves as the vanguard of a people's revolution, he quietly continued to insist that the role of the intellectual was to lead public opinion in favour of reform and to defend the civil rights of the citizenry against the powers of the state.[206] The intellectual's commitment, as Gallegos saw it, was to uphold truth and justice, not to 'prostitute the dignity of the intellect' to ideology.[207]

Yet he could not have come to prominence if it had not been for the unusual structural conditions of Venezuela, and some element of historical accident. In Venezuela, *caudillismo* lasted far longer than in other major Spanish American republics, with the result that when Gómez died in 1935, neither Venezuela's army nor its oligarchy were initially well placed to defend their own interests. At the end of the dictatorship, there were no organized political parties, apart from the clandestine Communist Party, and no civilian political institutions. The incoming President, General López Contreras, who had been Gómez's Minister of War, believed that democracy should be introduced gradually. However, oil wealth and Gómez's cautious modernization projects had combined to create a small urban middle class, which was able to take advantage of the temporary disorientation of the elites in order to build up AD as an effective political party with a solid base among organized workers and peasants. Within this unique context, a political role emerged for a prestigious intellectual – Gallegos – who had written a popular novel, avoided compromising himself with the dictatorship and limited his goals to reformism. However, the evidence suggests that had Betancourt not insisted on his former teacher's candidacy in 1947, the nomination might well have gone to Betancourt himself. Although Betancourt remained publicly loyal, he later made it clear in private conversations that he was convinced that it was Gallegos's lack of political ability which was mainly responsible for the military coup carried out in 1948 against AD by some of the same officers who had brought them to power three years earlier, and that AD's choice of Gallegos had been a mistake which was on no account to be repeated.[208] Gallegos's brief presidency should be seen as the exception that proved the rule suggested by Vargas Llosa: that Spanish American intellectuals were rarely admitted to the corridors of power.

The extent to which Spanish American intellectuals have acted as ambassadors for their nations has also been greatly exaggerated. Few governments adopted the policy of sending cultural figures abroad as official representatives, and when they did so it was usually in order to reward support or to add a veneer of prestige to the exile of a potentially troublesome voice from the local political scene; only a minority of intellectuals (mostly those who already enjoyed international renown) were its beneficiaries. The strategy was particularly favoured by revolutionary regimes. The post-1959 Cuban government gave Cuba's most famous novelist, Alejo Carpentier, who continued to express his support for the revolution until his death in 1979, a diplomatic posting in Paris, and tried unsuccessfully to contain Guillermo Cabrera Infante's increasing disaffection by making him cultural attaché to Belgium. In turn, the Popular Unity government in Chile made the mistake of sending the writer Jorge Edwards for what proved to be a disastrous three-month stint (from December 1970 until March 1971) as ambassador to Cuba, where state leaders were gearing up for a confrontation with intellectuals in the Padilla affair and accused Edwards, who was friendly with Heberto Padilla, of fraternizing with dissident writers.[209]

The policy of appointing intellectuals to diplomatic posts is perhaps most closely identified with post-revolutionary Mexico, although a close examination of the record shows that, even there, the strategy has been applied highly selectively, to famous intellectuals and usually at politically sensitive times. In the difficult period of the 1920s and 1930s, for example, the government avoided open rupture with Mexico's leading literary sage, Alfonso Reyes (1889–1959), whose commitment to universal humanism went against the grain of the revolutionary cultural nationalists, by awarding him a series of ambassadorships.[210] Reyes himself characterized his work as a diplomat as 'an important service beyond reproach, which assumes the nation to be an indivisible whole, and attends to the water line without interfering in what goes on inside the ship'.[211] The arrangement enabled both sides to keep their distance. The story of Reyes's 'rehabilitation', as told by the Mexican historian Daniel Cosío Villegas, is revealing. Apparently what happened was that, in 1938, President Cárdenas, finding himself confronted with an international embargo on purchases of Mexican oil after having nationalized the oil companies, asked Reyes to return to Brazil on a special mission designed to persuade the Brazilian government to break the embargo. The President appointed a civil engineer as head of the mission, on the grounds that Reyes knew nothing about oil, although, as it transpired, the civil engineer himself was no expert. Even thus hampered, Reyes reactivated old friendships to persuade the Brazilians to buy a small amount of Mexican oil, which had great symbolic value, and it was for this, according to Cosío Villegas, that Cárdenas felt obliged to reward Reyes with the presidency of the Casa de España which was established in Mexico in 1938 as a centre for intellectual refugees from the Spanish Republic. From then until his death, Reyes served as president of what was renamed the Colegio de México. The Colegio established a reputation as Mexico's most prestigious research institution; and it always received state funding (although much of its income later came from the Ford and Rockefeller foundations).[212] A less eminent, but more politically minded intellectual, Narciso Bassols, was sidelined by Cárdenas, who apparently found the Marxist's radical zeal inconvenient,[213] was concerned about the extent to which his autocratic ways had provoked confrontation with teachers' unions in Mexico City,[214] and kept him out of the country as ambassador to Britain (1935–37) and then France (1938–39). Several members of the disaffected *Contemporáneos* generation, all of whom were successfully co-opted by Mexican administrations after 1945, served as diplomats during the 1930s.[215]

The most notable example of a Mexican intellectual being appointed as ambassador is Octavio Paz, who made a particular point of emphasizing his position of critical independence.[216] Paz joined the Mexican diplomatic corps in 1943 by the well-trodden route of familial connections,[217] and, after a series of appointments abroad, mostly in Europe, and six years in the Mexican Foreign Ministry itself (1953–59), he was posted as ambassador to India in 1962. Coincidentally perhaps, this was a time when intellectuals were actively organizing themselves in opposition to the regime.[218] Paz always vehemently denied that his position as a diplomat compromised his role as a writer. But in the eyes of his critics, Paz's independence was tarnished, notwithstanding his resignation after the massacre of Tlatelolco in 1968, and the government knew this all too well. Moreover, the state succeeded in obscuring the circumstances of Paz's departure from the foreign service to the extent that his many enemies on the Left colluded in undermining the impact of his act of protest. According to one biographer's version, on 4 October 1968, two days after the massacre, Paz sent a letter of resignation to Antonio Carrillo Flores, Secretary of Foreign Relations. This was announced by the Secretariat on 18 October, in a communiqué stating, 'Señor Octavio Paz has requested to be relieved of his duties', as a result of which 'it has been decided that ambassador Paz will be allowed to leave the Mexican Foreign Service'. The following day, Paz refuted the implication of the official communiqué in his own public statement: 'I resigned, I was not fired.'[219] But the waters had been muddied, and, in the aftermath of Tlatelolco, some Mexican intellectuals dissipated nearly as much energy disputing the integrity of Octavio Paz as they directed towards condemning the actions of a ruling party that from 1970 onwards was to busy itself in promoting a *rapprochement* with them. Carlos Fuentes was rewarded for his staunch support of the presidency of Luis Echeverría (1970–76), in the face of criticism from the majority of intellectuals, by an ambassadorship to France (1975–77). However, the list of Mexican intellectuals serving as ambassadors scarcely extends beyond those names.

Militant opposition to the state by twentieth-century Spanish American intellectuals has largely been confined to small, left-wing parties or movements that lacked a mass base and therefore posed little threat. By promoting a few well-chosen intellectuals into posts that afforded prestige if not power, governments largely succeeded in persuading many other intellectuals that the potential for public influence existed for them too. However, on the rare occasions when individual intellectuals did succeed in attracting popular support, state leaders clamped down quickly. For example, the post-revolutionary Mexican government may initially have been prepared to give Vasconcelos a platform while he was willing to administer its goals, but as soon as he tried to establish an independent political position, it mobilized to neutralize his challenge. According to Daniel Cosío Villegas, Vasconcelos, whose political ambitions were stirring, resigned from the Ministry of Education early in 1924 at least partly because he was well aware that Obregón's designated successor as President, Plutarco Elías Calles, had no intention of allowing him to continue in the post. The central authorities then moved to thwart Vasconcelos's bid to become governor of his home state of Oaxaca, having no desire to see a 'famous and independent' intellectual establishing a strong local power base.[220] In the turbulent election of 1929, held in the aftermath of Obregón's assassination, Vasconcelos stood as an independent presidential candidate, having declined to found a political party.[221] Pledging honest government, which was deemed an inconvenient ideal by many Callistas, Vasconcelos travelled throughout Mexico on the campaign trail in a 'triumphal tour [which] took on the glamour of a plebiscite'.[222] Once Vasconcelos had taken the step (highly threatening, from the government's point of view) of making contact with the rebel Catholic Cristero forces in January 1929, President Emilio Portes Gil and his *éminence grise*, Calles, decided to enlist the services of the US ambassador, Dwight Morrow, to intimidate the Cristeros into a peace settlement and, simultaneously, undermine the philosopher's bid to be 'king'. After a manifestly fraudulent election, Vasconcelos fled the country, having been denied the opportunity of becoming the 'Mexican Sarmiento' he had apparently hoped to be.[223] Similarly, at another important historical conjuncture, as the institutionalization of the revolution in favour of business interests proceeded apace in the years following the Second World War, the federal government made it absolutely clear that it would not tolerate victory by the Marxist intellectual Vicente Lombardo Toledano and his Popular Party (which was supported by a few worker and peasant groups) in the local state elections of 1949. Lombardo Toledano's presidential candidacy foundered in 1952 amid government propaganda that he was a closet Communist.

In addition to denying intellectuals influence on policy-making, state leaders further undermined the intellectuals' claims to special consideration by themselves appropriating cultural symbols. As a general rule, the more a political leader was inclined to adopt anti-intellectual policies, the stronger was his tendency to indulge in public displays of erudition, invoking the authority of intellectuals (usually those who were safely long dead and, preferably, foreign) to legitimate his actions or statements. Perón, who branded most of Argentina's intellectuals as accomplices of the *vendepatria* oligarchy (accused of selling out the country) whose power he sought to challenge, nevertheless adopted the pen name Descartes and incorporated numerous intellectual references into his public pronouncements. In a speech to the first national congress of philosophy, held in 1949, he attempted to demonstrate that he was no philistine military man by mentioning virtually every leading Western philosopher from Hesiod to Heidegger.[224] Fidel Castro adopted a similar tactic in his famous trial speech in defence of the storming of the Moncada barracks in 1953. Claiming that 'History will absolve me,' his references ranged from characters in Balzac to Dante's Inferno, and included a four-page litany of heroic resistance to tyranny down the ages, citing such intellectual luminaries as Thomas Aquinas, Martin Luther, John Knox, Milton, Rousseau and Thomas Paine.[225]

From the 1920s onwards, it became explicit state policy in Spanish America to assume control over culture as well as education, aims that were incorporated into new constitutions. The Mexican constitution of 1917 stated that Congress was responsible not only for all levels of education 'throughout the Republic', but also for maintaining and regulating all 'institutions of scientific research, fine arts, and technical instruction; museums, libraries, observatories, and other institutes for the general culture of the inhabitants of the Nation'.[226] The Peruvian constitution of 1920 stipulated the state's prerogative to 'attend to the moral and intellectual progress of the country' and, more specifically, its responsibility not only to provide secondary and higher education but also to 'foster establishments dedicated to science, arts and letters'.[227] The 1933 constitution went further, bringing within the state's remit education at all levels, and entrusting the state with ensuring the maintenance of academic freedom and with safeguarding 'the archaeological, artistic and historic treasures' of the nation.[228] The Cuban constitution of 1940, introduced under Batista's first elected presidency, had an entire second section devoted to 'Culture', with one article (number 47) stating that 'culture, in all its manifestations, constitutes a primordial interest of the state'.[229] The most explicit link between culture and the nation-state was made in Argentina, where the Peronist constitution of 1949 proclaimed in article 37, which concerned the universities, that: 'What the state must give to every man is the means to think like an Argentine, so that he, as a man, may think how he likes.'[230]

In their quest to dominate the acquisition of cultural capital, governments across the region established networks of prizes and scholarships for intellectuals. In some countries, publishing houses were founded. Everywhere, ways were found to keep a relatively tight rein on the press. Official advertising was a vital source of revenue for many newspapers and periodicals; and public agencies often controlled the distribution of paper, newsprint or copies of the newspaper itself. As a result, most of the means for an intellectual to earn a living led ultimately back to the state. Unless they possessed a private income, intellectuals were almost invariably obliged to accept employment in an institution directly or indirectly controlled by the public authorities. This in itself had obvious implications for the potential independence of intellectuals, especially since distinctions between the state and the government have rarely been upheld in Spanish America. The Argentine writer Ezéquiel Martínez Estrada (himself an autodidact who worked in the postal service), painted a jaundiced but not inaccurate portrait of the state of affairs that persisted from the 1930s until the 1960s in Spanish American countries:

> It is true that there are in Buenos Aires what could be called specific structures dealing with science, art, and the liberal professions, but they are ... all ... ultimately sponsored or subsidized – somewhat secretly – by the government. If the intellectual wishes to clear a path in the jungle of interests mobilized by politics, he is obliged to offer his talent to the only bidders: journalism or public administration. Unable to derive benefit or joy from his work – which no one reads – he claims a subsidy, which automatically defeats him: he is but a collaborator.... Newspapers, universities, and salons maintain themselves by a complex system of interlocking interests; they protect each other, and throughout the entire chain flows only one blood and only one vital fluid: politics.[231]

The earliest arena for the struggle to control intellectual life between modernizing states and the intellectuals was the universities, and the outcomes of these battles were to prove crucial in determining the key role that the state played in intellectuals' lives. In this context, some general points need to be made about the university reform movement, which spread from Argentina to Peru, Chile, Cuba, Colombia, Guatemala and Uruguay. The university reform resulted in the granting of autonomy to universities, and was believed at the time to represent a significant advance in the intellectual community's bid to increase its independence of the state. The popular image of Spanish American universities from the 1920s to the 1960s, particularly the huge national institutions in the capital cities which attracted over half of the student population, was that these self-proclaimed 'ideal republics' were 'in active, articulate, and sometimes militant opposition to the state'.[232] As with other commonly accepted views of Spanish American intellectual life, this one is partly accurate. Néstor García Canclini points out that the reform movement established lay universities with a framework of democratic organization at an earlier stage than reformers in many European societies.[233] However, the widespread idea – as expressed, for example, by Jorge Castañeda – that the university reform movement resulted in 'increased university autonomy, student and faculty participation in the designation of administrators, [and] academic freedom [becoming] mainstays of Latin American universities' needs careful re-examination.[234] So, too, does the argument that 'the university community in Latin America ... has throughout this century been a leading force in the fight for democracy and freedom'.[235]

The first point to make is that university reform was not so much won by the reformists as *bestowed* by early modernizing states representing anti-oligarchic interests. By the 1920s, higher education had become a political issue in all five countries studied here, largely because of the emergence of a middle class that clamoured for access to education as a route to social mobility.[236] In the case of Argentina, Tulio Halperín Donghi and others have argued that Hipólito Yrigoyen's anti-clerical Radical government, elected by universal male suffrage in 1916 but without much support from intellectuals, saw university reform as a means of simultaneously defeating its own conservative enemies in the struggle for cultural hegemony, placating both the liberal oligarchy and the Socialists (who were also anti-Catholic) and meanwhile also obtaining support from the middle classes.[237] The student movement was able to achieve its aims because the Yrigoyen government was broadly sympathetic to them.[238] Corresponding arguments can be made about the relationship between the state and the reform movement in Peru and Cuba. In Mexico, as noted above, Portes Gil's granting of partial autonomy in 1929 is now generally interpreted as a move designed to sow confusion among the student support base of the independent presidential candidate, Vasconcelos.[239] Throughout the region, the removal of many university staff wedded to out-of-date teaching methods and curricula enabled anti-oligarchic governments to defeat at least some of the forces of cultural reaction. The introduction of a more modern syllabus enabled these governments to start training the professionals who they believed were needed to extend the state's role in economic development. It is also worth remembering that in countries where governments were not trying to appeal to the middle classes, movements for university reform were automatically repressed (for example, in Venezuela, Bolivia and Paraguay).

Historians of the reform movement have argued that states were in a better position to exercise control over the universities after the reform than they had been before.[240] Even when autonomy was formally observed, governments often simply traded direct channels of control for more indirect methods of manipulation. The universities' increased financial dependence on the state following the abolition of tuition fees was only the most obvious example of those indirect mechanisms. Equally important in this respect was the question of the politicization of the universities. On this issue, politicians took advantage of the fact that reformists were far more coherent about what the universities should not be than about what they should be.[241] The students' initial rebellion in 1918 was against the retention of incompetent and old-fashioned staff and antiquated teaching methods. Ultimately, however, the university reform took its aims far beyond the rectification of outdated and corrupt university practices: it claimed to be a national regeneration movement, and linked university democratization with a broad platform of anti-clericalism, anti-imperialism, Hispanic-americanism and ill-defined ideas about social justice. As a result of this enlargement of the reform movement's purpose, the original academic aims tended to become lost. The Argentine Socialist Alfredo Palacios observed that by the late 1920s, the reform had achieved a role for students in university governance and free attendance but 'the most important elements were [still] missing: the reorganization of teaching methods and the encouragement of intensive study'.[242] In consequence, 'student politics became inextricably linked with national politics and often served as a conduit to national office'.[243] Adopting the students' own definition of the universities as the crucible of the nation enabled governments to turn the universities into nationalist institutions which it was essential for aspirants to public office to attend. Granting autonomy to the universities at a time when they were highly politicized meant that there was little danger that they would take advantage of such autonomy to pursue independent, critical intellectual activity. Instead, under the umbrella of the modernizing states, universities became established as institutions in which youthful militancy could run its course while those same advocates of radicalism were making the social and political connections necessary for future advancement within the elite. Governments moved quickly to repress the most politically threatening outcome of the university reform: namely, the Popular Universities.[244] Again, their main concern was to prevent any identification by intellectuals with the masses from developing beyond the merely rhetorical.

After the Second World War, when public universities seemed to be in danger of becoming too radical, most governments simply changed tack and began to encourage the foundation of private institutions in order to dilute the political impact of militant student organizations. This dovetailed neatly with the need to meet growing middle-class demand for an expansion of higher education. Such initiatives were backed by the United States, particularly after the Cuban revolution, and many of the new institutions were organized along US lines. By and large, however, Spanish American governments were willing to allow their educated youth a few years of radicalism which until the polarization of the 1960s, could be contained without too much difficulty. Spanish American universities became the crucibles of professionals or politicians, but rarely of intellectuals. Thus the state took the lead, and university communities acquiesced, in creating a university ethos that attached more importance to power than to knowledge. Carlos Vilas's gently mocking account captures the extremes of politicization reached in the 1960s, by which time each subject had acquired its own ideological connotation:

> Sociology was, by definition, a left-wing course, if not revolutionary; law, of course, was right-wing. Psychology was also left-wing; anthropology was positively

reactionary. Political science wasn't clear. Economics was also more or less to the right, except when it was a question of 'political' economy, which was definitely on the left.[245]

The universities may have been centres of political resistance to various incumbent regimes, but they failed to challenge the fundamentally anti-intellectual structures of the state. The university reform movement was, ultimately, a thwarted attempt by the intellectual community to institutionalize a role for itself in creating popular national consciousness.

Conclusion

The Mexican anthropologist Roger Bartra recently made the following observation:

> Political power finds it inconvenient to deal with thinking intellectuals, restless, unstable people, who are always testing this or proving that. It is better and safer to deal with established professionals ... that is, with trustworthy people who practise without believing, who accumulate information rather than knowledge, who record but fail to understand.[246]

Throughout Spanish America, governments maintained conditions in which it was virtually impossible for intellectuals to establish independent critical communities that could have provided leadership to a civil society capable of challenging the legitimacy of the state. Anti-intellectual policies were implemented by a wide range of regimes: democratic, authoritarian, populist. The means varied, but not the ends, which suggests that it was the nature of the state (committed to intervention in pursuit of modernization) rather than the nature of the regime that was important in determining policies towards intellectuals. The 1920s were particularly important where cultural policy was concerned: regimes that were unable (or unwilling) to challenge the economic or social power of the oligarchies bolstered their claims to modernizing legitimacy by giving prominence to culture and education. They redefined 'culture' as no longer solely the preserve of an elite minority, but a necessary component of a nation-building project directed in the first instance at the emerging middle classes (who were themselves preoccupied with education as a means of social mobility) and, in the longer term, at least in theory, at the masses. It was the containment of intellectuals at an institutional level – the creation of state–society relations with an anti-intellectual bias – rather than either coercion or co-option that did most to stifle critical debate. Symptomatic of the relative success of state containment of intellectuals is the fact that the concept of 'civil society' did not acquire currency in Spanish America until the 1970s, once the full coercive power of the state had been unleashed by the military dictatorships.

From the 1920s until the 1970s, Spanish American states succeeded in creating a situation in which intellectuals became preoccupied with power rather than knowledge. It was not so much that 'civil society' was virtually nonexistent during most of this period, as Latin American intellectuals proclaiming its 'emergence' in the 1980s tended to imply; rather, it was that instead of civil society being clearly distinct from, and in opposition to, the state, as liberal thought anticipates, it tended more towards being included under the state's umbrella. In other words, the Spanish American experiences were much closer to Gramsci's formulation of civil society as a constituent part of the state. At the institutional level, the intellectual sectors of society were contained, mostly as specialists rather than generalists; meanwhile, Spanish American politicians restricted the influence of specific leading intellectuals through a variety of measures ranging from patronage to persecution. Intellectuals were marginalized, but not, at least until the 1960s, to the point where they felt that they had nothing to lose by moving into outright opposition. A precursor of this troubled twentieth-century relationship between intellectuals and the state occurred when the *pensador* Domingo Faustino Sarmiento became President of Argentina in 1868: his own draft inauguration speech was replaced by a version written by the statesman Nicolás Avellaneda, on the grounds that only an experienced politician was capable of manipulating the language of power. As the Argentine writer Ricardo Piglia has suggested, this is 'an apt metaphor' for the continual displacement of culture by politics that was to take place throughout most of the twentieth-century history of Spanish America.[247]

The Go-between:
The Role of the Intellectual in
Spanish America[1]

State policies in Spanish America established a framework that invited intellectuals to function as ideologues (either as co-opted supporters or ritual opponents); this chapter examines their varying responses. Spanish American intellectuals have represented each other as apostles and prophets, martyrs and heroes; their collective self-images draw on the vocabulary of the Bible and the battlefield. Nevertheless, the modern, secular idea of the intellectual that had developed in Europe (a role itself not wholly devoid of apocalyptic claims, of course) was consistently influential in Spanish America, with the archetypal figures of Hugo, Zola, Ortega y Gasset and Sartre acting as touchstones – although by no means the only ones – for Spanish American intellectuals' self-definition. There were three key periods of transition when notable shifts in the intellectuals' socio-economic position occurred in conjunction with the impact of major historical events and ideas, both regional and international, to prompt a rethinking of their role. In each period, one or two archetypes (although always contested) came to prevail. The crucial decades were: (1) the 1890s–1900s, when the role of the modern intellectual was first elaborated in the region (archetype: the *maestro* [mentor]); (2) the 1920s, when the role of the intellectual became radicalized in response to revolutions in both Mexico and Russia (archetypes: the *intelectual de vanguardia* [vanguard intellectual] or the *intelectual comprometido* [the committed intellectual]; and (3) the 1960s, when views about the political commitment of the intellectual became polarized under pressures catalysed by the Cuban revolution (archetype: the *intelectual militante* [the militant intellectual]). From the 1970s onwards, the traditional role of the socially committed intellectual has waned in Spanish America (as elsewhere), and a new archetype of 'the expert' has gained the ascendant. The following discussion focuses on the creation of this role around 1900, its expansion during the 1920s and its final disintegration in the 1960s.

The 1890s–1900s

The work of three leading figures from the late nineteenth century serves to illustrate how the image of the intellectual as *maestro* was developed: the Cuban poet, journalist and independence fighter José Martí (1853–95); the Nicaraguan *modernista* poet Rubén Darío (1867–1916); and the Uruguayan essayist José Enrique Rodó (1871–1917). They have all been subject to controversial interpretations. Martí has been depicted as a precursor of the twentieth-century figure of the *intelectual comprometido*.[2] Darío, who was for a long time acclaimed for his poetic gifts but attacked for alleged Symbolist-inspired decadence and a 'Gallic mindset',[3] has more recently been reinterpreted as the founder of a distinctively Spanish American modernism based on the reinvention of the Spanish language.[4] Rodó, whose essay *Ariel* (1900) was by far the most influential of early statements about the role of the Spanish American intellectual, has often been accused of being elitist and escapist.[5] It is suggested below that the work of each appears in a different light if it is considered in the context of their shared commitment to establishing the legitimacy of culture as a distinct sphere of activity in society. Darío himself noted while in Buenos Aires that all the intellectuals of his acquaintance were complaining of a sense of *decaimiento* (decline) and acknowledging their need to 'seek another role'.[6]

The use of the term 'intellectual' in Spanish America has been identified as early as 1892,[7] and it gained wide currency during the first decade of the twentieth century. Rodó enlisted it (probably for the first time) in 1900.[8] His compatriot Carlos Vaz Ferreira published a treatise entitled *Moral para intelectuales* in 1909 which (consciously echoing Diderot's *Le neveu de Rameau* [*c.* 1761]) prescribed how each profession could develop its own specific way of expressing a general morality.[9] Darío referred twice to intellectuals in his autobiography, published in 1912.[10] The social acceptability of the term in Spanish America was enhanced after it came into common usage in late-nineteenth-century France. The Dreyfus affair (1894–1906), Zola's 'J'accuse' and the supporting 'Manifesto of the Intellectuals' of 1898 were all eagerly discussed in educated circles throughout the region.[11] This reflected not only France's cultural ascendancy in *belle époque* Spanish America, but also the fact that the issues confronted by French liberal intellectuals (who were themselves a distinct minority among men of letters)[12] in their struggle against militarism and clericalism offered some parallels to their even more isolated Spanish American counterparts. The Dreyfus affair had particular resonance in the then intellectual capital of the subcontinent, Buenos Aires, where debates over the rights of immigrants had become heated.[13] After all, not only was Dreyfus, as an Alsatian Jew, perceived to be an outsider by strategic sectors of French society, but so was Zola, who himself came from Venice. The emergence of the modern intellectual as a significant figure in France served as an inspiration for a new generation of Spanish American writers and thinkers to define their own relationship to society.

The strongest point of identification with French intellectuals was the common preoccupation with social responsibility. This ethical concern dominated debates about the role of intellectual both in France and in Spanish America from the beginning of the twentieth century until the 1960s (when sociologists switched the emphasis to the occupational practices, interests and allegiances of the 'knowledge elite'). Historians of the Dreyfus affair highlight 'the similarity that exist[ed] between the Dreyfusards and the anti-Dreyfusards';[14] they concur that the dispute is best understood less as a conflict between Reason and Faith than as the result of rivalry between two sectors of an intellectual community: the aristocracy of culture clustered around the Académie Française (which by 1898 had refused Zola admission ten times) and the emerging meritocracy, the apogee of which was the École Normale Supérieure. The two sides were echoing a longstanding debate in French history over whether the state should be organized to favour the rights of the individual or the collective. But both groups defined themselves with reference to state and nation, and both accepted that intellectuality implied a certain obligation towards society; the key difference between them was that the Dreyfusards chose to identify specifically with the Third Republic's concept of the state, in defiance of the Church and the aristocracy. The Dreyfus affair 'gave to French intellectuals their sense of mission . . . [and] provided them with the tradition that they have to be in opposition to the greater part of French society';[15] but it should not be forgotten that, at least in its initial stages, their dissent received the all-important backing of the state. Indeed, one of the most important lasting consequences of the Dreyfus affair was that the fortunes of those who claimed to be 'intellectuals' became tied to the fate of the Republic (or the state) rather than the nation – nationalists had been *anti*-Dreyfus. The Third Republic's reforms, dating from the 1880s, of the Sorbonne and the *grandes écoles* were explicitly designed to promote the university as the secular successor to the Church and its academics as a 'republican clergy'.[16] After the Dreyfus affair, and for most of the twentieth century, 'French intellectuals could claim to represent a general interest as if by public statute'.[17]

Whereas the Dreyfusards successfully reasserted the eighteenth-century *philosophes*' claim to legislate public opinion based on a supposedly superior acquaintance with the processes of Cartesian Reason, the conditions for a comparable coup did not exist in less developed Spanish America. The region's middle-class intellectuals, who also faced exclusion from the economic and political elites, lacked the state-funded institutional base that cushioned their French counterparts. In Spanish America's underfunded universities, a reductionist version of positivism and its bias towards the liberal professions had been superimposed on to the oratorical formulas of a residual scholasticism, with predictably unilluminating results. A research base was almost nonexistent, particularly in the natural sciences, and remained so until the 1950s. Those who aspired to be intellectuals in early-twentieth-century Spanish America were nearly all writers, many of them autodidacts, who scratched together a living from a combination of journalism, translation, speech writing for politicians, and minor bureaucratic posts in public administration. The Peruvian philosopher Antenor Orrego described conditions in his country during the 1920s as follows:

> In Peru, one particular phenomenon shows the intellectual and spiritual poverty of the country. By the time literary or artistic work reaches the public it is already stale and out-of-date in terms of the thinking of its creator. There are no publishing houses to pay for the book or even to publish and distribute it effectively, nor is there a public with sufficient curiosity to interest itself in intellectual production. The author finds himself in the position of having to pay in order to be read. Intellectual labour here – more than in any other country – is truly heroic.[18]

Even in far more prosperous Argentina, Manuel Gálvez recorded, 'In this country, it's a great achievement to sell a thousand copies of a book. There are writers, even among the best, who don't sell even half that. The print runs are generally five or seven hundred, and only rarely do they sell out.'[19] In such a milieu, the term 'professional writer' did not imply a capacity to earn a living from writing, as in Europe, 'because [such a] phenomenon is unknown here', but referred instead to 'the man who dedicates himself mainly to literary work, who publishes books regularly and who, although he may not mean to live off his earnings as a writer ... tries, at least, to supplement his income with them'.[20] This poor material base for intellectual life meant that while Spanish American intellectuals could, like the Dreyfusards, stake a claim to the moral authority of an alternative priesthood, they found it difficult to win acceptance for this status on intellectual grounds alone.

Those who wished to distinguish themselves from the *pensadores* were confronted by the need to defend the validity of devoting themselves to one specialism – rather than ranging broadly across many fields as their predecessors had done – while at the same time making a bid for universalism. The tensions inherent in this shift were never fully resolved, as is borne out by the persistence of the essay as a major genre in Spanish American writing. Even so, the evidence suggests that the 1900s saw the final stage in the development of an independent secular intellectual community, a process that had taken over a century. A watershed in the differentiation of intellectual from political authority had been reached towards the middle of the nineteenth century, when the word *pensador* began to stand in its own right – apart from the qualifying '*caudillo*' – to refer to the composite figure of a journalist/philosopher/man of letters. Most of the *pensadores* were members of the elite who could write at leisure, but increasingly from this time onwards, a significant minority felt themselves to be social outsiders. Domingo Faustino Sarmiento (1811–88), who came from a previously illustrious provincial family that had fallen on hard times, especially after his father's desertion of the household when the future President was only fifteen years old, later described himself as 'alone against the odds'.[21] In *Mi defensa*, published from exile in Chile in 1843, he sought vindication over the heads of his enemies from 'the public, [which] deceived today, will do me justice tomorrow, when the facts are seen in their true light'.[22] In self-justification, Sarmiento suggested that the opposition he had faced was related to his impoverished background:

> I have always excited great antagonism and deep sympathy. . . . Since infancy my life has been a continuous struggle, due less to my character than to the humble position from which I began, and my lack of status. . . . My whole life has been one long battle, which has destroyed my body without weakening my soul, in the process steeling and fortifying my character.[23]

He added that, throughout his life, he had 'known no friends other than books and journals', a disadvantage he claimed to have turned to good effect in that his mind remained resplendent in its untutored, iconoclastic state:

> Having no teachers and being guided only by my own sense of justice, I have always been the adjudicator rather than the automatic admirer of a book's importance, its ideas, or its principles. From this shaky position came my independence of mind, and a certain propensity to develop my own ideas without reference to established authorities.[24]

Tulio Halperín Donghi has argued that Sarmiento's adoption of the Romantic myth of being 'a child of his works' (an expression which had recently come into vogue in Chile) enabled him to lay claim to a role as a possessor of privileged knowledge, as a prophet crying in the wilderness who could lead society to the promised land.[25] Despite Sarmiento's later successful reintegration into the Argentine liberal elite, the idea of marginality continued to resonate, in that it introduced the possibility, at least, of an educated man becoming independent of the state.

Two or more generations later, Martí, Darío and Rodó were all born into the emergent middle sectors of Spanish American society, and grew up outside the social and political elites. Martí was the son of Spanish immigrants; his father was a soldier who had received no formal education. Darío's family circumstances were also modest, and an additional barrier excluded him from elite Nicaraguan society: he was *aindiado* (partly of Indian descent). Rodó, despite the prevalent image of him as an aristocrat, was in fact a petty-bourgeois autodidact (as indeed were most members of what became known as the Generation of 1900 in Uruguay). His mother was from 'a patrician and well-to-do family',[26] but she married a Catalan businessman, whose declining economic fortunes meant that Rodó had to be transferred from private to state education. Two years later, when Rodó was only fourteen, his father died and he was obliged to seek work first in a scribe's office and later as a bank clerk.[27] He did later enrol at the university, but he abandoned his formal studies, partly for financial reasons and partly, it appears, from disaffection with a syllabus that required him to study science when he was interested in literature and history.[28] 'The advancement of human thought', he was later to observe, 'owes a good deal . . . to great *autodidacts*.'[29] There is evidence that he perceived himself to be an outsider, comparing his own upbringing unfavourably with that of the instigator of Uruguay's advanced welfare state, José Batlle y Ordóñez (President, 1903–07 and 1911–15), whom Rodó at first supported as leader of the Colorado Party but later broke with over the issue of constitutional reform. Batlle was the son of a distinguished former President, and had received 'the finest [education] available' at the English school in Montevideo and the university, including the standard wealthy young South American's sojourn in Europe.[30] In 1910, Rodó bitterly contrasted the lives of ease enjoyed by men such as Batlle with those of people like himself, who had little choice but to work for the state: 'Salaried public posts are the preserve of those of us who have not yet found a decent means of earning a living; they are not for those who are in possession of sufficient wealth to enable them to enjoy the luxury of living a life of eternal pleasure.'[31] Despite the fact that *Ariel* brought Rodó instant acclaim, and an invitation from the leading faction of the ruling Colorados to stand for Congress because 'your name alone [would] adorn the electoral platform',[32] he developed – indeed, perhaps cultivated – an acute sense of exclusion from influence in national affairs. In 1912, he was passed over as Uruguay's representative at the centennial celebrations of Spain's Cádiz Constitution for somebody of less intellectual distinction from the inner circles of government; this incident apparently left a lasting resentment in Rodó.[33] In 1916, he justified his stance on constitutional reform (opposition to Batlle's plans to introduce a plural executive, modelled on the Swiss Confederation, which Rodó believed would only consolidate the increasing monopoly over government exercised by the Colorado Party), by arguing that it was important to oppose 'the disastrous cliquishness of the political system; the deliberate exclusion from the work of government of the country's most representative intellectual and moral forces; the overwhelming personalism of the presidency'.[34]

In addition to their comparable social backgrounds, a second feature that Martí, Darío and Rodó had in common was their preoccupation with the inadequacies of intellectual life in Spanish America. Martí's ire was directed particularly against outdated university syllabuses: 'it is no longer enough ... to take a pointer and indicate cities upon maps ... or recite in chorus proofs of the earth's roundness ... or know that worthless chrono- logical history which one is obliged to learn in our universities and col- leges'.[35] The Cuban poet was a crucial transitional figure between Sarmiento, who saw art primarily as a vehicle for the indirect practice of politics, and the self-styled aesthete Darío (whom Martí referred to as his 'son'). Although he mocked the affectation of art-for-art's-sake dandyism,[36] and dedicated himself to the cause of Cuban nationalism, Martí helped to advance the emergence of a distinct creative sphere by insisting that politics should be kept out of art. He saw art as a 'source of splendid enchantments and of consolations with which to restore a spirit anguished by the bitter sorrows that life brings'.[37] Art could sustain the human spirit most effectively if it remained art and did not become politics, he maintained:

> The world is full of suffering, and the greatest artist is not the one who paints it in the best possible light ... but the one who uses the gift of composition to show the sadness of the world, and moves man to alleviate it.[38]

Martí always emphasized that, morally, the struggle for social justice should prevail over any dedication to art: 'Justice first, art second! When there is no liberty, the only justification for art and its only reason for existing is that it must place itself at liberty's service.'[39] Yet he saw no advantage to either art or politics in mixing the two: 'He who introduces politics and sociology into verse is no poet.'[40] The general purpose of art, in his view, was 'to enjoin people to love each other well, and to paint all that is beautiful in the world'; poetry, specifically, should be used, 'like a whip', 'to castigate ... those who seek to deprive men of their liberty'.[41] For Martí, social liberation was related to freedom of the imagination, but he upheld a clear distinction between the two and, unlike many twentieth-century Spanish American intellectuals, argued that political freedom had to pre- cede artistic freedom, and not vice versa: 'There will be no Spanish American literature while there is no Spanish America. To an undetermined people, an undetermined literature!'[42] Both in turn were dependent upon spiritual renewal: 'There can be no originality, nor can political freedom endure, until such time as spiritual freedom is secured. Man's first task is to reconquer himself.'[43]

In 1900, Rodó, who was also contending with a restricted cultural milieu, wrote: 'Intellectual life is desultory and difficult in this [part of] America. . . . What oppresses us is the lack of a public. . . . Politics absorbs [virtually] all intellectual energy, and the need to earning a living saps what little remains.'[44] Rodó found out how difficult it could be to create a forum for intellectual life when he launched the *Revista Nacional de Literatura y Ciencias Sociales* in 1895. According to his biographer and colleague on the journal Víctor Pérez Petit, this pioneering initiative to remedy the absence of opportunities to publish literary and intellectual works encountered myriad frustrations:

> We had to surmount the unsurmountable apathy of our men of letters: they all promised original work, but nobody wrote a line. It is true that we could not pay contributors. Getting articles out of them was like getting blood out of a stone; we had to besiege writers, visiting each one twenty times, convincing them that this was no ephemeral project, begging them virtually on bended knees for even one page.[45]

Subsequently Rodó campaigned as a congressional deputy for improvements in the economic basis for intellectual activity, such as copyright legislation and the elimination of taxation on imported books; he also tried to defend the freedom of the press and academic standards at the university.[46] In the midst of Uruguay's efforts to introduce an advanced system of welfare legislation for workers, Rodó pleaded the case for intellectuals. He argued: '. . . it is important that we should not forget, among the workers worthy of solicitous interest, the intellectual worker. . . . The writer is, generically, a labourer.'[47] One piece of legislation he repeatedly placed before Congress insisted that the roles of university professor and congressional legislator should not be deemed incompatible.[48]

Darío, famous for his Byronic lifestyle and his assertion of the value of art-for-art's-sake, was the cultural figure who did most to win social recognition in Spanish America for creative intellectual work as an activity in its own right. In an embittered article written from Paris in 1913, he lamented the inadequate facilities for cultural exchange within Spanish America and the fact that the governments of the region treated intellectual matters 'with disdain'.[49] He insisted on the importance of the specialization of literary activity: 'literature is only for the literati, just as mathematics is only for mathematicians, and chemistry for chemists'.[50] He wrote many articles of literary and artistic criticism, a considerable number of them about Spanish American writers (as also did Martí and Rodó). Darío was the first leading literary figure to publish an autobiography (in 1912),[51] in which he wrote disingenuously and distractedly of his mercurial literary and romantic fortunes, introducing the idea of poetry as a whole way of being, rather than merely one of the many accomplishments of a cultivated man. In 1913 he published *Historia de mis libros,* an account of the creative process involved in his three major collections of poetry (*Azul, Prosas profanas* and *Cantos de vida y esperanza*). Here, he was explicit about the 'period of arduous intellectual struggle which I had to undergo, together with my companions and followers, in Buenos Aires, in defence of new ideas and artistic freedom'.[52] In the course of his expositions of the influences and ideas behind each poem, he derided what he saw as the amateurism of the didactic, patriotic stanzas that had hitherto counted as poetry in Spanish America: 'an eternal song to Junín, an unending ode to the agriculture of the torrid zone' (the latter reference was to Andrés Bello's famous poem of 1826).[53] No previous Spanish American poet had shown so much dedication to the mastery of artistic technique.[54] Darío's desire to establish himself as a professional writer is tellingly illustrated by an incident early in 1902, when the young Spanish poet Juan Ramón Jiménez (1881–1958) approached him asking for an unpaid contribution to a fledgling *revista*. In reply, Darío tartly, albeit not unreasonably, demanded to know whether he was expected to 'work for the love of it', eliciting a letter of fulsome apology from the embarrassed Spaniard.[55]

In sharp contrast to these very material concerns, Darío represented intellectuals as gentlemen–scholars: for example, he refers to 'Ricardo Jiménez and Cleto González Viquez, members of what we will call the Costa Rican nobility, learned scholars, genteel men, immaculate gentlemen, both true intellectuals'.[56] Darío emulated the European Romantics in promoting an aristocracy of the spirit to defend artistic integrity against bourgeois commercial values. Throughout his autobiography, he draws on this idea to elaborate a specific social role for the poet, the particularity of whose gift, in his view, enhances a claim to universal authority. Much has been written about the literary influence on Darío of Victor Hugo, but in terms of style and metaphor Darío's work owes more to the Parnassian poets: what he mainly took from Hugo was the idea of the poet as the voice of God.[57] In a telling evocation of the Romantic myth of divine inspiration, Darío offers the reader an account of how his first verses came to be written:

[It was Holy Week,] and the streets were adorned with arches of green branches. . . . From the middle of one of the arches, at the corner of my house, there hung a golden pomegranate. When the procession of Our Lord Triumphant passed by, on Palm Sunday, the pomegranate opened up and a shower of poems poured forth. I was the author of them. I have been unable to recall any . . . but I know for sure that they were poems, poems which came to me instinctively. I was never taught to write verse. In me it was organic, natural, innate'.[58]

The fact that Darío took Holy Week as the backdrop for this depiction of his initiation into the creative process was not accidental. The Catholic

Church was still highly influential throughout Spanish America, where the processes that in northern Europe had already brought about greater secularization (urbanization, industrialization and the extension of state education) were still in their earliest stages. It was to the advantage of Spanish Americans who were seeking intellectual authority to cast themselves as alternatives to the priests rather than their direct opponents; it was also, in many cases, their personal inclination. Indeed, the role of the intellectual in Spanish America has yet to reach the heights of secularization that it scaled in eighteenth-century France. There are elements of religiosity inherent in all images of the intellectual, but instead of trying to appropriate the juridical authority of the priest (as had the *philosophes*), Darío chose to represent himself as an alternative conduit for the divine:

> In the enchanted Mass of my youth, I have recited my own antiphonies, my own chants and my own profane hymns. I needed more time, and less weariness of soul and heart, to emulate a skilled artisan monk and make my capital letters worthy of every page of the breviary. . . . Ring out bells of gold, bells of silver, ring out every day and summon me to the feast where the eyes of fire sparkle and the roses in the mouths bleed their incomparable delights. My organ is an old pompadour harpsichord to the tunes of which joyous forebears once danced their gavottes. And my perfume is the perfume of your breast, timeless censer of flesh, immortal Lady, flower of my rib.
>
> Man am I.[59]

A perception of the intellectual as a worshipper of physical as well as metaphorical beauty is one final aspect of Romantic mythology that was readily embraced in Spanish America. Darío encapsulates this attitude in the following lines from his autobiography: 'Then I sang the praises of "Julia's black eyes". Which Julia? I can't remember now. Pray indulge such ingratitude towards beauty. Because the woman who inspired the stanzas in question was undoubtedly beautiful.'[60] Built into the original self-definition was the assumption that an intellectual was male, because of the imagined link between creative and sexual potency. (During the early twentieth century, the Chilean Gabriela Mistral, who won Latin America's first Nobel Prize for Literature in 1947, was regarded as *una poetisa* [a poetess] rather than an intellectual. Mistral herself was uncomfortable with the idea of intellectuality. In clear distinction from Rodó's secular spiritualism, she embraced a religious, even mystical approach to life: 'So much learning and knowledge has come to me through the heart, not through the brain, that I would cultivate nothing in humanity but sensibility, and I would leave to atrophy a little that horrible, perverse, icy and antipathetic thing we call the brain.')[61] Even in the 1990s, well after the introduction of Anglo-American and French feminist ideas into Spanish America during the 1960s and 1970s, women still found it difficult to win recognition as 'intellectuals', even when they had succeeded in establishing themselves as writers, journalists or academics.

The importance of the new role of the independent creative intellectual in the early years of the twentieth century is well illustrated by the legendary contemporary renown that attached to the minor Chilean writer Augusto D'Halmar (1882–1950). At the height of his popularity D'Halmar, who had affected an aristocratic name,[62] reigned supreme as the most admired man in the university, the National Library, the *tertulias* (literary gatherings), the *revistas*, and the Ateneo (Athenaeum). A tall, slim, dandified figure, with flowing romantic locks, whose social gimmick was to appear at speaking engagements with his tiny white-haired grandmother on his arm, D'Halmar was celebrated by the country's literati as 'the Chilean Zola'.[63] (It was actually a rather inappropriate appellation given that Zola himself was somewhat lacking in what educated Chileans might have deemed the social graces.) This adulation had less to do with the quality of D'Halmar's writing than with the circumstance that he was the first Chilean to define himself as a writer *tout court*, rather than a writer–politician or a writer–diplomat or a gentleman–writer: 'after D'Halmar, writers no longer needed to be from the upper classes with an inherited fortune; [neither did they need to be] politicians . . .; nor impoverished bohemians . . .; nor bureaucrats. . . . They could live from their trade.'[64] In practice, as noted above, the incipient 'profession' of writer was more a question of image than reality: very few writers could actually live off their earnings – indeed, it was still common practice for the author to pay the publisher rather than the other way around. D'Halmar left Chile in 1907 to become consul to India, and supported himself through a combination of diplomatic posts and journalism in Europe, Africa and Asia before eventually returning home in 1934. Despite the miserable practicalities, however, the emergence of the *idea* of the professional writer was confirmation of the development, albeit uneven and fragile, of autonomous cultural activity. From this base in a specific intellectual pursuit, would-be 'intellectuals' hoped that they could launch a bid for national political influence. However, it proved impossible to separate culture from politics completely, for any attempt to do so in itself constituted a challenge to the status quo upheld by an elite that had hitherto monopolized both cultural and political authority.

In the early twentieth century, fears provoked by the rise of US power in Spanish America dovetailed with the intellectuals' need to resist the pro-European cultural orientation of the elites to inject new urgency into the theme of the region's cultural autonomy, which had been raised by *pensadores* since the wars of independence. At this stage of Spanish American development, cultural emancipation could not plausibly be declared on a national basis: the only foundation for a claim to a distinctive set of values was regional. This had an important consequence for Spanish American intellectuals in that it precluded them from making a bid for influence on the basis of superior mastery of Cartesian Reason. Reason was associated with Europe and the pro-European elites; in order to differentiate themselves, the region's intellectuals had to seek alternative values. Thus, in contrast to the United States, the role of the modern intellectual in Spanish America was consciously created in opposition to the established academic institutions, which were viewed as bastions of the sterile, imported doctrines of positivism and utilitarianism. Martí attacked *letrados* and despots in the same breath for betraying their peoples across Spanish America.[65] Darío included academics in his litany of those '*qui-ne-comprendent-pas*'[66] and his famous line 'Deliver us, Lord, from the academies' was adopted as a slogan by the self-proclaimed 'new men' of the 1920s.[67] Rodó too saw the academy as anathema to freedom of thought:

> What an enormous sum of energy . . . is required . . . for an individual conscience, left to its own devices, to break the iron grip of a secular authority supported by the weight of tradition, *magister dixit* (the voice of authority) and conventional wisdom, such as scholastic philosophy.[68]

In order to present an alternative to what he saw as inappropriate imported knowledge, Martí invoked the idea of natural being:

> . . . in America, the good governor is not someone who knows how the German or the Frenchman is governed, but someone who knows the elements that make up his own country. . . . For this reason, the imported book has been vanquished in America by natural man. Natural men have vanquished men of artificial learning. . . . The battle is not between civilization and barbarism, but between false erudition and nature.[69]

Martí based his own claim to authority not on superior intellectual powers but on his capacity to live authentically: in his prologue to *Versos libres* (1882), he assured the reader that these poems were written 'not in the ink of the academy, but in my own blood'.[70] He saw his verses as 'pieces slashed . . . from my own entrails – my warriors. Not one has come out of me overdone, contrived, over-elaborate, from the mind; instead, they come forth like tears from my eyes, like blood gushing from a wound.' The poet was to surrender his flesh, if only metaphorically. He was to be not only a Christ-like martyr, but also a military hero.

The vision of intellectuals as heroes was a recurrent theme in Spanish American writings from then onwards. It was related to two factors: first, the power that had been lost – twentieth-century intellectuals had little chance of combining military and intellectual power in the way that some of their forefathers had done. Rodó knew, for example, that circumstances would not afford him the opportunity to fulfil Bolívar's multiple roles as 'revolutionary, *montonero* [guerrilla fighter], general, military leader, tribune, legislator, president . . .'.[71] The emphasis on heroism was also a corollary of the image of the intellectual as a repository of moral values. As intellectuals lost the opportunity to be men of action, they reinforced their claims to a heroism of the spirit. In that context, creative works came to be celebrated less for their aesthetic value than for what they revealed about the greatness of the man who produced them. This tendency was displayed in Darío's encomium to Martí in a review of *Versos libres*:

> When I recall that pure man and kind friend, I admire that cosmic mind, that all-embracing soul, that profound and all-encompassing humanity. He had everything: he was a man of action and a man of vision, a man of ideals who lived life to the full; he experienced an epic death and, in his America, will know immortality itself.[72]

If the intellectual were to fulfil the role of bearer of the spirit of Spanish America, then he was required to embody a wholeness of being appropriate to a secular saint.

In their struggles against the elites, intellectuals began to look for social allies. One of the few to state this explicitly was the disaffected Peruvian aristocrat Manuel González Prada (1848–1918), who was the first in his country to assume 'a modern kind of intellectual responsibility', addressing himself to a public that included the workers, students and the emergent middle classes.[73] In 1905 he gave a speech denying the value of any theoretical distinction between intellectual and manual work, as Gramsci was later to do, and advocating an alliance between intellectuals and workers in the fight for social justice.[74] Martí and Rodó were less categorical, but the same concerns can be traced in their work: repudiation of the Romantic view of the common man as an irredeemable philistine, and a commitment to the raising of his consciousness through education. Even Darío, for whom it is harder to make a convincing case that he was at all interested in the masses, wrote a fulsome obituary of Zola apostrophizing him as 'the prophet of the proletarians'. It is worth noting that Darío made a point of drawing a distinction between Hugo, who dispensed his gifts from on high 'like a literary pope', and Zola, whom he characterized as 'an orphic and august musician of the multitudes'.[75] Darío's endorsement of Zola's humanity as ultimately more necessary to people than Hugo's genius is indicative of the Nicaraguan's own beliefs about the appropriate role for an intellectual in the early twentieth century.[76] For all his aestheticism, Darío identified himself as both a dreamer *and* a fighter.[77] In part, this is symptomatic of how European Romantic ideas had been interpreted in Spanish America. It was the later Romantics (Byron, Hugo, Scott) – devotees of a passion that was political as well as personal – who appealed most to the Spanish Americans, rather than the earlier generation (Goethe and Schiller) who saw art more as a refuge from the sordid pursuit of power. In

Spanish America, when poets or *pensadores* claimed to be visionaries they were not signalling a retreat from public life but precisely the opposite in that they were hoping for privileged access to political influence. Even the bohemian Darío expressed political opinions (albeit sometimes contradictory ones), not only in his journalism, but also in some of his poetry.[78] He admired the moral force of Zola's defence of Dreyfus, and in that context argued that it was the duty of the true intellectual 'of our time . . . to go into action for worthy causes'.[79] His assumption (and that of his audience) was not that his poetic gift absolved him from political responsibility, but rather that it endowed him with an enhanced understanding of politics. Halperín Donghi has noted: 'what Darío offers can be [simply] a rendering in resonant verse of the editorials he has read that morning, an exercise that endows those commonplace ideas with novel depth and meaning, not only in his eyes, but also in those of his public'.[80] But the important transition represented by Darío is that instead of mobilizing his poetic gifts to acquire political power, he enlisted politics to bolster his legitimacy as a poet.

There is also evidence in Rodó's work that, despite the widespread view that his ideal intellectual was a detached, contemplative figure, he too expected that intellectuals would have an interest in working with the masses. While there undoubtedly are elements of elitism in Rodó's work, his reputation as an ivory-tower escapist owes far more to the way his ideas were received by a generation captivated by the allure of a bohemian lifestyle than to what he actually wrote. (In passing, it is worth observing that the Welsh socialist Aneurin Bevan, who was never noted for his tolerance of elitism, found in Rodó his most important intellectual influence apart from Marx.)[81] In contrast to Martí, although in common with many *fin de siècle* European intellectuals, Rodó was pessimistic about the prospect of mass political participation, fearing above all 'the levelling effect' which could result in mediocracy. Nevertheless, he held that democracy was inescapable, not least because he argued that to reject democracy was to reject science.[82] This view revealed how strongly his version of idealist philosophy had been influenced by positivism. Indeed, although Rodó stated that positivism in Spanish America had been 'as poorly interpreted in its basic tenets as [it had been] bastardized in practice', he contended that it had brought some benefits to his generation, including 'due consideration of the realities of life; . . . an insistence on critical method; . . . respect for the circumstances of time and place; . . . [and] scorn for ill-considered objectives, sterile debates and naïve expectations'.[83] Rodó explicitly rejected both Ernest Renan's claim that the cultivation of moral and spiritual superiority was incompatible with democracy, and his promotion of an aristocratic republic of the loftiest intellects:

Given, then, that it's senseless to think, like Renan, that by destroying democratic equality we might bring about a more effective means of ordaining those who are truly morally superior . . ., it only remains for us to consider how to enhance and reform democracy.[84]

Rodó's quarrel was with utilitarianism rather than democracy; indeed, his main purpose was to establish how best democracy might be safeguarded. His concern was that if the spiritual development of the people were to be neglected, material strength would decide the outcome of power struggles, and democracy could prove counterproductive to establishing the meritocracy of culture and morality that he advocated. Rodó is often accused of promoting an aristocracy, but what he envisaged was closer to an aristocracy of merit intended to replace an aristocracy of wealth (a strategy comparable to that of the *philosophes*). He argued that democracy, 'like aristocracies, enshrines distinctions of superiority, but resolves them in favour of the truly superior qualities – those of virtue, character, spirit – and, without seeking to place those qualities in a class apart . . . democracy continually replenishes its own ruling aristocracy [of the spirit] from the life-giving source of the people, and makes that rule acceptable because it is based on principles of justice and love'.[85] For Rodó, the way forward lay in the extension of public elementary education – which he saw as 'a matter of supreme importance' – to create an aristocracy of merit:[86] 'The state's duty is to ensure that all members of society enjoy similar conditions in which they can attend to their own self-perfection.'[87] For Rodó, it was endeavour, rather than any intrinsic qualities, that constituted the true virtue:

When all the aristocratic titles founded on fictitious and outdated notions of superiority have turned to dust, there will remain among men only one claim to superior and aristocratic status, and that will be to be a worker. This is an aristocracy that cannot be prescribed, because the worker is, by definition, 'a man who works', in other words, the only kind of man who deserves to live.[88]

In an intriguing late work, Rodó located the seeds of democracy and 'the cradle of the nation' not in Montevideo, but instead in 'the bleak plains of the interior, where the heroic *montoneras* spread their instinctive love of freedom and their indomitable pride, catalysts of independence and democracy'.[89]

Rodó repeatedly maintained that he was advocating cultivation of the contemplative state not for its own reward, but rather as a means of preparing an appropriate moral basis for action.[90] He declared: 'I do not aspire to the "ivory tower", I take pleasure in the type of literature which, in its own way, is militant.'[91] He argued further that, in the process of attaining self-awareness, action was not only desirable but essential: 'action is not only an end in itself, but also the means for gaining that self-knowledge'.[92] The imagery of *Ariel* gives further clues as to how Rodó saw intellectual agency.

Prospero is represented as a *maestro*, not, as in the original play, a sorceror, or, as in Renan's *Caliban, suite de la Tempête* (1878), an intellectual leader. Throughout most of the text, his audience consists of students – either potential intellectuals or members of the intelligentsia – but at the very end, the masses make an appearance when the students flock out into the crowd. A familiar image of modernist alienation – the intellectual looking with horror upon the 'human herd' – is reversed by Rodó, who gives the final words – emphasizing the potential of the masses to achieve a more elevated life, if guided from on high – to the youngest student in the group: 'As the crowd passes by, I observe that although they do not look up at the sky, the sky looks down on them. Above their obscure and indifferent mass, like furrowed ground, something descends from on high. The vibration of the stars resembles the movement of the hands of a sower.'[93] Unlike many of his European contemporaries, Rodó did not see the great unwashed as beyond redemption. Indeed, he specifically stated that he was writing with them in mind: 'I wield my pen like a chisel destined to inscribe words and images on the soul of the multitude.'[94] There is, however, a level of violence inherent in this image, which is echoed in the metaphor of branding at the close of *Ariel*. In this context, Roberto González Echevarría has drawn attention to Prospero's final invocation: 'May the image of this bronze – engraved upon your hearts – play the same intangible but decisive role in your lives.'[95] In neither case is Rodó appealing to the efficacy of reasoned persuasion; force remains a latent element in his formulation of the role of the intellectual.

A more indirect indication of Rodó's view of the intellectual's relationship to the masses is given by the fact that he wrote *Ariel* as a dialogue. González Echevarría has argued that at no point during Prospero's speech do his students make any intervention – therefore all that the dialogic structure 'really allows is an enthronement of the voice of the master'.[96] But Rodó's adoption of the Platonic dialogue, in homage to the classical heritage he was claiming for Latin America, has a further and perhaps more significant implication in the context of Spanish American culture. It enabled him to challenge the primacy of writing, emphasizing the power of the voice and, therefore, of a more immediate, authentic kind of authority. The Peruvian critic Julio Ortega has observed:

> It should not be forgotten that, contrary to Derrida's strictures, in Latin America the spoken word represents not the language of authority but that of marginality. The written word corresponds to the law, and under its auspices the rules of society's dominant framework of thought are codified.[97]

By making Prospero master of the spoken rather than the written word, Rodó placed him in a marginal position from which he could reclaim the alternative legitimacy of an oral tradition, in opposition to the dominant elite culture. Implicit here is the idea that the marginalized intellectual could – and perhaps should – speak on behalf of the people of a nation, an idea that was given concrete expression in a speech given by Rodó as a Uruguayan representative at Chile's official celebrations of its independence centenary:

> ... never before have I so deplored the fact that, having acquired the habit of committing my thoughts to the cold and lifeless symbols of the written word, I possess neither the inclination nor the aptitude to express my ideas in that other way that springs naturally, warm and sonorous, from the lips, like a direct emanation of the spirit ...
> I should be here as the voice of a people.[98]

Contrary to the customary image of Rodó as a defender of the ivory tower, he proposed that the mission of the intellectual was 'to instil, in the souls of these peoples, a receptiveness to the legitimate authority of aristocracies of the spirit, for the guidance and government of the collective conscience'.[99] Rodó actually went further than envisaging the intellectual as the spiritual teacher of his people, and advocated political commitment, although he did express uneasiness about the loss of intellectual integrity risked by participating in political parties:

> Who ... does not recall, if he has a soul at all elevated above the ordinary, the tortures of adaptation; the personal resistance to the uniformities of [party] discipline; that intellectual anguish caused by the impossibility of distinguishing nuances and clarifying ideas in the crude forms of expression intelligible to the majority; ... the all-too-vivid sensation of the profound differences of thought and feeling which were given a false unity under a single programme and a single name?[100]

Even so, he viewed political parties as 'fatal necessities of action. Since we cannot think of suppressing them, let us aspire, so far as it is possible, to educate them.' He also advised writers to work for the press, which he referred to as 'the people's tribune',[101] noting that, in 'the peculiar circumstances of a nascent culture scarcely differentiated into specific areas of activity, the character of our intellectuality has been personified so far by the journalist: a type of encyclopaedic improviser, disposed, like the theologian of old, to find out about and pronounce upon everything'.[102] In a 1909 speech to the inaugural ceremony of the Montevideo press club, he denounced those who disdained journalism:

> To be a writer and not to have been ... a journalist, in a land like ours, is less a claim to superiority than a manifestation of egoism. It would mean never having felt reverberating in one's soul that imperious voice with which the popular

conscience calls upon those who wield a pen to come to the defence of common interests and common rights.[103]

Rodó's own politicization dated back to the Uruguayan civil war of 1897, as a result of which 'he [converted] straight away into what we would call today a *committed* writer'.[104] He went on to serve for eleven years as a deputy in the Uruguayan Congress. According to one biographer, when first elected to Congress Rodó deserted literature altogether in favour of politics:

> Temporarily abandoning his work as a writer, seduced by the opportunity for action which politics offers him, he wants to fulfil his mission with Catonian virtue. He no longer pursues literature now that he can do social work which is productive and useful for the people. It is not that he betrays or denies his former ideals . . .; it's that he yearns to take his vision of the ideal into politics and to put into practice what he has conceived in theory.[105]

Rodó proved to be ill-adapted to the compromises and confrontations inherent in congressional politics, however, and was not nominated for the elections in 1904. This failure left him depressed – 'to say goodbye to politics', he mused, 'would almost be like saying goodbye to the country, for our country and its politics are synonymous: there is no country outside politics' – and also meant that he was obliged to fall back on his family for financial support.[106] His attitude to politics was henceforth ambivalent. In 1907, having refused an offer to renew his teaching post at the university because he had decided to run again as a deputy, he wrote resignedly of 'that inescapable fact of South American life that compels almost all of us who pick up a pen to go into politics. And I do not consider this to be entirely a bad thing.'[107] He served a second term in Congress from 1907 to 1910, and was re-elected once more in 1910, only to find himself vetoed once more in 1913 because of his disputes with Batlle. Indeed, by this stage his political views had come to undermine the social status accorded by his literary achievements, which suggests that politics was at least as important to him as literature. One biographer wrote:

> . . . the political attitude adopted by Rodó placed him in an unusual position in his own country. He was recognized and esteemed by all; the most eminent men were proud to be his friend; his advice and ideas were beyond all price, but his life became dominated by bitterness and disappointment. His political friends of only a short time before turned their backs on him. . . . He shut himself up in his house and wouldn't see anyone apart from a few close friends.[108]

Despite his own increasing sense of acute isolation, Rodó was popular not only with students, but also with the general public. Crowds turned up to wave him farewell when he left for a visit to Europe in 1916, and when his remains were repatriated from Italy the following year a day of national mourning was declared and there was 'an unprecedented demonstration' of public grief.[109]

Far from being 'the representative of an exhausted nineteenth-century mentality',[110] in some ways Rodó's ideas were more modern than those of Martí or Darío: he insisted on the separation of intellectual and political activity, he recognized that many individuals found them hard to reconcile, yet he nevertheless maintained that political participation was an inescapable part of being a modern intellectual, at least in Spanish America, where politics tended to be all-consuming. His main concern was that political involvement should not eclipse intellectual creativity:

> I beg you to defend yourselves, in the midst of life's battles, against the mutilation of your spirit by the tyranny of one single, ultimately self-seeking objective. . . . Even in circumstances of material slavery, it is possible to preserve an inner freedom: that of reason and feeling. So do not try to justify the enslavement of your spirit with absorption in work or struggle.[111]

Rodó's incipient modernity has been highlighted by Carlos Fuentes, who suggests that he was outlining, albeit sketchily, the development of civil society when he wrote about the importance of 'the secular solidity of the social structure, a secure political order and . . . a culture that has taken deep root'.[112]

As the most dedicated participant in politics of these three key figures, Martí has been identified (particularly in Cuba after 1959) as a precursor of the *intelectual comprometido* of the mid-twentieth century. Martí's belief in the vital connection between an intellectual and his people was strengthened by a political incentive: the need for the Cuban independence movement to attract support from all social classes if it were to prevail over the rival elite factions of annexationists and autonomists. He was the first Cuban intellectual to present himself as a mediator between the people and the nation, elaborating a concept of *cubanidad*. Throughout his work, he claimed to speak on behalf of 'the Cuban', elaborating 'our' qualities and 'our' values.[113] Compare the use of 'the people' in Sarmiento's work, where the masses were referred to as an object.[114] In this, Martí made a key contribution to the evolution of the role of a modern intellectual in Spanish America. Even so, he 'stood nearer to the generation that preceded him than to his own',[115] and is better understood as the last leading example of the nineteenth-century model of the *licenciado–político* than as the first in a series of twentieth-century figures. This distinction, which may at first sight seem mere sophistry, is important in tracing the separation of political and cultural authority in Spanish America. Martí's life testified to the existence of new opportunities to earn a living from intellectual activity: he worked for a few years as a diplomat but most of his income came from journalism. As in Darío's case, the latter possibility arose out of being in exile from his native country, which enabled him to take advantage of the more developed cultural infrastructure of Mexico and the USA. In that respect, his experiences resembled those of his successors. But from his youth onwards he had campaigned against colonialism, and his political standing and intellectual authority grew in tandem, reinforcing each other: he was not invoking intellectual authority to claim political influence, as twentieth-century intellectuals have done. The particular historical circumstances of Cuba's struggle for political independence allowed someone from Martí's petty-bourgeois background to participate in the political life of his country to an extent that was far closer to the opportunities open to, say, Sarmiento in the 1860s than to those available to virtually any Spanish American intellectual in the twentieth century. Martí had long been sceptical about the potential impact of intellectual work on the fight for liberty: on returning to Cuba at the end of the Ten Years' War, he sounded distinctly pessimistic about what he could achieve: 'I'm going to be a lawyer, a farmer, a teacher; [in other words,] a weaver of legal formulas, a producer of foodstuffs, a disseminator of muddled ideas – lost in the froth of the sea.'[116] Later, he argued that liberty would not be won by any 'young Prospero' conjuring visions out of 'his fragrant tobacco'.[117] From 1892 onwards, Martí set aside his intellectual pursuits to devote himself full-time to the independence struggle. In doing so, he put into practice his earlier assertion that 'the only way to be a poet in an oppressed land is to be a soldier'.[118] Clearly stung by accusations of being an 'intellectual revolutionary, more of a writer than a fighter',[119] his conscience was apparently eased once he had become, in his own eyes, a 'useful man'.[120] In Cuba, Martí is remembered chiefly as a nationalist, that is, for his political rather than his intellectual contribution; his poetry is praised as a glorious adjunct to a heroic life. Rodó's reputation, on the other hand, despite his long and respectable political career, is based almost exclusively on his intellectual output. This shift in perception marks the emergence of the role of the modern intellectual in Spanish America.

The 1920s–1930s

In 1925, the Mexican intellectual and former Minister of Education José Vasconcelos was welcomed to Havana as a 'teacher, revolutionary and precursor'.[121] Between the already established images of the disseminator of knowledge and the herald of the future, the idea of the intellectual as a revolutionary became lodged. A key text was *Los tiempos nuevos*, by the Argentine philosopher José Ingenieros, in which he heralded the Bolshevik revolution as 'the spirit of renewal'.[122] He also celebrated the proposal made by Henri Barbusse (1873–1935) for an Internationale de la Pensée (1919) composed of 'workers of the mind', which was intended 'to renew moral, sociological and aesthetic values'.[123] According to José Aricó, this book became a bible for both socialist and democratic intellectuals.[124] *Hispanoamericanismo*, although not forgotten by intellectuals, was largely superseded by nationalism. Whereas Martí had identified republicanism, and Rodó education, as the means of reconciling *pueblo* and *nación*, by the 1920s many intellectuals found both these remedies wanting. Faced with ample evidence from Cuba of just how artificial independence could be, and (Mexico apart) increasingly excluded from influence on public education projects by populist takeovers of the state, many Spanish American intellectuals, with the example of the Mexican revolution in mind, began to pursue more radical solutions to the problem of national liberation.

The changing conception of the role of the intellectual in the 1920s can be traced clearly in the work of the Cuban writer, university reform leader and founder of the Cuban Communist Party, Julio Antonio Mella (1903–29). At first influenced by Rodó, Mella later adopted Leninist views. Unlike many of his contemporaries, Mella did not interpret Rodó as an advocate of ivory-tower intellectualism, but instead read him in much the same way as suggested earlier in this chapter, expressed in Barbusse's vocabulary: 'The worker of the mind is an intellectual. The worker! – that is, the only man who, in Rodó's opinion, deserves to live – is the one who brandishes his pen to combat iniquities.'[125] He drew on *Ariel* to support a distinction between the teacher who merely passes on book learning and the true *maestro*, whom he defined as 'he who moulds, like a skilful artist, the future of society in his classroom': 'Prospero invoking Ariel's winged genius, right at the end of his last lesson, in Rodó's immortal myth, exemplifies a true *maestro*'.[126] One indication of Mella's respect for Rodó is that he named a newly founded Polytechnic Institute in Havana after him. Initially, Mella himself emphasized the educator role for intellectuals that had been propagated by both Rodó and Martí: 'To free the people, that is the mission of the current generation; the people are slaves because they are ignorant of their rights, so let us teach them, let us drench them in all our knowledge, let us not allow Church and state education to infect them with the poison of insincerity and corruption.'[127] Furthermore, he maintained, 'Knowledge is a privilege that brings with it certain responsibilities. To have new ideas and not to make them known is a betrayal. To feel a deep spiritual disquiet and not to come down to the level of the popular masses in order to temper that unease in the daily struggles of today's society is pernicious stupidity.'[128] At this stage, Mella represented the intellectual as a catalyst, explicitly invoking Rodó. For example, in an article he wrote about Víctor Raúl Haya de la Torre's visit to Havana in 1923, Mella portrayed the Peruvian as a god-like figure, 'swift and evanescent, like a condor blazing a brilliant trail across the skies towards the eternal heavens', who embodied the virtues of both Mirabeau and the Messiah and yet still came among them 'as a jovial comrade, almost like a child, with a pure and ingenuous soul all of which he lays bare on the altars of friendship'. This life-giving being, sacrificing himself in the ardour of his mission to dissemi- nate heat and light to his fellow human beings, was, concluded Mella, 'the archetype of Latin American youth . . . Rodó's dream come true . . . Ariel'.[129] Like Haya de la Torre, Mella was a key figure in his local popular university, named after José Martí, which offered free education to workers, and where probably the most sustained and effective attempt was made by intellectuals anywhere in Spanish America to make contacts with working people. Mella specifically called upon students to become the 'apostles, heroes and martyrs' of their nations.[130] In 1924, his views were still that 'culture is the one True and Lasting form of emancipation',[131] and that opposition to the status quo was a necessary part of being an intellectual: 'Those who debase their thinking by becoming slaves to conventional wisdom or to ignominious tyranny should never be called intellectuals.'[132]

Later, however, after his conversion to Communism, Mella became increasingly sceptical about the possibility of intellectuals contributing to the revolution unless they were prepared to relinquish their cultural status in order to assume the role of professional revolutionary. He advised one potential comrade: 'if none of the existing professions offered by the bourgeois universities appeals to you, become a REVOLUTIONARY. Go to jail for an education.'[133] In 1927, Mella denounced the Mexican intellectual Vicente Lombardo Toledano for opportunism and ignorance of Marxism, wearily observing that most intellectuals were tarred with the same brush.[134] A year later, one of the main weapons in Mella's attack on the Peruvian APRA (American Popular Revolutionary Alliance) was withering scorn for its espousal of the revolutionary potential of intellectuals: 'Everyone knows that "intellectual workers" . . . are neither revolutionaries, nor anti- imperialists, nor proletarians, but members of the bourgeoisie or the petty bourgeoisie, and almost always allies of reactionary national capitalism'; students sometimes proved to be an exception to this rule, he observed, but even their radicalism usually evaporated 'once they had received their graduation certificates and begun to struggle for their "bourgeois daily bread"'.[135] Mella concluded that most intellectuals were reactionary by nature and that their calls for reform were motivated primarily by self- interest: 'The intellectual declares himself to be a rebel because of constant economic crises. . . . But the aspiration of the majority of these new- fashioned socialists is to improve and reform the capitalist system, in which yesterday they were doing fine but today, because of a particular crisis, they find themselves doing badly.'[136] By 1928, he had endorsed the Leninist position that a prerequisite of being a revolutionary was to renounce the status of being an intellectual: 'Anyone within a Communist Party who is still an intellectual, that is to say, anyone who "has not broken his links with the bourgeoisie", should break them at once or leave the party.'[137] Yet Mella did not go so far as his fellow militant Rubén Martínez Villena who announced, soon after joining the Cuban Communist Party in 1927, 'I am no longer a poet (although I have written verse)' and refused to allow a collection of his poems to be published by public subscription.[138]

By no means all Spanish American intellectuals shared Mella's conviction that a commitment to Communism required an abrogation of the role of intellectual. José Carlos Mariátegui and César Vallejo, for example, both of whom were founder members of the Peruvian Socialist Party, tried to preserve a distinct realm for the intellectual even in the context of committing themselves to socialist revolution. Discussing the work of Henri Barbusse, whom he had met in 1919, Mariátegui approvingly noted his 'spiritual outlook'. Indeed, Barbusse's lofty vision of the intellectual's responsibility to stimulate 'a revolution of the spirit' met with a far warmer response among many Spanish American intellectuals than did the more prescriptive injunctions to intellectuals to work as propagandists of the revolution from the Soviet Commissar of Culture, Anatoli Lunacharsky.[139] Socialist revolution was interpreted in Spanish America as something potentially far greater than a redistribution of the means of production; in Mariátegui's words: 'For the poor, the Revolution . . . will be not only the attainment of their daily bread, but also the attainment of beauty, thought and all the consolations of the spirit.'[140]

For Mariátegui, the corollary of this view of revolution as a vehicle for redemption was that receptivity to revolutionary ideas was a matter of spiritual preparedness as much as intellectual conversion. Intellectuals, perhaps more so than workers, had to embrace socialism with more than their minds if they were to avoid regressing into reactionary positions:

> . . . one cannot arrive at revolution by a coldly conceptual route alone. Revolution is more than an idea, it is an emotion. More than a concept, it is a passion. In order to understand it, a fundamentally spiritual approach is needed, a particular state of mind. The intellectual, like any other idiot, is subject to the influence of his surroundings, his education and his self-interest. . . . His intelligence does not function freely. . . . An intellectual's reactionism, in a word, has its origin in the same . . . roots as the reactionism of a shopkeeper.[141]

The influence of the French syndicalist Georges Sorel (whom Mariátegui later nominated his ideal type of intellectual – 'outside party discipline, but faithful to a superior discipline based on class and method, he serves the revolutionary idea'),[142] is evident here. Sorel argued that intellectuals, by the very nature of their being intellectuals, were too committed to the processes of objective reason to be useful agents in a process of revolutionary transformation in which he attributed a primordial role to the irrational power of myth. But Mariátegui did not follow Sorel in dismissing intellectuals as 'idlers and parasites' who were fundamentally authoritarian by nature and more likely to hinder than to help workers on their road to revolutionary consciousness; on the contrary, like Barbusse, he reserved 'a special place for intellectuals in the forthcoming world revolution'.[143]

Mariátegui refuted the idea that intellectuals could 'keep themselves *au dessus de la mêlée*', and condemned those who loftily held themselves to be 'more or less absent from history' but yet still had the 'hopeless egocentricity' to believe that their inspiration alone would enable them to furnish the masses with a new vision of society.[144] He registered his approval that Barbusse had joined the French Communist Party, noting that, 'intellectuals who are truly revolutionary have no alternative but to accept a role in collective action'.[145] Yet Mariátegui continued to insist on the importance of maintaining a distinctive role for 'the intellectual' rather than allowing it to be subsumed in the role of revolutionary. Unlike Mella, he never advocated relinquishing the position of intellectual. Mariátegui was concerned not only with what the intellectual could do for the revolution, but also with what the revolution could do for the intellectual. He argued that it was necessary for intellectuals to sustain a capacity for speculative thought by founding it 'on a belief, a principle, which may make it a factor in history and progress'. It was only then, Mariátegui suggested, that the intellectual's maximum creative potential could be realized.[146] Mariátegui insisted on the value of intellectual activity in its own right in opposition to the prevailing climate of left-wing opinion which tended to see intellectual work in instrumental terms.

Mariátegui (like Rodó) was an autodidact and described himself as 'extra-academic if not anti-academic'.[147] This rejection of academia was not unusual among his intellectual contemporaries, partly because most of them had started out as journalists, partly because the previous generation had been so closely identified with the University of San Marcos. As the Peruvian press expanded during the first two decades of the twentieth century, it became 'a sort of chink in the cultural monopoly exercised by the oligarchy, through which came many young people from the provinces with a radical outlook'.[148] Mariátegui averred: 'I have raised myself up from the level of journalism to political philosophy, by means of an effort to transcend my surroundings that indicates a certain determination to oppose, with all my strength, dialectically, their backwardness and vice'.[149] Throughout his work, he reiterated the importance of intellectual professionalism. He usually described himself as 'an intellectual' instead of adopting what had become the more usual left-wing appellation, 'intellectual worker'.[150] He never departed from his early view that 'artists and professionals are all the more useful and valuable to the revolution to the extent that they remain artists and professionals'.[151] For Mariátegui, it was vital to sustain the intellect as an area of common ground that transcended ideological differences: 'I believe that it is easy for men who think clearly and know their own minds to understand and appreciate each other, even when they are opposed. Especially when they are opposed.'[152] (This comment was made in reference to the right-wing Argentine poet Leopoldo Lugones, who was to declare himself a Fascist in 1929 and from whom Mariátegui could hardly have been more distant ideologically.) In 1927, Mariátegui and his brother founded a publishing house, Editorial Minerva, which was one of the earliest in Peru and provided the main source of funds for his journal *Amauta* (the title was a Quechua word meaning 'teacher and sage').[153] As he explained in the first editorial, he envisaged *Amauta* not so much as a tribune for revolution as a crucible for the new spirit of the age:

> This magazine . . . represents . . . a movement, a spirit. A current of renewal has been felt for some time in Peru, ever more vigorous and unmistakeable. The instigators of this renewal are called vanguardists, socialists, revolutionaries, etc.. . . . But above and beyond all that differentiates them, all these spirits emanate what brings them together and unites them: their will to create a new Peru within a new world. . . . The movement – intellectual and spiritual – is little by little acquiring the character of an organic whole. With the appearance of *Amauta* it enters a phase of definition. . . . *Amauta* will sift through the men of the vanguard – militants and sympathizers – until the wheat is separated from the chaff. It will produce or precipitate a phenomenon of polarization and concentration.[154]

The aim of the magazine, Mariátegui stated, was 'to pose, clarify and understand Peruvian problems through the application of a rigorous and scientific method of analysis' but, he added, 'we will always think about Peru in the context of the rest of the world. We will study all the great movements of renewal – political, philosophical, artistic, literary, scientific. All human life is ours.'[155] *Amauta* was intended to function as a new ideological forum in which the divides in Peruvian cultural life between indigenists and 'Europeanizers', nationalists and cosmopolitans, were transcended. Mariátegui was proud to receive recognition for *Amauta* from intellectuals who could by no means be described as left-wing, and maintained an editorial policy of refraining from direct comment on Peruvian politics as much out of philosophical commitment as from the need to evade censorship.[156] By 1929, it was widely held that 'the cultural centre of up-to-date Peruvian society was not the University of San Marcos, but the magazine *Amauta*'.[157]

The difficulties intellectuals throughout Spanish America faced in trying to sustain both cultural and political activity in the face of restrictive state structures and fractured intellectual communities are well illustrated by Mariátegui's experiences during the last three years of his life. In June 1927, his relationship of uneasy coexistence with the government came to an end when Leguía accused him of fomenting a Communist conspiracy (apparently the first time that the Peruvian state had denounced a Communist threat)[158] and arrested him. From jail, Mariátegui wrote a letter to *La Correspondencia Sudamericana*, reflecting both the aspiration of Spanish American intellectuals to lead public opinion and the obstructions they encountered in doing so: 'It is my duty to protest before Latin American opinion against the false accusations made by the Lima police . . . circulated without any rebuttal except for a single letter of mine, since, as is well known, all the press is under government control or censorship.'[159] The available evidence suggests that at this stage Mariátegui had no links with the Communist International (Comintern); indeed, the first approach from Moscow was made in late 1927, possibly as a result of Leguía's attack.[160] But Mariátegui's developing contacts with the Comintern brought him no relief from increasing isolation, especially after the increasingly Stalinized organization had moved into its ultra-leftist 'third period' in 1928. At the famous Conference of Latin American Communist Parties, held in Buenos Aires in June 1929, which Mariátegui was too unwell to attend, his submissions were attacked for departing from the orthodox line on a variety of counts. In his opening address to the conference, the Argentine Comintern bureaucrat Vitorio Codovilla denounced the Peruvians for taking insufficient advantage of a chance to thwart US policy by provoking a popular revolt against Washington's attempts to mediate the territorial dispute with Chile over Tacna and Arica; the Peruvians responded that they had not mentioned the problem because, in their view, the masses were indifferent to 'such manifestations of patriotism'.[161] Other points at issue were the role of imperialism in Latin America (for the Comintern, it served to prop up feudalism; according to the Peruvians, it had brought capitalism), the role of the peasantry (deemed petty-bourgeois by the Comintern, part of the proletariat by Mariátegui), the role of the indigenous peoples (according to orthodoxy, Peru was a society of several nationalities; for Mariátegui, the indigenous population was the crucial foundation of a united Peruvian nation), and the nature of the revolution appropriate to a country like Peru (democratic–bourgeois versus socialist). But in the context of Mariátegui's increasingly bitter polemic with Haya de la Torre during 1928–29 over APRA's policy of seeking to incorporate the 'national' bourgeoisie into a revolutionary alliance, his delegates found themselves too isolated to risk severing links with the Comintern. The Soviet connection – albeit inimical – still lent the prestige of international solidarity to their position, in contrast to APRA's break with Moscow and the Comintern's subsequent denunciation of its policies. The polemic with APRA had already left Mariátegui in a minority position among the Peruvian Left, a situation that was exacerbated by the fact that a group had emerged in Cuzco, seeking to organize a Communist Party independently of Mariátegui. He found himself battling on three fronts: against APRA, against the Comintern, and against factions within the revolutionary movement in Peru. What was worse, at *Amauta* a division emerged between those who opted for political militancy and those who persisted in their intellectual vocation: 'Thus emerged an opposition between the projects of the "politician" and the "intellectual", a division of labour that had not existed for Mariátegui and which, to the contrary, he had striven to avoid.'[162]

In a revealing aside about his well-known rupture with Haya de la Torre, Mariátegui deplored not only the APRA leader's susceptibility to 'the demons of political bossism and personalism', but also his cavalier approach to questions of political vocabulary:

> You cannot imagine how much I have suffered over those manifestos by the supposed central committee of a supposedly nationalist party. Language is not of the slightest importance to Haya; but it is to me, and not for literary reasons but ideological and moral ones. If we do not distinguish ourselves from the past at least in our political language, I have a well-founded fear that, in the end, through mere adaptation and imitation, we may finish up by not differentiating ourselves at all except [in terms of] personalities.[163]

In turn, Haya de la Torre used the term 'intellectual' against Mariátegui, in an attempt to discredit his political ideas: 'My fraternal objections to Mariátegui were always based on his lack of a sense of realism, his excessive intellectualizing and his almost total lack of any sense of effective action.'[164] Mariátegui's critics dubbed him 'the intellectual', in explicit contrast to Haya de la Torre, to whom the *aprista* literary critic Luis Alberto Sánchez 'dedicated an emotive biography entitled *Haya de la Torre o el político* [*Haya de la Torre or the Politician*], as if he had been the only one among his contemporaries'.[165] The problem was compounded after the dispute with the Comintern in 1929; in the eyes of Communist stalwarts such as Luis Humbert-Droz or Vitorio Codovilla, Mariátegui was the quintessential 'intellectual' who had to be subjected to permanent vigilance to preclude betrayal of the revolutionary cause.

It is hardly surprising that even among those Spanish American intellectuals attracted to Marxism, there was a significant minority determined to defend the fragile cultural autonomy that had been evolving in their nations since around 1900, who declined to obey the directives of Soviet socialist realism to use art as a vehicle for propaganda. Like Mariátegui, César Vallejo rejected Julien Benda's idealization of 'pure intelligence',[166] maintaining that the intellectual was inevitably and rightfully implicated in politics,[167] although he agreed with Mella that 'intellectuals are rebels but not revolutionaries'.[168] Vallejo argued that the purpose of art was not to change what happened at the ballot box or the barricade but to touch the depths of people's political sensibilities, to create 'in human nature a new raw material for political action'.[169] Only art, he suggested, could effect this long-term regeneration of the spirit: 'If the artist were to renounce creating [work that taps] what we might call the inchoate political elements in human nature, confining his role to a secondary, sporadic one of disseminating propaganda or manning the barricade, to whom would it then fall to bring about that great miracle of spiritual transformation?'[170] Vallejo endorsed political commitment for intellectuals, but to his mind it lay not only in activism but also in intellectual endeavour itself. In the context of the Spanish Civil War, he proclaimed: 'We writers are the ones who are responsible for what happens in the world, because we have the most formidable weapon, which is the word.'[171] But, like Martí, Vallejo stipulated that the introduction of any particular political creed into art would undermine its intrinsic potential to revolutionize man's spirit:

> The socialist poet does not reduce his socialism . . . to the insertion of jargon from economics, dialectics or the laws of Marxism. . . . The socialist poet assumes, by preference, a sensibility that is organic and, in itself, implicitly socialist. . . . The only man who will create a socialist poem is one whose main concern is precisely not to serve a party interest or a historical class contingency, but who lives a personal, everyday socialist life. . . . For the socialist poet, then, a poem is not a spectacular display, instigated at will in the cause of a political creed or a propaganda exercise, but rather a natural and simple function of human sensibility.[172]

Vallejo cited Mayakovsky as an example of an artist who '[by] submitting to an artistic programme taken from historical materialism . . . created only verses lacking intimate warmth and feeling, the products of external mechanical forces and artificial heating'.[173] In any case, it was impossible for creative writers to write as propagandists, Vallejo contended, because how their works were interpreted was beyond their own control. In an oft-quoted passage, he stated, 'As a man, I may sympathize and work for the Revolution, but as an artist [my experience is that] it is out of anybody's hands, let alone my own, to control the political meanings that may be hidden in my poems.'[174]

By the end of the 1930s, only in Argentina, where oligarchic patronage lasted longer than elsewhere in the region, was there still a significant minority of intellectuals sustaining the view that an intellectual's main loyalty was to his spirit, and that his only true *patria* was the international community of cultivated minds.[175] This group was influenced by José Ortega y Gasset, who argued that politics was a mere reflection of the fundamental social and cultural realities; he also advocated an aristocratic role for his intellectual generation which he saw as destined to topple Reason from its pedestal and utilize it to enhance rather than control vitality (the theory of 'vital reason').[176] While the impact of Ortega y Gasset's *Revista de Occidente*, which from 1923 onwards was the main source of European ideas for most

Spanish American intellectuals, is hard to overestimate, it was only in Buenos Aires that his view of the intellectual as aristocrat of the spirit exercised a major influence.[177] In general, Benda's famous call for intellectual detachment met with little response in Spanish America. In most Spanish American countries, Marxist-Leninist ideas were the cloak in which intellectuals draped their aspirations to dissent. Leninism, which located revolutionary consciousness in a vanguard party rather than, as Marx had done, in the proletariat, demarcated a clear role for intellectuals as the critical conscience and political organizers of the revolution. The 1920s saw the emergence of a discourse of *lo nacional-popular*; for some intellectuals, this became radicalized into what became known as the national-revolutionary myth, according to which national integration was to be forged through anti-imperialist and anti-oligarchic struggle. The new archetypes were the *intelectual de vanguardia* or – as support for popular nationalism became increasingly embroiled with cultural legitimacy beyond the realm of the Marxist parties – the *intelectual comprometido*.

This conception of the social responsibility of the intellectual in Spanish America was to persist into the 1940s and well beyond. Neruda's memoirs, *Confieso que he vivido* (1974), provide a useful illustration of how culture and political commitment came to reinforce each other in sustaining an intellectual's prestige. In the opening scene, 'The Chilean Forest', Neruda draws on much the same Romantic mythology that permeated Darío's autobiography to present himself as emerging like some prehistoric man from the forests of deepest Chile. This passage, which concludes, 'From those lands, from that mud, that silence, I set out to roam, to sing my way through the world,'[178] emphasizes his identification with the land of his birth. This telluric 'return to the roots' establishes his claim to be quintessentially Chilean. Having located his birthplace in the crucible of the national soul, Neruda then marks himself out as different from his fellow mortals: 'The boys at school neither knew nor cared that I was a poet.'[179] After several chapters describing his early adulthood outside Chile, Neruda recounts his return in 1943 – literally to his country, and metaphorically to his people. He presents his decision to stand as a senator for one of the poorest regions of Chile in terms of a clearcut choice between siding with the elite or with the masses:

> The country had not changed. Fields and sleepy villages, desperate poverty in the mining areas and the smart set swanning around in their Country Club. It was necessary to choose between them.
>
> My decision brought me persecution but it also brought me moments I'll never forget.
>
> How could any poet have regretted it?[180]

The significance of this passage lies in his claim to have taken this decision not as a man or a revolutionary, but as a poet. Neruda is explicit about how revolutionary commitment enhanced his position as a poet, enabling him to establish a relationship with the workers (the greatest prize he ever won, he stated) and to identify himself as the voice of the oppressed: 'I have come, through hard lessons in aesthetics and a long search through the labyrinths of the written word, to be the poet of my people.'[181]

But even in the late 1920s, seeds of doubt about what it meant to be a revolutionary intellectual in Spanish America were the first signs of the contradictions that were to flower in the 1960s. For example, in one article published in *Amauta*, the author hailed Rosa Luxemburg as 'the great revolutionary', and went on to ask, 'But was she really an intellectual? She was not, because to be an intellectual is, by definition, to be deformed, to see everything through the rigid prism of cerebral abstraction, and Rosa Luxemburg was a woman in whom all the human faculties were equally developed.'[182] The tensions inherent in the conflicting demands upon Spanish American intellectuals to sustain both cultural work and political commitment, and to be both the repositories of the spirit and heroic defenders of the people, were exacerbated throughout the 1940s and 1950s, and were finally to reach breaking point during the 1960s. Intellectuals' claims to authority over cultural matters were increasingly subject to challenge in the years after the Second World War because of the expansion of state education, the extension of mass electronic media into the region, and the manifest popularity of films, comics, television shows, etcetera – particularly those from the USA – which many intellectuals condemned as yet another manifestation of imperialism. But it was events in Cuba that were to provide the catalyst for the disintegration of the role of the *intelectual comprometido*. Public support for social reformism and nationalism enabled many Spanish American intellectuals to reconcile the conflicting pressures on them before 1959, but after Castro's triumphal march into Havana – which was interpreted as a practical demonstration of the limitations of the *intelectual comprometido* – rhetorical measures no longer sufficed.

The 1960s

The Cuban revolution was attractive to many intellectuals not only politically and ideologically, but also culturally. Castro's early initiatives to establish Havana as the cultural centre of Latin America proved important in helping to overcome the parochialism that had characterized the region's intellectual life in the late 1950s (according to José Donoso: '[In no country did anyone know] what was being written in other Latin American countries, especially because it was so difficult to publish a first novel. . . . All the publishing houses were more or less poor and, in the larger countries, prejudiced in favour of foreign literature').[183] The new Cuban government established Casa de las Américas, which launched a yearly literature prize and a monthly review, to create new networks of communication among intellectuals; its impact was soon felt, as described by Antonio Skármeta:

> Winning the prize didn't mean one's books would be stocked in bookstores throughout Latin America – because the commercial blockade made these small details its business too – but it did permit the prize-winning book to reach the hands of interested critics, journalists, writers, and professors. Thousands of books flew through the mails constituting a kind of clandestine map of the continent's new narrative and poetry.[184]

But Spanish American intellectuals' longstanding claims to be the natural mediators between the elites and the masses were made far more difficult to sustain by the success of Castro's guerrilla offensive against Batista, unaided and indeed criticized by the Marxist-Leninist vanguard party in which intellectuals were prescribed a key role. Intellectuals could no longer view the masses as an abstract, inert entity (the *pueblo*), but had to start considering them as critical consumers of culture and protagonists of revolution. This trend was strengthened by the establishment in the 1950s of institutes for the study of the social sciences (mostly sociology and economics), the research findings of which convinced many intellectuals that popular revolution was a scientific inevitability. Since the Cuban strategy had succeeded in overthrowing the old order, it became increasingly difficult for intellectuals to justify not committing themselves wholeheartedly to revolutionary militancy. It was no longer plausible for intellectuals to say, as Vallejo had done in the 1920s, 'as a man, I'm a revolutionary, but as a poet, I'm a free spirit'. The Cuban revolution had appropriated the role of 'vigilant conscience' of poverty and exploitation that the intellectuals had until then ascribed to themselves.[185] The Salvadoran poet and guerrilla fighter Roque Dalton (himself murdered by comrades-in-arms) argued that the intellectual was henceforth obliged 'to respond to his own avant-garde words with deeds so as not to betray *himself*, in a continent where moral superiority is one of the few credentials the people demand before they will listen to those who solicit their support'.[186] Intellectuals came under pressure to purge themselves of their 'original sin', as Che Guevara called it, of elitism.

Internationally, debates about the political responsibility of the intellectual were dominated by those who advocated a leading role for intellectuals in the national liberation of their countries. One champion of this view was C. Wright Mills, who taught a course comparing Marxism and liberalism at UNAM in 1960. Frantz Fanon's arguments about the need for intellectuals in former colonial countries to create a national culture were also influential,[187] although analogies between Latin America and the decolonizing countries of Africa and Asia were shaky, as many Latin American intellectuals argued. The worldwide shift in emphasis towards political commitment in place of critical awareness as the crucial variable for intellectuals had been signalled during the debates in the 1950s between Sartre and Camus. Most Spanish American intellectuals had identified with Sartre's idea of the *intellectuel engagé* rather than with Camus's disinterested observer and anti-hero:[188] they wanted to be revolutionaries, not just rebels.

According to Sartre's concept of commitment, it was not enough for an intellectual to indulge in general condemnations of oppression: his denunciations had to be specific and the product of rigorous methodological analysis of concrete historical circumstances. The Argentine critic Adolfo Canitrot has argued that the absence of such analysis explains why no Spanish American intellectuals '[managed] to become a Sartre, because the ethical imperative [did] not extend beyond itself and because at times it [was] combined with a certain ideological innocence'.[189] The very possibility of reconciling Sartre's vision of literature as an agent of liberation with the preservation of intellectual freedom existed only in a society that guaranteed freedom of expression (it was elusive enough even there, as Sartre himself came to acknowledge). Indeed, as early as 1964, Sartre had stated in an interview that while Western intellectuals could fulfil their duty towards the world's starving by writing about them, intellectuals from the Third World were obliged to go out and teach them. This was a dictum that caused at least one Spanish American intellectual, Mario Vargas Llosa, severe disillusionment with his erstwhile hero.[190] Increasingly, Spanish American intellectuals found themselves obliged to choose between adopting a stance of critical distance, in which case they became politically redundant, or devoting themselves to politics, in which case they risked losing moral authority. Mella's words about the impossibility of reconciling the roles of revolutionary and intellectual were proving prophetic.

As the *maestro* element of the intellectual role receded, the aspect of revolutionary rose to the fore. During the 1960s, the Spanish American archetype of an intellectual metamorphosed from the *intelectual comprometido* to the *intelectual militante*.[191] The theoretical reformulation of the intellectual's role that followed acquired all the more cachet for having been written by a young French disciple of Althusser, whose ideas were in vogue in the social science faculties of Spanish American universities. Régis Debray, who was then an ardent supporter of Fidel Castro, attempted to distil a theory of general revolutionary strategy from the experiences of the Cuban revolution. He argued that intellectuals should immerse themselves in the life of a guerrilla *foco* (a small group of committed fighters) and, by living among the people, shed their bourgeois attitudes in order to be transformed into true revolutionaries.[192] His ideas were promoted by the

Cuban government, which published his *Revolution in the Revolution* in 1967, with an unusually high initial print run of 200,000.[193]

In *Revolution in the Revolution*, Debray repeatedly invoked the name of Simón Bolívar, the original *caudillo–pensador*, as an exemplary model of a scholar who renounced his books for a life of military action. Somewhat reluctantly, Debray conceded that intellectuals did have a part to play in the socio-economic revolution that would constitute the second independence of Latin America. However, he insisted that they could make themselves fit to assist in the liberation of their peoples only by 'commit[ting] suicide' as intellectuals.[194] Echoing Castro's own views, Debray blamed intellectuals and their 'physical weakness', 'lack of adjustment to rural life', 'ideological constraints' and '[lack of] flexibility' for setbacks during the Cuban revolutionary war of 1956–58.[195] In a revolutionary strategy that emphasized the importance of armed insurrection to the virtual exclusion of political work, he argued, military skills were paramount. Debray left his readers in little doubt that intellectuals who considered themselves to be revolutionaries should at once take up arms and not allow any residual contemplative tendencies to deter them from killing the oppressors. It was no longer sufficient for intellectuals to proclaim revolutionary words and values: henceforth they had to perform revolutionary acts. Should they end up martyrs, so be it. Mario Vargas Llosa captured the spirit of the times in a tribute to Javier Heraud (1942–63), a young Peruvian poet killed in guerrilla warfare: 'I am sure that . . . he fell as heroes fall, exuding courage, at once serene and exalted, beautifully tranquil'.[196]

Debray's writings both tempted and goaded Spanish American intellectuals into pursuing their identification with the people to its logical, apocalyptic conclusion. How could intellectuals identify any culture worth defending, he demanded, when 'fascism, oligarchies, [and] military castes' were in power?[197] The Uruguayan writer Mario Benedetti explained the dilemma as it was seen in Spanish America at the time:

> The most urgent task for revolutionary intellectuals is perhaps to cease to function as an untouchable caste, and to integrate themselves into the people to whom they belong. . . . Inscribing themselves in an intellectual elite, feeling themselves to be a sacrosanct and maligned clan, makes it almost inevitable that their priority will be individualism, [in other words] . . . liberty in its bourgeois sense, that kind of liberty which the creole oligarchs, the *Reader's Digest* . . . and the Peace Corps have no problem in defending.[198]

To many Spanish American intellectuals, in the light of how populism had raised expectations but failed to meet them, it seemed that revolution was both inevitable and imminent, and the question was to decide which side they were on. Those who followed Debray's advice to become militants in effect abandoned their role as intellectuals. As one Chilean academic has argued, with hindsight, 'In the sixties, there were no intellectuals. Because of the wide acceptance of Marxism, it was discredited, even "ugly", to be one. We were all militants and the intellectuals painted slogans on walls.'[199] Similarly, José Aricó has asked: 'What was the experience of armed violence in Latin America other than an attempt by radicalized left-wing intellectuals to assume control of politics?'[200]

Many intellectuals resisted the pressures to renounce their position as intellectuals and devote themselves to the revolution. Instead, they argued, in more or less extreme terms, in favour of preserving some degree of autonomy for culture. Some, for example Gabriel García Márquez and Carlos Fuentes, maintained that they were ultimately more effective as propagandists of revolution if they preserved their reputation as independent intellectuals. Others, such as Octavio Paz and Mario Vargas Llosa (despite his initial enthusiasm for revolutionary militancy),[201] insisted that if they had to choose between being revolutionaries and intellectuals they would opt for the latter, although both subsequently found it impossible to preserve political detachment. What these two opposing groups had in common was the availability of an alternative to being an *intelectual militante*: they could become celebrities in their own right. Within their own countries, a degree of popular success was at last possible because an expansion in higher education had by the late 1960s or early 1970s given writers what they had always lamented that they lacked, namely a mass base. More important, the literary 'boom' stimulated a level of interest in Latin American literature that created opportunities for them to achieve international renown.

In effect, these charismatic, cosmopolitan celebrity intellectuals tried to sustain the role of spokesman of the people and bearer of national identity that had been established in the 1920s. Different circumstances demanded that some modifications had to be made: the idea of national identity was not so much discarded as subsumed into a resurgent regional identity aimed at evading the contradictions between nationalism and internationalism. The 1960s saw the revival of turn-of-the-century *hispanoamericanismo*, this time expanded to include Brazil in *latinoamericanismo*, a development related to the fact that many Brazilian intellectuals took refuge in Spanish American countries, especially Chile and Mexico, after the 1964 coup, which helped to bridge the gap between the two hitherto largely separate intellectual traditions. Spanish American intellectuals represented key emblematic texts such as García Márquez's *Cien años de soledad* [*One Hundred Years of Solitude*] (1967) as works that functioned simultaneously at local, national and continental levels.[202] Intellectuals, who for several decades had been (more or less sophisticated) proponents of cultural nationalism, now embraced a regionalism that could be reconciled with demands from the Left to be internationalist, while at the same time enabling them to maintain

their claims to be prophets of identity. During the 1960s, the idea of a
'Latin American' intellectual was often invoked, as in the following observation by Julio Cortázar: 'the most significant writers [he cites Martí,
Sarmiento, Neruda, Miguel Ángel Asturias and García Márquez] . . . are
characterized . . . by one common feature, which is precisely the search for
our Latin American identity'.[203]

But by seeking to perpetuate a role the foundations of which were by
then visibly crumbling, these celebrity intellectuals were in effect creating
an obstacle to the rethinking of the role of intellectuals that began in
Spanish America in the 1980s. The conflicts between political solidarity and
critical thought inherent in their approach made their position increasingly
untenable, particularly after such contradictions publicly surfaced during
the Padilla affair (see page 27). The support of non-Cuban intellectuals for
Castro's regime had peaked at a 1968 Cultural Congress in Havana, which
was attended by most of the well-known Spanish American literati along
with a respectable number of European luminaries. At this congress, Mario
Benedetti argued that the mission of the intellectual within the revolution
was 'to be something akin to its vigilant conscience, its imaginative interpreter, its appointed critic'.[204] It sounded plausible. At this stage, most
intellectuals outside Cuba were prepared to turn a blind eye to signs of
increasing cultural repressiveness from a regime they knew to be under
considerable international pressure, especially because on top of the US
embargo a slow-down in Soviet oil supplies was inflicting extra hardship on
the Cuban economy. But after the government's failure to achieve its much-
vaunted target of a ten-million-ton sugar harvest in 1970, despite having
switched virtually the entire labour force from the production of other
goods into sugar, it was harder for intellectuals to continue ignoring the
cultural consequences of Cuba's deteriorating economic and political situation. One year later, the Padilla affair proved to be the defining moment.
When Western and Spanish American intellectuals sent two letters of protest
about the poet's imprisonment and subsequent self-incrimination, Castro
roundly denounced them as 'decadent bourgeois'. By then, some intellectuals had already experienced qualms about Castro's support for the Soviet
invasion of Czechoslovakia. Now, in the light of his rebuff to their intervention in the Padilla affair, they were forced to choose between accepting the
right of the Cuban government to manage its internal affairs as it wished,
even if this meant imprisoning and intimidating fellow intellectuals, or
breaking with the revolution. There was no opportunity for intellectuals to
take up Benedetti's suggestion that they should act as the Castro regime's
'vigilant conscience'. Those who favoured non-interference in the affairs
of the revolution, for example, Cortázar and García Márquez, had in
practice relinquished their right to criticize the revolution. As far as the
Cuban government was concerned, moral authority resided not in the

pronouncements of intellectuals but in the logic of the people's revolution. After the Padilla affair, the Cuban authorities emphasized that the role of the intellectual was henceforth to be subordinate to the dictates of the Communist Party. Once this position had officially been made explicit in mid-1971, it was no longer easy to sustain with any great deal of conviction the idea of a marriage between intellectual and revolutionary activities. Politics had subsumed culture once again.

The continuing difficulties Spanish American intellectuals faced in trying to act as independent social critics are illustrated by the case of Octavio Paz, who has explicitly identified himself with the tradition of the French moralists.[205] Paz always accepted that he could not escape the issue of political commitment, although throughout the 1960s and 1970s he resisted pressure to relinquish his critical independence in favour of any particular political cause. In the 1970s, he argued that it was anathema to an intellectual to submit to either 'a party or a church', and wrote that, for him, criticism was 'a *free* form of commitment'.[206] Paz contended that a writer could fulfil his political calling only if he kept apart from the political fray itself: 'The political function of the writer depends on his position as a man who does not get mixed up in politics. The writer is neither a man of power nor a man of party: he is a man of conscience.'[207] But much of Paz's work indirectly reveals the precariousness of such a position in Spanish America, where to 'know oneself to be on the margins',[208] as Paz advocated, may lead an intellectual to become so marginalized as to be politically irrelevant, thereby in turn diminishing his status as an intellectual.

That Paz felt moved constantly to reinforce his intellectual authority is significant in itself. In the foreword to his collection of political essays *El ogro filantrópico*, for example, he reaffirmed a universal authority by disclaiming a specialist knowledge: 'My reflections on the state are not systematic and should be seen instead as an invitation to specialists to study the subject.'[209] Again, in the Foreword to a later collection of political writings, *Tiempo nublado*, there was the rhetorical denial of authority that served above all to enhance it: 'I am not a historian. My passion is poetry and my occupation, literature; neither the one nor the other grants me authority to give my opinion on the upheavals and disturbances of our times.'[210]

Most telling of all were Paz's reiterated attacks on those of his fellow Spanish American intellectuals whom he deemed to be insufficiently critical. His call for more rigorous criticism came to be a ritual in itself, which at first sight appeared to substantiate his own claim to be a voice in the wilderness. But, ultimately, his attacks on other intellectuals rebounded to undermine his own independence. In 1978, Paz claimed that Mexican academics and writers were fulfilling a function in the post-revolutionary state comparable to the complicity of the friars and clerics with the colonial state of New Spain: ideology had simply replaced theology.[211] He then went on to argue: 'Fortunately Mexico is a society that is becoming increasingly plural, and the exercise of criticism – the only antidote to ideological orthodoxies – increases in the same measure as the country diversifies.'[212] While on the one hand blaming intellectuals in general for not being critical enough, he then denied them, collectively, any credit for the increase in critical debate he identified in Mexico; instead, he attributed this to structural changes beyond their control. In other works, Paz met this objection by stipulating that certain individuals who adopted the role of independent critic had contributed to those changes, whereas those blinded by ideology had not.[213] But his need to condemn intellectuals collectively reflected a highly limited room for manoeuvre. By using the inclusive 'we' when attacking his colleagues, Paz was adopting a rhetorical substitute for the self-criticism he abjured all Spanish American intellectuals to undertake: 'before undertaking a critique of our societies, ... we Spanish American writers must start by criticizing ourselves. The first task is to cure ourselves of our intoxication with simplistic and simplifying ideologies.'[214] But many people would argue that a few years later Paz himself succumbed to a simplistic ideology by lending his support to President Carlos Salinas de Gortari's implementation of neo-liberal economic policies.

Conclusion

In a region where the possibilities for acquiring cultural capital have been relatively restricted, participation in the discourse of *lo nacional-popular* became an essential, indeed often overriding, legitimating device. Under these conditions, Spanish American intellectuals tried to sustain a modern role, not least because their own experience was one of modernity, albeit peripheral. But this was a role which in its original manifestation, in late-nineteenth-century France, was founded both on the existence of a state that permitted the functioning of an active civil society, and a commitment to Cartesian rationality. Spanish American intellectuals did not so much reject rationality altogether (as suggested by Martin Stabb)[215] as maintain an ambivalence towards it that severely undermined their efforts to act as independent social critics. Cartesian Reason has been less than hegemonic for most of the twentieth century in Spanish America, where it has been regarded – at least since the late nineteenth century – with a degree of suspicion as an imposition from the more developed world. Twentieth-century Spanish American intellectuals have propagated the idea that their nations simply cannot be understood in terms of rational 'European' standards. The idea of an alternative rationality has been a common strand of Spanish American twentieth-century culture, from Rodó's *Ariel* to Vasconcelos's 'cosmic race' to the cult of 'Macondismo' that sprang up around

García Márquez's *Cien años de soledad*. Attitudes towards history reflect this same ambivalence towards European Reason: Enlightenment-based ideas about lineal, 'progressive' history, with all their implications for the practice of historical writing, have never been fully accepted in Spanish American intellectual circles. This is not to argue, as does Octavio Paz, that all Spanish America's ills can be attributed to the Enlightenment having passed it by.[216] It is important to recall that European Reason *was* important to the men of letters of the post-independence period, not least because the idea that Reason could subdue history was an idea with understandable appeal to liberals wishing to free their societies from corporate power. However, Spanish Americans soon began to question the applicability of Enlightenment ideas to their circumstances, and Romanticism was a strong influence on Spanish American men of letters from the 1830s onwards. Even so, the Romantic movement in Europe was itself only a partial rejection of Enlightenment: while Romantics rejected the idea that Reason was the only or even the fundamental virtue, arguing that the emotional and spiritual experiences of mankind should not be discarded, they retained several key aspects of the Enlightenment, not least of which was a belief in the privileged position of the intellectual. In Spanish America, the reception of Romanticism revealed a corresponding ambivalence towards Reason, and it was not until the late nineteenth century that ideas about an alternative rationality began to emerge. The evidence suggests that the explicit rejection of Cartesian rationalism was a strategy adopted by emerging professional intellectuals to defend their own position as modernization gathered pace. But this strategy meant that the very role of the Spanish American intellectual was founded on shifting sands. The role of all modern intellectuals is imbued with contradiction because, in practice, most modern societies have expected their intellectuals to fulfil a dual function as both preservers of tradition and agents of change. But whereas in Europe intellectuals were able to reconcile these potentially conflicting demands with relative ease, the distortions of peripheral modernity made it far harder for Spanish American intellectuals to do so.

A useful way of thinking about the options available to modern intellectuals is Zygmunt Bauman's distinction between 'legislators' and 'interpreters'. Bauman associates the 'legislator' function with the condition of (European) modernity, and sees the 'interpreter' role as the maximum that intellectuals who are not content to confine themselves to specialisms can hope to achieve under conditions of postmodernity.[217] He argues that the strategy originally adopted by the *philosophes* to bridge the past and the future was to promote themselves as 'legislators' (the term was Rousseau's). In Europe, the development of nation-states, capitalism and science combined to create a significant social role for 'intellectuals' as 'legislators' of opinion. In contrast, conditions have never existed in Spanish America for intellectuals to enjoy the authority of 'legislators' in this sense. During the early to mid-nineteenth century a few leading Spanish American men of letters acted as legislators in the literal sense that they drafted constitutions and laws. But these men were *letrados* or *licenciado–políticos*, not intellectuals in the modern sense.

Given that it has been argued recently that Spanish American cultural life has displayed signs of a precocious postmodernity, it is worth pausing to explore the counterfactual question of whether it might have been feasible for early-twentieth-century Spanish American intellectuals to adopt the role of interpreter. This role is dependent upon the legislator in a way analogous to the dependence of postmodernity on modernity: it retains a legislative element, albeit in reduced form, because of the need to establish the authority of any one interpretation over another. But, more important for the argument here, the interpreter role is dependent on the recognition of equality between different traditions. This did not exist in early-twentieth-century Spanish America where questions of culture were still posed in terms of 'civilization' and 'barbarism'. Moreover, the act of interpretation implies knowledge and understanding of both parties involved; it is an active intervention in the sense of an act of construing meaning. This in turn implies the availability of the means to sustain an independent position. While Spanish American intellectuals were often ascribed an almost holy aura because of their supposed capacity to act as the 'enlightened interpreters of the obscure yearnings of the masses',[218] their sphere of operations was constrained to the extent that it was to prove very difficult for them to achieve such positions during most of this century. José Martí may well have been, as Mella characterized him, 'the interpreter of a need for social transformation at a particular moment',[219] but Martí's experience represented the close of an era, not the beginning.

Unable to attain the authority of 'legislators', and in too precarious a position to risk basing their claims to influence on being 'interpreters', twentieth-century Spanish American intellectuals instead usually steered a course somewhere between the two, adopting a strategy of mediation. They tried to act as 'go-betweens' in multiple ways, mediating between elites and masses, nations and peoples, and Latin America and the developed world. But this term 'mediation', which is commonly and often uncritically used in discussions about the role of Spanish American intellectuals, has both a strong and a weak meaning. In its strong sense, the word implies active intercession between two parties; in the weak sense, it simply means being a passive conduit between them. As a defensive recourse, mediation is not wholly without advantages: at least in its stronger sense it enables a challenge, albeit limited, to the status quo, which has perhaps been exploited most effectively in terms of the relationship between European and Spanish American cultures. Even then, it remains a fundamentally limited and self-defeating strategy because, ultimately, it is founded on a tacit acceptance of the hierarchies of power it is supposedly trying to subvert. Roberto Schwarz has argued, 'Mediation . . . is a cultural comfort, but not a historical solution to the real problems of power.'[220]

It is therefore misleading to place too much emphasis on what Alain Touraine has called the 'excess autonomy' of the intellectual in a dependent country.[221] The identification of an expanded role for the Spanish American intellectual as the 'substitute' for civil society (in itself a dubious claim) too easily becomes subsumed into arguments claiming that the region's intellectuals have enjoyed a considerable degree of political power. Angel Rama, for example, has suggested that intellectual specialization at the beginning of the twentieth century offered Spanish American intellectuals opportunities to assume a spiritual leadership that went beyond the confines of party politics.[222] But this (like the characterization of Spanish America as precociously postmodern) is to exaggerate the opportunities available to the region's intellectuals for most of the twentieth century, and to ascribe an unwarranted level of privilege (having greater capacity for what Barthes called 'jouissance' – passion and play) to situations that were historically conditioned by distinctly limited room for manoeuvre. The very expansiveness and vagueness of the intellectuals' role as prophets and spiritual leaders (Rodó's idea of the 'cure of souls')[223] made it harder for them to defend the besieged domain of intellectuality. One Chilean academic lamented, 'we have no intellectual tradition', in reference to his view that in Chile (and, by extension, it can be argued, throughout Spanish America) no clear distinction had been sustained between political militancy and political theorizing. In Europe, by contrast, he continued, even Gramsci, 'in spite of being tremendously politically committed . . . was always capable of distinguishing his strictly political tasks from his tasks as a thinker'.[224] Silvia Sigal has argued that twentieth-century Spanish American intellectuals tended to speak not for themselves but 'as spokesmen for other entities: People, Nation or Revolution'.[225] In the process of identifying an agent of history to which they could ally themselves, intellectuals forestalled any possibility of instigating real change by maintaining the supposed agent of any such change as a prisoner of abstraction and ahistoricism. This idea will be explored in detail in Part II.

Part II

Intellectual Discourses of Popular Nationalism

4

The Ideology of Bi-culturalism

We are not Europeans; we are not Indians; we are but a mixed species . . .

Simón Bolívar, 1819[1]

In early twentieth-century attempts to identify 'the people' who might constitute 'the nation', the idea of a divided origin came to prevail. Before the emergence of modern intellectuals, debates about ethnicity had been couched in different terms. Towards the end of the nineteenth century, a number of *pensadores* had drawn on social Darwinist theories which supplied ruling elites with an alleged rationale for a series of policies geared towards 'whitening' their populations. These strategies ranged from European immigration to assimilation of so-called 'undesirable' black and Indian peoples through education and modernization, and even to outright extermination (for example, in the military campaigns conducted against Indians by the state in Chile [1869], Argentina [War of the Desert, 1879], and Mexico [1880–84]). With rare exceptions, until the early twentieth century Spanish American *pensadores* and statesmen promoted exclusionary, elite nationalisms founded on identification with Britain, France and/or the United States in the case of liberals, and Golden Age Spain in the case of conservatives. They argued that the Indians within their borders should be regarded (and regard themselves) as members of 'a nation parallel to the Spanish-Creole one';[2] they had little or nothing to say about other ethnic groups. This type of creole nationalism was closer to patriotism in its lack of a popular dimension. In contrast, from the early twentieth century onwards, in virtually all Spanish American countries, intellectuals advocating more inclusionary nationalisms proposed popular national identities on the basis of the resurrected idea that the people were a distinctively 'mixed species' and should be celebrated as such, even if only rhetorically. Reacting against the social Darwinism and racial pessimism usually (although not invariably) associated with the dominant ideology of positivism, and influenced both

by Rodó's *Ariel* and by European idealist philosophies, across the region
new generations of intellectuals – virtually all of whom were themselves
predominantly white – began to elaborate archetypes of bi-culturalism.
(Arguably, just as women were excluded almost by definition from the status
of being an intellectual in Spanish America,[3] so Indians and blacks found it
equally difficult to secure such recognition.) Cultural nationalism came to
displace the former narrowly political sense of nationhood, and nationalism
throughout the region acquired an ethnic component which had hitherto
been largely absent. To illustrate these processes, this chapter compares
Mexico, Peru and Argentina.

Mexico

Mexico is widely regarded as the most successful of Spanish American
countries in its efforts to establish a national identity based on bi-culturalism. Florencia Mallon suggests persuasively that the Plaza de las Tres
Culturas in Mexico City (where the government has erected a monument
to the two heritages – Spanish and indigenous – that are officially held to
infuse the third, *mestizo*, culture of modern Mexico) could never have been
built in Peru or Bolivia.[4] The very existence of this public symbol of dual
origin implies a degree of éclat in creating a mythology of national ethnic
integration, although its location in a small square some way from the city
centre intimates that *mestizaje* (racial mixing) is still less than central to a
ruling political party dominated by an almost exclusively white elite. Some
telling criticisms have been made of Mexican *mestizaje* and *indigenismo* (pro-
Indianism): Alan Knight and Florencia Mallon, among others, have argued
convincingly that the post-revolutionary policy of promoting *mestizaje* was part
of the Sonoran state's overall project of modernization, which was intended
to turn supposedly 'backward' Indian peasants into a 'modern' *mestizo* labour
force.[5] That is, *mestizaje* was a modernizing ideology, committed to the
eventual elimination of the forms of cultural expression championed and
sponsored by *indigenismo*. Nevertheless, the post-revolutionary Mexican state
did consolidate a cult of *mestizaje* as one of the twin planks of Mexican
nationalism (the other being opposition to the United States). Mexico is
also commonly thought of as the Spanish American nation in which
intellectuals have enjoyed the most influence on state policy, and its official
celebration of *mestizaje* is conventionally associated with José Vasconcelos's
book, *La raza cósmica* (1925). Can it be concluded, then, that Mexico's
relative efficacy in founding a national identity on bi-culturalism should be
attributed to the input of intellectuals?

The idea of two cultures is deep-rooted in Mexican history. Luis Villoro
has identified three main historical stages in Mexican thinking about the

country's indigenous peoples: (1) the conquest, when their culture was perceived negatively, mainly because of its immediacy; (2) the independence era, when indigenous culture was reduced to a remote past and therefore could safely be re-evaluated positively; and (3) the post-revolutionary period, when, for the first time in Mexican history, indigenous culture was celebrated not only for its past greatness but also for its present potential contribution to the creation of a national identity.[6] No longer categorized as alien and separate, Indian culture was envisaged by the *indigenistas* of the 1920s as a crucial constituent of any distinctive *mexicanidad*. Villoro concluded that the first thinker to make this move from exclusion to (an at least symbolic) inclusion of the Indians was the anthropologist Manuel Gamio (1883–1960), who – almost alone among intellectuals – had championed Zapata.[7]

Most of the policies carried out in the name of official *indigenismo* in Mexico bore the mark of Gamio's ideas. Nevertheless, his career illustrated just how difficult it was even for intellectuals who supported the revolution to make their voices heard during the 1920s and 1930s. Unlike the *ateneistas*, Gamio had never rebelled against his liberal and positivist intellectual formation, although it was to acquire a patina of romantic nationalism during the post-revolutionary euphoria of the early 1920s. His approach to relations between intellectuals and the Mexican state remained essentially in line with that of the pre-revolutionary *científicos*. He argued that the state needed knowledge about its people in order to govern well: 'The ruler should have the sociologist as a guide.'[8] He has been appropriately categorized as someone who saw himself as 'a social scientist who sought to deploy his professional expertise in service of the Mexican people and the Mexican state'.[9] He advocated more influence for 'men of science',[10] but somewhat unscientifically maintained that they should be 'Mexicans of good faith'.[11] He did not seek political power, but was an able archaeologist and anthropologist who wished to secure state funding for the technical investigations that he saw as a prerequisite of good government. In other words, he was content to confine himself to the role of technical 'expert' without harbouring aspirations to become a 'legislator' or even a 'mediator'.

The Mexican state's treatment of Gamio, who had no desire to challenge its power, illuminates the context in which dissidence had to operate in the aftermath of the revolution. Gamio's key work was an essay, *Forjando patria* (1916), in which he set out his ideas for Mexican integration, summarizing them as follows: 'Fusion of races, convergence and fusion of cultural characteristics, linguistic unification and economic equilibrium among social groups.'[12] Strongly influenced by Justo Sierra, one of the few leading positivists who had rejected social Darwinism and prescribed *mestizaje* as the key to Mexico's future, Gamio sought a positive re-evaluation of the contribution of Indian cultures to the nation, but his ultimate commitment was to their assimilation. This vision of a culturally if not racially *mestizo* Mexico evidently captured the imagination of the revolutionary leader General Álvaro Obregón. Gamio's granddaughter and biographer relates an anecdote from 1916, which described Obregón asking someone if he had read *Forjando patria*. When the reply was in the negative, Obregón rejoined, 'Well, you should. It's a work of fundamental importance. It made a great impression on me and I intend to buy a hundred copies to distribute among my friends.'[13] One of the recipients of those copies was reputedly Plutarco Elías Calles (not that this did its author much good when Calles became President, as will become clear below). Even during Obregón's presidency (1920–24), however, Gamio found it difficult to persuade the state to back his schemes to promote the integration of the Indians. He used to tell a revealing story about his relationship with Vasconcelos, then Secretary of Education, according to which his request for support to open craft workshops for Indians provoked the following response: 'Look Manuel, I'll give you whatever you want for archaeology, but not for those Indians.'[14]

As an archaeologist, Gamio lent considerable prestige to the Mexican state. When the results of his pioneering excavations at the pre-Aztec metropolis of Teotihuacán were published in 1922,[15] his work attracted international acclaim. Gamio's connections in the United States (dating back to his studies at the University of Columbia under Franz Boas from 1909 to 1912) meant that his personal world renown incidentally enhanced the credibility of the Obregón government (which struggled along without recognition from Washington until the very end of 1923) as a patron of scientific progress. Despite all this, Gamio found it impossible to secure state funding for a similar excavation project in the Valley of Oaxaca. Government support for his archaeological work stopped altogether with the transition from Obregón to Calles in 1924, and did not resume until 1942, when he was made Director of the newly established Inter-American Institute for the Indigenous. On this appointment, he wrote a letter to his US mentor, Franz Boas, lamenting, 'Since 1925 ... I have been working without any real enthusiasm, because although I've done responsible jobs which were quite well paid, I have been unable to devote myself fully to the studies of society that have given me so much satisfaction.'[16]

Despite his lack of political ambition, Gamio did try his luck at the game of politics in the hope of securing Calles's support for his work. On a visit to the United States in 1924 he sounded out US opinion on Calles's presidential candidacy. His subsequent report testifying to the high esteem in which Calles was held by various public figures in the United States was leavened with the reminder that the endorsement of several US scholarly institutions stemmed from their belief that Calles would continue to sponsor 'the social and economic emancipation of the Indian'.[17] But Calles, once in office, instead of letting Gamio continue as Director of Anthropology, invited him to be Sub-secretary of Public Education. When Gamio begged leave to decline on the grounds that he wanted to continue with his archaeological work, Calles insisted on his acceptance, arguing that it would be unpatriotic to refuse.[18] The subsequent events have all the appearance of a deliberate attempt to discredit Gamio and force him into exile. As told by his granddaughter, the story was as follows.[19] Within a few months of his arrival at the Secretariat of Public Education (SEP) early in 1925, it was drawn to Gamio's attention that school furniture was being bought from a US concern at grossly inflated prices. Gamio informed Calles and presented his resignation; the President refused to accept it and, instead, appointed him head of an investigation into corruption at SEP. Gamio soon realized that those involved included the incumbent Secretary, José Manuel Puig Casauranc, who enjoyed the protection of Calles. Once again, Gamio tried to resign; this time, Calles claimed to be too busy to see him. Gamio then sent detailed allegations to various newspapers, which published them to a degree of public outcry, whereupon he was summarily dismissed. After only a few months in office, he fled into exile in the United States, and soon afterwards heard rumours of public allegations in Mexico implicating him in the loss of a valuable collection of coins from the National Museum.[20] It was only when, in the following year, 1926, the US Social Science Research Council awarded Gamio a grant to study the effects of Mexican immigration, that Calles deemed it politic to send a message via the Mexican ambassador guaranteeing the archaeologist's safety in Mexico.

Gamio's career continued to be a frustration of his real interests. From 1929 until 1932, he worked as the Magistrate of the Supreme Council for Internal Defence and Security, showing goodwill by publishing work on delinquency and penal issues. Even during Cárdenas's presidency (1934–40), Gamio did not influence policy to the extent that might have been expected. Cárdenas's speeches on the indigenous question did contain echoes of Gamio's ideas, and in later life he wrote a brief appreciation of Gamio's work.[21] In turn, Gamio was a Cárdenas supporter, helping him to draw up his campaign policies and speaking out against Calles's intrigues. But even Cárdenas, who is thought of as the most *indigenista* of all Mexican presidents, saw the indigenous question primarily in terms of class rather than race, and paid serious attention to specifically ethnic issues only during the relatively brief period when his priority was to unify peasant organizations into the National Confederation of Peasants (CNC) founded in 1938. Earlier, Gamio had been involved in the Institute of Socialist Orientation, which helped to draw up plans for socialist education,[22] and the idea of integral education for the Indians was his. But he was not invited to participate in Cárdenas's much-vaunted Department of Indian Affairs (which in any case was always restricted to a small budget). As with his appointments to the education sector, Cárdenas preferred to keep intellectuals at a distance from his *indigenista* policies.[23] Overall, before 1940, post-revolutionary

Mexican governments were reluctant to give Gamio the resources with which to pursue his policies for integrating the Indians, while finding it politically convenient to appropriate his vision of the incorporation of Indian communities into a modern Mexican nation.

Compared with Gamio's experience, a far more marked degree of selectivity was shown by the Mexican state towards the ideas promulgated by José Vasconcelos. In confining Vasconcelos's messianic continental vision of Ibero-American *mestizaje* to the borders of Mexico, the state completely neutralized the force of his original argument.[24] Vasconcelos's essay *La raza cósmica* [*The Cosmic Race*] (1925), which was primarily an intellectual refutation of Spencerian ideas privileging the Aryan and denigrating the *mestizo* races, was conceived on a regional scale with universal implications. Neither *La raza cósmica* nor the subsequent *Indología* (1927) was written to address *mexicanidad*, but rather to establish Latin America's place in world culture. Indeed, Vasconcelos regarded national identity as a spurious issue for Spanish American countries: 'We have within our continent all the elements of a new human race; a law will select factors for the creation of superior types, a law that will operate not according to national criteria but by a yardstick of universality and beauty.'[25] One of his chief lines of argument was that the Spanish American 'race' had thwarted the realization of its potential by giving way to the 'sin' of 'local patriotism' and the 'puerile satisfaction of creating Lilliputian nations'.[26] He envisaged Latin America as the 'cradle of a fifth race' which would synthesize the finest qualities of the four existing races (black, Indian, Oriental and white) and would therefore be better able to realize his internationalist ideal ('more capable of true fraternity and a genuinely universal vision').[27] The Americas, once the site of the legendary civilization of Atlantis, were destined, Vasconcelos suggested, to generate a visionary civilization distinguished by aestheticism and universalism. The United States had lost out to Latin America in this respect, he maintained, because Anglo-Saxons 'committed the sin of destroying those [other] races, whereas we assimilated them, which gives us new rights and new hopes regarding a mission unprecedented in History'. The racial mixing that would bring about the development of the 'cosmic race' was to be determined by an ethereal selection process involving 'the spiritual factor which has to direct and accomplish this extraordinary undertaking'.[28] Mariátegui commented – not unfairly – thus:

> The racial mixing extolled by Vasconcelos is precisely not the actual mixing of Spanish, indigenous and African races that has already taken place in the continent, but rather a purifying fusion and refusion of those peoples, from which process will be born, with the passing of the centuries, the cosmic race. The actual, living *mestizo* is not, for Vasconcelos, the model of the new race . . . but only barely its precursor.[29]

As far as Vasconcelos was concerned, it was certainly not the existing Mexican people ('that poor hybrid race which we are')[30] who constituted the cosmic race.

The important point about both *La raza cósmica* and *Indología* was that they did not discuss Mexican national identity, but rather the possibility of Spanish American union. For Vasconcelos, 'the very thesis of the existence of a future race rests on a norm of universality'.[31] The main dualism that preoccupied him was not indigenous versus European, but Anglo-Saxon versus Ibero-American. In this respect, his vision was not bi-cultural but multicultural. The 'cosmic race' was dependent precisely upon the idea that all the known races had mixed in Ibero-America, which made the Ibero-Americans 'the first example of a positively universal race'.[32] In any case, Vasconcelos soon began to question the positive value attached to his own concept of *mestizaje* (even his preface to *Indología* raised doubts), at least in reference to Spanish America. In 1944, he declared his theory of the 'cosmic race' to have been erroneous: 'And one of my inanities, perhaps one of my most notorious mistakes, was the thesis . . . which expressed faith in our mixed race and its potentially great future.'[33] By the time the second edition of *La raza cósmica* appeared in 1945, Vasconcelos had developed a distinction between 'fertile' and 'suspect' types of *mestizaje*, the former occurring between similar races (for example, Europeans in the United States), and the latter between dissimilar races, that is, the Indian and the Spaniard. In the latter case, he warned, only the intervention of the 'spiritual factor' could bring about a beneficial outcome.[34] Vasconcelos never had any time for *indigenismo*, concluding that 'a counterfeit *indigenismo*' was as great a threat to 'Mexican' culture – which for him was synonymous with 'all things creole, that is, culture of Hispanic type' – as were the Anglo-Saxon influences he held to be so pernicious.[35]

According to Daniel Cosío Villegas, Vasconcelos's views on national identity during the early 1920s were that Mexico did not yet constitute a nation because it lacked common experiences and values; and that misceg-enation was not likely to bring about unification even in the longer term because whites were no longer mixing with Indians. The only way to achieve national unity, Vasconcelos proposed, was through a policy of common education for all Mexicans.[36] This aspect of Vasconcelos's strategy for national integration was undermined by his replacements at the Secretariat of Education, namely the corrupt José Manuel Puig y Casauranc (Secretary, 1924–28 and again 1930–31) and Moises Sáenz (Sub-secretary, 1925–28 and 1928–30). Sáenz, who took most of the policy decisions, was not only a pro-US Protestant minister but also an *indigenista* who introduced separate schooling for Indians. Calles's appointment of Sáenz could hardly have been better designed, in the event, to repudiate all that Vasconcelos had stood for as Secretary of Education.

Mexican state leaders extracted from Vasconcelos's work his arguments for the assimilation of the Indian, and quietly dropped his corollary that the salvation of the white man also lay in *mestizaje*.[37] That Vasconcelos's ideas had a degree of influence on Mexican statesmen is not in question (compare, for example, his argument, 'The Indian has no gateway to the future other than the gateway of modern culture' with Cárdenas's proclamation, 'Our indigenous problem is not a question of how to keep the Indian "Indian", nor of how to make Mexico indigenous, but rather of how to make the Indian Mexican.'[38]) But the main impetus of Vasconcelos's intellectual project – that is, towards universalism – was systematically ignored. Although he maintained that, for countries like Mexico, the contemporaneous realities made patriotism a necessary defence against the supremacy of the imperialist white man, he also argued that such patriotism should pursue 'vast and transcendental ends'.[39] One of Vasconcelos's few consistent intellectual stands during a long and ideologically variegated career was against the chauvinistic nationalism embraced by the post-revolutionary state in the name of his ideas.

Samuel Ramos (1897–1959) has been described as the first Mexican intellectual for whom the search for national identity became 'self-conscious and interpretive' rather than 'descriptive and naïve' as it had been previously.[40] From a middle-class Michoacán family, he is usually associated with the intellectual Generation of 1915, although he also contributed to the journal identified with the subsequent generation, *Contemporáneos*, and was more attuned to their cultural idealism than to the practical élan of his contemporaries. Having reached young adulthood during the course of the Mexican revolution, Ramos was largely self-taught. His essays of the 1920s reveal a staunch resistance to the anti-intellectualism then dominant in pro-revolutionary circles (what he later referred to as 'the abandonment of culture').[41] He was preoccupied with preserving the autonomy of the intellectual realm in the face of pressures to become an activist, and was convinced that what Mexico most needed was a generation that could effect moral and spiritual regeneration.[42] He lamented, 'In Mexico, whenever anyone ventures to preach the principles of intellectual rigour, he is soon slapped down on the grounds that what our country needs is not theory, but good practice, not words, but deeds.'[43] On assuming the editorship of *La Antorcha* from Vasconcelos in 1925, Ramos immediately changed the subtitle from 'Review of letters, art, science, industry' to 'Review of modern culture', and he insisted on the importance of its being just that.[44] Arguing that Rodó's message of spiritual redemption had failed to resonate because 'the *maestro*' had adopted too light, too sweet and too classical a tone,[45] Ramos manifestly hoped to represent himself as the new bearer of Spirit (Ariel) who would thwart the triumph of materialistic values in Mexico. Ramos's allegorical essay 'The Sunset of Ariel' (1925) suggested that Rodó himself had fallen into the error of succumbing to the Spirit's mastery, whereas Ramos's own imagined future prophet, he predicted, would succeed in taming Ariel and obliging him to redeem mankind.[46]

All these concerns crystallized in Ramos's famous attack on his former teacher, Antonio Caso, in 1927.[47] The attack was made in the second of three articles that Ramos wrote on Caso, and prompted a rather self-congratulatory reply from the older man.[48] The first article, published in 1922, had been adulatory, as might have been expected from a young student writing about his *maestro*; the third, in 1946, was to be an obituary, and offered a more measured assessment of Caso's contribution to philosophy. The dispute partly reflected changing philosophical trends in Mexico, Caso having been influenced primarily by French thinkers, Ramos by Germans; it was also a quarrel between generations. Above all, it bore the hallmarks of the insecurity of those times for Mexican intellectuals who were not prepared to become propagandists of the revolution. The main thrust of Ramos's attack was that Caso was anti-intellectual, both in his philosophy (intuitionism, which Ramos argued was lacking in rigour) and in his pedagogy (designed, according to Ramos, to create model citizens rather than inquiring minds).[49] Caso took refuge in a belief in intuition, Ramos alleged, 'to compensate for his critical weakness'.[50] Ramos maintained that what he saw as Caso's obeisance to 'the rigid and conventional mould of academic style',[51] and his habitual citation of other philosophers ('for him, infallible authorities'),[52] undermined Caso's claims to be preaching a new philosophy for post-revolutionary Mexico. The attack focused on Caso's representative status as the philosopher-king of Mexico in the 1920s. (Ramos refrained from public criticism of his other mentor, Vasconcelos, partly because of the latter's help in his own intellectual career, partly because he admired Vasconcelos's achievements as Secretary of Education, but mainly, perhaps, because Vasconcelos always saw himself more in the tradition of the nineteenth-century statesman–*pensador*, Sarmiento.) Ramos's own bid for the crown was only too apparent, and it is not surprising that Caso responded with an equally personal attack denying the claims of the pretender. Caso catalogued what he saw as Ramos's defects, including a misunderstanding of positivism, an 'unforgivable superficiality which makes me doubt his competence as a philosophy teacher', and 'a rigid, false intellectualism'.[53] He even picked him up for spelling mistakes: 'Señor Ramos . . . writes Henry, as in the English, when discussing the great . . . French philosopher, Henri Bergson'.[54] Caso then proceeded to list what he saw as his own achievements as an intellectual, notably an international reputation and, above all, professional status – 'I can support myself with my earnings from books on metaphysics and lessons in philosophy.'[55] Caso concluded, 'I am not concerned with arguing the case for philosophical ideas that take into account "the needs of the country". . . . What interests me is to think.'[56] Behind these *ad hominem* arguments lay an acute awareness on the part of both men of the difficulties involved in maintaining a position of intellectual independence in what Ramos condemned as 'a country in which the discipline of intellectual activity is lacking'.[57]

The Mexican state's co-option of intellectuals after the Second World War and the high-profile role of Vasconcelos in the early 1920s make it easy today to forget the degree of anti-intellectualism in Mexico under Calles and Cárdenas. Calles, who took a highly rationalist view of government, was dedicated to the elimination of all opposition to the urban, industrial, literate nation-state he was determined to build. During his presidency (1924–28), intellectuals were welcomed if they chose to collaborate as technicians, but were rapidly marginalized if they tried to promote themselves as technocrats or to venture any public criticism of policy (as the example of Manuel Gamio shows).[58] The volatile cultural nationalism that Obregón had permitted to flourish became overtly politicized as Calles sought to represent the expanding 'revolutionary' state as the idealization of national reality. It was also during this period that the notion of *mexicanidad* took shape.[59] Calles saw himself as 'a realist' whose preference was for beauty in its natural state: 'I like to admire a landscape in the countryside and not on a canvas; I prefer to admire the beauty of a woman's form not in her likeness, but in the woman herself.'[60] He remained unmoved by culture (remarking that although he had met Diego Rivera a few times, it had never even occurred to him to discuss painting with Mexico's leading muralist),[61] but he understood its political significance. During his time in office – 'a presidency at war'[62] – the revolutionary state did not achieve cultural hegemony. However, Calles envisaged the National Revolutionary Party (PNR), founded in 1929, as the major means to this end, intending it to 'penetrate the soul of the people and sculpt the heart of the *patria*, arrive at the intimate sentiment of the *pueblo* and help it to shake off the yoke of its errors and superstitions'.[63]

This was the context in which Samuel Ramos's famous national character essay *El perfil del hombre y la cultura en México* [*Profile of Man and Culture in Mexico*] was published in 1934. The immediate impact of this work is attested by the fact that the first edition quickly sold out; a second was printed in 1938 and a third in 1951.[64] Henry Schmidt raises the question of why Ramos's treatment of *mexicanidad* attracted so much attention even though he had said 'little on the problem of national identity that had not been said since 1920 and hinted at since 1900 and earlier',[65] and attributes it to the book's 'synthetic power that intensified the national diagnostic'.[66] Perhaps this was so, but there is another factor to take into account, namely that, by the time *El perfil del hombre y la cultura* appeared, Mexican intellectuals were seeking to challenge the vision of national identity trumpeted by officialdom, at least partly in order to protect their own position *as intellectuals.* At one level, the essay was a sustained attack on the post-revolutionary state's ideology of *indigenismo.* Ramos's view was: 'To represent Mexico without the Indian is false, but it is equally false to represent it only with the Indian.'[67] He repudiated the glorification of pre-Columbian culture promoted by the ruling party, contending that the 'monumental artistic style of the pre-Cortesian age reveals a lack of imagination, [and is] almost always dominated by a ritual formalism'.[68] It reminded him of Egyptian art, the distinguishing feature of which was rigidity, he argued; not 'a demonia-cal rigidity in which man's capacity for trembling in reverence, that most estimable of human qualities, reaches its sublime moment of transcendence and attains an equally sublime repose', but instead 'another kind of rigidity, which is restrained, arid and based on an internal apathy and a lack of sensitivity to the most profound resonances of life', traits that could also, he believed, be found in the Indian.[69] Instead of adopting the official view of the Indians as heirs of a great civilization, he saw them collectively as altogether apart from civilization: 'If the Mexican Indian seems unable to assimilate to civilization, it is not because he is inferior to it, but, rather, distinct from it. His "Egyptianness" makes him incompatible with a civiliza-tion the law of which is development.'[70] Ramos claimed that individuals could assimilate, but 'only . . . when the individual is separated from the social group into which he was born'.[71] While he did not condone the unthinking importation of European culture into Mexico, he contended that 'the plan to create a pure Mexicanism is equally misguided'.[72] His position was that Mexicans were deceiving themselves if they thought that they could escape European influence: 'In order to turn its back on Europe, Mexico has taken refuge in nationalism . . . which [in itself] is a European idea.'[73] What was needed, he argued, was for Mexicans to select those foreign ideas that could usefully be applied in Mexico: 'I understand Mexican culture to mean world culture made *ours,* living inside us, express-ing our inner selves.'[74]

As has been noted in earlier studies, Ramos's work was influenced by psychoanalysis, in particular the work of Alfred Adler and his theory of the inferiority complex. What has not previously been dwelt upon is Ramos's bid to fulfil the role of therapist to the Mexican nation. He opened one chapter, 'Psychoanalysis of the Mexican', with Nietzsche's query about how much reality humankind could withstand, warning readers that although they might not like the picture of themselves that he was about to paint, self-recognition was a salutary first step towards change.[75] His premiss was that the psychoanalytical tenet that repressed negative characteristics would continue to impede self-realization unless identified and confronted: 'in the case of the Mexican, we think that it is harmful for him to remain ignorant of his own character, which is so contrary to his destiny, and the only way forward is precisely for him to take cognisance of that. The truth, in cases such as this, is more salutary than living in a state of self-deception.'[76] Assigning himself the role of diagnostician, Ramos warned his readers that it would be necessary to go beyond 'the more salient features of the Mexican character' so that 'we can probe deeply until we discover its hidden causes, in order to find out how to transform our inner being'.[77] His criticisms were well-meant, insisted Ramos, and therefore should be received in a like spirit:

> The aim of this work is not to criticize the Mexicans out of malice; we believe that every Mexican is entitled to analyse his inner self and to take the liberty of publishing his observations, if he becomes convinced that [such reflections], whether disagreeable or not, will be beneficial to his fellow Mexicans. People who are not used to criticism think that anything short of praise is an attack on them, when very often praising them is the surest way to go against their real interests and to cause them lasting harm.[78]

This attitude enabled Ramos (like a psychoanalyst) both to identify with and simultaneously distance himself from his subject – in this case, the Mexican people. Having already placed the people at one remove by discussing them in terms of an archetype, 'the Mexican', Ramos then increased the critical distance by using the authorial 'we' to accentuate the otherness of his fellow citizens: 'It would be to abuse our argument to deduce from it an opinion which the [existing] Mexican finds depressing, for we cannot take responsibility for his present character, which is the result of a historical destiny beyond his control.'[79] Again, like an analyst, the author rejected responsibility for the current state of the subject, which he attributed to past experience rather than present circumstance. He thereby elevated himself to a position of authority, but then elected to withhold judgement, and in doing so prepared the ground for a move back towards identification with the people. The passage continued: 'It is not very gratifying to feel oneself to be in possession of a character such as is painted below, but it is a relief to know that it can be changed in the same way as one changes a suit, since that character is borrowed, and we wear it like a disguise to conceal our real selves, about which, in our view, we have nothing to be ashamed.' In this sentence, Ramos built up to a point of complete identification with his subject ('we wear it like a disguise to conceal our real selves'), which was immediately qualified by a distancing phrase in the authorial voice, 'in our view'; this gap, in turn, was closed over by a renewed assimilation of the author and his audience: 'we have nothing to be ashamed about'. This dialectic was sustained throughout, allowing Ramos to challenge the state's claim to identify with the people, by placing himself in their position, while at the same time maintaining the distinction that he considered due to an intellectual. Ramos repeatedly insisted that his work on Mexican national identity was original precisely because of its intellectual rigour:

Others have already talked about our race's sense of inferiority, but nobody, so far as we know, has systematically availed himself of this idea to explain our character. What this essay attempts to do, for the first time, is to make methodical use of this time-honoured observation, rigorously applying Adler's psychological theories to the Mexican case.[80]

Despite his resistance to the cultural nationalism promoted by Mexican leaders, Ramos's ideas dovetailed crucially with theirs in his acceptance of a racialization of the distinction between traditional and modern: 'within the country two different worlds coexist, scarcely touching each other. One is primitive and inhabited by the Indian, the other is civilized and the preserve of the white man.'[81] Ramos reproduced the long standing stereotypes of the passive Indian, resistant to all change,[82] and the arrogant, individualistic Spaniard.[83] This convergence in bi-culturalism enabled state propagandists ultimately to reincorporate Ramos's dissenting vision of *mexicanidad* into their own. His account of *mexicanidad*, like the state's, was premissed on *mestizaje*. In a challenge to official orthodoxy, Ramos chose to exclude the Indians from his discussion, arguing that they played only a passive role in contemporary Mexico, acting as 'a chorus that bears silent witness to the drama of Mexican life'.[84] But in concentrating on the *pelado*, the urban rather than rural *mestizo*, and casting him as 'the most elemental and the most clearly delineated expression of national character',[85] Ramos was in effect realizing the revolutionary party's modernizing vision of Indian peasants becoming *mestizo* labourers. The fact that Ramos's image of the *pelado* was not wholly positive became less important than the fact that he put flesh and blood on an ideal and thereby helped to make it seem a potential reality. By the time that Ramos proposed his vision of Mexico, he was writing in the context of an already well-established official version of national identity. The only critical option available to him was to challenge the government's positive image of racial mixing, with the result that his book became associated with the idea of a Mexican inferiority complex which he himself vehemently rejected. Although observing that many Mexicans felt inferior, Ramos was explicit that: 'We do not claim that such inferiority is a fact. We do not believe in the theory of inferior races, which was sustainable only as long as the value of European culture was deemed to be absolute. . . . Our idea should not be taken as yet another example of Mexican self-denigration.'[86] As it transpired, however, his work was received as exactly that.

Ironically enough, by the end of the Second World War, all those who had earlier resisted a policy of narrow cultural nationalism were incorporated into the Mexican establishment. Vasconcelos, invited to select his own post in Avila Camacho's administration, became director of the National Library; Alfonso Reyes was ensconced as director of the Colegio de México.

Ramos, who – it should be remembered – had occupied a secure niche at the National Preparatory School since 1921, was made Director of UNAM's Faculty of Philosophy and Letters in 1945, and Co-ordinator of Humanities from 1954 until his death in 1959. From 1949–52 the study of Mexican identity was at its apex, sponsored by the state and directed by Ramos, who was widely credited – and certainly saw himself – as the originator of *lo mexicano*.[87]

Octavio Paz's essay of 1950, *El laberinto de la soledad* [*The Labyrinth of Solitude*], which was written – like Ramos's *El perfil del hombre y la cultura* and, indeed, Vasconcelos's *La raza cósmica* – as a work of dissidence against the prevailing climate of cultural nationalism, suffered a fate comparable to Ramos's book, and with even less justification: by selective quotation, an essay that discussed the Mexican case in terms of a universal dilemma became famous as the definitive study of *mexicanidad*. Admittedly, it is not hard to find the stereotypes of *mexicanidad* in the text: the Mexican represented as a 'solitary' being who is nevertheless a lover of 'festivals and public gatherings', 'a being who shuts himself away and keeps himself to himself: both his face and his smile a mask', a being who was 'seduced' by death.[88] Despite this, however, the impetus of Paz's argument is to take Mexico beyond inward-looking self-preoccupation to a comprehension of its experience in universal terms. The essay builds up towards a declaration of Mexico's new-found cultural independence:

> The Mexican hides behind many masks, which he then flings aside on days of celebration or mourning, in the same way as the nation has broken free of all the forms which were suffocating it. . . . In only a few short years we have exhausted all the historical forms which Europe possessed. Nothing is left to us but nakedness or lies. . . . We are, finally, alone. Like all men. . . . There, in the truth of the open void, transcendence also awaits us: in the outstretched hands of other solitary beings. For the first time in our history, we are the contemporaries of all men.[89]

Paz subsequently denied that *El laberinto de la soledad* was an essay on the philosophy of *lo mexicano*, insisting that it was written as 'a book of social, political and psychological critique within the French tradition of "moralism"'.[90] Paz always insisted that he did not believe in *mexicanidad*, arguing in favour of the importance of historical conditioning: 'The Mexican is not an essence but a history.'[91] That said, there is evidence that he, too, attached explanatory value to the stereotypes of a bi-culturalist framework of thought, as illustrated by the following observations about the Massacre of Tlatelolco (themselves immediately preceded by another repudiation of the concept of *mexicanidad*): 'For a long time I thought that Mexican violence was a result of the conquest. But I am more and more persuaded that such violence is even more ancient in origin. Although the Spanish heritage has to be taken into account, in truth the roots of our violence are to be found in the Aztec world.'[92] Once again, the force of dissidence was tempered by the implicit acceptance of a state-sponsored version of national identity based upon the bi-culturalist divide.

The Mexican governments of the 1920s and 1930s systematically misappropriated and bowdlerized the ideas of independent intellectuals in order to promote a crude cultural nationalism which was precisely the opposite of what the intellectuals themselves advocated. This was partly because one consequence of the Mexican revolution was to postpone the emergence of a generation of intellectuals who identified themselves as spokesmen of national identity. The *ateneista* generation (Vasconcelos, Antonio Caso, Alfonso Reyes), who had been advocates of a spiritually oriented national rebirth, gave way in the 1920s to the policy-oriented zeal of 'the seven wise men',[93] as they became known.[94] One consequence of the revolution was that, initially, the gap between state and nation (people) which, by the 1920s, had been identified in Argentina, Chile, Peru and Cuba, was deemed to exist in Mexico only barely, if at all. For many of the Mexican intellectuals of the early 1920s, identification with the state became synonymous with identification with the people. Believing (mistakenly, as it was to prove) that opportunities were available for them to participate *as intellectuals* in the revolutionary process, this generation of Mexican intellectuals saw no need to create myths of national identity establishing themselves as mediators. Their immediate inheritance was the work of the *ateneistas*, which (in direct contrast to the corresponding generation in Argentina) had been characterized by its emphasis on a continental rather than a national perspective: Vasconcelos and Reyes, in particular, conceived *lo mexicano* in terms of *lo americano*. It was not until the political shocks of 1928–29 (the assassination of President-elect Obregón, the fraudulent electoral defeat of Vasconcelos and the creation of the Partido Nacional Revolucionario) that intellectuals in Mexico began to identify a divide between state and nation. Only in the 1930s did some of them, most notably Samuel Ramos, try to establish themselves in the by-then-prevalent role for the Spanish American intellectual as architect of national identity. (Alternative strategies for the Mexican intellectual, based on critical intellectual endeavour, were advocated at the time, but were almost impossible to realize in the political climate of the 1930s.)[95] As a result, in the crucial period of the late 1920s and early 1930s, it was the state that forged *mexicanidad,* creating the image of a nation founded on *mestizaje,* a version of national identity from which most independent Mexican intellectuals at the time continued to dissent. Thus it was that the formation of Mexican national identity after the revolution resulted primarily not from the involvement of intellectuals, but instead from early state intervention in the process. In turn, however, the state's misappropriation of their ideas was assisted by the intellectuals themselves, who continued to perpetuate the stereotypes of bi-culturalism. In seeking to invert official images, intellectuals ultimately succeeded only in reinforcing them.

Peru

Developments in Peru were in some respects ahead of those in Mexico (with which they can most usefully be compared in relation to bi-culturalism), but in other ways behind. The concept of *peruanidad* emerged far earlier than that of *mexicanidad* (which was mainly a product of the 1920s). The causes of this lay in Peru's disastrous defeat by Chile in the War of the Pacific (1879–83), which Peruvian leaders attributed at least in part to a stronger sense of national identity in Chile. In particular, the issue of what role the Indians should play in the Peruvian nation was brought into sharp focus as the elites began to ponder the contribution that an army of Indians might have made to victory.[96] Like Mexico, Peru had a leading positivist who rejected theories of racial pessimism: Manuel González Prada (1848–1918). But whereas in Mexico Justo Sierra had taken refuge in promoting miscegenation, González Prada identified a need for more radical solutions to the problem of national integration, and advocated that the Indians of Peru should take up arms against their oppressors.[97] Unlike Mexico, Peru had experienced a war motivated primarily by racial tensions, albeit during the colonial period (Tupac Amaru II's uprising in 1780); and also unlike Mexico, Peru has never had an Indian President. In post-revolutionary Mexico *indigenismo* was primarily cultural, a strategy used by the new creole governing elite to establish a hegemony clearly distinct from the pro-European cultural orientation of the *porfiriato*, and to distract attention from the assimilating intent of its nation-building ideology, *mestizaje*. In contrast, in Leguía's Peru (1919–30), battles between *hispanistas* and *indigenistas* became highly politicized and radicalized.

By then, Peru had fallen behind Mexico in the pace and degree of its modernization. As a result, the prominent Peruvian intellectual group at the start of this century, the Generation of 1900, also known as the *arielista* or 'futurist' generation, were all aristocrats who identified with the oligarchy, unlike the corresponding middle-class *ateneistas* in Mexico. Peruvians like Víctor Andrés Belaúnde (1883–1966) and Francisco García Calderón (1883–1953) did not consider themselves professional intellectuals and had no interest in elaborating an inclusive nationalism involving *lo popular*. González Prada's radicalism bypassed his immediate successors to influence the Centenary Generation of the 1920s. The vacuum left behind by the *arielistas* meant that when the concept of a popular Peruvian nationalism first began to be developed in the 1920s it became imbued with

Marxism and, as a result, the target of anti-Communists. In this respect Peru was unique (Mexico had its proletcult in the 1920s, but there the Marxist input was subsumed by a state-led nationalism based on Mexico's own revolution). Debates about Peru's future were all refracted through the prism of a perceived contradiction between Communism and nationalism. The raw political conflicts that underlay the competing visions of national identity put forward by Marxists and their opponents helped to solidify the banal dualism of *indigenista* versus *hispanista*. This ideological construct and its attendant stereotypes, established in the 1920s, dominated Peruvian intellectual life, historiography and politics for at least the next four decades, largely because it served the interests of the state as well as the intellectuals. Moreover, it has proved remarkably difficult to extirpate, despite the valiant efforts of several influential Peruvian intellectuals from the 1970s onwards.

The extent to which a 'bipolar' vision of Peru ('Indian highlands, white and *mestizo* coast; white and *mestizo* cities, Indian countryside')[98] became entrenched in the 1920s can best be illustrated by two specific debates. In both cases the protagonist was José Carlos Mariátegui. The first was his 'polemic' with Luis Alberto Sánchez, conducted in the pages of the Lima journal *Mundial* early in 1927; the second concerned Mariátegui's *Siete ensayos de interpretación de la realidad peruana* (1928) and the explicit rebuttal it prompted from Víctor Andrés Belaúnde in his own book *La realidad nacional* (1930).[99] A close reading of these disputes reveals that, at root, both were about far more than their ostensible pretext, which was the future of *indigenismo* in Peru. Not only were competing visions of national identity at stake, but also different conceptions of the role of the intellectual in constructing that identity.

The debate with Sánchez was triggered when Mariátegui published three articles in *Mundial* on '*Indigenismo* in national literature'.[100] In these, he compared Peruvian literary *indigenismo* with '*mujikismo*' in pre-revolutionary Russia and argued that it could play an analogous role in relation to the first phase of social agitation that had paved the way for the Bolshevik revolution. In a strident refutation of the first two of these articles, an Indian supporter of the Leguía government, José Ángel Escalante (1883–1965), published 'We, the Indians...', in the Lima daily, *La Prensa*.[101] Escalante was a highly successful Indian aristocrat, a leading newspaper proprietor in Cuzco, congressional deputy for Acomayo Province and, allegedly, a leading member of Peruvian freemasonry.[102] Having begun his involvement with *indigenismo* in the politically indeterminate and paternalistic movement that emerged in Cuzco during the 1900s, by 1923 he had come to believe that Leguía was far more likely to meet Indian needs than a clique of vanguard intellectuals, and was correspondingly scathing about the new-found fascination of *costeño* writers (from the coast) with the indigenous. In that respect, he made a few telling points: that *indigenistas* from the coastal cities rarely bothered to get to know the Indians in their own environment, or to ask them how they saw their future; that intellectuals tended to talk about the 'indigenous question' or the 'indigenous problem' when in fact 'there are many "questions" and various difficult "problems" regarding the indigenous race';[103] and that the situation of Indians in Cuzco was not the same as in Cajamarca or Ayacucho or various other regions of the country. Escalante argued that phrases such as 'racial slavery' and 'exploitation by the *gamonales* (local bosses)' had become clichés, and his article vigorously refuted the common stereotypes of passive, fatalistic Indians stupefied by coca and alcohol. But his legitimate complaints about the lack of complexity with which white intellectuals tended to approach Indian societies were undermined by the fact that his own article was not entirely devoid of cliché itself ('the European conqueror, greedy for riches'), and likewise depended upon unqualified divisions between coast and mountain, exploiter and exploited. Correspondingly, his uncritical adherence to official *indigenismo* and a facile anti-Communism undercut the potential radicalism of his vision of a Peru redeemed by the 'Great Race'. Escalante represented Leguía's assumption of the presidency in 1919 as 'a defining moment in the history of the Peruvian Indian' asserting that 'today, in the remotest corners of the Republic, the authorities are taking the Indians' side'.[104] By 1927, when Escalante wrote this article, there was little doubt that scant justification for this claim remained, even if it could – arguably – have been upheld during the early, more reformist stage (1919–23) of Leguía's *oncenio*. Even so, Escalante concluded that 'we, the Indians' would reject the attempts of the *indigenista* vanguard to lead them, because the Indians had already found scope for implementing their own remedies 'within current government ideology'.[105] A subsequent article of his was an even more blatant propaganda piece in support of Leguía.[106]

It is important to bear in mind that it was this official, state-sponsored *indigenismo* against which both Sánchez and Mariátegui were reacting. Leguía's policies had divided the intellectual *indigenista* movement, both within Cuzco (Escalante's switch to Leguía prompted other leading *indigenistas* from Cuzco to resign from his newspaper, notably Luis Valcárcel) and between Cuzco and Lima. Official *indigenismo*, which was seized upon as an opportunity for further militancy by peasants who had launched a wave of protests during the 1910s, also hampered either provincial or national intellectuals from forging enduring links with peasant movements. The limited evidence available suggests that peasant leaders were skilful at exploiting the tensions between state *indigenismo* and intellectual *indigenistas* in order to further their own aims. They were quite prepared to work with intellectuals, but they also attended the government-sponsored annual

Indigenous Congresses (1921–23), which were conducted in Quechua, and they also besieged the official Organization for the Protection of the Indigenous Race, established in 1922, with their complaints. Peasant leaders strengthened their own positions by establishing themselves as 'intermediaries' between their followers and the organizations of both official and alternative *indigenismo*, and 'whenever conflict broke out, the intellectuals invariably called for calm . . . whilst the peasant leaders got on with organizing the movement'.[107] In the context of this fractured *indigenista* movement, the issue dividing Mariátegui and Sánchez was that while Mariátegui supported the alternative *indigenismo* of the avant-garde, arguing that it was one component of national redemption, Sánchez rejected that too, on the grounds that it retained simplistic divisions and was therefore fundamentally anti-national. The so-called polemic began when Sánchez (drawing some of his arguments from Escalante's 'We, the Indians . . .') published an article, entitled '*Indigenista* Hotchpotch', which set out his arguments against the avant-garde and directly accused Mariátegui, by name, of setting up an implicitly false opposition between colonialism and *indigenismo* 'as if it were a matter of bulls, boxers, cocks or colliding trains'.[108]

The opening paragraph of Mariátegui's reply to Sánchez betrayed just how important issues of intellectual status were in shaping these debates. Instead of addressing the issue of *indigenismo* directly, he began by picking up on the opening sentence of Sánchez's article, which was: 'We coastal people, or rather, we writers from the coast . . .'. Mariátegui launched straight into an attack on Sánchez for lumping all 'writers from the coast' together, 'without excluding himself', slyly suggesting that one reason for this was that otherwise 'his article could not have begun with the word "we"'; in other words, Sánchez would not have been able to present himself as an insider to the debate.[109] More important, Mariátegui argued, the all-embracing 'we' imposed false coherence on what was still the subject of contention among Lima intellectuals, and indicated that Sánchez had failed to understand what was implied by a critical response to ideas: 'I should like to remind Sánchez', the self-taught Mariátegui admonished the established university professor, 'that a programme does not come before a debate but after it.'[110] But as far as Mariátegui was concerned, the underlying cause of their difference of opinion was that Sánchez remained a 'spectator' to *indigenismo* while he himself was 'one who fights, one who struggles'.[111] This claim was founded on Mariátegui's Marxist conception of the necessary interdependence of theory and practice. In contrast, Sánchez's rejoinder, which acknowledged that he did indeed remain a spectator for the reason that 'I have no alternative but to look on, as long as the stage is occupied by the puppetmaster manipulating his puppets,'[112] was consistent with his own belief (derived from liberalism) that thought should precede action. As his subsequent career in APRA was to show, Sánchez was not averse to militancy:

he announced that he might 'venture to take my first steps as "a combatant, as one who struggles"' once what he saw as sterile debates had been resolved.[113] But instead of responding directly to Mariátegui's challenge to clarify his ideological position, Sánchez rounded on him for having accepted a scholarship to Europe instead of staying in Peru, as Sánchez himself had done, 'obscurely and fruitlessly, unsuccessfully if you like' writing about national problems.[114] He also accused Mariátegui of assuming the role of a 'preacher' and declared, 'I do not get annoyed with those who contradict me, because I do not [pretend to] speak *ex-cathedra*.'[115] In short, each of the two intellectuals claimed that he was prepared to engage in genuine debate while the other one was not.

Both parties continued to devote more energy to sparring about their respective intellectual and ideological status than to responding to the few substantive points either of them had made. The key point about this 'polemic' is that it was not one in the sense of a controversy over doctrine or belief, but was merely an *ad hominem* argument. On precisely those grounds, Mariátegui opted out fairly quickly, claiming, 'I have rarely got involved in arguments with individuals; my arguments are with ideas.'[116] His final word on the subject was wholly devoted to refuting Sánchez's assertion that *Amauta* was not fulfilling its self-assigned ideological role: this last salvo of Mariátegui's actually said nothing at all about *indigenismo* or Peruvian national identity.[117] The highly personalized nature of this dispute was symptomatic, above all, of the precarious position of the would-be professional Peruvian intellectual in the 1920s.

Different but related issues were involved in Belaúnde's response to Mariátegui's *Siete ensayos* (1928). The intellectual generation gap – perhaps the word 'gulf' more accurately captures its extent – between these two men was explicitly raised as an issue in both their works. The younger Mariátegui attacked the previous 'futurist generation' for 'living in the past', arguing that Belaúnde and his ilk represented 'a momentary restoration of colonialism and *civilismo* in Peruvian thought'.[118] Belaúnde opened *La realidad nacional* (1930) with a statement accusing Mariátegui of treating the *arielistas* with 'manifest injustice'.[119] Most of his chapter on 'The Indian Problem' was devoted to countering what he referred to as 'Mariátegui's gratuitous claim that I am linked by education and temperament to Peru's feudal caste'; he said relatively little directly concerning the indigenous people. Pointing out that he came from Arequipa, and arguing that it was not 'an aristocratic city, but the heartland of middle-income gentlemen-farmers', Belaúnde insisted that he did not identify with the *civilista* oligarchy. In support of this claim, he cited his commitment to Christian democracy, his reaction against positivism and biological determinism, the influence upon him of the social reformism espoused by David Lloyd George, and his later belief in a society based on the institutions of organic Catholicism, the family and the *gremio* (professional association).[120] Belaúnde could also have buttressed his self-defence with the fact that he had been a member of the mildly reformist National Democratic Party (in existence from 1915 to 1919). Nevertheless, it could well be argued (as Mariátegui had implied) that Belaúnde was part of the *civilista* establishment of the Aristocratic Republic: he held the statutory teaching post at the University of San Marcos, was involved in founding the Catholic University in 1917, and became an eminent diplomat (ultimately serving as President of the United Nations General Assembly in 1959). Belaúnde did not claim to be a professional intellectual and he certainly did not identify with 'the people'. He considered himself to be a social Christian whose approach to the Indians was to advocate assimilation through education and jobs, and to hope (as late as 1945) that European 'whitening' through immigration would speed up the process of imbuing the Peruvian masses with Western culture.[121] His fundamental antipathy to Marxism – he accused Mariátegui of distorting Peruvian reality by viewing it through 'the rigid creed of pseudo-scientific socialism'[122] – and his refutation of Mariátegui's versions of the conquest and independence of Peru led him to misread Mariátegui's views of the indigenous question. Yet he insisted that his generation was essentially reformist and modern, partly because of their reassertion of idealism in line with intellectual developments in France, Germany and Italy, but, above all, because of their emphasis on nationalism.[123] This indicates the extent to which intellectual credibility had become bound up with questions of national identity.

In this volatile context of highly politicized debates, it is perhaps not surprising that work adopting a more complex approach to Peru's indigenous peoples became subject to oversimplification. Two major distortions of Mariátegui's ideas, dating back to the 1920s, have remained commonplace to the present day. The first was that he advocated a return to the Incas. As is well known, Mariátegui rejected the view that what he, too, referred to as 'the Indian problem' could be understood by means of 'ethnic' criteria (or indeed in 'administrative, legal, . . . moral, educational or ecclesiastical' terms).[124] Instead, he argued, it was fundamentally an economic issue with its roots in the 'feudal' regime of the *gamonales* (local bosses), against which all liberal reformist measures would always prove to be wholly ineffectual.[125] For Mariátegui, to define the issue of the Indians in ethnic terms was equivalent to adopting the imperialist ideology of superior and inferior races, by which the white man justified his acts of conquest:

> It has invariably tended to serve the interest of the ruling class – first Spanish, then creole – to explain the condition of the indigenous races with arguments about their inferiority or their primitivism. In this, that class has done nothing

but reproduce, with respect to this internal national question, the white man's
rationale for his treatment . . . of colonial peoples.[126]

By justifying exploitation on the basis of being more advanced, he maintained, Peru's dominant class, who 'share the contempt felt by white
imperialists towards Indians, blacks and mulattos',[127] used 'the racial problem . . . to conceal or to close their eyes to the continent's real problems'.[128]
(In this, we can trace the beginnings of the concept of internal colonialism
which was to become salient in the thinking of the 1960s.) As Mariátegui
defined it, the problem was one of land, and the solution had to go beyond
a democratic-liberal land reform to embrace common (state) ownership of
all lands as the only means of destroying the power of the *gamonales*. He
certainly perceived a form of primitive Communism in Inca methods of
working the land. Whatever problems historians have subsequently identified with this idealized version of Inca society in itself, it still does not follow
from this that Mariátegui confused what he referred to as 'Inca Communism' with modern Communism.[129] Indeed, he specifically stated that the
Inca way of life had been destroyed by Spanish colonization and that
modern Communism, the product of an industrial society, was an altogether
distinct idea.[130] His argument, far from promoting a return to the Incas, was
that Indian communities had been obliged to maintain a communal way of
life since Peruvian independence because this had proved to be the best
way of defending themselves against liberal government encroachments on
their land. Mariátegui emphasized that these Indian communities, some of
which had responded to the intrusion of capitalism by turning themselves
into economic co-operatives, were far more effective as modern units of
production than the still-'feudal' *latifundia*.[131] Equally, he did not oppose
the idea of education for the Indians; he simply argued that it stood no
chance of being effective while the power of the *gamonales*, who preferred
to keep Indians in a state of ignorance and alcoholic stupor, was still intact:
'Modern schooling . . . is incompatible with the feudal large landed
estate'.[132] Mariátegui declared that an improved future for the Indians (and
all other oppressed Peruvians) lay in a socialist Peruvian nation. He rejected
the Comintern's call for indigenous peoples to found separate states, which,
he argued, would only be bourgeois Indian states with the same internal
contradictions as any other bourgeois structure.[133] Like all Marxists, Mariátegui defended the benefits of modernization and progress, from which he
wanted the Indians to benefit within the context of revolution: in an article
of 1927, for example, he referred to 'Western civilization, the science and
technology of which only utopian romanticists could see as anything but
magnificent additions to modern life to be preserved at all costs'.[134] He was
no atavist. Moreover, in his later political writings, Mariátegui called into
question the main assumption underlying the rigid division of Peru into

Spanish and Indian cultures, namely the association of the whites with modernization and the Indians with backwardness (a prejudice that, incidentally, at the time went unchallenged by Mexican intellectuals). He pointed out, for example, that the *latifundia* hardly constituted an agricultural advance: in the matter of how to farm the difficult terrain of the Andes 'the white man's rule represents no advance on aboriginal culture, not even technologically'.[135] Indians had adapted perfectly well to modern industry, he argued; indeed, it was precisely because they were 'attentive and sober' workers that capitalists liked to employ them.[136]

A second misrepresentation of Mariátegui's thought lay in the claim that he equated the Indians with the Peruvian nation. On the one hand, the Comintern accused him of reducing the Indian problem to the peasant problem. On the other hand, both Belaúnde and Sánchez attacked him for supposedly saying that the future of the nation lay only in the Indian. Sánchez wrote, 'Mariátegui has written countless articles exalting the Indian, basing Peru's salvation on him alone.'[137] Belaúnde accused Mariátegui of advocating a 'racial nationalism',[138] in line with the dictates of world revolutionary strategy, which assigned primary importance to the rebellion of the oppressed races. In his view, radical *indigenistas*, among whom he included Mariátegui, erred in their alleged belief that 'the Indian is not only an essential part of Peru's nationality, but the nationality itself'.[139] Creating a nationality along racial lines did not cause problems in countries like India or China, he argued, where the overwhelming majority of the population were of the same ethnic origin; but it would lead to major difficulties in *mestizo* Spanish America, where 'the application of racism is not the affirmation of nationality but its disintegration or rupture'.[140] But having made this point, in the next line Belaúnde reaffirmed the same dualism in inverted form when he claimed that racial nationalism would lead to barbarism in Peru because it would involve sacrificing those members of the population – namely, the descendants of the Spanish – which 'through biological and spiritual inheritance, belong to Christian civilization'.[141]

Part of the confusion surrounding Mariátegui's views on the relationship of the Indians to the Peruvian nation lay in the perceived contradiction between socialism and nationalism, which he himself denied.[142] Mariátegui argued only that the Indians had to be 'the foundation of Peru's nationality'.[143] The main reason for this was simply their situation – at least, as Mariátegui saw it – as the majority of the oppressed masses living within the national territory: 'the Indian problem is the problem of four million Peruvians. ... It is the problem of the majority. It is the problem of nationality.'[144] In fact, there was no agreement in Peru during the 1920s about what proportion of the population was Indian. Belaúnde asserted that 'the majority' was *mestizo*.[145] There was no national census taken between

1876 and 1940, which perhaps partly accounts for the discrepancies of information in contemporaneous discussions of the indigenous population, although in 1920 an estimate now deemed by Peruvian historians to be fairly reliable pitched the country's population at over 4 million, the majority of whom were thought to live in rural areas and speak Quechua or Aymara.[146] Although the migrations from the *sierra* to Lima that initiated a process of cultural *mestizaje* began in the 1920s, they had not accounted for more than about 100,000 people by the end of that decade.[147] Mariátegui was almost certainly closer to the truth with his estimate that four-fifths of the Peruvian population could be considered 'indigenous and peasant'.[148] That was the basis upon which he argued: 'Our socialism would not be . . . Peruvian – it would not even be socialism – if it did not declare solidarity first of all with the claims of the indigenous peoples.'[149] Any revolutionary strategy that ignored the Indian/peasant masses (for example, that advocated by the Comintern) was in Mariátegui's view doomed to failure.

As a nationalist, which for him implied being a socialist revolutionary, Mariátegui saw *indigenismo* as one manifestation of a redemptive spirit heralding a new revolutionary age. But it was always only a part of the envisaged transformation which, he stated, would '[draw] on both native feeling and universal thought'.[150] Throughout his work, Mariátegui sought to reconcile the national and the cosmopolitan.[151] He wanted to adapt a European idea – socialism – to bring about a national transformation which, for him, could not but entail redemption from poverty and repression for the Indians, given that they constituted the majority of the oppressed. The anticipated benefits were not to be restricted to the Indians, however, but were conceived by Mariátegui as extending to all the oppressed people of Peru: 'The claim that we uphold is that . . . of the working classes, with no distinctions between coast and mountain, or between Indians and people of mixed race.'[152] Mariátegui specifically rejected 'Indianism', arguing that to place faith in 'autochthonous racial forces' to create a new American culture was to fall prey to 'the most naïve and absurd mysticism'. It was, he added, 'senseless and dangerous' to try to counter anti-Indian racism with a nebulous messianic faith – in itself equally racist, in his opinion – which overestimated the potential role of Indians in the rebirth of Spanish American nations.[153] Again, he insisted on addressing the economic causes of social divisions: 'Any possibilities for the Indians to elevate themselves materially and intellectually are dependent upon a change in social and economic conditions. They are determined not by race but by economics and politics.'[154] Mariátegui stated that the issue of race could not be ignored, and had its part to play in the resolution of the overall problem of exploitation. Leaders who were themselves Indians and spoke Indian languages would be needed to persuade their companions to militancy, he argued.[155] But he insisted that 'the ethnic problem' was 'totally fictitious

and imagined'.[156] Fundamentally, Mariátegui saw racial integration as a
political issue and in that sense he transcended the bi-culturalist divide.

Even so, there were some respects in which Mariátegui's thought was
constrained by bi-culturalism. Most important, the overall emphasis of his
work sustained the basic dualism of Indian/rural/*sierra* versus white/urban/
costa, and he never fully addressed the validity of arguments in favour of a
more complex version of Peruvian reality (although there is one reference
in the *Siete ensayos* to the idea that *mestizaje* was not just a question of
'resolving a duality, that of Spanish and Indian' but 'a complex variety'
including blacks and Chinese, neither of whom, he argued, 'have yet
contributed cultural values or progressive energies to the formation of
nationality').[157] But in response to Sánchez's challenge to answer the
question 'do you believe that the solution [to Peru's problems] lies . . . in
the opposition between coast and mountain?',[158] Mariátegui dismissed the
issue:

> How can Sánchez ask me if I reduce the whole Peruvian problem to the
> opposition between coast and mountain? I have testified to the duality born of
> the conquest in order to affirm the historical necessity of resolving it. My ideal is
> neither colonial Peru nor Inca Peru but an integrated Peru.[159]

In so doing, he implicitly accepted an analysis based on Peru's supposed
racial divide as a given, and reinforced that dualism in his denial that
indigenismo was a product of Lima: 'It is not "we the coastal people" who are
agitating. . . . It is the authentic mountain people.'[160] Both Belaúnde and
Sánchez suggested that racial distribution in Peru was far more complex
than the duality of coast and mountain allowed. In Sánchez's words, 'the
coast itself is full of indigenous people, who are more superficial and more
"*costeño*" than we *costeños*'.[161] In any case, no agreement existed on what was
meant by 'Indian' or 'creole'. Sánchez mused: 'From a cultural and ethnic
point of view, there are "Indians" who are wholly *mestizo* and "creoles" who
are completely indigenous. Because of this, I have come to suspect that
Indian characteristics are the result neither of birth nor culture, but rather
of social circumstances and economic situation.'[162] Belaúnde also devoted
several pages to an analysis of the complexity of Peru's patterns of ethnicity,
claiming that: 'The opposition between coast and mountain is not as radical
as Mariátegui portrays it.'[163]

It was Mariátegui's discussions of cultural manifestations of *indigenismo*
that left him most vulnerable to his critics. He tried to redefine the term,
extending it beyond the common meaning of 'concern with the indigenous
peoples' in an attempt virtually to equate it to the intellectual emancipation
of Peru. Any Peruvian artist or writer whose work Mariátegui deemed not to
be imitative of European styles was identified by him as an example of
indigenismo, which he saw as 'the manifestation of a complex spiritual

phenomenon ... expressed variously but equally coherently by Sabogal's painting and Vallejo's poetry, by Valcárcel's translations and Orrego's philosophical speculations, in all of which can be observed a spirit purged of intellectual and aesthetic colonialism'.[164] But whereas José Sabogal's murals (influenced by the Mexican movement) and Luis Valcárcel's visions of Indian millenarianism could uncontroversially be classified as *indigenista*, in the usual sense of the word, the label is less applicable to Antenor Orrego's Bergsonian meditations and seems wholly inappropriate to Vallejo's experimental vanguard poetry. In the case of Vallejo, Mariátegui was obliged to resort to stereotypes in order to sustain the case that he was 'the poet of ... a race', asserting that Vallejo's verse bore the pessimism and nostalgia of the Indian. In effect, Mariátegui acknowledged the forced nature of his own argument when he conceded that, as far as Vallejo was concerned, 'indigenous feeling is at work in his art perhaps without his knowing or even wishing it to be so'.[165]

Mariátegui's work is marred by a basic contradiction in that while from a political point of view he defined 'the indigenous question' in terms of land and power, from the perspective of an intellectual trying to create a popular national identity, he represented the Indians as the bearers of Peru's great past and the embodiment of the autochthonous. In this vein, he fell into the bi-culturalist trap of implying that there was some pristine so-called 'indigenous' spirit to be recovered: 'Virtually all that remains of Tawantinsuyu is the Indian. . . . The biological material of Tawantinsuyu shows itself, after four centuries, to be indestructible and, in part, immutable.'[166] As noted above, from the 1930s until the 1960s, debates in Peru on the 'Indian question' were 'confined to stereotypes established in the 1920s'.[167] Alejandro Marroquín has argued that after a state policy of repressing worker militancy in the early 1930s, the radicalized, class-conscious *indigenismo* that Mariátegui had tried to promote gave way to an *indigenismo* that was 'integrationist and culturalist' and represented the 'Indian question' as a cultural rather than a political or economic issue.[168] This shift partly reflected the influences of US anthropology and Cárdenas's approach to *indigenismo* in Mexico, and above all mirrored the priorities of a state run in the interests of the oligarchy. But it was made possible by the failure of any intellectual of the 1920s, including Mariátegui, wholly to break free of the constraints of bi-culturalist thinking and shift the ground of debate.

The depth of the cultural divisions in Peru, and the role played by some intellectuals in sustaining them into the 1970s, was nowhere illustrated more clearly than in Mario Vargas Llosa's public critique of the novels of José María Arguedas (1911–69), the leading Peruvian *indigenista* writer of the twentieth century, whose first language was Quechua. This incident was also telling about the extent to which white intellectuals have claimed a monopoly on rationality. Vargas Llosa took Arguedas's work as the subject of his inaugural speech on becoming a member of the Peruvian Academy of Language in 1977. Stating at the outset that one of his reasons for accepting the invitation to join the academy was in order to 'express the pride every Peruvian should take in speaking Spanish', Vargas Llosa then proceeded to discredit Arguedas's representation of Indian life.[169] Using the conceit of claiming literary originality for Arguedas and 'rescuing' him from charges of being merely a documentary writer, Vargas Llosa argued that the violence Arguedas depicted in Indian life was more a projection of his own brutal childhood experiences than an image of sociological reality.[170] The commonplace (and hard-to-refute) argument that *indigenistas* were often guilty of cliché was elaborately reworked by Vargas Llosa to reaffirm his own conviction that the most promising hope for Peru's future lay in its Hispanic past, which had given it 'a history, a culture and experiences that guarantee our modernity and our dialogue with the rest of mankind'.[171] Vargas Llosa has repeatedly alleged that twentieth-century Peruvian intellectuals have failed to contribute positively to national political development because of their ideological conformity,[172] but arguably the problem lay elsewhere: in their intellectual conformity and their inability to break out of a highly restricted framework of debate. In an attempt to transcend the stale dichotomy between *hispanistas* and *indigenistas*, since the early 1970s revisionist work has tended to challenge the very idea of any united 'Peru', the '*peruanidad*' of which could be articulated. As Alberto Flores Galindo put it: 'From 1920 to 1986, there has been a transition from the feverish search for an inner being, which in reality was a mirror in which the personal desires of certain intellectuals were reflected, to the discovery of others: the multiple faces of a country made up of a variety of cultural traditions.'[173] Given this perceived level of fragmentation, it is perhaps not surprising that the myth of free market economics has taken such a hold in Peru.

Argentina

In the immigrant society of early-twentieth-century Argentina, bi-culturalism had a much less clearly identifiable social base than in Mexico or Peru. Argentina's native Indian population had been virtually eliminated during the War of the Desert (1879), reduced from an estimated 5 per cent of the national total in 1869 to 0.7 per cent in 1895; people of African origin, who had constituted 25 per cent of Argentines in 1838, made up fewer than 2 per cent by 1900.[174] Argentina's national population doubled from 3.9 million to 7.8 million in the twenty years leading up to the First World War, reflecting the influx of approximately one million Italians, 800,000 Spaniards, 94,000 Russians and Poles (often classified together because the majority of both groups were Jewish), 86,000 French, 80,000 '*turcos*' (people from the Ottoman Empire), 40,000 British and Irish, and 35,000 Germans, not to mention 18,000 Bolivians and 86,000 Uruguayans.[175] This was 'the most overwhelming immigrant invasion in the history of the modern age'.[176] And yet a bi-culturalist framework of thought came to dominate the debate about national identity in early-twentieth-century Argentina just as it did in Mexico and Peru where the reasons were far more readily apparent.

The explanation for this can be found in the increasing hostility of the liberal-dominated establishment towards immigrants, whom they identified as a major cause of social and labour unrest. By the late nineteenth century, most Argentine writers sympathetic to the liberal elites were openly opposed to immigration: even Sarmiento, the great exponent of European settlement as an engine of nation-building, reconsidered when he saw the consequences of his own policies, although in fairness it should be noted that he had always advocated far more comprehensive programmes of assimilation than were implemented by Argentine governments after 1880. Similar reservations were expressed by early-twentieth-century intellectuals, many of whom continued to support the policy of immigration while condemning the behaviour of the immigrants themselves. José Ingenieros, himself the son of Italians, commended the liberal elite's ideal of 'whitening'.[177] Yet none of them produced a comprehensive critique of government policies, which were inimical to a successful immigration strategy (immigrants found it hard to secure land, housing or credit, and were denied political rights).[178] The furthest any intellectual went was to insist on the importance of 'a national education' to 'Argentinize' the newcomers.[179]

The most significant response to immigration from among Argentine intellectual circles came from the Centenary Generation. These writers, most of whom had grown up in the provinces,[180] identified the widening gap between the liberal elite's exclusive 'we are white and European' nationalism and the social tensions caused by immigration as an opportunity for them to influence the nation's self-image. The leading figures were the novelist and biographer Manuel Gálvez (1882–1962) from Paraná, and the literary historian Ricardo Rojas (1882–1957) from Tucumán. The self-taught modernist poet Leopoldo Lugones (1874–1938) from Córdoba is sometimes identified with this generation. Neither Lugones himself nor the Centenary Generation writers would have accepted his inclusion among their ranks: as Gálvez makes clear in his memoirs, they quarrelled several times.[181] However, their contributions to the creation of Argentine national identity had sufficient features in common to warrant consideration together.

Although these were not men of the Left, they had little in common politically. As a student, Lugones was briefly a socialist but soon moved to the Right; eventually, in 1929, he declared himself a Fascist; his two consistent positions were a vehement anti-clericalism and disparagement of Spain. He was vehemently opposed to the Radical governments of Yrigoyen, and actively supported General José Uriburu's military *coup d'état* of 1930. Gálvez was a committed Catholic and Hispanophile, basically a conservative who came to admire Mussolini; he was prepared to lend his backing to Yrigoyen, but expressed far more enthusiasm for Uriburu's brief experiment in corporatism. Rojas, the most liberal of the three, was ambivalent about Yrigoyen's increasingly populist style but baulked at the 1930 coup, which he publicly condemned, and subsequently joined the Radical Party. However, their common position as aspiring professional intellectuals caught between a *europeizante* (Europeanizing) elite that despised local culture and an immigrant community in pursuit of material gains ultimately proved to be more significant to the development of their nationalist thought than were their various political views. The extent to which they were concerned with achieving status as professional intellectuals is evident in Gálvez's memoirs. Gálvez was one of Argentina's few professional novelists in the early twentieth century and, exceptionally, was able to make a living from his writing. He also devoted much of his time and energy to building up intellectual institutions, persisting with a series of largely doomed publishing ventures in the 1920s, founding the Argentine branch of the PEN Club in 1930 and helping to establish the Argentine Academy of Letters in 1931.[182] But it was Lugones who won official recognition as the first professional Argentine writer: for a time his birthday was celebrated as 'The Day of the Writer',[183] although Gálvez sniped that Lugones did not publish often enough to warrant that appellation.[184] Gálvez's reiterated insistence that his intellectual generation was the first to be both professional and nationalist suggests just how closely these issues were related in his mind.[185] He described what he saw as 'our heroic struggle against our surroundings, [which are] materialistic and spiritually bankrupt, foreign-oriented and contemptuous of all things Argentine, indifferent towards intellectual and spiritual values'.[186] Despite their upper-class backgrounds (albeit impoverished by Argentina's financial crash in 1890), the Centenary Generation's experience of being disdained as provincial outsiders by the *porteños* compounded their existing determination as professional intellectuals to differentiate themselves from the nation's elite. Lugones, for example, declared himself to be a lifelong foreigner in Buenos Aires.[187] The cumulative effect of all these factors was a shared dissent from the liberal vision of the Argentine nation, which had consistently denigrated the country's Spanish heritage, its popular traditions, and the mixed-blood masses.[188] Influenced by Rodó's *Ariel* and the Generation of 1898 in Spain, these three writers rejected the dominant intellectual matrix of liberal-positivism and offered themselves as leaders of a movement of 'spiritualization of the national consciousness'.[189] Gálvez expressed a view with which they all concurred when he wrote in the prologue to his centennial publication that their type of nationalism had nothing in common with 'the laughable speeches made at patriotic festivals nor with that national megalomania which sustains itself with the illusion of stupendous greatness'.[190]

It is therefore questionable to refer to these writers as 'traditionalists', as does David Rock,[191] because despite their basically reactionary politics and their evocation of nostalgia and tradition, they were engaged in a fundamentally modernizing endeavour. Gálvez defended himself against the charge of traditionalism in a preface to the fifth edition (1930) of *El solar de la raza* [*The Lineage of the Race*]. He insisted that he was committed to modernity, claiming that his book had a right to be considered 'highly modern . . . in its spiritual anxiety, its sense of character, its love of energy'.[192] He explicitly denied that he was advocating that Golden Age Spain should act as a model for modern Argentina: he merely wished to draw the attention of 'the Argentines – who are so materialistic' to 'some examples of spirituality'.[193] The resistance of these writers was not to modernity *per se*, but to the Argentine elite's vision of it. While Gálvez, for example, opposed the so-called 'progressive nationalism' of the liberal sector of the oligarchy, he also rejected the 'historical nationalism' of the conservatives who dreamt of restricting immigration. What he envisaged was a 'modern Argentina' based on immigration but conserving 'a reservoir of Argentine-ness'.[194] All three writers wanted to challenge Sarmiento's location of 'civilization' in the cities and 'barbarism' in the countryside. They argued that the conviction – entrenched in the minds of wealthy *porteños* – that Argentines were of pure European descent was 'a serious falsification of history' and simply 'absurd'.[195] Instead they advocated a cultural nationalism that, even if it could not be described as 'popular' in the sense of being in favour of the people,[196] did ground itself on an identification of, if not with, *lo popular*. In the terms and conventions of their times, such views could by no means be considered traditionalist.

In a series of articles written in 1906 for the Buenos Aires elite's daily newspaper, *La Nación*, Ricardo Rojas, who had been strongly influenced by Herder and his concepts of *Volk* (an authentic people) and *Volksgeist* (collective spiritual force), argued that 'the old concept of the *patria* has been replaced by . . . the concept of nationhood'.[197] He warned prosperous, *belle-époque* Argentina that the true strength of a people would henceforth depend upon its sense of nationality rather than the wealth of its territory. Argentina, he argued, needed to advance beyond the mere possession of formal political sovereignty to forge a genuine collective consciousness through 'knowledge of its geography, its history and its destiny'.[198] Rojas later explicitly identified the intellectual as his preferred vehicle for guiding the nation into a state of self-awareness. In the prologue to *Eurindia* (1924), where Rojas set out his vision of a cultural synthesis between the indigenous and the European, he represented himself in Romantic terms as the unknowing conduit of the vision of 'Eurindia': 'I know not whether this word came to my ears in the voice of the sea, or if I heard it in the wind of the night ... or if it rose up from the subconscious depths of my very soul.'[199] He then suggested that the country's current emphasis on cosmopolitanism was historically destined to be corrected in a 'nativist restoration by means of the intelligence'; the resulting new autochthonous culture for Argentina would 'be consummated in a philosophical and artistic renaissance, the proximity of which is already apparent'.[200] But, in order to represent the intellectual as the incarnation of this new national spirit, Rojas was obliged to compromise his own commitment, as an intellectual, to a rationalist approach. This tension between the idea of mediation in the weak sense (a passive channel) and the strong sense (an active intercessor) had already been indicated in an earlier work by Rojas. In his prologue to *Blasón de plata* (1912) [*Silver Shield*], Rojas had told the reader that he had not set out to write a conceptual work but one of pure emotion, which 'was formed within the core of my being'.[201]

Rojas is credited with popularizing the term *argentinidad*. The appeal of his vision lay in his representation of Argentine nationality as 'primarily spiritual rather than racial'.[202] This enabled him to reclaim the Spanish heritage of creole Argentina (provincial communities, Church and family) without welcoming the far-more-recent Spanish immigrants who were still arriving. Rojas recast the standard divide of the times between cultural nationalism and cosmopolitanism in terms of what he called 'Indianism' (meaning everything native to Argentina, including the Spanish-descended creoles) and 'exoticism' (everything imported – from liberal ideas to French novels and English tea parties). He specifically proposed the contrast of Indianism/exoticism as a nationalist alternative to Sarmiento's civilization and barbarism; and, like Sarmiento, he maintained – not very convincingly – that his binary opposition could decode the whole of Argentine history, 'even that which has not yet taken place'.[203] The ideological weight attached to the distinction was exposed when Rojas had to confront the fact that Argentina's railways and utilities were built by foreign interests (mostly the British). Indignantly denying that this was an example of 'exoticism', he represented these developments as 'a work of international solidarity', on the grounds that 'European investments ... would not have come without our guarantee of order and our support for progress'.[204] This convoluted rationale was necessary if Rojas were to retain the idea that foreign-built (and foreign-owned) utilities were part of 'our progress', but it undermined any meaningful distinction between what was native and what had been imported.

There are elements of a pluralistic Argentine identity in Rojas's work, as Fredrick Pike notes.[205] Rojas did increasingly tend to complement an ethnic conception of national identity with an invocation of civic values. He observed that 'the Argentine society that brought about our emancipation' had been made up of people of a variety of ethnic origins: peninsular

Spaniards, American Spaniards, a minority of other Europeans, Indians, blacks, *mestizos, mulattos, zambos* (who were half-Indian, half-black) and other mixtures.[206] He argued that the potential unifying forces among so much ethnic diversity, which had been aggravated during the early twentieth century by the 'new miscegenation' brought about by immigration, were 'the community of the land and the community of the ideal'.[207] The concluding paragraph of *Blasón de plata* was a call for men 'of all oppressed races and all democratic creeds' to go to Argentina and 'strengthen with your multiple voices the Argentine song' of liberty.[208]

In this context of his interest in the non-ethnic foundations of nationhood, Rojas's book *La argentinidad* (1916), which was written to celebrate the centennial of Argentina's achievement of independence, is especially telling about the difficult logic of his dissent from the liberal imagining of the Argentine nation. As the subtitle states, the book purported to identify the emergence of 'our national consciousness' during the Wars of Independence (1810–16).[209] The crucial point about this work, perhaps the key text of Argentine cultural nationalism, is that Rojas did not seek to refute liberal values as the basis for Argentina's national identity: rather, democracy and liberty were represented as the fundamental tenets of *argentinidad*.[210] Rojas identified *argentinidad* as a progressive force: 'the same one that drives us to complete our independence and bring about genuine democracy'.[211] His challenge to the early-twentieth-century Argentine elite lay in his attribution of liberal values not to the established heroes of the liberal pantheon (Moreno, Rivadavia, Deán Funes etc.), whom he dismissed as 'those who theorized from foreign doctrine', but instead to 'all the peoples of Argentina'.[212] *Argentinidad* was, therefore, represented by him as *mestiza*. Rojas made much of the fact that the *mestizo* town of Santiago del Estero was the first after Buenos Aires to declare in favour of independence, arguing that it was the 'subaltern peoples' who 'defended the manifest destiny of our nationhood'.[213] It was, he claimed, the ordinary people, 'the illiterate *gauchos* and the violent *caudillos*', who rose up against the monarchy proposed by *porteño* liberals, thereby conserving what Rojas identified as the historic mission of the Argentine people to govern themselves 'without kings, and with the *patria* open to all men . . . implementing its democracy in an ever broader embrace of justice, beauty, science and liberty'.[214] He contended that 'neither the Indian, nor the *gaucho*, nor the Spaniard, separately, embodies the whole of the national spirit'.[215] But all the imaginative force of Rojas's moves towards the idea of an Argentine identity based on common values was ultimately undermined by the underlying bicultural framework of his overall approach:

> Exoticism is necessary to our political growth; Indianism to our aesthetic culture. We want neither *gaucho* barbarism nor cosmopolitan barbarism. We want a

national culture to act as the source of a national civilization; an art that is the expression of both phenomena.

Eurindia is the name of this ambition.[216]

The main difficulty faced by the Centenary Generation in their expositions of cultural nationalism was to locate an archetype of *argentinidad*. The fact that Argentina's Indians had been exterminated need not, in theory, have been an insuperable barrier to their being resurrected as a symbol of *lo popular*. (Many Indians were massacred in Chile during the 1860s but this did not prevent subsequent intellectuals from preserving the image of them as the heroic founding fathers of the nation.)[217] But the fact was that the myth of the noble savage had never taken hold in Argentina. Whatever their own views (Rojas at least rather admired the Indians),[218] the Centenary Generation writers (who were still dependent upon the oligarchy for intellectual patronage) must have realized that they were unlikely to persuade the Argentine elite to embrace any version of *argentinidad* based on the Indian, however insecure creoles might have felt in the face of immigration.

The *gaucho* provided the perfect solution, enabling elite Argentines to distance themselves from the 'taint' of Indian blood while at the same time claiming the authenticity of the indigenous. *Gauchos* were of mixed race; in fact, many of them had Negro blood, although it is impossible to ascertain if the total was as high as the estimated one-fifth of US cowboys in the southwest who were black.[219] The *gaucho*, who in the eyes of nineteenth-century liberals had been a symbol of barbarism and backwardness, was fixed in national iconography by Rojas, Lugones and Gálvez as the incarnation of an authentically Argentine spirit. As in the case of *mestizaje* in Mexico, the ideas of these twentieth-century Argentine intellectuals were not entirely new; the equation of the *gaucho* with 'our race' can be found as early as 1870 in Lucio Mansilla's *Una excursión a los indios ranqueles*.[220] What *was* new was their identification of the *gaucho* with archetypal *argentinidad*. Conveniently for the purposes of the nationalists, *gaucho* poetry spanned the history of the Argentine nation, dating back to the Montevideo-born Bartolomé Hidalgo (1788–1822) during the Wars of Independence. The main focus of attention for the cultural nationalists was José Hernández's epic narrative poem about *gaucho* life, *Martín Fierro* (1872) and its sequel, *Vuelta de Martín Fierro* (1879), which were anointed as the fundamental works of Argentine literature in Gálvez's centennial publication *Diario de Quiroga* (1910) and Rojas's pioneering *Historia de la literatura argentina* (1917–22).[221] Above all, in 1913, *Martín Fierro*, which was highly popular in rural areas but had hitherto been ignored in Buenos Aires, was brusquely forced upon the attention of the *porteño* elite by Leopoldo Lugones in a series of public lectures.

Lugones's lectures, attended by the President, Dr Roque Sáenz Peña, were 'among the highlights of the Buenos Aires 1913 social season',[222] and were immediately reprinted in *La Nación* and soon published in book form as *El payador*. In the prologue, Lugones attacked those same 'smartly turned out university men . . . who branded me as uncouth' for their inability to appreciate 'the difference between the virile *gaucho*, roaming the *pampa* with no master, and the wretched riff-raff of the city'.[223] Lugones's attitude towards his audience betrayed the insecure outsider's mixture of contempt and simultaneous longing for approval: in this respect, it was not insignificant that he was an autodidact. Daring the critical establishment to reject his assessment of *Martín Fierro* as the national epic, he alleged that 'those who count syllables and welcome clichés' lacked the understanding to appreciate 'that creativity which is torn from the living entrails of the language . . . that freedom of the great horseman of the *pampas*'.[224] It was the barely literate rural people, argued Lugones, who had first recognized the national genius of José Hernández. The governing elite of a country 'where the cultured people do not buy books by national authors' was too corrupted by commercial and utilitarian values, Lugones maintained, to acknowledge *Martín Fierro* as the founding epic of Argentine literature.[225] But, he concluded, obliging his elite audience to identify themselves both with the culture of the *gauchos* and with Lugones himself as one of the 'cultured', 'when our *gauchos* rejoice in the poem that also delights we cultured people, it is because both we and they can envisage a real *gaucho* who thinks and says beautiful, interesting, picturesque and exact things'.[226] Lugones's conception of his own role as a go-between in the creation of national identity was unequivocally stated at the close of his final address: 'I congratulate myself on having been the agent of an intimate national communication between the poetry of the people and the cultivated minds of the upper class; for it will be thus that the national spirit is formed.'[227]

In a deft rhetorical manoeuvre that made it virtually impossible for the *porteño* elite to reject his *gaucho* version of *argentinidad*, Lugones inserted the leading lights of the liberal pantheon of heroes, Mitre and Sarmiento, into the tradition of *gauchismo*. Completely undercutting Sarmiento's celebrated distinction between the 'civilization' of liberal Buenos Aires and the 'barbarism' of the *caudillo*-led pampas, Lugones mischievously lauded Sarmiento for combining qualities he himself had declared incompatible. At the same time as being 'masters in *gaucho* arts', Lugones declared, Mitre and Sarmiento were at the same time fluent in 'the English of the federalists and the French of Lamartine'. By his order of words, Lugones managed to imply that their acquaintance with the *gaucho* way of life was by far the most significant accomplishment of these two founding fathers of the Argentine nation. Their political and social distinctions were presented as being of altogether lesser importance: 'leaders of *gauchos* on the *pampas*, they were at the same time government statesmen and landed gentlemen'. 'Thus', Lugones reminded his audience, 'in his youth, Mitre used to break in colts; Sarmiento was a mine-worker.'[228] Manuel Gálvez went even further, provocatively arguing, in support of his contention that Sarmiento had been 'the most Argentine of all', that Sarmiento 'bore all the marks of the barbarism of his times', that he 'adored barbarism', and that 'were it not for his cultural talents he would have been a *caudillo*'.[229]

Lugones's casting of Argentine national identity in a bi-culturalist mould can be seen as particularly ironic in the context of his view, expressed in a private conversation with Alfonso Reyes in 1913, that Argentina, along with the United States and Australia, had been founded on a different basis from the nations of Europe. Reyes quotes him as saying:

> You Mexicans, are almost like the Europeans; you have traditions, you have historical accounts to settle, you can *jouer à l'autochtone* with your Indians, and you retard your progress by trying to reconcile your differences of race and caste. You are peoples who look back. We look to the future: the United States, Australia and Argentina, the nations without history, we are the peoples of tomorrow.[230]

And yet it was Lugones who, along with Gálvez and Rojas, was primarily responsible for inciting Argentina to '*jouer à l'autochtone*' with the *gaucho*.

The legacy of the Centenary Generation was mixed. These writers imagined a national identity based on a bi-culturalist depiction of *argentinidad* at a time when vast numbers of its potential citizens were immigrants who sought to retain their diverse cultural identities. What was particularly marked about the way that they formulated Argentine national identity was their avoidance of any concept of pluralism. In an immigrant society, intellectuals proposed an antimony of indigenous (that is, Argentine) versus foreign (that is, European or North American). A degree of past miscegenation during the early colonial period, the descendants of which – the *gauchos* – had been marginalized in the nineteenth century, was accepted and even celebrated in order to ignore the contemporaneous racial and cultural mixing brought about by immigration. Even so, accounts that identify these early-twentieth-century Argentine intellectuals as ideologues of the Argentine elite and argue that their cultural nationalism was used by that elite 'to justify its continued dominance' are not wholly convincing.[231] In the short term, perhaps, the cultural nationalists' evocation of a *gaucho* past enabled the oligarchy to maintain hegemony by disguising it under a veneer of populism. But, in the longer term, their celebration of *lo popular*, even if only at the rhetorical level, was to undermine the liberal concept of nation. The political consequences were seen first when the leader of the Radical Civic Union (UCR), Hipólito Yrigoyen, adopted some of these ideas, blended with Krausist conceptions of an 'organic' nation with the state as arbiter between competing interests.[232] Yrigoyen described the UCR as a 'movement of national opinion' and went so far as to claim: 'In the truth of our ideals and the virtue of our sentiments we are the *patria* itself.'[233] In government, the Radicals not only identified with native folk traditions (including those of the Indians) but also established a 'Day of the Race' on the anniversary of Columbus's discovery, in order to celebrate the nation's historic link with Spain.[234] Later, Eva Perón heralded the *descamisado* as the reincarnation of the *gaucho*.[235] Indeed, subsequent versions of Argentine nationalism were all constrained by the rigid dichotomy of indigenous versus European, which bore so little relation to the nation's historical experience.

Conclusion

Bi-culturalism – the inscription of national identity in terms of a hybrid cultural formation – encouraged intellectuals to gloss over all other sources of division such as class, region or history. Intellectuals helped to sustain the dualism of indigenous/European, and its correlate backward/modern, both of which obscured the complexity of the changes brought about by Spanish America's process of modernization. The cultural rediscovery of oppressed groups by intellectuals followed on from, or went in tandem with, the calculated destruction of their political power by modernizing states. Across the region, an unsought recognition of the past cultural achievements of these social groups was bestowed in a forced exchange for their relinquishment of existing customs and practices. The Aztec empire could be represented in murals and manifestos alike as the glorious ancestry of the modern Mexican nation, but its descendants were perceived as impediments to economic development. In Chile, only a few Mapuche survived the 'pacification' programmes of the 1860s to 1890s to become living reminders of the proud Araucanian warrior of that country's semi-invented past. By the time that black culture had begun to be celebrated by Cuban intellectuals in the 1930s, Afro-Cubans 'had lost much of their strength and political power', not least after the crushing of the black uprising in 1912.[236] Likewise, the *gaucho* could be rehabilitated as the incarnation of the proud, noble and free Argentine spirit, but in historical reality he was hounded off the *pampa* by land-hungry developers in the late nineteenth century. The marginalizing of these groups served to enhance – indeed, was arguably a prerequisite for – their symbolic value in differentiating post-colonial national identities. Lugones's conclusions about the *gaucho* are revealing:

> His disappearance is a good thing for the country, because he contained an inferior element in the indigenous part of his blood; but his definition as a national type accentuated irrevocably, that is to say, ethnically and socially, our

separation from Spain and the constitution of our own distinct personality. Hence the Argentine, despite being of the same physical type and speaking the same language, is completely different from the Spaniard.[237]

This casting of the debates in cultural terms meant that the possibility of change was always sustained, albeit indefinitely postponed; the implicit racialization of the divide meant that it, and by analogy all other divides, took on an aura of immutability – resolvable at the rhetorical level (by intellectuals) but not in reality. It was no coincidence that Rodó, the first Spanish American to elaborate a modern role for the intellectual, was also the first major thinker to move from 'scientific racism' to a 'historical conception of race'.[238] This shift in perspective enabled intellectuals to fix the images of Spanish American identity in historical stereotypes that permanently needed their explication and mediation. In misrepresenting 'the people', intellectuals made it all the more difficult for any popular voices to be heard. Moreover, the paucity of intellectual debate and criticism left the way open for states to impose unchallenged their own repressive versions of national identity. By the 1960s, it had become a commonplace that the only unities possible for Spanish American nations were either mythical or military.

From *Ariel* to 'Caliban':
Anti-imperialism among Spanish
American Intellectuals

'Gentlemen, I have to be anti-imperialist out of sheer pride.'

Carlos Monsiváis[1]

The preoccupation with anti-imperialism caricatured by Carlos Monsiváis was particularly intense during the three decades following the Spanish-American War of 1898, which saw a proliferation of anti-imperialist tracts by Spanish American writers, most of whom advocated a degree of Hispanic-American union, or at least co-operation, as the best defence against US expansionism. Of course, neither of these themes was new. The Monroe Doctrine (1823) had signalled that the United States intended to seek some kind of influence over their 'southern brethren', but was vague about both its nature and its extent.[2] Throughout the nineteenth century Spanish American voices – albeit relatively isolated ones – were raised in warning against the as yet unclear ambitions of the United States. The idea of Spanish American union had an equally long pedigree, originating with Bolívar and the failed Congress of Panama (1826), and resurrected at intervals when the weakness of Spanish American countries was sensed to be particularly acute. The leading mid-nineteenth-century example was Juan Bautista Alberdi's project for an 'American league'.[3] Concern about Spanish America's cultural autonomy also dated back to Bello, Sarmiento and Alberdi, who had all made declarations of intellectual independence similar to Ralph Waldo Emerson's for the United States.[4] But these had in no way implied either a hostility towards other cultures or a sense of their own inferiority; in fact, quite the reverse, in that each of these thinkers had confidently envisaged a great future for Spanish America in terms of cultural achievement. Some liberal *pensadores* may have perceived a potential threat from the United States, but by far their main emphasis was on identifying features of its model of development that the Spanish American nations could usefully emulate, just as they were trying to follow in the footsteps of England and/or France. For example, Francisco Bilbao criticized the US leaders for believing themselves to be 'the arbiters of the earth', but the main thrust of his argument was overwhelmingly favourable to the United States, which he eulogized as 'the luminary of the world', the modern equivalent of ancient Greece.[5] Bilbao represented the United States as 'the creative nation', and claimed that it had 'the most original of modern literatures', the 'best historians' and the 'best philosophers' – an image that contrasts starkly with the prevailing twentieth-century Spanish American view of the United States as materialistic and uncultured.[6] Whereas for many leading *pensadores*, the best way to advance the cause of the *patria* had been to introduce a degree of cosmopolitanism, it became increasingly difficult for any twentieth-century Spanish American intellectual to advocate imitation of 'the West', or indeed, to approach a discussion of the United States from any position other than one of denunciation. In seeking to explain these changes in perspective, the starting point, as with so many other debates in twentieth-century Spanish American cultural history, is José Enrique Rodó's essay *Ariel* (1900).

The *Arielista* Response to Imperialism

Rodó has often been criticized for his allegedly simplistic reduction of US imperialism to a cultural phenomenon of materialism and utilitarianism.[7] Rodó himself publicly refuted this interpretation on several occasions, claiming that what he had been trying to do was 'to expound the need to maintain an ideal in their lives which could prevent all the different peoples, but especially those of the Americas, from becoming materialistic and embracing the corrupting influence of mercantilism'.[8] The main argument of his essay, Rodó contended, was that Spanish America needed to conquer the materialism within itself in order to realize its potential greatness. In *Ariel*, he stated specifically that he did not wish to reject the US model altogether, merely to caution Spanish Americans against embracing '*nordo-manía*' (mania for all things northern) to the extent that their own identity which, according to Rodó, was *Latin*, became obliterated.[9] He saw the United States as a model of industry, but not of civilization.[10] Nowhere in the text did he explicitly make the link between the United States and Caliban which 'was ascribed more and more widely to [his] essay'.[11] (Carlos Fuentes has recalled 'oratorical contests' during the 1940s and 1950s in which Rodó was usually quoted as the 'blithe Latin American fighting off brutish North American Caliban'.)[12] However, both Caliban and the United

States were identified in the text with utilitarianism, and it is hard to rescue Rodó from the charge of propagating stereotypes in the light of his assertions that 'the United States can be thought of as the embodiment of the word utilitarian',[13] that the descendants of the puritans were indifferent to the ideals of truth and beauty, and that the US education system had produced a nation of 'widespread semi-culture and a high culture marked by profound torpor'.[14] Indeed, Rodó reinforced stereotypes not only of the United States but also, by implication, of Spanish America.

Most important, Rodó couched his defence against imperialism in cultural terms. In allegorical form, he argued that Latin America's striving for culture, 'this new sense of intellectual dignity', would enable the region to overcome its troubled past: 'the hour is already nigh when the poet's heroic child will no longer gesticulate wildly to the passer-by in quest of "gunpowder and bullets"; instead, he will smilingly accept, straight out of his hands, a delicate flower and a melodious songbird, symbols of beauty and gentleness'.[15] Oscar Terán has suggested that Rodó revived the classical opposition betwen *ocio* (a state of serene contemplation to be cultivated within the sacred realm of each man's interior world) and *negocio* (business) in order to liberate culture from economics.[16] Indeed, Rodó's emphasis on spiritual and intellectual distance should be understood partly in the context of his desire to establish culture as a distinct field of activity. *Arielismo*'s preoccupation with racial and cultural values also has to be set in the context of the then-dominant European intellectual trend ascribing superiority to the Anglo-Saxons: Gustave Le Bon, for example, in *The Psychology of Socialism*,[17] had claimed that the best hope for Spanish America lay in conquest by the United States. Rodó's aim was to challenge a hierarchy of race in which the peoples of Spanish America were not highly placed. The consequence for anti-imperialist thought, however, was an emphasis on a cultural threat – and, correspondingly, a cultural response – over an economic threat.

Rodó, who called in Part II of *Ariel* for the individual intellectual to maintain universal values in an age of increasing material specialization, correspondingly argued in Part V that societies, too, needed to nurture '*inner* independence – of personality and of judgement – [which] is one of the most valuable forms of self-respect'.[18] The process of acquiring such independence, he argued, involved developing the capacity to discriminate between what was useful and what was not in any particular foreign idea.[19] What Spanish America lacked, above all, was 'critical awareness'.[20] Cosmopolitanism, for Rodó, was a 'necessary condition of [Spanish America's] growth'.[21]

Rodó's according of priority to culture inescapably led him to deny the value of nation-states in the Spanish American context, since the only plausible way to invoke common cultural values at that time was on a regional basis: 'I have always believed that in our America it was not possible to talk about many *patrias*, but only of one great *patria*; ... the American *patria* transcends the national *patria*.'[22] Although one Uruguayan critic has argued, as part of a spirited and often convincing defence of Rodó against the standard charges of idealism and elitism, that Rodó's Americanism evolved beyond the cultural into a political strategy in his advocacy of Spanish American union,[23] there is little evidence to substantiate this view. The basis of Rodó's *hispanoamericanismo* was cultural: 'Neither Sarmiento, nor Bilbao, nor Martí, nor Bello, nor Montalvo are writers from any one particular part of America: they are all citizens of an American republic of letters.'[24] It also had a racial dimension, albeit imprecisely formulated: 'we, the Latin Americans, have a racial inheritance, a great ethnic tradition to maintain, a sacred link which binds us to immortal pages in history'.[25] Nowhere did he analyse the opportunities or the difficulties involved in forging Hispanic American union: he offered a vision, not a blueprint. Indeed, it could be argued that by virtually equating intellectual and political union, Rodó reduced the scope for realistic debate about the latter.

The intellectuals' initial casting of the debate about imperialism in cultural (rather than political or economic) terms led to the creation of Spanish American nationalisms that were based on a sense of inferiority, on the idea that Spanish American experience was best represented as in some fundamental way *lacking*, and that dependency was therefore an inevitability. In a discussion of Russian nationalism, Liah Greenfeld refers to this kind of negative national self-image and its consequences as *ressentiment*, by which she means a 'rejection of the West based on envy and the realization of the all-too-evident, and therefore unbearable, inferiority'.[26] Greenfeld identifies three nineteenth-century Russian reactions to *ressentiment*, all of which found parallels in early-twentieth-century Spanish America. The first was a continued advocacy of imitation; the second was shame; and the third, by far the most common, was denial. For those who chose the route of denial, the next stage was to present equality as undesirable, to damn the West as an inappropriate model and to attack those of their compatriots who persisted in admiring Western culture. All three responses, even the latter, ultimately retained the idea of the West as the touchstone of self-definition.

In twentieth-century Spanish America, an important minority continued to advocate cosmopolitanism and universalism, arguing that genuine intellectualism was incompatible with nationalism. The more simplistic and snobbish in this category merely trumpeted their right to read the European classics in preference to the literature of their own countries; the more thoughtful of them suggested that Spanish American countries could achieve self-understanding only through an appreciation of universal culture. Alfonso Reyes, for example, argued, 'The only way to be profitably national is to be hospitably universal, for the part was never understood without the whole.'[27] The response of shame can be found in the writings of some of the racial pessimists,[28] but had largely died out, along with the influence of social Darwinism in Spanish America, by the 1930s. As in Russia, the dominant Spanish American reaction to an emerging sense of inferiority was a denial of the superiority of Western culture and a corresponding assertion of allegedly autochthonous virtues. *Arielismo*, with its ambivalence towards Reason, was comparable to the Russian nationalists' rejection of rationality in preference for 'life so full of feeling that one could choke on it, the inexpressible, the unlimited, the hyperbolic'[29] – in short, the great Russian soul. In Spanish America, however, although there were isolated attempts to reassert the value of natural man (for example, in early Martí),[30] the dominant stream of thought did not so much deny the superiority of European culture as lay claim to being the true repository of it. Spanish American intellectuals, themselves mostly of European ancestry, did not wish wholly to reject Western models, because, by implication, they would have also been relinquishing any claim to be judged – potentially favourably – on the Western terms upon which their national project was based. In order to avoid the traps of cultural relativism, therefore, early-twentieth-century Spanish American intellectuals called on the classical heritage, representing *Latin* America as an alternative expression of the Western tradition, a reservoir of the Renaissance virtues of rhetorical and poetic skill, and the world's crucible of aestheticism. This idea that Latin America had special qualities that made it superior to the West was only the reverse side of the coin of the idea that it was deficient in comparison.

Rodó offers a perfect example of the first two stages of *ressentiment*, moving from an apprehension of inferiority ('A definite outline of a "personality" is lacking, it seems, in our collective character') to an assertion of unspecified racial and cultural superiority: the 'great ethnic tradition'.[31] However, Rodó did not proceed to condemn the United States and Western Europe outright and take refuge in a defensive nationalism, as had happened in nineteenth-century Russia. Where he differed from the Russian nationalists was in his insistence that cosmopolitanism need not impede Spanish America's realization of its historic cultural mission. The *arielista* model sought to transcend nationalism and promote one kind of foreign influence (European) over another (US). Thus, the link between anti-imperialism and national sovereignty, which had been insisted upon by Martí, was broken.

If Rodó baulked at the third stage of *ressentiment*, trying to avoid a crude anti-Americanism, many of his followers were less subtle in their approach. In the wake of *Ariel*, to be an intellectual was to be anti-imperialist; and to be anti-imperialist was to be anti-American. Spanish American anti-imperialism developed on the basis of the *arielista* claim that, if Spanish America could not be economically equal to the United States, it might at least be spiritually superior. Darío's poem 'Salutación del optimista' (1905), heralding the dawn of the Latin race, was highly influential in crystallizing this reductionist approach to the relations between the two Americas. As early as 1896, Darío had associated the United States with Caliban, arguing that 'Caliban reigns on Manhattan island, in San Francisco, in Boston, in Washington, in the whole country'.[32] In his article responding to the Spanish-American War, 'El triunfo de Calibán' (1898), Darío characterized the men of the United States as 'buffalo with silver teeth' who did nothing but 'eat, eat, calculate, drink whiskey and make millions'.[33] The Venezuelan writer Rufino Blanco-Fombona (1874–1944) propagated the stereotypes of the United States as 'incapable of the fine arts and lacking in ideals',[34] and insisted that the struggle within the Americas was not between classes but between races.[35] The Colombian novelist José María Vargas Vila (1860–1933) wrote his anti-imperialist tract Ante los bárbaros [In the Face of the Barbarians] (1916), in the form of nearly 250 pages of sermonic blank verse. Hatred of the yankee, he intoned, 'must be our maxim,/for, since that hatred is our duty, an imperative duty,/to renounce it is to renounce life'.[36] José Vasconcelos saw the arielista response as flawed: 'If the Yankees were no more than Caliban, they would represent no great threat. What's really serious is ... that they are also wont to surpass us spiritually.'[37] Nevertheless, his analysis, too, was founded on the premiss that the clash between the United States and what he referred to as Ibero-America should be understood almost exclusively in terms of Anglo-Saxon versus Latin culture.[38] Inasmuch as it was discussed at all by these authors, actual US policy was equated with filibustering.[39] The limitations of arielismo as a framework for anti-imperialism are highlighted by the work of two other leading intellectuals who produced an alternative response to the rise of US influence in Spanish America: José Martí and Manuel Ugarte.

José Martí

Martí has both been acclaimed as a prophet of Cuba's lengthy struggle against US domination ('the most fervent, the most astute, the most steadfast of all our anti-imperialists')[40] and attacked for having sustained an idealism and romanticism that ultimately betrayed the alleged 'colonization' of his mind by European ideas.[41] Martí's analysis of Cuba's colonial relationship with Spain has been justifiably criticized for its lack of structural content, and its narrow focus on a clash of values between the two cultures.[42] There has been a tendency, especially in post-revolutionary Cuban historiography, to gloss over similar shortcomings in his analysis of US relations with Spanish America. Martí's attitude towards the nation that he famously epitomized in his last letter as 'the monster' did not constitute the complete rejection that his Marxist-Leninist admirers imputed to him.[43] Instead, it was characterized by the ambivalence that has marked the response of the majority of twentieth-century Spanish American intellectuals to their northern neighbour, an attitude 'oscillating between admiration and fear'.[44] It is also the case that some of Martí's anti-imperialist writings were highly romantic in tone, above all, his declaration of Spanish American cultural independence, 'Nuestra América' ('Our America') (1891). In this, he called for a halt to the unthinking importation of ideas:

> [America] is suffering from the pointless effort of trying to reconcile the discordant and hostile elements inherited from a despotic and perverse colonizer with the imported ideas and methods that have hindered our progress towards logical government, because of their lack of any sense of local realities. . . . No book by any European or any Yankee has yielded the key to the enigma of Spanish America.[45]

Correspondingly, he argued that the region needed its educational institutions to be geared towards its own specific requirements:

> The European university has to give way to the American university. The history of America, from the Incas onwards, has to be learnt inside out, even at the expense of remaining ignorant of the splendours of Ancient Greece. Our Greece is preferable to the Greece that is not ours. It is more necessary to us.[46]

Although Martí insisted on the importance of critical thinking ('Peoples have to make a practice of self-criticism, because to be critical is to be healthy')[47] and identified the 'new men of America' as those who read 'in order to apply, not to copy',[48] his emphasis on the need for 'our America' to create an authentic identity was easily reducible to a rejection of all foreign influences. Martí propagated the Romantic opposition between imitation and originality: 'The youth of America . . . realize that there is too much imitation, and that creation holds the key to salvation. The wine might be made from plantain, but even if it turns sour, at least it is our own wine.'[49] Many of his epigrams ('our America comes neither from Rousseau nor from Washington, but from itself')[50] ostensibly support what was to prove one of the most divisive ideas in twentieth-century Spanish American culture, namely that there could be nothing in between the authentic and the derivative, no option other than a dishonourable mimeticism or full and glorious autonomy.

Despite his vulnerability on these points, Martí sketched out a framework for anti-imperialist thought that was far more subtle than the *arielista* model which later came to dominate Spanish American intellectuals' thinking about imperialism. His formulation of anti-imperialism differed from subsequent versions, both *arielista* and Marxist, in four important respects: his commitment to analysing differences within the US policy-making establishment; his insistence that an attack on the sovereignty of one Spanish

American country should be deemed an attack upon them all; his refutation of racial stereotypes; and, finally, his elaboration of a nationalism and a regionalism that was not based on *ressentiment*, that is, which did not categorize Spanish America as inherently lacking.

Martí's experience of living and working in the United States as a journalist had given him a far more sophisticated understanding of US politics than was possible for most of his Spanish American contemporaries, and he knew full well that 'the United States' was in practice no monolith in its policy-making. He sought to publicize his view that there was by no means a consensus in the United States over imperial policies, and that one vital defence strategy for Spanish American countries lay in manoeuvring to exploit political differences within Washington.[51] In an article entitled 'The Truth about the United States' (1894), Martí opened with the argument that Spanish Americans should not purposely exaggerate the faults of the United States 'out of a desire to deny it all virtue', but 'nor should these faults be concealed or proclaimed as virtues'.[52] Martí declared that he sought to 'aid in the understanding of political reality in America, and to . . . correct with the calm force of fact the ill-advised praise (pernicious when carried to extremes) of the North American character and political life'.[53] In articles on a whole range of topics, from the Haymarket Martyrs to women's suffrage in Kansas, he did just that.[54] In this sense, Martí can be said to have acted as 'an interpreter' of the US political process not only for Cuba but also – because of the syndication of his journalism – throughout the whole of Spanish America.[55]

Just as Martí argued that US imperialism threatened all of 'our America', correspondingly he held that winning independence for Cuba and Puerto Rico was a crucial element in the struggle to block US expansion and secure the independence of all Spanish America.[56] He argued that Spanish American countries made a great mistake in looking at their relations with the United States in isolation from each other. In an article published in 1883, 'The Commercial Treaty between the United States and Mexico', he suggested that reciprocal tariff concessions between those two nations posed an economic risk to all other Spanish American countries that traded with the United States. Given that Mexico, with its comparatively broadly based economy, produced most of the goods upon which the export economies of Central and South American states relied, Martí argued, it was probable that Mexico, as the favoured recipient of US investment, concessions and infrastructural development, would capture the US market at the expense of other Spanish American countries. His particular concern was that Mexico would displace Cuba from the US sugar market, if the Louisiana sugar producers successfully opposed Cuban imports but failed to block sugar supplies from Mexico because of the growing number of significant US interest groups that would benefit from free trade with Mexico. In a conclusion that would still be applicable over a century later, in the context of the North American Free Trade Agreement (NAFTA), Martí warned that although it was possible that the United States would conclude similar trading agreements with other Spanish American countries, this could not be said to be a probable scenario.[57]

Martí wrote extensively about the economic aspects of imperialism, at a time when such issues were not routinely analysed. His article on the first Pan-American Congress, an event instigated by US Secretary of State James Blaine and held in Washington in 1889–90, concentrated on the economic imperative behind Blaine's invitation. The US government, 'glutted with unsaleable merchandise', was trying to find a way to secure South American markets for US industrialists while protecting US mining and agricultural interests from South American imports, Martí claimed.[58] In 1891, he stated unequivocally his view that economic dependence would inevitably result in political dependence: 'Anyone who says economic union is saying political union. The nation that buys, commands.'[59] This connection may seem commonplace nowadays, but in making it Martí was going against the grain of much contemporaneous thinking in Spanish America, which saw no necessary relation between close economic links with a developed power and any threat to political sovereignty. Despite his emphasis on economics, Martí also cast the major threat from the United States in terms of cultural misunderstanding: 'The scorn of our formidable neighbour, which has no knowledge of us, is the greatest danger to our America.'[60] In that sense, it could be argued that Martí prefigured the *arielista* emphasis on the cultural components of imperialism, except that his conclusions were political. In one of several articles arguing against Pan-Americanism, he noted that US policy-makers believed in the superiority of Anglo-Saxons over Latins, in the inferiority of Indians and blacks, and in the idea that Spanish American peoples were mostly made up of Indians and blacks. Until such misconceptions had been countered and the United States had learned to hold Spanish Americans in higher esteem, he concluded, it was hardly likely that Spanish America would have anything to gain from economic and political union with the United States.[61] Furthermore, Martí neither accepted negative US evaluations of Spanish American culture, as did the racial pessimists, nor attempted to invert social Darwinist stereotypes, as did the *arielistas*. Indeed, exceptionally for his era, Martí denied the validity of race as a category, which he saw as an invention of 'sickly *pensadores*' who 'breathe new life into the races found within the covers of books, which any fair-minded traveller or well-disposed observer will seek in vain in the justice of nature, where the universal identity of man stands out in victorious love and turbulent desire'.[62] His view was that: 'There are no races; there are only the various modifications of man in details of form and habits, according to the conditions of climate and history in which he lives. . . . Both Latins and

Saxons are equally capable of having virtues and defects; what does vary is the peculiar outcome of different historical groups.'[63] In his opinion, it was only '[s]uperficial men who have not explored human problems very thoroughly' who were 'prone to amuse themselves by finding substantial variety between the egotistical Saxon and the egotistical Latin, the generous Saxon and the generous Latin, the Saxon bureaucrat and the Latin bureaucrat'.[64] Instead, he devoted considerable energy to denying the validity of any such stereotypes about Cubans or Spanish Americans in general. Responding to an article in the US press that had reproduced all the clichés associated with the Black Legend of the Spanish as lazy, greedy, superstitious and brutal, Martí wrote a letter to the editor of the New York *Evening Post* rejecting the image of Cubans as a people of 'wretched vagabonds or immoral pygmies . . . useless, verbose people, incapable of action, enemies of hard work'.[65] Far from being an 'effeminate' people, as alleged in the US article, Martí argued, Cubans had fought like men, indeed sometimes like giants, in order to liberate themselves from tyranny, and they deserved the respect of those (namely, the United States) who had refused a request for aid in that struggle (a reference to the US refusal to back Cuban independence fighters during the first war of 1868–78).[66] Cubans were as well prepared as the people of the United States to be citizens of their own nation-state, insisted Martí, even in terms of their respect for private property:

> The average Cuban's knowledge does not compare disadvantageously with that of the average US citizen. The complete absence of religious intolerance, the Cuban's love for the property acquired by his own labour, and his familiarity in both theory and practice with the laws and procedures of liberty, prepare the Cuban well to rebuild his own country on the ruins in which he will receive it from his oppressors.[67]

Martí repeatedly maintained that the political instability of nineteenth-century Spanish America was not, as often alleged, an indication of the region's incapacity for progress, but indeed of precisely the opposite: 'the same wars for which out of pure ignorance those who do not know [our America] reproach us, are our peoples' mark of honour, for they prove that our peoples have not hesitated to expedite the path of progress with the spilling of their blood'.[68] Far from the nineteenth-century history of Spanish America being a failure, he argued, it was quite the reverse: 'Never in history have such advanced and compact nations been created in such a short space of time.'[69] Indeed, in comparison to its northern neighbour, Martí suggested, Spanish America had done a lot more to realize its potential from far less auspicious beginnings:

> . . . the North American character has gone downhill since the winning of independence, and is today less human and virile; whereas the Spanish American character today is in all ways superior, in spite of its confusion and fatigue, to

what it was when it began to emerge from the disorganized mass of grasping clergy, [inappropriate] ideology, and ignorant or savage Indians.[70]

Martí was clear-sighted about the turbulence of Spanish America's past, but he attributed the region's problems to neither of the customary scapegoats, namely the colonial legacy or the racial divide, arguing instead that most of the difficulties stemmed from misguided attempts to adjust Spanish American realities to foreign models.[71] There was nothing intrinsically amiss in Spanish America, in his view. Indeed, like many of his forebears, he saw a bright future for the region if it could only overcome a misplaced sense of inferiority: 'Oh, on the day when the Hispanic American mind commences to shine, it will shine like the sun – the day when we consider our present provincial existence as dead.'[72] Neither did Martí fall into the opposite trap of insisting that Spanish America was innately superior to the United States: according to him, the two regions were simply different. In that context, as far as Martí was concerned, it was only natural that a Spanish American should celebrate the grandeur of his own part of the Americas, however much he, as a man of liberty, might be prepared to concede greatness to the United States. Speaking in New York of 'Mother America', he put it thus: 'however great this land may be, and however anointed in the eyes of the free men of America may be the land in which Lincoln was born, for us . . . the America in which Juárez was born is greater, because it is ours and because it has been less fortunate'. Spanish America should be esteemed for its merits, and honoured for its sacrifices, he argued.[73] The defensiveness of *ressentiment* held no attractions for Martí.

Manuel Ugarte

The works of the Argentine Manuel Ugarte (1878–1951) demonstrate that a more political response to the rise of US imperialism continued to present a possible alternative to *arielismo*'s emphasis on culture.[74] Ugarte was born into a privileged *porteño* family, began to frequent café society as a young man, and became one of the most prolific writers of his generation. Identified as one of the *modernista* Generation of 1900, Ugarte's considered reaction to his contemporaries' growing preoccupation with *lo nacional* turned out to be quite different from their promotion of cultural nationalism.[75] His anxiety about the intentions of the United States towards Spanish America was first awakened during a visit of several months to the USA in 1899. In Ugarte's first anti-imperialist article, 'El peligro yanqui' (1901), the influence of *arielismo* can be detected: 'Even the most elevated minds that do not attach any great importance to national borders . . . must incline towards combating the growing influence of Saxon America in Latin

America.'[76] *Arielista* stereotypes were to linger on into later works: for example, in 1910, he contrasted 'cold North America' to 'the warm America of Spanish origin, Italian influence and French culture'.[77] But Ugarte made his position political from the outset, arguing that 'to stand by indifferently', while the region's culture was 'supplanted by US influences would be to take a step backwards in our slow march towards the progressive emancipation of mankind'.[78] Already influenced by the French reformist socialist Jean Jaurès (1859–1914), Ugarte claimed that the kind of society to be fought against had achieved its maximum realization in the United States. US influence, he said, should therefore be resisted because 'Along with the industrial feudalism that submits a whole province to the will of one man, prejudice against inferior races would also be exported to us. . . . The great empires represent a negation of liberty.'[79]

Ugarte embarked on a two-year tour of the region (October 1911–July 1913), specifically in order to alert Latin American public opinion to the imperialist threat. He declined to curtail this trip early in 1913, despite having received an invitation from the Argentine Socialist Party (PSA) to stand as a senatorial candidate, in the conviction that his influence as an intellectual would outweigh any he might wield as a politician.[80] Ugarte later reflected: 'I have never sought public office. . . . My mind's tendency was never to discipline, but rather to dissidence, founded on sincerity.'[81] The main theme of his speeches was that the threat posed by the United States was only as great as Latin Americans allowed it to be; he emphasized their failure to resist US expansionism thus far, and argued that 'our ills were the work less of the greed of foreigners, than of our own incapacity for struggle'.[82] His view was that the United States, in its imperialist expansion, was only obeying the same laws of self-preservation underlying the territorial ambitions of the Romans, the Spanish under Charles V and the French under Napoleon, but 'we, by ignoring the threat, by failing to reach any agreement to meet it, showed signs of an inferiority that in the eyes of authoritarians and determinists was tantamount to justifying the assault upon us'.[83] He expressed bafflement that Latin American leaders had not protested against the US annexation of Mexican territory (1846–48) or the Platt Amendment (1901), and lamented that President Theodore Roosevelt's ominous words, 'We have begun to take possession of the continent' had been met with an equally ominous silence in Latin America.[84] Like those whose nationalism was founded on *ressentiment*, Ugarte represented Latin Americans as 'lacking', but his distinctiveness lay in his identification of the lack as political (and therefore open to relatively fast remedy) rather than cultural (and, by implication, modifiable only in the longer term by means of education) or racial (innate and unchangeable). Like Martí and Rodó, he saw Latin America's weakness as stemming from its division into republics:

What could have been a great Latin force capable of intervening effectively in international debates, defending the interests and the worldview of a solidly united group, was reduced to a painful clamouring of weak bodies which either fought among themselves or exhausted their energies in pointless revolutions, lacking the material or the moral strength to be worthy . . . of the respect of great nations.[85]

In contrast to many of his contemporaries, who confined themselves to generalized denunciations of the United States – and particularly its culture, or alleged lack thereof – Ugarte cited examples of US policies towards Latin America to substantiate his arguments. Had Latin Americans forgotten, he demanded, the incident of the battleship USS *Wilmington* exploring the Amazon in 1899, the US attempt to control territory disputed by Peru and Bolivia, its 'support' for Panama's secession from Colombia in 1903 (a prerequisite for building the Panama Canal), or its aid to opponents of the Venezuelan leader Cipriano Castro merely because he was deemed unreliable by Washington?[86]

Ugarte specifically rejected the prevalent *arielista* stereotypes of the materially successful United States offset by a spiritually superior Latin America, arguing that Latin America's alleged advancement in that respect was far from proven: 'The United States, apparently so "money-minded and profit-oriented", or so we are commonly told, has made universally famous the names of Walt Whitman, Whistler, William James, Edison, and a hundred others. . . . More's the pity that we cannot begin to say the same.'[87] He repeatedly insisted that Latin America had 'everything to learn' from the United States and, moreover, was in need of US economic and technical assistance.[88] Indeed, the illusion of spiritual superiority was 'as childish as it was pernicious', he argued, and itself the greatest obstacle to Latin America's realizing of its true potential.[89] In his opinion, if Latin Americans were to constrain themselves by these stereotypes, they would be condemning themselves to a lack of material progress whereas, he contended, Latin American countries would be better advised to emulate the example of the Japanese who, when obliged to open up to Western culture in the mid-nineteenth century, adapted those ideas they found useful and began to compete commercially.[90] He stated: 'This example, of which we can never sufficiently remind ourselves, can inspire us to ready ourselves in all different spheres to take the levers of the country's life into our own hands.'[91] Instead of asserting cultural superiority, he maintained, Latin Americans should try to ensure that their relationship with Washington was founded on principles of mutual respect. Thirty years before Robinson and Gallagher first raised the issue of the importance of collaborative local elites in the consolidation of imperialist power,[92] Ugarte wrote:

If the United States has not shown us more respect, it has perhaps been because of the obsequiousness with which we have always bowed down before them, and also because of the selfishness with which we have postponed the advantages of union in favour of the short-term interests of one man, one oligarchy or one particular region.[93]

At a time when the understanding of imperialism was in its earliest stages worldwide, and when Spanish American intellectuals more often than not reduced anti-imperialism to anti-Yankeeism, Ugarte's work explored the wide-ranging effects of US imperialism on politics, economics and culture in Spanish America. Whereas most anti-imperialist intellectuals of the time concentrated on the more direct manifestations of imperial power exemplified by US military interventionism in the Caribbean and Central America, Ugarte was concerned to alert South Americans to the latent threat posed to them as well. Just because territorial conquest of those more southerly countries was militarily impossible, he emphasized, they should not consider themselves immune to the dangers of US imperialism, which he defined as 'a perennial claim to moral superiority, progressive economic infiltration, a claim to protect our independence which has proved useless in practice, dissemination of the English language and the parading of their leadership of the hemisphere before the Europeans'.[94] He argued that US political influence in South America was already disproportionate to its commercial importance to the region (which, he estimated, was far less than Europe's, with South American countries importing only about one-eighth of their goods from the United States before the First World War).[95] From this, he inferred that the United States wanted to create dependency throughout the region.[96] Ugarte warned that the idea – promoted by US advocates of Pan-Americanism and commonly accepted among Spanish American elites – that the United States was the guardian of Latin American liberty against the European threat was a dangerous self-delusion, resulting in self-denigration and a sense of inferiority.[97]

Ugarte was well aware of the importance of economic factors in imperialism, as *El porvenir de la América Latina* (1911) made clear. He noted that imperialism had changed in character, with commercial conquest overtaking military control,[98] and, unlike most of his contemporaries, he tried to counteract the prevailing sense that US expansionism was an inevitable and irresistible force. Ugarte pointed out that, a century after independence, most of South America's trade was still with Europe; like Martí, he emphasized the importance of preserving commercial neutrality as a 'guarantee of independence'.[99] To stave off the advance of US trade and capital, he advocated nationalization of public services, mines and insurance companies. To undermine the US project of Pan-American union, Ugarte urged Spanish American nations to strengthen their connections with Europe and promote a greater degree of unity among themselves.[100] He anticipated that regional integration was likely to be a protracted process, but insisted that

gradual steps – including congresses, diplomatic envoys, commercial trea-
ties, communications agreements and arbitration bodies – would have a
cumulative effect.[101] A good starting point, he suggested, would be if
national newspapers were to devote less space to events in Paris and London
and more to what was happening in other parts of their own region.[102] He
concluded that it was wilfully obstinate of Spanish Americans to remain
disunited in the face of the US threat.[103] As a parting shot, anyone inclined
to dismiss the idea of Spanish American union as merely the 'dreams of a
poet' was admonished to remember that 'hitherto, poets have in reality
done much more for union than the authorities have'.[104] This book had
great impact throughout Spanish America, where many intellectuals formed
committees to work for regional integration, albeit to little tangible effect.

Ugarte's life was particularly revealing about the cultural context in
which Spanish American anti-imperialist thought developed. His career
illustrated just how difficult it was for an early-twentieth-century Spanish
American intellectual to reconcile the contradictions between cosmopolitanism and nationalism. Despite (or perhaps because of) the fact that Ugarte
was known throughout the region, and was probably the most renowned
Spanish American writer of his generation in Europe,[105] no Argentine
publisher would accept any of his works on anti-imperialism until after his
death in 1951. His advocacy of Argentine neutrality in the First World War,
which was based on a refusal to accept the 'civilizing' pretensions of
imperialism, led to his being reviled in his own country as an enemy of
progress. After going into a long exile from Argentina in 1919, he initially
managed to earn a living from journalism and royalties from Spain, but
experienced severe financial hardship during the 1930s. Moreover, the
Argentine government refused to award him the national prize for literature
on the grounds that his work had all been published outside Argentina,
despite lobbying on his behalf by luminaries such as Gabriela Mistral, José
Vasconcelos, Rufino Blanco-Fombona and Francisco García Calderón.[106]
For political reasons, literary recognition in his native land was denied to
Ugarte during his lifetime.

Ugarte's involvement in politics was fraught with frustration in its own
right, quite apart from the problems it caused him in his professional life.
On returning to Buenos Aires from his journey around the continent in
1903, Ugarte had joined the Argentine Socialist Party (PSA). The distinguishing feature of Ugarte's commitment to socialism was that he consistently argued that, in Latin America at least, reformist socialism was
compatible with nationalism. Even when he later came to believe (during
the First World War) that nationalism in developed Europe was a retrogres-
sive force, he maintained that in underdeveloped Latin America 'There is
no incompatibility between socialism and *patria*.'[107] He saw nationalism as
only a stage in the development of the human spirit, which would ultimately

free itself from 'regional selfishness'. In the meantime, however, a sense of nationality was 'an indispensable condition of man's integral development'.[108] Indeed, nationalism was necessary in order to combat imperialism: 'The most urgent task is to establish lasting agreements among the parties within the nation and among the threatened nations of America, in order to stop facilitating the onrush of the Yankees.'[109] On becoming a member of the PSA, Ugarte immediately launched a campaign to wean the party off its enthusiasm for internationalism and its disdain for Latin American cultures. In 1903, he was also involved, along with José Ingenieros, in drawing up a labour code for the Roca government. For this, he was disparaged as a bourgeois collaborationist by the PSA, which then tried to defuse this dispute with one of its best-known members by deputing him to attend the forthcoming congress of the Socialist (Second) International in Amsterdam. Within only six months of arriving back in Argentina, Ugarte found himself setting sail for Europe.[110] His dispute with the PSA was to continue for most of the rest of his life, largely founded on his belief that the socialism espoused by Juan B. Justo and his supporters had 'little to do with Argentina'.[111]

Ugarte was not entirely alone among Argentine socialists in his views about the relationship between socialism and nationalism. In 1908, Enrique Ferri initiated a polemic in the PSA's newspaper *La Vanguardia*, arguing that a socialist party should be the product of the country in which it operated, and attacking Justo for drawing all his ideas from Europe. Ugarte intervened with an article entitled 'As Socialists, Should We be Anti-patriotic?' in which he spelt out the extent to which, for him, patriotism inevitably implied anti-imperialism. He emphasized that he also deprecated patriotism's cruder manifestations:

> I, too, consider myself an enemy of the brutish kind of patriotism . . . that drags the multitudes to the national border to subjugate other peoples; . . . of the arrogant kind of patriotism that consists of thinking ourselves superior to others, admiring even our own vices and despising anything from abroad; . . . and of ancestral patriotism . . . which is equivalent to the tribal instinct.

But there was a worthier and more modern form of patriotism, he maintained, which was the type that 'makes us defend, in the face of foreign intervention, the autonomy of the city, the province, the State, the free disposal of ourselves, the right to live and govern ourselves as it seems best to us'.[112] In an editorial of 1911, *La Vanguardia* retorted that conjuring up the 'bogeyman' of Yankee imperialism did little to help the oppressed of Latin America to liberate themselves from 'internal tyranny and *possible* external pressure', and that the best way to oppose US capitalist expansionism was to awaken the consciousness of the Latin American proletariat.[113] Most socialists' wariness about nationalism stemmed from their interpretation of it as a device used by the Argentine oligarchy to restrict political participation, especially by immigrants. Justo argued that there was no necessary contradiction between nationalist and internationalist commitments, but in the context of its challenge to the ruling class, the majority of the PSA preferred to sustain a commitment to internationalism.[114] Ugarte was dismissed as the PSA's delegate to the Socialist International, and the leadership made various attempts to discredit him. Formally expelled from the party in 1913, Ugarte was eventually persuaded to rejoin in 1935, but his sympathies for the emerging popular nationalism of Raúl Scalabrini Ortiz and Arturo Jauretche (whose ideas were also rejected by the PSA) ultimately led to his resignation the following year. Ugarte came to see Perón as a convert to his own political ideas ('It is not that I have accepted the government's doctrine, it is that the government has come round to my way of thinking'),[115] but his attempt to work for the first Peronist government ended in failure (see Chapter 2) and he died in Nice, probably by his own hand, in 1951.

Like Rodó, Ugarte maintained that the true *patria* for any Spanish American consisted not in one particular nation-state, but rather in the whole of Spanish America, and was based on 'the entirety of habits, memories and preferences' deriving from a common origin, language and conceptions about life.[116] He saw the existing nation-state boundaries of the region as the outcome of the *caudillo*-dominated politics and the rudimentary communications of the independence period.[117] In the belief that many of the smaller Spanish American countries, in particular, were unlikely to be able to sustain sovereignty on their own, Ugarte advanced the view that regional unity was 'the secret of all victories'.[118] Like Martí, he denied that any basis existed for an alliance with the United States,[119] arguing that for Latin Americans to acquiesce in Pan-American union was 'the most dangerous self-deception of all'.[120]

In accordance with the intellectual climate of his times, Ugarte held that economic progress was dependent upon cultural development. He did not dispute the idea that US imperialism entailed a cultural imposition, and was vehement in his defence of the view that Spanish America should preserve its own linguistic and cultural identity in the face of the US onslaught,[121] but he did not follow the *arielistas* in reducing imperialism to a cultural threat. Indeed, he regretted that, 'Forgetting that in international affairs there is no place for sentiment, our point of view was, from the outset, more literary than political.'[122] Like Martí, Ugarte challenged prevalent stereotypes about the peoples of Spanish America, arguing that the turbulence and violence of their nineteenth-century history did not necessarily imply the inferiority commonly imputed to them by US and European advocates of racial hierarchies. Invoking the analogy of the undisciplined student whose wayward brilliance ultimately secures him a future of great distinction, he saw these difficult beginnings as a portent of great promise for Spanish America: 'The uprisings for which we are so greatly reproached are simply the palpable manifestations of a creative impulse.'[123] Ugarte's view was that Latin Americans would not strengthen their capacity to resist the US threat either by escaping into an imaginary superiority or by allowing themselves to be intimidated by the doubts that contemporary racial theory raised about their position in the human hierarchy;[124] in other words, he rejected both *ressentiment* and shame.

Marxist Models of Anti-imperialism

From the 1920s onwards, as the contradictions between cosmopolitanism and nationalism sharpened in Spanish America, intellectuals hoping to uphold a commitment to both had to perform an increasingly precarious balancing act. Either an intellectual was considered to be seduced by foreign ideas, and therefore a lackey of imperialism and the oligarchy, or he was held to be a defender of national traditions: it was deemed well-nigh impossible to reconcile the two. Marxism – with its discourse of an internationalism on the side of the underprivileged – provided a partial way out of this dilemma, which helps to explain why it established a strong hold in Spanish American intellectual communities. Marxist-influenced Spanish American writers of the 1920s explicitly set out to dismiss *arielismo's* representation of anti-imperialist struggle as cultural resistance and replace it with a more politicized sense of anti-imperialism. Among both *arielistas* and Marxists, there were some intellectuals who propagated versions of anti-imperialism based on *ressentiment* and others who cultivated a more complex analysis of the issues. The famous disputes over the nature of imperialism between the two leading Peruvian Marxist intellectuals of the 1920s, Víctor Raúl Haya de la Torre and José Carlos Mariátegui, bear re-examination in this light.

It is important to note the circumstances in which Haya de la Torre's main book on anti-imperialism, *El antimperialismo y el Apra*, was produced.[125] Eventually published in 1936, it had mostly been written in 1928, in response to an article attacking APRA by the Cuban Communist Julio Antonio Mella. Mella, following the Comintern, which was about to enter its hard-line Third Period (1928–35) of eschewing any alliance and attacking all manifestations of 'reformism', had lambasted APRA for inventing a new type of fascism and using anti-Yankeeism as a smokescreen for capitulation to the interests of British imperialism.[126] Haya de la Torre's intended response originally echoed the title of Mella's article 'What is Arpa (*sic*)?', and it was noted in the introduction to *El antimperialismo y el Apra* that the title of Haya de la Torre's work could equally well have been *What is Apra?*[127]

Indeed, as it transpired, this was what most of his book was about. Having rejected the *arielista* analysis of the imperialist threat as a conflict between races (Anglo-Saxons versus Latins) or cultures, and argued that nor could it be understood as 'a question of nationalism',[128] Haya de la Torre contended that 'the instrument of imperialist domination in our countries is the state'.[129] In his view, all Latin American states were under the control, direct or indirect, of foreign powers, and national sovereignty was only apparent: 'Those who control our production, sell our currency, impose prices on our products, preside over our finances, organize our work and regulate our wages are themselves the economic subjects of the great imperial powers.'[130] Thus far, Haya de la Torre did not diverge from the Comintern analysis. However, for obvious reasons, he wished to escape the Comintern's conclusion that Latin American activists should await either the overthrow of capitalism in those parts of the world where it had achieved a more mature state, or the development of proletarian consciousness in their own countries. Instead, Haya de la Torre identified a dual character to Latin American economies, with the advanced imperialist sector counterbalanced by a backward national sector that was disconnected from imperialist penetration, still in feudal mode, and constituted 'our true base of resistance'.[131] For Haya de la Torre, then, the anti-imperialist struggle was primarily a question of expanding nationalist forces to the point where they could overthrow the existent state power, and consequently required the creation of a political party incorporating workers, peasants, intellectuals and the 'national' bourgeoisie.

Despite Haya de la Torre's belief that 'imperialism is, essentially, an economic phenomenon that displaces itself on to the political plane in order to proclaim itself',[132] his analysis of the political manifestations and consequences of imperialism was sketchy at best. He represented Spanish American nationalism as merely a tool of the governing classes for dividing Spanish America and thereby aiding imperialism by preventing Spanish American unity.[133] He saw little need to analyse specific US policies, dismissing Roosevelt's Good Neighbour initiative, for example, as 'only a policy'. He judged, 'It will free us for now from interventions, but that has nothing to do with imperialism as an economic phenomenon.'[134] Haya de la Torre was highly prone to economic reductionism. Moreover, he never defined what he meant by the term 'anti-imperialism': at one point, it seemed to be restricted to economic nationalism ('an anti-imperialist consciousness . . . is the consciousness of *Indo-American economic nationalism*');[135] at others, it was expanded to include workers' control of the state, the socialization of production and the federalization of Latin America.[136] Most of this, his main book about imperialism, was devoted to justifying his break with the Comintern. It contained little about how APRA should set about creating its anti-imperialist front, and even less analysis of imperialism itself, which was restricted to a couple of pages of figures on US investments in Latin America.[137] This was notwithstanding the fact that Haya de la Torre attached great importance to the role of intellectuals from both parts of the Americas in the anti-imperialist struggle (he was attacked by the president of Profintern, Aleksandr Lozowsky, for valuing the participation of US intellectuals above that of US workers).[138] He regarded the contribution of intellectuals as 'definitive',[139] on the grounds that imperialism was a truly complicated phenomenon and the workers were very ignorant.[140] Yet Haya de la Torre's own formulation of anti-imperialism was so vague and all-embracing as to compromise severely its validity, as a tool either of theoretical understanding or political action.

This was one of Mariátegui's main points of dispute with Haya de la Torre. Mariátegui denounced the tendency for anti-imperialism to become a catch-all slogan which, he argued, was used by certain political interests (he referred specifically to APRA) to obscure the class struggle.[141] In itself, he insisted, anti-imperialism did not constitute a programme or even a political movement for liberation; indeed, anti-imperialism was not necessarily linked with radical social change at all. Mariátegui believed, for example, that imperialist interests could perfectly well have accommodated the undermining of the Latin American landowning oligarchy by means of land redistribution, given that the resulting small proprietors would have been just as likely to co-operate with imperialism.[142] Denying APRA's claim that a 'national' bourgeoisie could be recruited to the anti-imperialist struggle,[143] Mariátegui concluded, like Ugarte, that it was the non-formal nature of US imperialism that enabled it to prosper and provoke so little resistance: 'As long as imperialist policy is able "to manage" the feelings and formalities attached to the national sovereignty of these states, and as long as it does not see itself as obliged to resort to armed intervention and military occupation, it will certainly be able to count on the collaboration of the local bourgeoisies.'[144]

Mariátegui also remained sceptical about the orthodox anti-imperialist project of Latin American unity. He believed that the incomplete formation of individual nations in Latin America, and the paucity of economic links between them, precluded any effective regional body.[145] The project was essentially an intellectual one and not, therefore, in Mariátegui's view, a particularly high priority. He identified the revolutionary spirit that he saw connecting the young throughout Latin America as far more important than any attempts to foster intellectual unity.[146] While not wholly rejecting the idea of a congress of Latin American writers, he could muster only lukewarm enthusiasm, suggesting that anything might conceivably emerge out of such an assembly with the sole exception of 'a vibrant plan for an organization of Spanish-American thought'.[147] In any case, he argued, however eloquent the supporters of *hispanoamericanismo*, their appeals to 'sentiment and tradition' were unlikely to prevail over Washington's own project for regional co-operation, Pan-Americanism, which was founded 'on financial interests and trade'.[148] For Mariátegui, the main feature of the United States was that after the First World War it had become the 'axis of capitalist society' and was 'predestined for maximum capitalist development'.[149] Yet, he largely avoided economic reductionism, producing a number of journalistic articles analysing the economic and political ramifications of US imperialism, particularly in Central America,[150] where he believed the repeated experience of US military interventionism made the local bourgeoisie more ready to oppose imperialism than their counterparts in South America.[151] If these analyses of imperialism were not numerous, and did not constitute a major part of his work, that was because, for Mariátegui, effective opposition to imperialism would be a consequence of the overthrow of capitalism in Spanish America, not (as for Haya de la Torre) the other way around: 'Against capitalist, plutocratic, imperialist North America, it is possible to pit effectively only a Latin or Ibero-America that is socialist.'[152]

Mariátegui categorically rejected the *arielista* claim to Latin American cultural superiority over the United States, arguing that 'Rodó's myth . . . has never had a useful or creative effect on anyone's soul.'[153] It was not primarily differences of language, race or spirit that divided the two Americas, Mariátegui argued, but their different positions within the world capitalist order.[154] Moreover, he added, and not without justification, APRA's 'alarmist and messianic sermons' on the struggle between 'Indo-America' and the United States drew primarily not on economic analysis, but on 'racial and sentimental factors'.[155] Apart from anything else, Mariátegui's close friendship with Waldo Frank had made him unsympathetic to the idea of a stark contrast 'between a materialist Saxon America and an idealistic Latin America'.[156] After all, he pointed out, the United States had produced not only the 'imperialist spirit' of Theodore Roosevelt but also Henry Thoreau's 'spirit of humanity'.[157] Like Martí, Mariátegui believed that there was no reason for Spanish American intellectuals to translate their opposition to US economic expansionism ('the Empire of Dawes and Morgan')[158] into a rejection of US culture which, he argued, offered Spanish Americans many valuable examples of independence of mind and spirit.[159] Mariátegui had no patience with the extremes of *ressentiment*: although in his view it was good for Spanish American intellectuals to base their region's identity on a belief that it was destined to be the seat of a future civilization (he rather approved of Vasconcelos's *La raza cósmica*), he saw any claims that Latin America was about to replace Europe (or even that it had already freed itself from the intellectual hegemony of Europe) as 'absurd and presumptuous'.[160] In an article of 1925 questioning whether there existed a body of distinctively 'Spanish-American' thought, Mariátegui disputed a call from the Argentine Marxist Alfredo Palacios for Spanish America to declare its cultural independence from Europe. Mariátegui was no enthusiast of Oswald Spengler's *Decline of the West* (1918–22), which became 'a huge best seller' in Spanish America because 'this text, which was reactionary in Europe, had unforeseen revolutionary effects in Latin America, where it strengthened and affirmed those who were criticizing all things European in order to vindicate the true origins of our culture'.[161] His position was that Spanish America was not even yet ready to cut itself off from European ideas ('Spanish American thought is generally no more than a rhapsody composed of motifs and phrases from European thought'),[162] let alone on the verge of overtaking Europe, which might have been in economic decline but was far from culturally decadent. He warned his contemporaries that, 'Spanish America should neither suppose itself to be on the verge of replacing Europe nor assume the intellectual hegemony of the Europeans to be exhausted and surpassed.'[163] The opposition between mimeticism and originality was a red herring, Mariátegui argued. It did not matter, for example, he claimed, that the independence leaders in Spanish America had taken their ideals (liberty, democracy, sovereignty of the people) from a European repertory; what was important was that they had used those ideas effectively to further the interests of their own people.[164] Like Ugarte, Mariátegui cited the example of Japan, which 'demonstrated how easily peoples of a different race and tradition from the Europeans [could] appropriate Western knowledge and adapt to Western production techniques'.[165] Similarly, it did not matter to him that socialism was an idea born in Europe, because he saw its application as universal.[166] For Mariátegui, it was incumbent upon the intellectual to resist the temptations of what he regarded as facile cultural nationalism.

But Mariátegui's call for *arielista*-style caricatures to be replaced with an analysis of historical reality fell mostly on deaf ears for a further three decades. Anti-imperialist thought in Spanish America was characterized from the 1920s onwards by a division into two strands: *arielista* and Marxist-Leninist. There were two partial exceptions. The first of these occurred in Argentina, where neither of those two models was dominant at the same time as in other parts of Spanish America, although elements of both can be detected in the work of Raúl Scalabrini Ortiz. The second was in Cuba, where both *arielismo* and Marxism-Leninism were moderated in the 1920s by the revived influence of José Martí.

Raúl Scalabrini Ortiz

Anti-imperialism in Argentina did not originate among progressive left-wing intellectuals, as it had done in Cuba and Peru, but instead 'developed on a web of conspiracy theories of the type that were fundamental to the political tactics and techniques of the ultra-Right'.[167] It did not figure prominently as an issue in intellectual debates until somewhat later than in the other four case studies, not until the 1930s, by which time Argentina was under right-wing rule in the wake of the Uriburu coup of 1930. Previously Yrigoyen, for whom anti-imperialism was a major theme, had largely captured the popular constituency for economic nationalism, especially with his founding of Latin America's first state-owned oil company, Yacimientos Petrolíferos Argenti-nos (YPF) in 1922.[168] When it was eventually aroused, the anti-imperialist animus among intellectuals was focused almost exclusively on the British role in Argentina, notwithstanding the fact that the 1920s had seen a sharp increase in US investment. This attack on the relationship with Britain was almost unprecedented in Argentina. Although signs of anti-British senti-ment had emerged during the Baring Crisis (1889–90), it had rapidly receded. Most of Ugarte's anti-imperialism had been directed against the United States, not Britain; indeed, he has since been criticized for allowing his preoccupation with combating US influence to obscure his vision of the effects of European, particularly British, imperialism in Argentina and elsewhere in South America.[169] Before the First World War, he depicted European commercial influence as beneficial, partly because he did not deem the several European powers to be any threat, regarding them as counterweights to each other in the competition for markets; and partly because he strongly identified Latin America with Europe and believed that Europe's cosmopolitanism lay at the root of Latin America's distinctive spirit.[170] However, these arguments should be set in the context of his main purpose at that time, which was to refute US claims that Washington's policies were designed to protect Latin America from European powers.[171] Later, as Argentina began to experience serious economic repercussions from the First World War, Ugarte extended his critique of US policies to encompass other imperialisms. In 1916, his short-lived newspaper *La Patria* (which quickly succumbed to a combination of censure from the pro-European intelligentsia and police intimidation)[172] declared its opposition to 'any act of an imperialist character . . . from wherever it may have come'.[173] His denunciation of the railway companies, whose interests he deemed contrary to those of the national economy, and of the dominance of British merchants and shipping over Argentina's wheat trade presaged the attitude of young intellectuals in the 1930s. Ugarte's solutions were the same too: trade diversification, industrialization, economic nationalism, popular sovereignty and national culture. He was virtually the only prior Argentine influence acknowledged by the popular nationalists of the 1930s,[174] but it must be acknowledged that he was never as specific in his critique of British imperialism as in his attacks on the United States. Most of his fellow Socialist Party intellectuals were even more reluctant to denounce the British presence in Argentina, which they saw as a necessary stimulus to the bourgeois capitalist development held to be a prerequisite to socialism. The cultural nationalists (Rojas, Lugones and Gálvez) saw nothing amiss in Argentina's economic links with Britain.[175] Their anti-foreign ire was almost exclusively cultural, and was reserved largely for immigrants (above all, they feared the 'Italianization' of Argentina) and the elites whom they regarded as in thrall to foreign ideas. The only bastions of anti-imperialism in the Argentina of the 1920s were the Communist Party (PCA), which regularly lambasted the Standard Oil Company,[176] and a few intellectuals such as José Ingenieros, whose influence – like Ugarte's – was greater abroad than at home. Ingenieros dismissed *arielismo*'s view of the United States ('The danger of the United States lies not in its inferiority but in its superiority; it is to be feared because it is large, rich and enterprising') and his analysis of US imperialism was well-informed, but his only proffered strategy of resistance was to call on 'the moral forces' of Spanish America.[177] As Mariátegui had pointed out, such an approach was unlikely to succeed against imperialist inducements and blandishments, at least given the weakly developed state of the 'public opinion' that Ingenieros hoped to form.[178]

During the 1930s, however, a new generation of intellectuals from middle-class backgrounds began to challenge the prevalent liberal consensus on Argentine history and politics (an amalgam of ideas, values and tenets known as *mitrismo*, after Bartolomé Mitre [1821–1906], who was elected the first constitutional President of a united Argentina in 1862, and was also the nation's first major liberal historian). From 1935 onwards, these young intellectuals were centred on FORJA, a breakaway group from the Radical Party. They saw General Uriburu's overthrow of Yrigoyen in 1930 as more than a mere military coup: for them, it represented an unwelcome reconfiguration of the alliance between British imperialism and the Argentine state which, in their eyes, had been undermined by the First World War and *yrigoyenismo*.[179] The signing of the Roca–Runciman Pact in 1933, which reformulated the economic link with Britain on manifestly less advantageous terms for Argentina, presented them with an opportunity to turn the tide of public opinion. FORJA intellectuals came to the conclusion that their own minds had effectively been 'colonized' by the sector of the Argentine oligarchy that had been dominant from 1853 until 1916: 'we were the offspring of a cultural formation built on a systematic obscuring of the truth, which proposed precisely that we should remain ignorant of the decisive factors involved in fulfilling our destiny'.[180] Indeed, by the 1930s, it was only among the intelligentsia that a *mitrista* version of Argentine reality was still hegemonic. One leading member of FORJA, Arturo Jauretche, noted, '*Mitrismo* had been defeated as a political force both on the battlefield and at the ballot box, but it still held sway as an intellectual force.'[181]

It was in this context that a series of works appeared that were strongly

critical of the British role in Argentina. One of the main examples was Raúl
Scalabrini Ortiz's *Política británica en el río de la Plata* (1939),[182] in which he
blamed Britain for most of his country's problems, ranging from 'the
railways, a fundamentally anti-progressive factor', to the state of the Argentine press: 'journalism, instrument of British domination'.[183] He argued
that, from 1853 onwards, Argentina's history was 'the history of British
economic penetration',[184] the most notable feature of which he identified
as corruption. Scalabrini Ortiz has been justly taken to task for failing to
place the undoubted corruption taking place in the British railway companies operating in Argentina within any broader socio-economic context,
or indeed to offer any explanation for it other than a demonizing of the
British, which one recent critic argued reached such extremes that some
passages of *Política británica* were 'on the verge of systematic delirium'.[185]
This is a standard critique of Scalabrini Ortiz, from which it is hard to find
grounds for dissent.

However, what is particularly noteworthy about Scalabrini Ortiz's work
for the purposes of my argument here is that his primary concern was for
the spiritual regeneration of the Argentine people. The influence of
Ricardo Rojas's geographical determinism and invocations of a tellurian
spirit of *argentinidad* are clearly evident throughout Scalabrini Ortiz's writing.[186] His first major book, published to great acclaim and commercial
success in 1931, was not one of the denunciations of the British role in
Argentine development for which he later became well known, but a
meditation on Argentine sadness and, above all, the solitude of the *porteño*,
entitled *El hombre que está solo y espera* [*The Man who is Alone and Waits*].[187] In
this work, Scalabrini Ortiz explicitly rejected the cultural stereotypes created
by the earlier generation of Argentine nationalists, arguing that to continue
'disinterring creole characters who have long since perished, [such as] the
gaucho, the colonial *porteño*, the Indian' showed 'an irreverence bordering
on the macabre'.[188] Comparing 'today's inhabitant of Buenos Aires' to a
drop of water, which is composed of hydrogen and oxygen but bears no
resemblance to either, Scalabrini Ortiz asserted the possibility of a reinvention of Argentine identity, liberated from its racial and cultural origins: 'the
porteño son of a European father is not the descendant of his parent, apart
from in the physiology that may be supposed to have been thus engendered.
He is not his father's son, he is the son of his country.'[189] It is in this context
that Scalabrini Ortiz expressed, albeit in a confused way, a desire to strip
Argentina bare of 'deceptive European conventions'.[190] The most enduring
effect of this work, Juan José Hernández Arregui argued, was that the
collective Argentine man evoked by Scalabrini Ortiz 'no longer [thought]
about Europe'.[191] Scalabrini Ortiz's essay was founded on a desire for
liberation that was primarily cultural: 'Why is it thought desirable for us to

be other than we are? . . . Why should we imitate the decadent peevishness of some Frenchman or other?'[192]

Even in those works in which Scalabrini Ortiz analysed Argentina's economic relationship with Britain, he sought economic independence not so much in order to gain benefits in terms of national economic progress or improvements in the welfare of the people, but rather on the grounds that, without it, the Argentine spirit would be insubstantial and therefore incapable of sustaining itself. His generation, in his view, saw themselves not as romantics but as 'mystics of reality', who identified their mission as the creation of 'the necessary conditions for the development of an autochthonous spirit'.[193] According to Scalabrini Ortiz, it was spiritually imperative for Argentina to return to its own reality, and this required an unshakeable determination among Argentines to see themselves as they really were.[194] For him, the economy was 'a means of sounding out the heart of a people': just as it was impossible for an individual human spirit to survive without a body, so it would be impossible for a national spirit to come to life 'in a collectivity of men whose economic links are not bound up in a common destiny'.[195] He saw the Depression of the 1930s as salutary, in that it had broken the existing national spirit and thereby created the conditions for the emergence of a revitalized manifestation thereof, 'vested in the truth of the land and for that very reason more powerful'.[196] Under the influence of this new spirit permeating the Argentine land, both class and sectoral differences were evaporating, according to Scalabrini Ortiz, to create a united front against the common enemy of British imperialism: 'Cattle-breeders and agrarian farmers had arrived at the same conclusions. Powerful landowners and wretched sharecroppers were united by the same sense of desperation and impotence.'[197] It was, he said, the Argentine people's predilection to disdain material wealth in favour of 'an unexpressed vocation for mysticism and a metaphysical approach to the world' that had made it so easy for foreign capitalists to exploit them;[198] but even though the people were unaware of the detrimental economic consequences of foreign ownership, they had none the less come to sense it as a pressure threatening their liberty;[199] thus, economic nationalism was being born in the people.[200] Now the people were 'without weapons to defend themselves' and, therefore, 'in this condition of suffocation, for the first time they are turning towards the state, which is the sum of many individual desires'.[201] Scalabrini Ortiz's influence on Peronism was evident in Eva Perón's *Historia del peronismo*, where she rejected the claim that Peronism was materialist by invoking the idea that the Argentine people were 'submerged . . . by a process of exploitation that . . . has not only been material, but also spiritual, since it prevented them from discovering either their own values or their own potential'.[202]

Scalabrini Ortiz's anti-imperialism, like that of Rodó and of Darío, was primarily the result of a cultural *malaise*, not a political analysis, and the consequences were similar. He rarely mentioned the impact of US imperialism on Argentina, despite the fact that commercial and economic ties between the two nations had increased dramatically during the 1920s. US industrial investment in Argentina had risen from $40 million in 1913 to $100 million in 1924 and $355 million in 1929, which made Argentina the third-largest recipient of US venture capital in Latin America (after Cuba and Mexico).[203] By 1929, although Britain still had the largest overall share of Argentine trade, the United States – significantly – had displaced Britain as the leading supplier of Argentine imports (whereas in 1913, Britain had provided one-third of Argentina's imports and the United States only one-seventh, by 1929 the US share had risen to one-quarter while the British portion had shrunk to one-sixth).[204] None of this was mentioned by Scalabrini Ortiz, who satirized what he saw as the foolish self-indulgence of the *porteño* intelligentsia in dismissing virtually any citizen of the United States as 'a troglodyte who travels by aeroplane', but failed himself to develop a more nuanced view.[205] It was not until the late 1950s that Scalabrini Ortiz devoted any sustained attention to the role of US imperialism in Argentina.[206] The same tendency to neglect the importance of the United States can be found in the work of all the *forjistas*. Thus, while it was the case that before FORJA, as Jauretche put it, 'the phantom of the Yankee . . . served to conceal the reality of the British',[207] it was equally true that the *forjistas'* concentration on a waning British presence obscured recognition of the waxing US threat to the point of virtually eclipsing it.

All Scalabrini Ortiz's discussions of British economic policy towards Argentina were couched in terms of what he saw as Europe's repeated attempts to annihilate the 'spirit of America'. Just as the 'autochthonous races' were exterminated during the conquest, he argued, so the *gaucho* had been wiped out by European immigration. When the American spirit re-emerged in the sons of European immigrants, he continued, presumably in a reference to the effects of the Depression in Spanish America, 'Europe is preparing to exterminate these new Americans without delay, by means of bodily emaciation, anaemic weakness, despair and humiliation of the spirit'. It was the duty of the nationalist intellectual, said Scalabrini Ortiz, to draw attention to this continual extermination of the non-European.[208] In arguing this, Scalabrini Ortiz revealed once again the close link between the adoption of anti-imperialist ideas and the intellectuals' own self-definition. However, the meaning of 'the American spirit' in Scalabrini Ortiz's work was defined in terms even vaguer than in most invocations by other Spanish American intellectuals. 'America', he claimed, was 'a feeling, a state of the soul', 'America' was 'the essence of the people'; 'America' was 'what remained present, not what has passed away . . . what is coming, not what has gone . . . what we will do, not what we have done'.[209] Unsurprisingly, in

Scalabrini Ortiz's books the tensions between Argentine nationalism and Hispanic-americanism were never resolved. As part of a challenge to the Argentine elite's pro-Europeanism, he claimed that Argentina was 'a typical example of America', its problems being those of 'the whole of this martyred continent'.[210] But instead of concentrating on the problem that Argentina did indeed share with the rest of the continent, namely the rise of US power, Scalabrini Ortiz ignored this to launch a vituperative attack on the relationship with Britain, which in many respects had made Argentina's economic development distinctive from that of its neighbours. As a result, he obscured understanding both of the ways in which Argentina's relations with the outside world were comparable with those of other Latin American countries, and of the ways in which they were not.

Cuban Views:
Julio Antonio Mella and Emilio Roig de Leuchsenring

In José Martí, Cuba had produced the first leading critic of the United States in Latin America, but once Cuba had become a republic in 1902, anti-imperialism declined and did not reappear as a significant element in intellectual debate until the 1920s, notwithstanding the high level of US interventionism in Cuba and the Platt Amendment's veto over Cuban sovereignty. During the interim years, a few isolated works by veterans of the Independence War (1895–98) were published, reflecting concern at the lack of freedom that had been the ultimate outcome of Cuba's anti-colonial struggle.[211] One leader of the Independence War and participant in the Constitutional Convention of 1901, Juan Gualberto Gómez, gave a detailed and convincing analysis of how certain clauses in the proposed Platt Amendment compromised Cuba's independence and contravened both the US Congress resolution of 19 April 1898 (which had promised that Cuba would become a sovereign republic once freed from Spanish colonial rule) and the Treaty of Paris, both in spirit and in letter.[212] The majority of early-twentieth-century Cuban intellectuals, however, were positivist liberals by philosophical inclination, and found themselves caught between wanting to *hacer patria* (build their own nation) and believing that the USA was the epitome of modern progress. As had happened elsewhere in Spanish America during the 1820s, the first post-independence generation of Cuban liberals looked to non-Spanish foreign models, in their case, mainly the United States, to counter what was by then perceived as the decadent influence of Spain. The leading example of this was the *Cuba Contemporánea* group, which formed Cuba's intellectual elite from 1913 (when the journal was founded) to 1923. *Cuba Contemporánea* attached priority to the promotion of cultural autonomy over economic or political independence, and

Martí's idea of an interrelationship between economic, political and intellectual emancipation was effectively abandoned. Ann Wright has concluded that the abstractions of cultural nationalism enabled these intellectuals to avoid the contradictions inherent in espousing patriotism while supporting the Platt Amendment.[213] In their supplanting of the economic by the cultural, these intellectuals were comparable to *arielistas* elsewhere, even though the anti-US element of *arielismo* did not become significant in Cuba until the Generation of 1923 became dominant. As Wright suggests, the idea that it was possible to *hacer patria* by non-political means was deeply flawed and resulted in the substitution of 'moralising for politics'.[214]

It was not until the 1920s, when the collapse of sugar prices led Cubans to question the benefits of a system of monoculture that hitherto had brought a degree of prosperity, that serious critiques of US policy towards Cuba began to appear in print. The legacy of Martí's contribution to anti-imperialist thought then became apparent. In the 1920s and later, even those Cuban intellectuals who were basically toeing the Comintern line were more sophisticated in their approach to the United States than many of their counterparts in other Spanish American countries. The best example of this was Julio Antonio Mella, who helped to found the Anti-Imperialist League of the Americas along with the Cuban Communist Party in 1925, supported the Comintern's position on anti-imperialism, and put his name to a succession of manifestos that were long on denunciation and short on analysis of US policy.[215] Although Mella did not challenge the orthodox Comintern view of Latin American governments as mere lackeys of imperialism,[216] in his own writings he demonstrated a relatively well-informed understanding both of US politics and of the different types of policies adopted towards Latin America by the Republican and Democrat parties. Analysing the 1924 presidential election in the United States, he argued, 'The Democrats' imperialism would be open and brutal like German imperialism, not veiled and hypocritical like that of the English, the tendency which the Republicans seem to follow.'[217] Mella was perceptive about the distinctive character of US imperialism, arguing that it was neither based on military conquest, like the Roman empire, nor on commercial dominance, like the British empire, but instead functioned on the basis of 'absolute economic domination with political guarantees when they appear to be necessary'.[218] These points may seem self-evident to us, looking back from the end of 'the American century', but they were rarely made in Spanish American anti-imperialist writings of the time, which focused mainly on the activities of the marines. He was also perceptive about US diplomatic manoeuvring: for example, in his analysis of the Sixth Pan-American Congress, held in Havana in 1928 (an article strongly reminiscent of Martí's account of the First Pan-American Congress of 1889), Mella deftly made the case that the United States had tried to manipulate the agenda to ensure that matters such as non-intervention would not be discussed.[219] Since those days, the Cuban anti-imperialist tradition has sustained a focus on imperialist policy-making which has been lacking in most other Spanish American countries. This longstanding awareness of the complexities of US politics may be one factor that helps to explain why the post-1959 government has been able to manoeuvre relatively successfully in its fraught relationship with Washington.

Martí's influence was apparent not only in the writings of Communists such as Mella, but also in the work of Emilio Roig de Leuchsenring (1899–1964). He was a lawyer and journalist who began his intellectual career as a contributor to *Cuba Contemporánea*, but later became sufficiently radicalized to join the Protest of the Thirteen in 1923 and the Grupo Minorista (Minority Group), although, unlike other leading *Minoristas*, Roig de Leuchsenring himself never joined the Communist Party. In 1919 he gave a speech to the Cuban Society of International Law, later published, on the US occupation of the Dominican Republic in 1916. This was the first serious, sustained analysis of US policy towards the Caribbean to appear in Cuba since 1898.[220] Relating financial and political interference to armed intervention, it had 'a profound impact amongst intellectuals, both within Cuba and without'.[221] From the early 1920s until his appointment to the office of Historian of the City of Havana in 1935, Roig de Leuchsenring's work combined historical analysis of US–Cuban relations with political critiques of contemporaneous policies, which he defined as imperialist. In 1927, for example, he published a pamphlet criticizing President Machado and the Cuban Foreign Minister for, in his view, betraying the internationalist legacy of Martí by kowtowing to the US President over arrangements for the Sixth Pan-American Conference.[222] In the last of these historical–political works, *Historia de la Enmienda Platt* (1935), Roig de Leuchsenring argued that the Reciprocity Treaty of 1934 should be repudiated by the Cuban people, just as the Platt Amendment had been, on the grounds that it only accentuated Cuba's position as a neo-colony of the United States.[223] More recent historians have concurred that, although 'the new treaty certainly contributed to Cuban revival' because of the reduced duties on sugar, it 'dealt a severe blow to Cuban efforts at economic diversification' and 'ultimately re-established US primacy in the Cuban economy'.[224]

In the light of Roig de Leuchsenring's comments on the Reciprocity Treaty, it was hardly surprising that Batista, who had overseen its negotiation, took steps to divert the historian's anti-imperialist energies. Batista's offer, in 1935, of the official post of Historian of the City of Havana was politically astute: after taking up that appointment, Roig de Leuchsenring's publications largely consisted of monographs on the development of Havana or relatively uncontroversial works devoted to the struggle for independence or to Cuba's founding fathers, Máximo Gómez and José

Martí.[225] His anti-imperialist commitment was channelled into extolling the anti-imperialism of Martí (in elementary form),[226] or, alternatively, in his famous *Cuba no debe su independencia a los Estados Unidos* [*Cuba Does Not Owe Its Independence to the United States*] (1949), into a historical rather than a contemporary political analysis. Following the Cuban revolution of 1959, Roig de Leuchsenring was finally able to publish a lengthy indictment of US policy towards Cuba from the early nineteenth century until the Platt Amendment, which had previously been subject to censorship.[227]

Roig de Leuchsenring was undoubtedly influential in helping to ensure that 'several generations of Cubans [were] made aware of the true character of the relations . . . between the United States and Cuba'.[228] *Cuba no debe su independencia a los Estados Unidos* is said to have been one of the books carried by Che Guevara in the Sierra Maestra.[229] Its conclusion became the linchpin of revisionist historiography and revolutionary ideology:

> Cuba owes its independence not to the United States of North America, but instead to the efforts of its own people, with their steadfast, unshakeable will to put an end to the injustices, abuses, discrimination and exploitation they suffered under the despotic colonial regime and to attain liberty, democracy, justice, culture and civilization.[230]

Nevertheless, there is one respect in which Roig de Leuchsenring's work testifies to the limited success of post-independence Cuban intellectuals in building on the foundations laid by Martí for an informed anti-imperialism and a nationalism not based on *ressentiment*. Whereas Martí had combated racial stereotypes, Roig de Leuchsenring did much to reinforce them, at least in his early work. In a lecture given in 1924, comparing colonial and republican Cuba, Roig de Leuchsenring argued that 'almost all the public ills and vices' the independence fighters had hoped to eliminate had resurged in the republic.[231] Although he attributed the depravity of the colonial period to the malignant influence of the Spaniards (thereby propagating the commonplace liberal idea of Spanish decadence as the cause of Cuba's ills), he failed to make the connection between Cuba's problems at that time and its neo-colonial relationship with the United States. Instead, he represented the US presence as an additional difficulty which had exacerbated Cuba's problems, rather than as a main causative factor in itself.[232] For example, he criticized Cuban political parties – not unfairly, it must be acknowledged – for being 'without programmes that could differentiate them from each other, and without ideals to recommend them',[233] but failed to relate this sorry state of affairs to the fact that the United States had disbanded the leading party in the struggle for independence, the Cuban Revolutionary Party (PRC), which had certainly not been lacking either in ideas or ideals, during its first military occupation (1898–1902). Nor did he observe that the parties lacked distinctive political

bases. Likewise, he deplored the circumstance – again, with some justification – that the Cuban public purse had 'become little more than a
patrimony for those who figure at the head of the government';[234] but he
did not even raise the issue of the high level of US economic penetration
which had effectively closed off most other routes to enrichment for the
Cuban bourgeoisie. At this stage, his anti-imperialism was limited to anti-
interventionism (lamenting the 'enormous harm caused to us by the
frequent and tolerated meddling . . . of the North American government in
our internal affairs').[235] Roig de Leuchsenring located the main problem in
Cuban weaknesses, and made no attempt to explain these in terms of the
country's structural relationship with the United States. The extent to which
such self-denigration compounded stereotypes in the United States is
revealed by an editorial in the *Washington Post*, written in response to Roig's
pamphlet. Acknowledging that the Cuban's arraignment of his country was
severe, the newspaper proclaimed that since it came from 'an important
authority', this view of Cuba could not be dismissed, and the only judicious
conclusion to be drawn was that 'the lessons of loyal and efficient self-
government have not yet been completely learned by the Cuban people'.[236]

Roberto Fernández Retamar's 'Calibán'

In 1971, Roberto Fernández Retamar's essay 'Calibán' openly brought
together the *arielista* and the Marxist models of anti-imperialism. The Cuban
Marxist's rewriting of Rodó was particularly revealing because it showed that
the two modes of thought were not as incompatible as had usually been
thought or indeed as Fernández Retamar's text itself claimed. Fernández
Retamar attacked 'the colonial Rodó', arguing that his 'misplaced' implicit
identification of the USA with Caliban had dramatically underestimated the
dangers posed to Spanish America by Washington.[237] Yet his own analysis of
Spanish America's cultural dependency amounted to little more than a re-
positioning of Rodó's stereotypes trapped within the same dualism of
authentic versus inauthentic. Whereas in Rodó's *Ariel*, Ariel had represented
idealism, Caliban utilitarianism and Prospero the intellectual, mediating
between the two, in Fernández Retamar's 'Calibán', Caliban was recast as
the hero, representing the colonized people, Prospero as the colonialist,
and Ariel as the intellectual. The choice of myth in itself reveals how closely
the trajectory of anti-imperialism was bound up with the question of the
legitimacy of intellectuals.

'Calibán' was written just after the Padilla affair in 1971,[238] and is
presented by Fernández Retamar as an intervention in the debates the affair
had stimulated about the role of the intellectual in a popular revolution. In
his view, the affair 'ended up by pitting . . . a few bourgeois European

intellectuals . . . with a visible nostalgia for colonialism' against 'the leading Latin American writers and artists who reject both overt and covert forms of cultural and political slavery'.[239] (Again, the term 'intellectual' is made to carry negative connotations.) For Latin Americans, he maintained: 'There is no true opposition between Ariel and Caliban: both are slaves in the hands of Prospero, the foreign sorceror.'[240] The famous lines from Shakespeare's *The Tempest* in which Caliban rages that the only gain he has experienced from having been taught language is that he knows how to curse his conquerors are taken by Fernández Retamar as a metaphor (the most apt possible, he claimed) for Latin America's history: 'What is our history, what is our culture, if not the history and culture of Caliban?'[241] Fernández Retamar equated this 'culture of Caliban' with 'our genuine culture', which (in a somewhat circular argument) was deemed to be:

> the culture developed by the *mestizo* people, those descendants of Indians, blacks and Europeans that Bolívar and Artigas understood how to lead; the culture of the exploited classes, the radical petty bourgeoisie of José Martí, the poor peasantry of Emiliano Zapata, the working class of Luis Emilio Recabarren . . .; the culture of the 'starving masses of Indians, landless peasants and exploited workers' referred to in the *Second Declaration of Havana* (1962), the culture 'of the honest and brilliant intellectuals of whom there are so many in our suffering lands'. . . .[242]

In superimposing notions of class on to a dichotomy of authentic versus inauthentic, Fernández Retamar effectively reduced cultural criticism to questions of political alignment. For example, he argued that Carlos Fuentes's emphasis on linguistic experimentation in his literature was in itself a manifestation of colonialist attitudes: 'it amounts to telling us that our current narrative – like those from the ostensibly contemporary capitalist countries – is a linguistic feat more than anything else'.[243] Fuentes, along with Mario Vargas Llosa, and unlike Gabriel García Márquez and Julio Cortázar, had withdrawn his support from the Cuban revolution after the Padilla affair. That same linguistic experimentation by the boom novelists had been hailed by many intellectuals as confirmation of the maturity of an 'authentic' Latin American culture. From either perspective, Fernández Retamar's essay highlighted the limitations of both *arielismo* (which represented anti-imperialism as spiritual and cultural resistance) and Marxism-Leninism (which viewed it in terms of class struggle).

Conclusion

'Imperialism' – ill-defined and ill-analysed – has been blamed for many of Spanish America's problems, including the inability of the region's intellectuals to fulfil a social function as independent critics.[244] It has often been remarked that the attitudes of twentieth-century Spanish American intellectuals towards the United States have been marked by a profound ambivalence, with contempt and admiration in almost equal measure.[245] The conclusion usually drawn from this is that the ineffectual nature of their anti-imperialist response stemmed from this ambivalence. Instead, the problem lay mainly in the tendency of early-twentieth-century Spanish American intellectuals (partly as a result of the precariousness of their own social position in relation to pro-European elites) to couch their anti-imperialism either wholly in terms of a racial/cultural clash or exclusively in terms of class struggle.

This fracturing of the anti-imperialist movement had three major consequences for the development of anti-imperialist thought in Spanish America. First, analysis of actual US policies was largely neglected, with the result that the true breadth and depth of US penetration – both direct and indirect (through multinational corporations and international financial institutions) – were not explored. Even the rapidly increasing influence of US popular culture in Spanish America, which began in the 1920s, was not discussed in any systematic way by the region's intellectuals until the 1960s. Correspondingly, the crucial issues of the relations between the various forms of imperialist domination (economic, political, cultural and so forth) and the potential for emancipation therefrom, which Martí had touched upon, were neglected by his successors, less so in Cuba but more so elsewhere in the region. Spanish American intellectuals have analysed imperialism not so much as a set of interrelating policies, but rather as an ideology – as either Americanization or capitalism.

Second, the restriction of the debate about US imperialism to a clash of cultures, and the conflating of all types of dependency into cultural dependency, resulted in a Spanish American intellectual tradition that denied – or at least ignored – the importance of material progress. What became referred to among its exponents as 'reconquering the language' of the former colonial power came to seem an acceptable substitute for more tangible forms of action in protest against the imperialist practices to which twentieth-century Spanish America was subject. Even when the Cuban revolution finally brought material questions to the forefront again, many intellectuals continued to emphasize metaphorical issues. In the 1960s, the commonplace idea that a writer's choice of language had potentially revolutionary implications was taken to extremes. The hardly distinctive (and highly debatable) claim that writing was itself a fundamentally revolutionary act became transmogrified into the far more unusual and more dubious idea that writing was *the* fundamental act of any revolution. If only a linguistic revolution could be achieved, it was argued, then social and political utopia would not be far behind. The Peruvian writer Manuel Scorza put it as follows:

> The novel in Latin America, in countries ruled permanently by censorship and terror, has become the first free territory. For me the first free territory of America is not Cuba; Cuba has undertaken an important political experience, but the first truly free territory of America is the Latin American novel . . . which has created a new way of looking at reality. For me this is crucial, because if Latin America is to carry out its great political project, it must first liberate its imagination.[246]

Scorza's claim that intellectuals were the only ones who could bring true liberation to their peoples implied that whatever the politicians did would be irrelevant unless the intellectuals had previously been successful in their own self-appointed task of rewriting Latin American reality. In this vision, the mediation – or reconquering – of language became a substitute for all other kinds of liberation.

Third, the limited framework within which debates about imperialism were conducted from the 1920s until the 1970s set up a dichotomy of overwhelming enemies versus all-powerful friends. In the twentieth century, Latin America's international relations have been characterized by a continual pursuit of powerful benefactors and special relationships, notwithstanding the equally persistent refusal of both the United States and the European powers (either singly or, more recently, collectively) to fulfil this role. In an article published in 1994 criticizing these 'delusions and mirages', Alberto van Klaveren cited the example of a recent book, entitled *América Latina se ha quedado sola* [*Latin America Has Remained Alone*] the title of which was explicitly taken from Gabriel García Márquez's Nobel Prize acceptance speech of 1982.[247] This book, van Klaveren argued, typified the self-image of helplessness still lingering on in Latin America.

The main problem with adopting an attitude towards the outside world based on *ressentiment* is that it is founded on extremes: either foreign influence is completely shunned, or it is wholly embraced. Correspondingly, the process of identity formation within Spanish America (both regional and national) was riven by an arguably false dichotomy between nationalism and cosmopolitanism. In this atmosphere, the possibility of 'equal but different', raised by Martí in the late nineteenth century, could no longer be realized. As a result, no measured evaluation of the role that foreign ideas might play in the region's development was achieved. More important, no capacity to adapt foreign ideas to local circumstances emerged. Just as the debt crises of the 1980s showed how 'underdeveloped' Latin American economies were in terms of their capacity to withstand external financial shocks, so the same decade revealed how open the region still was to the unquestioning assimilation of fashionable foreign panaceas. (While I would not wish for a moment to discount the extent to which monetarist policies were imposed on Spanish American governments by international financial institutions during the 1980s, it has to be recognized that the ideological conversion to Washington consensus economics rapidly became widespread throughout the region's political elites.) It is worth speculating that, had earlier debates within the intellectual community been more sophisticated and subtle, the recent extremes of neo-liberalism in Spanish America might have been precluded.

History as Hieroglyphics

[T]he nationalist metadiscourse is wont to impede or hamper the relations Mexicans have with their past and with world history: history is reduced to hieroglyphics, to static symbols destined to glorify national power and to tranquilize reason.

Roger Bartra, 1987[1]

The most significant consequence of the semi-modernization of intellectual life in Spanish America lay in the extent to which it constrained the writing of history. From the 1920s until the 1960s, history in Mexico and Peru was debated almost exclusively in a context of bi-culturalism; in Argentina and Cuba in terms of anti-imperialism; and in Chile, where a mythology of popular national identity never took root, within the framework of a theory of national decline. Thus, in twentieth-century Spanish America, the nineteenth-century tendency to write history in order to win immediate political advantage (a feature that was hardly absent from the European and US historiography of that period) not only persisted, but was accentuated at the expense of critical enquiry and analysis by the interventions of 'cultural *caudillos*'. This chapter seeks to illustrate how official policies on the role of history in nation-building dovetailed with the intellectuals' quest for cultural identity to reinforce highly politicized historiographical traditions in Spanish America. At its most extreme, history was appropriated by politics on the one side and culture on the other – and reduced to ideology.

The importance of the intellectuals' versions of Spanish America's past was brought into sharp relief by the persistence of a weak institutional base for the study of history until the 1960s. In contrast to West European countries, Russia and the United States,[2] modernizing Spanish American states (with the partial exception of Mexico in the mid-twentieth century) took few initiatives of any lasting significance to create national communities of historical scholars. Not only were resources lacking; so was political will. History was not securely established in Spanish America as a professional

academic discipline based in universities and research institutions until well
after the Second World War.

Three key elements have been identified as crucial to the development
of professional history in nineteenth-century Europe and the United States;
all of them were absent in Spanish American countries before the 1940s.[3]
First, the organization of professional societies to maintain and regulate
standards was important to the development of historical studies in both
Europe and the United States: key examples were the British Royal
Historical Society, which was founded in 1868 and turned itself into a
professional organization during the first quarter of the twentieth century,
and the American Historical Association, dating from 1884. Even today,
there are no real equivalents of these independently based organizations
in Spanish America. Instead, while academies of history were founded in
most Spanish American countries, these rapidly became guardians of official
history, highly defensive of one narrow interpretation of the nation's past,
and conservative in both methodology and topic.

Second, in no Spanish American country before the Second World War
was there a leading historical journal that commanded broad respect from
a range of historians. In Germany, the *Historische Zeitschrift*, founded in 1859,
had provided a crucial forum in which the development of professional
standards could be tested, as subsequently did the comparable French *Revue
historique* (1876), the *English Historical Review* (1886) and the *American
Historical Review* (1895). In Spanish America, Alfonso Caso's *Revista Mexicana
de Estudios Históricos* attracted some acclaim but lasted only from 1927 to
1928, and was anyway mostly devoted to archaeology and ethnography.
When it reappeared in 1939 as the *Revista Mexicana de Estudios Antropológicas*,
this new title was a rather more accurate reflection of its contents. It was
not until 1951 that Daniel Cosío Villegas established *Historia mexicana*, which
has continued to be published regularly until the present day. In Argentina,
the National Board of History (the bastion of liberal historiography,
founded in 1893 and constituted as the National Academy of History in
1938) started publishing a *Boletín* in 1924 and *Investigaciones y Ensayos* in
1966, but these publications were never generally recognized as being
broadly representative of a historical profession. Similarly, in Cuba the
Anales de la Academia de la Historia de Cuba, initiated in 1919, reflected only a
limited, increasingly conservative sector of national historiography, as did
the *Boletín* produced by Chile's Academy of History from 1933 onwards.
This was even more the case with the *Revista Histórica* published from 1906
to 1967 by Peru's Academy of History. In comparison with the weak state of
history journals, literary and cultural reviews of high repute were founded
throughout Spanish America during the 1910s–30s.[4]

Elsewhere, the third major feature of professionalization had been the
provision of training for historians: here again the Germans were first,

introducing a three-year research doctorate early in the nineteenth century. The United States followed suit in 1861, at Yale, and the French introduced a similar system at the beginning of the twentieth century. Oxford and Cambridge (with their customary resistance to innovation) finally did the same in 1917 and 1920 respectively. In Spanish America, however, before the Second World War, history functioned primarily as a secondary aspect of other disciplines: law, philosophy or literature. From the late nineteenth century until the 1940s, a modified version of positivist social science as represented by Spencer and Comte was taught in Spanish American universities. The result of this was that, whereas in nineteenth-century Europe history established its legitimacy as a discipline separate from sociology, in Spanish America sociology effectively displaced history. Even as history began at last to become established as a subject in Spanish American universities after the Second World War, it found itself under immediate challenge from the ascendant social sciences, which in Spanish America appropriated the legitimacy of empiricism that history had conserved in Europe. The legacy of the social sciences (based on methodologies developed in the United States) derived from their apparent promise to offer much-needed solutions to the problems of the present. From this perspective too, history was regarded as marginal. Deemed to be a discipline with 'no epistemological respectability', history was thought to be limited to providing the illustrative material necessary to support the structural analyses of social science.[5] Research training in history was still weak even in the 1990s in Spanish America. Mexico was probably the most advanced in this respect, at least partly because of the influx of refugees from Spain during the late 1930s following the fall of the Spanish Republic – these included the leading historians José Gáos and Rafael Altamira, who made a major contribution to professionalizing Mexican historical studies.[6] The prestigious Colegio de México, which had been established in 1939 principally to accommodate the refugees, established a small programme of annual scholarships for graduate work, but this was exceptional. Elsewhere in the region, progress was slow: as late as 1984, the University of Chile – widely held to be one of the best in the region – offered only a master's degree in history, not a doctorate.[7] Most Spanish American students hoping to pursue a career in historical research applied to do their graduate training abroad; those who were successful often chose to stay abroad once they had qualified.

This protracted development of historical scholarship in the region partly reflected the very real difficulties involved in trying to write history in the Spanish American republics, particularly during the first few decades after independence. The destruction wrought by the wars of independence had left very little documentation available to potential historians. This was one reason why the ideas about 'scientific' historical method that emerged from

Germany in the 1830s, which were to have a determining influence on the development of historical professions in Europe and the United States, had little impact in the region. It was difficult to follow Leopold von Ranke's famous injunction to tell history as it really was in a continent where, as Andrés Bello put it, 'the history of a country does not exist, apart from in scattered, incomplete documents, and in vague traditions'.[8]

The problems were in part logistical, but they were also political. One aspect of Ranke's thought that did appeal to Spanish American liberal nation-builders was his rejection of the then dominant Enlightenment view of history as based on an a priori philosophy.[9] Enlightenment thinkers had argued that history was governed by a series of laws analogous to those that ordered the natural world, and that it was necessary only to identify the workings of such laws for humankind to continue advancing towards a state of perfection. In contrast, Ranke, like Hegel, represented history as the revelation of God's will. In Spanish America, the liberals of the immediate post-independence years were reluctant to accept the Enlightenment view of history-as-progress because its determinist implications would have obliged them to attach positive value to the Spanish colonization, whereas they wished to represent the colonial period as the yoke that had held them back, and independence as their liberation. Spanish Americans rejected German empiricism but were attracted by German idealism, which in its varying manifestations continued to be influential until at least the 1940s. The link between philosophy and history which had been broken in Europe by the mid-nineteenth century lasted far longer in Spanish America: in fact, well into the twentieth century. This was almost exactly the opposite of what happened in the United States, where historians tended to be dismissive of philosophies of history until as late as the 1970s.[10] It was almost as if Ranke's ideas were split into two parts when they reached the Americas: his methodology went to the United States while his idealist philosophy went to Spanish America.

A more apparently scientific approach to history, which had spread from Germany to Britain and France by the 1860s, arrived in Spanish America in the 1880s with the advent of positivism. The consolidation of central governments during the 1860s and 1870s stimulated an increase in historical writing and the foundation of the 'nationalist' schools of history in the major countries of the region. The political triumph of liberalism was reinforced by the influence of positivism, which became the main intellectual current during the last two decades of the nineteenth century, particularly in those countries where strong secularizing movements had left an ideological vacuum, namely Mexico, Chile and Venezuela. But Spanish Americans were highly eclectic in what they borrowed from positivism: hardly any writers of history went so far as to accept Comte's idea of inevitable historical development; instead they continued to interpret national events in terms of a blend of 'revolutionary and rational natural law and [the] idealism of the independence movements, as modified by the romantic liberalism of the early nineteenth century'.[11] Positivism was received less as a stimulus to empirical research than as a framework with which to reformulate the search for laws of history. It did, however, act as a spur to the gathering of some impressive collections of documents.[12]

Positivism also prompted the writing of the first major national histories.[13] As exercises in overcoming research difficulties, these were remarkable achievements in themselves, but as encyclopaedic accumulations of data, usually without references or indications of sources, and with little analysis of cause and effect, they did have severe limitations. The legacies of legalism, Romanticism and positivism dictated that early-twentieth-century historiography was elitist (concentrating mainly on the military exploits or political acumen of great men), legalistic (emphasizing the Enlightenment idea of natural law), national (with very little comparative perspective), and largely confined to the compilation of undocumented information within a weak, or nonexistent, explanatory framework. Many of these early nationalist historians were members of the elites who tailored their accounts of the nation's past to their visions of its future. In oligarchic societies, where members of the small educated elite were regular visitors to each other's houses, national history was regarded with the same kind of fraught intensity that often characterizes a family history. For Victoria Ocampo, the Argentine aristocrat and founder of the leading cultural review *Sur*, for example, 'Argentina's history . . . was the history of our families.'[14] There was a corresponding tendency to appraise historical figures rather as one might weigh up a potential in-law to see if they merited being accepted as 'one of the family' or not. In Spanish American countries run by oligarchic states, 'official' history consisted of an uneasy blend of hagiography and cataloguing.

Given all this, it is hardly surprising that many early-twentieth-century Spanish American intellectuals perceived severe flaws in the efforts of their nations' historians. Criticisms were particularly strong in Argentina: the writer Ezéquiel Martínez Estrada, who became famous for his essays on Argentine national character, argued in 1933 that 'No one [had] told the truth' about any of the leading names in Argentine history. 'Their authentic figures [were] taboo,' he protested, remonstrating that 'data [were] gathered in the same manner as stamps [were] collected', which resulted only in 'an inventory of the chattels of the hero's home'.[15] More mildly, Manuel Ugarte observed that, 'we gather facts with great enthusiasm, [but] we almost always forget to study the causes that underlie them'.[16] Across the region, Spanish American intellectuals rejected positivist historical method, which they associated with elite nationalisms, and started exploring alternative ways of approaching the past through psychology, philosophy and fiction.

Mexico: History as Essentialism

It is in post-revolutionary Mexico that the displacement of history by culture can most clearly be traced. In contrast to the French or Russian revolutions' repudiation of the past, the Mexican revolution '[was born] together with a fervent defence of the past'.[17] Mexico's strongly, at times vehemently, anti-clerical post-revolutionary leaders looked to recapture the aura associated with religion and to channel it into a pro-revolutionary nationalism. Initiatives to promote the study of history itself came relatively late, however, at least a decade after state support had been granted to the mural artists, who promoted a version of popular history, and the anthropologists, notably Manuel Gamio, who saw indigenous culture as the foundation of nationality.[18]

The crucial period was from 1946 until the early 1960s, when the relationship between Mexican intellectuals and the state was at its least problematic in the twentieth century. A series of works appeared on *mexicanidad*, sponsored by the state, which are highly revealing about how politicians and these intellectuals enjoyed a shared perspective on the relationship between history and culture. A recent article by Aurora Loyo analysing some of these official publications offers some perceptive insights.[19] An edited book on Mexico and culture published by the Secretariat of Public Education in 1946 carried a prologue written by Jaime Torres Bodet, then Secretary-General of UNESCO (1946–48) and a former Secretary of Foreign Relations (1943–46) and Secretary of Education (1940–43). He set out the premises of *mexicanidad* as follows:

> ... our culture has up to now followed a course, along its most important lines, very similar to that traced by our history. Both are on an upward curve, albeit with interruptions and the occasional fall, towards the authentic. And it should be understood that here we do not conceive of the authentic in a limited sense, as the traditional or the folkloric, but as all that which we will be when we become what *only we* can be.[20]

As his prologue continued, Torres Bodet increasingly used the terms 'history' and 'culture' as if they were synonymous. Having identified the intellectual as the means of bridging the gap between high culture and 'living culture', he claimed that it was only the intellectual who could arbitrate on what was authentically Mexican, concluding that the intellectual was 'a depositary for that part of a people's historic dignity which can neither be replaced nor renounced'.[21]

Professional historians wielded very little influence in Mexico during the 1940s and 1950s, when the major questions of Mexican history became set in a philosophical mould. Various articles about history in Mexico written in the early 1950s reveal how much ground historians had been obliged to concede. *Historia mexicana*, a journal launched by the Colegio de México to provide a forum for professional history, carried one piece in which a historian noted that two main paths of historical interpretation were currently being forged in Mexico. The first path was condemned for having '[taken] refuge' in Lucas Alamán and 'made resentment the basis of its conduct'. (Alamán was a conservative historian, who had produced his main work just after Mexico's defeat at the hands of the United States in the Mexican-American War [1846–48]; not surprisingly, he emphasized the negative aspects of Mexican history.) The second approach to history, by contrast, was heralded as 'the new school, of Man and Culture, which penetrates our essences and investigates and explains the reality of our historical consciousness by means of a philosophical approach to our problems'.[22] Another historian argued, in a presentation to the Congreso Científico Mexicano in September 1951, that 'in Mexico, history has the serious responsibility of helping us to understand more fully *what is essential to us*'.[23] *Lo mexicano* (the essence of being Mexican) became the touchstone for anyone writing about Mexico's history: according to Emilio Uranga, who became closely associated with the term, '*lo mexicano* is today, as the Enlightenment was during the eighteenth century, the guiding idea of our culture'.[24] Uranga cited three works he deemed to be crucial to initiating the study of *mexicanidad*: Samuel Ramos's *El perfil del hombre y la cultura en México* (1934); Gabriel Méndez Plancarte's prologue to his own essay *Humanistas del siglo XVIII*, [*Humanists of the Eighteenth Century*] (1941), a literary study of eighteenth-century Jesuit writers; and the first volume of Leopoldo Zea's *El positivismo en México* [*Positivism in Mexico*] (1943). Uranga noted that none of these authors was a professional historian but argued that even so, 'all three have made important historiographical contributions executed along the lines of what they call, in a move clearly designed to provoke, historical method'.[25] History was openly subordinated not only to nationalism but also to culture.

The new, officially sanctioned version of Mexico's history was exemplified by Silvio Závala's work, especially in his essay entitled 'Síntesis de la historia del pueblo mexicano' ['Synthesis of the History of the Mexican People'] (1946).[26] Here, 'Mexico' was represented as if it were an immutable entity that had existed since migrants from Asia had settled in the region over 20,000 years previously, and lain dormant during three hundred years of colonial rule, to be awakened to national historical consciousness only after independence and brought to full selfhood by the revolution. In a marked departure from nineteenth-century Mexican historiography, in which both liberal and conservative historians had identified the Spanish Conquest as the starting point of Mexican history and independence as the foundation of the Mexican nation,[27] post-revolutionary accounts of Mexican history returned to pre-Columbian times. On the colonial period, Závala gave more or less equal weight both to defending the pre-Columbian indigenous civilizations from the traditional charges of having 'vegetated in apathy and passivity' and to rescuing the Spanish from the Black Legend. This paved the way for him to emphasize not only the latent 'racial mixing which was called upon to play an important part in the new country's history', but also 'an active two-way process of transculturation in which each party brought influences to bear on the other'. Independence was quickly glossed over as the result of a process of spiritual evolution – the disaggregation of an 'American' from a 'European' consciousness – in order not to introduce any inconvenient sense of historical interruption to Mexico's supposedly continuous progress towards self-realization. On the nineteenth century, Závala largely followed Justo Sierra, a progressive liberal-positivist who strongly opposed corporate interests, saw the future of Mexico in the strengthening of its middle classes, and advocated secular state education and *mestizaje*. The Porfiriato was attacked, as was then standard practice, for 'its obsession with all things European'; however, it was acknowledged that the dictatorship had achieved a degree of modernization which enabled Závala to preserve the impression of sustained historical advance in economic if not political development. Crucially, however, there had been no change in land-use under Porfirio Díaz. The Mexican revolution was represented as inevitable, therefore (a 'natural fruit of that dictatorship'), because 'the countryside had not been emancipated either from the economy of the large landed estates or from the servitude of the labourers'. The notion of the Mexican revolution as the protean realization of full collective self-consciousness was reinforced by the failure to mention any of the revolutionary leaders by name. It was almost as if history had stopped at the revolution (the most recent item in Závala's bibliography was Justo Sierra's *México: su evolución social* [1900–01]). Závala's essay concluded with a litany of the benefits the revolution had brought to peasants and workers, above all, its achievements in extending popular education. Census figures from 1930 were cited to show that 'the process of racial mixing which absorbs both the Indians and the whites is continuing'. Finally, it was claimed that through the evolution of an art and thought oriented towards 'autochthonous characteristics', 'the Mexican is beginning to discover himself'.[28]

One intriguing aspect of the subsuming of history to culture and, in particular, to philosophy, was that it enabled post-1945 Mexican governments to neutralize the virulence of the nationalism that their predecessors had encouraged in the 1920s and 1930s. During the 1940s, the state began to represent Mexico's new-found self-awareness as harmonious with its aspiration to play a responsible role in the international community. The emphasis of the previous decade on the myth of *mestizaje* as the basis of Mexican national identity was gradually modified into a claim that the main foundation of *mexicanidad* was humanism. Mexican historians continued to make ritual reference to *mestizaje* ('Only through *mestizaje* is it possible to arrive at a full understanding of our past'),[29] but increasingly it was superseded by a more expansive humanism which came to be promoted as the cardinal value of *lo mexicano*.

It has been argued that in the years immediately after the Second World War, when the Mexican post-revolutionary state was increasingly successful in overcoming its former international isolation, 'for the first time, the intellectual's aspiration towards universalism [coincided] with historical trends in our country'.[30] The most significant works in this context were those in a series entitled 'México y lo mexicano', edited in the 1950s by Leopoldo Zea of the Faculty of Philosophy and Arts at UNAM. Zea's own contribution, which opened the series, was entitled *Conciencia y posibilidad del mexicano* and represented the nation's past in terms of existential struggle. Casting Mexican history as a dialectical struggle between European and indigenous conceptions of the world, Zea maintained that:

> Throughout this history we can see the Mexican struggling because he recognizes his right to the only true universality, his humanity. The Revolution for Independence, the Revolution known as the Reform and that which we now, significantly, call the Mexican Revolution, are increasingly self-conscious expressions of this desire.[31]

However, the most influential work arguing that humanism was the foundation of *mexicanidad* was Uranga's essay 'Optimismo y pesimismo del mexicano' ['Optimism and Pessimism of the Mexican'] (1952).[32] Drawing particularly on Méndez Plancarte's prologue to his literary study of eighteenth-century Jesuit writers, Uranga claimed that the importance of Méndez Plancarte's essay lay 'in [its] having highlighted humanism as the field in which to harvest the meaning of being Mexican'. But 'this humanism', continued Uranga, 'has been unnecessarily restricted to its Graeco-Latin manifestation, that is, to the "humanities"'; the way forward to an exploration of *mexicanidad* was to pursue what was implicit in *mestizaje*, namely that the indigenous ancient cultures of Mexico had as much claim as the Christian tradition to be considered examples of humanism.[33] The work of this mid-century generation of intellectuals represented a transition from the inward-looking evaluation of Mexican culture of before the Second World War to the embrace of a more externally oriented approach. One noteworthy indication of this was that both Uranga and Zea commended Alfonso Reyes, who had been regarded as a cosmopolitan traitor at the height of Mexican cultural nationalism and then rehabilitated in the late 1930s,[34] as the supreme contemporary example of Mexican humanism.

Despite the increasing emphasis in works about *mexicanidad* on Mexico's right to be accepted 'as a suitable member of the great universal family',[35] the international interests of the Mexican state were not at this stage worldwide. During the Second World War, Mexico's economy had become increasingly integrated with the United States, and its post-war industrialization strategy relied heavily on US support.[36] This provided the motive for the Mexican government's efforts to mitigate the aggressive nationalism that had characterized Mexican cultural and political discourse before the war. Zea defended Mexico against accusations of 'extreme' nationalism by arguing that this had been a natural reaction against European dominance.[37] During the revolution, Zea declared, it had seemed as if 'Mexico was turning in on itself with such determination that it denied all external connections'.[38] But, he argued, this was Mexico's profoundest moment of self-knowledge. It followed, according to Zea, that the origin of Mexican nationalism lay not in any desire to cut itself off from the world, but in precisely the opposite, namely 'the most human and legitimate of aspirations: the right to be recognized as a free and sovereign people'.[39]

An even more telling example of history being appropriated to serve the immediate political interests of the Mexican state was Závala's essay 'El mexicano en sus contactos con el exterior', ['The Mexican in His Contacts with the Outside World'], written in the early 1950s.[40] The impetus behind this work was that 'in the construction of the "Mexican" recently begun in the Faculty of Philosophy and Letters, there ought to be a chapter on foreign relations'.[41] The essay analysed Mexico's links with Africa, the Orient, Spanish America, the United States and Europe, each in turn. Of the first two little remained, Závala argued, neither being any longer a 'living presence'.[42] Neither did he dwell long on Spanish America, merely noting that the historical and cultural parallels between Mexico and other Spanish American nations were not reinforced by contemporary economic or political contacts, and concluding, 'The Spanish American [route] . . . is an exit to the outside world that is more potential than real,' the benefits of which were 'of a spiritual rather than a practical nature.'[43] The influence of the United States, Závala argued, was in contrast both real and growing; he made it clear that he regarded Mexico's relationship with the United States as its most important external connection, implying that Mexico needed to moderate its attitudes in order to take advantage of the favourable conditions for an improvement in relations during the 1950s. A mention of the Mexican-American War was balanced by a plea for recognition of the (unspecified) help the United States had given Spanish America 'in consolidating its autonomy from metropolitan Europe, in guiding its political organization along republican lines, and in strengthening the sense of an

American community'.[44] He condemned Mexican stereotypes of the United States (rather than US stereotypes of Mexico), and discussed Mexican ignorance of the United States (rather than US ignorance of Mexico). Regarding Europe, Závala separated out Spain from more general European influences. Although he made passing reference to the historical debate between exponents of the Black Legend and its critics, he declined to take sides, noting merely that 'in the contemporary world, a country like Mexico can acknowledge its historical and cultural links to European Spain and, at the same time, out of interest in the values of the modern world, seek out innovations in science or matters of taste from other European countries ... or elsewhere in the Americas, such as the United States'.[45] In other words, Mexico did not intend to let historical and cultural links interfere with its cultivation of good relations with any other country that could help it to industrialize. Závala concluded that Mexico should remain faithful to 'the humanist legacy ... not to a deceptive nationalism, the only outcome of which would be a closing in on itself or a retreat from the universal'.[46] Once again, historical questions were sacrificed to the need to provide the Mexican one-party state with the requisite ideological justification for its policies.

Peru: History as Prophecy

Peru's historiography has been recently characterized by two of the country's leading revisionist historians, Alberto Flores Galindo and Magdalena Chocano, as history as 'what-might-have-been'. This epithet reflects the one feature common to all thinking about history in Peru, namely a 'deep discontent with what has actually happened'.[47] Jorge Basadre, one of Peru's most eminent historians of the twentieth century, encapsulated this approach when he wrote, 'The history of Peru in the nineteenth century is a history of lost opportunities and wasted possibilities.'[48] According to Chocano, the idea that Peru was somehow fatally flawed dates back to the aftermath of the War of the Pacific (1879–83). Peru's ignominious defeat by Chile had prompted a new generation of intellectuals to deny historical continuity and assert the need to reject all that had gone before in order to start anew. In a radical version of this critique, Manuel González Prada denounced the previous generation, arguing that the national disaster had been the result of oligarchic domination which excluded the majority of Peruvians from participation in national affairs.[49] Chocano suggests that it was primarily in order to deflect this guilt from the oligarchy that the historian José de la Riva Agüero (1885–1944), himself a descendant of the colonial aristocracy, formulated the idea of Peru's history as 'a series of possibilities squandered, and of promising opportunities missed as a result of the frivolity and inconsistency of youth'.[50] Responsibility was therefore removed from any one sector of Peruvian society, and deflected on to a vague collective entity, 'Peru'.

Riva Agüero's book *La historia en el Perú* (1910) marked the beginning of modern historiography in Peru,[51] and was widely read among the following two generations of intellectuals. Riva Agüero, who was convinced that history's role was to bring about national moral regeneration, also played an important role in establishing the framework of bi-culturalism that came to dominate Peruvian history. Like other members of the *arielista* generation such as Víctor Andrés Belaúnde, Riva Agüero saw *peruanidad* as a potential unity to be realized through *mestizaje*. In 1916, he gave a speech on the Inca Garcilaso de la Vega, whom he lauded as the prototype of future Peruvian man.[52] Thus the idea of *mestizaje* became strongly identified with the Hispanic tradition. But many of the intellectuals from the following Centenary Generation were critical of Riva Agüero and Belaúnde. As *indigenistas*, they argued that Peru was not a nation but merely a country in which two distinct cultural traditions – the Western and the indigenous – had existed in opposition to each other since the Spanish conquest.

As Peru's intellectual community became increasingly divided between *indigenistas* and *hispanistas* (see Chapter 4), both sides began to view Peru's history through a 'what-if?' prism. For the *indigenistas*, the basic question was 'What if the Spaniards had never come?', while for the *hispanistas* it came down to 'What if the Indians were not there?' Unsurprisingly, it was the latter version that was consolidated into official history during the 1930s, when the Peruvian oligarchy regained full control of the state. A new nationalist Right adopted Riva Agüero, who by then had become a Fascist sympathizer, as their intellectual inspiration. His earlier enthusiasm for *mestizaje* transmuted into a celebration of Spanish conquest and colonization as Pizarro replaced the Inca Garcilaso as his central hero. What became known as *hispanidad* – consecration of all Spain's works in Peru – consolidated its own traditions as Riva Agüero found disciples among young intellectuals who feared the emergence of the masses.[53] The Instituto Riva Agüero, established in 1947 to renovate conservative historiography, modelled itself on Seville's School of Spanish American Studies. Hispanicism, which inserted Peru into the Western, Christian tradition, was dominant in Peruvian historiography from the 1930s to the end of the 1960s.

The split between *indigenistas* and *hispanistas* was mirrored in the development of two distinct intellectual traditions: Peru is one of the few countries in Spanish America where the provinces have developed their own distinctive approach to questions of national identity. According to Manuel Burga, 'While to be an intellectual in Lima was to be Frenchified, Europeanized, a connoisseur of foreign languages, provincial scholars [have always felt] under pressure to discover themselves in order to raise the indigenous to academic status.'[54] It was during the early years of the Leguía government (1919–30) that Peruvian intellectuals from the provinces first turned their attention to 'an exhaustive inventory of our Andean particularities' which was 'the way chosen to discuss the national problem'.[55] In this drive to create distinctive Andean traditions, historical accuracy was not always the highest priority: 'The indigenous was the historic, the pre-Hispanic, the millenarian, the traditional. When these terms did not coincide, recourse was made to "invention".'[56] People like Luis Valcárcel – who created a Department of Anthropology at the University of San Marcos in 1946 and in 1959 introduced the term 'ethno-history' into Peru – Emilio Romero and Julio C. Tello (1880–1947) laboured with few resources and little recognition to piece together information about Indian societies. Official history held sway, and it is probably fair to conclude, as did Flores Galindo, that the best work from the *indigenistas* concerned the study of folklore rather than of history.[57]

Official history and ethno-history continued to work in isolation from each other until the late 1960s, when the former finally lost the support of the state under the anti-oligarchic military government (1968–75) led by Juan Velasco Alvarado. Under the military regime, the Academy of History virtually stopped functioning, the *Revista Histórica* was hardly published and the Instituto Riva Agüero saw its seminar audiences dwindle away.[58] A few years earlier, in 1965, a new 'popular' version of Peruvian history had been launched as a direct challenge to official history, when José María Arguedas started the journal *Historia y Cultura*. This group recast Peruvian history away from the glories of the Spanish civilizing mission to argue, in contrast, that all the country's ills had begun with the European intrusion. The group saw the Inca empire as the moment of greatest glory which nothing in the history of Peru as an independent nation had surpassed. This interpretation has since succeeded in displacing the traditional version of history, largely due to the efforts of Peru's radical schoolteachers. According to Magdalena Chocano, however, the radicals who attempted to challenge official history in the 1960s fell into the same trap of seeing Peru's history through the 'what if?' prism. They argued that the dominant class had repeatedly failed to take its opportunities to become a national bourgeoisie; but, contended Chocano, given that the Peruvian Left also had a record of missing its opportunities, 'the idea of the failure of the dominant class stopped being a motivation and a moral incentive that sustained a desire to transform history, and became one element in a resigned explanation for impotence in the face of events'.[59] Flores Galindo agreed, arguing that the new focus on the Inca empire as a glorious part of Peru's history was only an inverse image of the old picture of Spanish colonial rule as the apex of Peruvian achievement. Guillermo Rochabrun (not himself a historian) has argued that the element of fatalism in the 'lost opportunities' paradigm of the

1930s to the 1960s was exacerbated in the 1970s by emphasis on the 'colonial legacy', and in the 1980s by a preoccupation with 'Andean utopias'. This continuing sacrifice of history to nostalgia and prophecy offered no effective resistance to the Right's rejection of collective memory in favour of individualistic rationality.[60] The efforts of the 1960s to explore some of the areas neglected by official history stimulated new approaches which are likely ultimately to undermine the pretensions to dominance of history-as-prophecy, but it should be noted that most of the new 'history from below' has been written within other disciplines (for example, work by the linguist Alfredo Torero or the anthropologist Stefano Varese). The heritage of Riva Agüero – that 'obsessive preoccupation with the nation' – was still very much in evidence during the 1990s.[61]

Argentina: History as Politics

From the 1930s until the 1960s, Argentina's political culture was suffused with two competing sets of stereotypes related to different conceptions of the nation's past.[62] The first, and initially dominant, framework was referred to variously as the liberal, official or *mitrista* school of history. Although Bartolomé Mitre (1821–1906) himself expressed rather more subtle views in his pioneering historical works of the middle-to-late nineteenth century, the conventions of *mitrista* historiography came to be as follows: the colonial period was to be assessed in terms of Spanish obscurantism and cruelty (the Black Legend); Argentina had been launched on its path towards civilized existence when the revolution of May was declared by *porteño* liberals in 1810; the first national heroes were Bernardino Rivadavia (President of the United Provinces of Río de la Plata from 1826 to 1827) and his fellow liberals, who tried, albeit unsuccessfully, to introduce the principles of the Enlightenment as a basis for ordering the newly independent nation; the subsequent dictatorship of the barbarous *caudillo* Juan Manuel de Rosas was proof of the reactionary tendencies of most local creoles; civilization finally triumphed in the River Plate with the defeat of Rosas by Mitre at the Battle of Monte Caseros in February 1852; liberal government from then onwards until 1916 brought order and prosperity in the context of a mutually beneficial financial and commercial alliance with Britain; but all this pro-gress had been stalled by immigration and its consequences, especially the extension of the suffrage in 1912 to all male Argentine citizens, which had led to what liberals decried as the demagoguery of Yrigoyen.

A liberal version of history was consolidated in late-nineteenth-century Argentina more strongly than in any other Spanish American country. According to Juan Bautista Alberdi, *mitrismo* achieved the status of 'a Koran, which it was an unwritten law to observe, on pain of excommunication for the crimes of barbarism and despotism'.[63] Conservative thought, although far from absent, as Nicolás Shumway has demonstrated,[64] never developed in Argentina to the extent that it did in either Chile or Mexico. The symbiotic nature of the relationship between liberal history and the state was well illustrated by a draft bill sent by the National Academy of History to the Ministry of Justice in 1942. This marshalled historical evidence to support demands that liberal nationalist iconography should be maintained, and specifically that the national flag should remain blue and white, as it had been created by Manuel Belgrano; that the national shield should continue to be a reproduction of the seal used by the General Constituent Assembly of 1813; and that the national anthem should continue to be a version approved in 1860.[65]

It was not until the 1930s, when Argentina's oligarchy resorted to authoritarianism and then electoral corruption in an attempt to re-establish its rule, that the hegemony of the liberal version of Argentine history was seriously called into question.[66] Inevitably, given the close links between this view of history and oligarchic government, the historical revisionism of the 1930s not only had political implications, it also had political goals. As one of its leading proponents, Arturo Jauretche, argued, 'the need for historical revisionism arose out of the need for a national political idea. . . . Thus, revisionism saw itself as obliged to go beyond exclusively historical ends.'[67] Revisionists belonged to two political camps: right-wing nationalists (influenced by the French monarchist and anti-Dreyfusard Charles Maurras [1868–1952]) who rejected liberalism's disparagement of Argentina's Catholic and Hispanic traditions, and popular nationalists who challenged liberalism's exclusion of the masses.[68] Both groups identified the fundamental cause of internal political weakness as an abdication of national interests to the foreigner,[69] and took their analysis right back into pre-independence times to demonstrate a long legacy of the oligarchy betraying the country to British imperialism. Revisionism was institutionalized with the foundation, in 1938, of the Juan Manuel de Rosas Institute for Historical Research.[70]

Liberal official history had been dominated by three legends: 'the black legend of Spanish America, the blue law of the "enlightened" and the red law of Rosas'.[71] The revisionists set out to challenge all three. They recast Rosas, who had been portrayed by liberals as a manifestation of reaction and barbarism, as the incarnation of Argentine virtues unsullied by foreign influences, an economic nationalist and an anti-imperialist (although in fact he was an Anglophile, whom the British helped to escape to exile in England after his defeat in 1852).[72] Most important for the argument here, however, was the extent to which debates about the role of intellectuals became irrevocably entangled with reinterpretations of Argentine history. As popular nationalist revisionists sought to refute the importance of the *ilustrados* (the learned) in Argentine history, a lasting stigma became attached to the idea of 'an intellectual'. Popular nationalists promoted the term 'intelligentsia' to distinguish themselves from Argentina's 'liberal' intellectuals – from Sarmiento to the university reform movement, *Sur* and *La Nación* – all of whom the 'intelligentsia' condemned for their betrayal of the 'true' Argentine values allegedly incarnated in Rosas, Yrigoyen and, later, Perón.[73] From the 1930s onwards in Argentina, even to identify oneself as an intellectual was to invite accusations of supporting the *vendepatria* oligarchy and imperialism against the interests of the people. Arturo Jauretche, for example, disowned his role as an intellectual: 'I do not accept being defined as an intellectual. . . . [I]t is enough for me . . . if someone thinks that I am a man with national ideas. If forced to choose between being an intellectual and being an Argentine, I vote for the second.'[74] By the late 1950s, after two anti-intellectual Peronist governments, even the term 'intelligentsia' had become tainted: in 1957, in a best-selling book entitled *Los profetas del odio y la yapa* [*The Prophets of Hatred*], Arturo Jauretche excoriated the Argentine 'intelligentsia' for having facilitated 'the process of constituting the [nations of South America] as dependent countries' because of the intellectuals' own attachment to 'universal' values.[75]

This attribution of lack of patriotism to intellectuals caused severe problems for a group of Argentine writers associated with the literary journal *Contorno*, which published ten issues from 1953 to 1959. These young men (David and Ismael Viñas, Tulio Halperín Donghi, Noé Jitrik, Adolfo Prieto, Leon Rozitchner, Oscar Masotta and Juan José Sebreli) were all middle-class; the majority were from Buenos Aires and Jewish-born. They studied at the University of Buenos Aires, mostly in the Faculty of Philosophy and Arts, during the Peronist years. By family tradition and philosophical inclination, they were natural Radical Party supporters, who were initially hostile to Perón because he was supported by the corporate weight of the Church and military. Later, as will be explored below, their position became more ambivalent.[76] Strongly influenced by French existentialism (a Spanish edition, published in 1950, of Sartre's *What is Literature?* became 'required reading' for them,[77] and the title *Contorno* echoed Sartre's concept of *situation*,)[78] they were the first generation of Argentine intellectuals who were prepared both to identify themselves as critical intellectuals and to place themselves on the side of the national-popular. They sought to become politically involved while remaining true to the spirit, and to keep culture and politics more or less in balance.

The one intervention in formal politics made by the *Contorno* intellectuals turned out to be a disaster: their declaration of support for Arturo Frondizi in the presidential elections of 1958.[79] This intervention, however, has to be understood in the context of this generation's vexed relationship with Peronism. In the aftermath of his overthrow in 1955, they had mixed feelings: having experienced the stultifying atmosphere of a

Peronist-controlled UBA, they could hardly have been wholeheartedly in favour; but they did identify with Perón's rhetoric against elitism and imperialism, and they unambiguously welcomed his incorporation of the working class into politics. The outright condemnation and abuse of the Perón couple by aristocratic intellectuals such as Borges (who mocked Eva as 'the blonde fairy' and denounced Perón's regime as a 'long period of infamy' and 'a nightmare')[80] was not an option for a generation that wanted to align itself with the masses. The *Contorno* group struggled to contend with the dilemma posed by the accumulating evidence that Perón had won the staunch allegiance of 'the people' for whom intellectuals claimed to speak. Given that Peronism had successfully established a monopoly over the 'national-popular tradition', expostulations of *rabia* (incoherent rage) at the very mention of Perón's name were deemed by the new generation to be indicative merely of the increasing bankruptcy of *Sur*'s emphasis on high culture. After 1955, many of the new generation of left-wing Argentine intellectuals identified with Perón at least in so far as they too were critical of the *mitrista* tradition. The *Contorno* group remained suspicious, however, of Peronist corruption, demagoguery and intimidation, all of which worsened with the rise of the Peronist union resistance after 1955. But the vehemence with which the incoming military regime sought to extirpate Peronist influence reinforced a stark dichotomy of Peronism/anti-Peronism which left anyone with more complex reactions in a marginalized position, lacking a clear identity. In venturing to finesse this difficulty, the *Contorno* group came to advocate the incorporation of the middle classes into Peronism, which explains why they decided to support Frondizi (who had done a deal with Perón to secure votes from the exiled ex-President's supporters). Their views on Peronism, which were published in issue 7/8 of *Contorno* in 1956, should be read in the light of their desire to act as intermediaries between the middle classes and the workers, trying to induce each to overcome their hostility to the other.[81]

The *Contorno* writers have been severely criticized, both at the time and subsequently, for their political attitudes. Some of these criticisms were similar to those meted out by the orthodox Left to French existentialists (for example, accusations that they emphasized human subjectivity, the power of ideas and morality over material forces; and replaced the party as revolutionary vanguard with the moral leadership of the intellectual). Other objections arose from the belief that these Argentine writers' interpretation of Sartre's concept of guilt prompted them less to 'greater sensitization and sympathy for Argentina's underdogs' than to a feeling of 'self-pity' for their own position 'as petit-bourgeois intellectuals in a system that had relegated them to a marginal position'. This, William Katra argues, was an attitude that was 'hardly [to] be compared to the altruistic "guilt" of Sartre'.[82] Of course, the Argentine intellectuals faced a very different *situation* from the

French: as Katra has pointed out, social and political conditions in France made the idea of collaboration between workers and intellectuals realistic (shared experiences in the Resistance during the Second World War, an advanced degree of class consciousness, and a system of public education that created a common cultural outlook), none of which existed in Argentina. In general, however, there is some foundation for the frequently encountered criticism that the *Contorno* writers were overpreoccupied with themselves and their own role, and had too much of a penchant for lapsing into subjectivity.[83] It is also hard to dispute José Aricó's view that after the overthrow of Perón in 1955 many left-wing Argentine intellectuals devoted their energies to convincing themselves that they had to accept 'as the only possible reality, the new Peronism that was reconstituted from outside the power of the state', instead of creating the conditions for 'self-criticism of [their] society geared towards overcoming its past'.[84]

For the purposes of this argument, however, the main point of interest lies in identifying the extent to which the *Contorno* group's misjudgements of both Frondizi and Peronism stemmed from the fact that their thinking was constrained by two sets of opposing historical stereotypes, derived from *mitrista* history on the one hand, and revisionism on the other. Revisionist nostrums went virtually unquestioned within left-wing Argentine cultural circles during the late 1950s. The clichés used to counter the liberal stereotypes have been summarized by Oscar Terán as follows: 'Rivadavia is the eternal "ideologue" who wanted to destroy the Catholic and Spanish legacies; it is a matter of great regret that *Facundo* is still read in the schools; Rosas represents a healthy nationalist response; England pulls all the strings behind the scenes, and where this sibylline imprint can most clearly be traced is in the politics of the railways.'[85]

The popularity of these ideas was partly a consequence of Perón's own appropriation of revisionist tenets. Perón skilfully drew upon each of the two types of nationalism (right-wing Catholic and popular/anti-imperialist) articulated during the 1930s, both of which subscribed to similar versions of historical revisionism. The reappropriation of history for political purposes was a consistent feature of Peronist propaganda (though while he often invoked General José de San Martín and Martín Fierro, Perón evaded the central controversy by avoiding mention of Juan Manuel de Rosas).[86] To take just one example that illustrates how history, politics and the role of the intellectual became inextricably intertwined, consider the ramifications of the official commemoration, in 1950, of the centenary of San Martín's death. José Aricó has suggested that Perón's decision to celebrate the conservative, monarchist San Martín – rather than the traditional pantheon of liberal independence heroes – was taken not only for political purposes but also to demonstrate 'the cultural hegemony achieved by a political force which was traditionally opposed to the world of intellectuals'.[87]

Liberal-democratic, socialist and Communist intellectuals duly sought to meet Perón's implicit challenge to their authority as intellectuals by launching a campaign in 1951 to rehabilitate the utopian socialist and poet Estebán Echeverría, who had died in exile in Uruguay one hundred years earlier. This attempt to revive the supposedly 'democratic' doctrine of the Generation of 1837 was their indirect way of protesting against Perón's authoritarianism by reasserting the values of the liberal tradition. As it transpired, however, Echeverría was not a convincing choice for the role of defender of democracy, having expressed the view that the people's sovereignty was best left in the realm of the symbolic, at least until education became universal.[88] Incidents such as this had made it plausible for Perón to condemn the liberal and traditional left-wing intellectuals in the Socialist and Communist parties as anti-popular. The *Contorno* intellectuals had no wish to be tarred with the same brush.

The *Contorno* writers certainly tried to transcend these sterile polemics. In an article of 1952, Juan José Sebreli explicitly attacked the dichotomy between 'blues' (liberals) and 'reds' (revisionists), arguing that the latter's proposal that Argentines should reject their rational half in the name of blood, land and authenticity simply inverted the liberals' prescription that Argentines should discard the irrational in favour of Reason and Western culture.[89] Both parties, he claimed, made the mistake of assuming that there was only one fixed truth, and both sustained false oppositions between logic and history, society and nature, reason and life – in other words, between civilization and barbarism.[90] In a similar plea for more subtlety of outlook, the editorial of *Contorno*'s special issue on Peronism declared, 'we have deliberately taken the risk of saying: this from Peronism, yes; this from Peronism, no'.[91] But the editorial also revealed the extent to which this generation saw its political predicament in existential terms:

> So we wanted to see what kind of a thing was this complex and debatable phenomenon that the country had gone through. . . . And equally we wanted to set ourselves the task of applying reason to what had happened, but [we wanted to do so] from within, writing as individuals who have been drenched by the rain, not as if we were claiming to be dry, intact and citizens of the world. We feel uncomfortable inside our own skins. . . . [W]e have no right to take shelter in the suspect shadow of a liberty that represents as yet no more than the arguments of those who are well-fed and the counter-arguments of those who are starving.[92]

The struggle for cultural hegemony in which they were engaged was made very evident when *Contorno*'s edition on Peronism was published – in direct response to *Sur*'s own exceptional issue devoted to politics.[93] The contents of *Contorno*'s reply were concerned far less with Peronism than with the cultural and political predicament of that particular generation. Leon Rozitchner's contribution, 'Proletarian experience and bourgeois experience', mainly discussed how intellectuals should align themselves in the class struggle; Osiris Troiani's 'Examination of conscience' was a Sartrean meditation on his own 'absent generation'; Ismael Viñas wrote about 'Fears, complexes and misunderstandings'; and Sebreli produced a testimony of his trajectory towards support for Peronism; only Tulio Halperín Donghi – the only one to appear in both *Sur* and *Contorno* – concentrated on the Peronist movement itself. With respect to Perón, the *Contorno* intellectuals shared *Sur*'s contempt, an attitude that was betrayed even when trying to refute *Sur*'s dismissal of him. Oscar Masotta wrote: 'It is not a question of arguing about whether Perón was a clown or not. It is a question of describing the conditions that made it possible for a clown to govern us for ten years.'[94] This was from an article largely devoted to an attack on *Sur* or, more accurately, to personal abuse of Victoria Ocampo ('It is important, it seems to us, to point out here that Victoria Ocampo knows only two modes of communication: shouting and praying').[95] Like the *Sur* intellectuals, the *Contorno* group both ignored the fact that so many Argentines had repeatedly voted for Perón and reduced the question of Peronism to the question of Perón.[96] Rozitchner's account of why the proletariat followed Perón echoed Sarmiento's explanation of *gaucho* support for the *caudillo* Don Facundo Quiroga. Rozitchner portrayed the masses as duped and manipulated by Perón, who had offered them false hope of liberty. According to his article, the proletariat, having learned that the powerful were dominant, 'believed that they could be liberated only by another dominant leader'. Perón gave the proletariat 'the illusion of their own power', Rozitcher argued, concluding, 'Only a man like Perón could do it, because being a military man, accustomed to power, he knew which strings to pull to manipulate those forces that are always prone to seduction, blandishment and self-interest.'[97]

In one sense, the *Contorno* writers' whole project was based on a denial of history. Their longing for a radical break with the past (a critic later characterized them as 'parricides')[98] echoed Peronism's own myths about its origin, which were also founded on a supposed rupture with the liberal-dominated past and the regeneration of 'true' Argentine values embodied in the *descamisados*.[99] Katra has pointed out, however, that much of their analysis of Peronism was based on ahistorical categories 'reminiscent of Mallea's nostalgia or the anti-modern anarchism of Martínez Estrada'.[100] When they did move beyond essentialism to a more historical approach, they remained caught in the framework established in the 1930s, echoing revisionism's attacks on all that liberals held sacred. Beatriz Sarlo has argued that, by making it possible to rethink Peronism, the *Contorno* group and others from the Argentine Left 'opened a new chapter in the history of Argentine intellectuals'. She maintains that their interpretation was not merely a symmetric opposition to *Sur*'s rejection of Peronism, and that it

raised 'a set of valuable questions, governed by the idea ... that events as
they had been lived in the first Peronist decade were resistant to summary
analysis'.[101] In terms of the legacy the *Contorno* group bequeathed to the
social democrats of the 1980s, perhaps this argument is valid, but it remains
the case that at the time, their attempt to break the mould of Argentine
thought had little impact, and they proved unable to sustain a position as
critical intellectuals. Most of them went on to establish themselves as
professional academics; only David Viñas continued to make interventions
from an avowedly universalist standpoint. Overall, the *Contorno* group offers
one of the clearest examples of a generation of Spanish American intellectuals who found that their own social predicament as intellectuals impeded
their capacity to realize the intellectual task they had identified for
themselves.

The opposition between *mitristas* and popular nationalists that had begun
in the 1930s continued to cast a shadow over Argentine intellectual life into
the 1970s. One manifestation of this was the public prominence enjoyed by
Arturo Jauretche, who despite his own rejection of the label 'intellectual'
has none the less been identified by many of the Argentine intelligentsia as
one of the most influential intellectuals in Argentina between 1958 and
1972.[102] Although he was disparaged by intellectuals for not having any
professional base as an economist, a historian or a creative writer, his
defence was that he was representative of the average Argentine: 'I am in
no sense an intellectual, merely a compatriot who sees the affairs of his
nation through Argentine eyes and from the standpoint of the masses, who
were formerly supporters of Yrigoyen, latterly of Perón.'[103] He cultivated a
reputation as an iconoclast, challenging the social codes and mores of an
Argentine cultural establishment still imbued with liberalism. Most of
Jauretche's 'polemics' concerned interpretations of Argentine history, and
all were played out within battle lines drawn up in the 1930s.

These polemics often became vicious. While appearing on a television
programme in 1971, Jauretche referred to Dr Carlos Saavedra Lamas, who
had been Minister of Foreign Affairs during the 1930s and had won the
Nobel Peace Prize – Argentina's first Nobel Prize – for his role in negotiat-
ing a settlement to the Chaco War (1932–35) between Bolivia and Paraguay.
What Jauretche actually said is not recorded, but he evidently mentioned
Saavedra's allegedly close links with British economic interests, specifically
Royal Dutch Shell in Paraguay. In Bolivia, US interests were dominant, in
the form of Standard Oil of California, and Jauretche's apparent imputation
was that Saavedra had ensured that British interests were safeguarded in the
treaty. Saavedra's niece duly had a letter published in *La Nación*, defending
her uncle's reputation, to which Jauretche replied, in a journal article, that
apparently she divided historical personages into two categories: 'those who
have descendants and those who do not, because the former can be

defended by a relative and the latter . . . must rot in isolation'.[104] The elite's claim to see Argentine history as if it were family history was analogous to their tendency to regard the nation as their family property, Jauretche alleged.[105]

An even more telling incident was Jauretche's response to criticism of the first film ever made about Rosas, entitled *Juan Manuel de Rosas* and shown in 1972. The film provoked predictable outrage in the two newspaper bastions of liberalism, *La Nación* and *La Prensa*, but was also criticized by the historian Félix Luna, author of books on Perón that were certainly not in the *mitrista* mode of demonology.[106] In his own journal, *Todo es Historia*, Luna welcomed the breaking of the taboo on Rosas, but argued that the film was weakened by its tendency to caricature any character who was not *rosista*. Current historiography was finally going beyond this schematic approach, he stated, arguing, 'Going back to revisionist exaggeration is as negative as returning to liberal mendacity.'[107] Jauretche's response was to claim that liberal 'history' went beyond history to become what he called a 'politics of history', and that revisionism was fighting a war against a well-entrenched enemy that already had on its side 'all the statues, all the portraits, in all the squares and in all the schools'. In such circumstances, Jauretche argued, there was no place for the 'equanimity' of the historian because 'the objective means of forming opinion are not equable'.[108] Sigal drily notes that Jauretche's fame 'certainly did not bring about any alteration in the rules governing the discipline' of history.[109] In a situation in which history had become not just politicized but politics in itself, any attempt to sustain a position of critical independence was open to attack as weakness, acquiescence or betrayal.

Chile: History as Nostalgia

Twentieth-century Chilean intellectuals inherited a comparatively strong historiographical tradition from the nineteenth century: in contrast to other Spanish American republics, the Chilean state had encouraged the establishment of a community of historians in the University of Chile since the 1840s. An institutional basis for professional history (even including a central office of statistics founded in 1843) was established far earlier in Chile than in the other four case study countries in this book. Nineteenth-century Chilean historians believed themselves to be more methodologically advanced, more objective and more professional than their counterparts in other Spanish American countries. Allen Woll has demonstrated in his study of nineteenth-century Chilean historiography that this supposed professionalization of history as a discipline (which came down to the imparting of methodological skills at the University of Chile or the National Institute) did not in practice prevent the use of history for political purposes, although it was often used as a shield for it.[110] Chile's historians successfully promoted the idea that their country's history, unlike that of its neighbours, was one to inspire respect and emulation, arguing that under a conservative, centralizing constitution (1833), Chile had avoided the high levels of social conflict and militarism experienced in most other Spanish American republics. As Woll has pointed out, Chile is unusual in Spanish America in that the state has honoured historians, building monuments and statues to the leading names of nineteenth-century Chilean historiography, most of whom were also statesmen.[111]

It appears to be all the more remarkable, therefore, that the most influential works of Chilean history during the twentieth century were not written by historians, and that the dominant image of Chile's history came to be one of national decline. Cristián Gazmuri has identified the main proponents of the theory of *decadentismo* as Luis Galdames (1881–1941), Alberto Edwards (1874–1932) and Francisco Encina (1874–1965).[112] These writers, none of whom was a professional historian, were influenced by the idea of decadence present in the work of many early-twentieth-century European thinkers, most explicitly Oswald Spengler, whose *Decline of the West* was published in Chile in 1923. Edwards acknowledged that Spengler's views had affected him profoundly; Encina persistently denied any influence of Spengler in his own work. Particularly in Edwards's case, however, the outline of his version of Chilean history can be traced as early as 1903,[113] and arguably Spengler simply enabled him to lend the kudos of a leading European philosopher to his own ideas about Chile. The defining event that had confirmed the already growing doubts among the educated elite about Chile's political institutions was the civil war of 1891, which culminated in the triumph of the *congresistas* and the shock of President Balmaceda's suicide shortly afterwards. In the succeeding Parliamentary Republic (1891–1920), the role of Chile's hitherto strong executive was sharply reduced. The *decadentista* interpretation represented Chile's history as one of inexorable decline from the great days of the Portalian republic, when strong government had allegedly brought order, hierarchy and progress to the nation. This conservative myth persisted notwithstanding Chile's political achievements in the twentieth century, notably a relatively smooth transition from oligarchic to middle-class government in the 1920s–30s, and the maintenance of constitutional government until 1973. Chilean conservatives succeeded, for well over half a century, in convincing not only the oligarchy but also the rising middle classes of this version of the nation's past.[114] Indeed, Chile's twentieth-century historiographical tradition is distinctive in Spanish America for the strength of a conservative view of history, which endured into the 1960s and is not without its more recent exponents.[115]

A precursor can be identified in the educator Luis Galdames, whose *Historia de Chile* was published in 1906–07, so that at least two generations were introduced to Chilean history through his work (it continued to be reprinted until 1974).[116] He outlined the ideas that later came to constitute the myth of *decadentismo*: that Diego Portales might have been authoritarian but he had at least ensured stability; that the constitution of 1833 was the 'first and most glorious tradition' of the conservative party; and that under the Parliamentary Republic 'it was never possible to undertake methodical and continuous government work'.[117] But Galdames, who was from a middle-class background, found Chile's governance after 1920 to his liking. He saw Alessandri's election as a victory for 'advocates of a profound social and political change, in the sense of a broader "democratization" of national institutions'.[118] In editions of the *Historia de Chile* that appeared after 1920, Galdames revised his theory of *decadentismo* so that it ended with the Parliamentary Republic, and, in the eighth edition – of 1938 – he finally renounced it altogether: '[Chilean] decadence does not exist. Here are four centuries of history to belie that idea.'[119]

Alberto Edwards had grown up in Buenos Aires and was from an aristocratic background, although as an adult he was obliged to work for a living: 'he was not rich, and he had to go into public administration after a brief passage through Parliament'.[120] He was a scholar, mainly of geography, but did not see himself as an intellectual in the modern sense. His book *La fronda aristocrática* [*The Aristocratic Frond*] (1927),[121] one of the best-known interpretations of Chilean history, contended that Chilean society (by which he meant the elite) had inherited from the colonial period a set of values that coalesced into Chile's 'national soul' during Portales's authoritarian rule. In Portalian Chile, aristocracy was defined less by inheritance than in terms of the 'moral quality of preferring public order to chaos',[122] so it was not wholly implausible for Edwards to represent this period as an aristocracy of merit. In his view, it was the introduction of liberalism and French culture during President José Joaquín Pérez's government (1861–71) – bringing new values that were essentially in conflict with Chile's true being – that led to a weakening of the national spirit. With the triumph of liberalism in 1891, and the subsequent Parliamentary Republic, Edwards believed that Chile entered into a definitive decline, in which the 'national soul' became distorted by bourgeois parliamentarianism and policies such as free mass education. Edwards was even more dismayed by the entry of the Chilean middle classes into politics in 1920; he was unable to accept that men without any political tradition could possibly govern competently. The only way out for Chile, as he saw it, was Caesarism, and he agreed to act as Minister of Education in the government of the dictator Carlos Ibáñez (1927–30).[123]

The most controversial of the three creators of *decadentismo* was Francisco

Encina, whose critique of foreign economic penetration in Chile, *Nuestra inferioridad económica* [*Our Economic Inferiority*], was published in 1912. Later, his twenty-volume *Historia de Chile* (1940–52) made him probably the most popular Chilean historian of the twentieth century (the total print run came to about 200,000).[124] He was not an intellectual in the sense used in this book: he benefited from family inheritance to establish himself as a wealthy commercial agriculturalist by his early thirties, and never sought to earn a living from his writing. However, it is inaccurate to portray him as simply an ideologue for Chile's land-owning class.[125] His family was part of the commercial bourgeoisie that had emerged during the regime of Manuel Montt (1851–61), a new sector of the elite whose wealth came from business rather than land ownership. Convinced that Chile's economic future lay not in agriculture but in industrialization, he attacked the upper classes for their preference for foreign goods, comparing their attitudes unfavourably (and probably also inaccurately) with those in Argentina where, according to Encina, people were proud to say 'made in Buenos Aires'.[126] Encina served as a deputy for the National Party, which represented this commercial sector, from 1906 to 1912, apparently without much enthusiasm or effect. He was one of a younger, nationalist generation who, without being socially radical, saw the need for the extension of popular education and limited labour legislation. Frustrated with the endless machinations and compromises of the existing parties in the Parliamentary Republic, this group (Encina, Edwards, Guillermo Subercaseaux and others) formed the National Union, later called the Nationalist Party, in 1915. Their programme included measures to restore the pre-1891 balance of power between executive and legislature, economic nationalism, the independence of state education from political influence, and steps to ensure that the University of Chile extended its remit beyond the provision of professional training to become a centre of research and scientific progress.[127] It was a great mistake, Encina contended, for Chilean intellectuals to try to apply European education systems in Chile without introducing some national content.[128] He also criticized the importance Chileans attached to the liberal professions which, in his view, had such a monopoly on social status that they soaked up 'not only the special talents, but all talents'.[129] Likewise, he attacked Chilean intellectuals for sustaining the prejudice that industrial entrepreneurship required no talent.[130]

As its title implies, *Nuestra inferioridad económica* was an indictment more of Chile than of the imperialist powers. Encina's view was that foreign capital had taken such a strong hold in Chile because of 'an extraordinary economic ineptitude in the national population'.[131] In seeking the causes for this, he veered between social Darwinism (attributing the problem to racial mentality) and liberal-positivism (blaming it on what he saw as Chile's 'detestable and inadequate education').[132] There is no doubt that Encina propagated racial stereotypes, representing Chilean workers as vigorous, proud and intelligent but hindered by 'Araucanian atavism', which made them 'incapable of the regular and sustained work' achieved by 'the most evolved peoples' (that is, Britons and North Americans).[133] He did not consider the possibility that the presence of foreign capital might have constrained the development of national entrepreneurial activity, insisting on precisely the opposite: namely, that foreign penetration was an effect of Chilean inferiority with respect to capitalist development.[134] But while maintaining that foreign investment had brought more rapid progress to Chile than would otherwise have been possible, he identified two fatal drawbacks: the Chilean people (or at least the elites) had been taught to consume before they had learned to produce, and the national spirit – that is, according to Encina, the moral force behind economic vitality – had been destroyed.[135] Increasing contact with 'foreign civilizations' would, he argued, serve only to exacerbate Chileans' sense of inferiority and weaken their capacity to compete still further.[136]

National character was a major theme of his *Historia de Chile*, and although Encina never subscribed explicitly to the myth of *decadentismo*, he reproduced it in all the essentials. However, the influences on his work of Edwards and the nineteenth-century historian Diego Barros Arana have been subjects of considerable dispute. Although it has been demonstrated convincingly that Encina's *Historia de Chile* adopted not only the periodization used by Edwards but also the main arguments about national decline,[137] Encina vehemently denied that he had been influenced by Edwards, arguing that the influence had in fact been the other way around. More important, although Encina attacked Barros Arana's *Historia general de Chile* (1884–1902) for methodological weaknesses, arguing that it was little more than a compilation of facts, he manifestly owed a huge debt to Barros Arana's work.[138] Encina's public expressions of contempt for Barros Arana moved even a highly sympathetic biographer to rebuke him: 'As a historian, Encina had made good use of Barros Arana's work and his disrespect was an irritating injustice.'[139]

Encina may have been contemptuous of intellectuals, but he was always anxious to claim academic distinction for himself. A law graduate with little formal training in historical method (a self-styled 'simple bohemian of thought'),[140] he appropriated the legacy of nineteenth-century professionalism in history in order to lend legitimacy to his work. In his first historical work, an encomium to Portales, published in 1934, Encina argued that it was because of the inability of intellectuals to appreciate Portales's genius that he did not enjoy the influence he deserved: 'the apostle's influence was limited by the intellectuals' lack of understanding of him'.[141] Encina mythologized Portales, arguing that his 'transcendental' importance in Chilean history lay not in his achievements as a state-builder, but in his incarnation of the 'creative genius' and 'national spirit' of the Chilean people.[142] General Pinochet was later to appropriate this Portalian myth, representing himself as the reincarnation of the 'nation's ancestral values'.[143]

A conservative interpretation of history, propounded by men who were neither historians nor intellectuals but more typical of the nineteenth-century figure of the *pensador*, succeeded in establishing dominance for most of the twentieth century in Chile. In seeking an explanation for this, we should bear in mind that an intellectually vibrant conservatism developed partly because it was plausible to believe in conserving aspects of the past: Chile's nineteenth century *was* far less turbulent than that of most of its neighbours. But it reflected, above all, the weakness of any intellectual challenge from cultural nationalists who tried to elaborate an idea of *lo popular*. After the events of 1891, which had raised questions about Chile's much-vaunted political stability, a few middle-class intellectuals tried during the 1900s to introduce an ethnic element into Chile's national identity with the archetype of the *roto* (poor labourer), supposedly an amalgam of Gothic and Araucanian ancestries. The most notable example was *Raza chilena*, published in 1904 by Dr Nicolás Palacios (1854–1911), who argued that Chileans were the result of miscegenation between conquerors who were descended not from the Spaniards but the Goths and the Araucanians.[144] Palacios's *mestizo* never acquired the archetypal status accorded to the *gaucho* in Argentina, and a later attempt to turn the Chilean *roto* into a national hero also failed.[145] Thinkers who identified with the oligarchy won the battle for hegemony of ideas with only minor challenges from middle-class intellectuals during the first three decades of the twentieth century. The oligarchy relinquished political power in the 1920s, but it can be said to have retained ideological hegemony for at least another two decades, just as many historians have argued that it retained economic power. In contrast to other Spanish American countries, where popular national identities (*argentinidad, mexicanidad*) were promoted by middle-class intellectuals, there was little discussion of *chilenidad*. Instead, conservative terminology – ideas of a 'national soul', which lacked a popular dimension – remained dominant. When Chile's national unity was once again shattered by the events of the early 1970s, a new interest in *lo chileno* became manifest, but once more it was the preserve of the Right.[146] Throughout the twentieth century, conservatives maintained a virtual monopoly on Chilean national identity.

In 1971, the historian Ariel Peralta Pizarro (1939–) published an attack on the theory of national decline entitled *El mito de Chile* [*The Myth of Chile*]. It was dedicated to 'the country's new leaders, whose actions should annihilate the myths that made Chile a nation with a truncated destiny'.[147] He attacked the Centenary Generation as 'vociferous but isolated individuals clamouring with bold and chauvinist hysteria for Chile's moral decline'.[148] What this book revealed, above all, however, was the very persistence of the myth of national decline: Peralta offered little more than another version thereof. For him, the point at which Chile entered into decline was in the mid-nineteenth century, when 'by historical anomaly, an ill-understood liberalism introduced the myth of democracy into the collective soul'.[149] Since then, generations of Chileans, comforting themselves with the belief that 'we are by definition democratic', had turned their backs upon 'autochthonous culture' and 'hidden values', accommodating themselves to being 'the apocryphal sons of Western culture'.[150] Chile would be saved, he concluded rather unpersuasively, by '*machismo*, the irreplaceable vertebrae of the psychic health of all Latin Americans'.[151] In its tone, Peralta's book, which claimed to be attacking the theory of *decadentismo*, echoes Encina's *Nuestra inferioridad económica*, which claimed to refute it: yet, the thinking about Chilean history of each work is limited by its framework.

Cuba: History as Political Liberation

Cuba's late independence, in 1898, meant that the idea of historical consciousness being closely related to different conceptions of a country's future was established before Cuba became a nation, rather than afterwards as had largely been the case in other Spanish American countries. The second half of the nineteenth century had seen a widening gap between histories of Cuba written by pro-Spanish Cubans, who continued to insist on the benefits of Spanish colonialism, and those written by creole separatists, who began to emphasize its exploitative elements, for example, by discussing slavery.[152] Immediately after independence, steps were taken, firstly by the US occupying forces and subsequently by republican Cuban governments, to create an institutional basis for professional history. The first US military government appointed Vidal Morales y Morales head of the archives, and in 1902 he initiated publication of the *Boletín del Archivo Nacional*, the earliest archival review in the region to maintain continuous publication.[153] From the early days of the republic, emphasis was placed on the collation of documents. This in itself was an anti-colonial issue, since many of the documents relating to Cuba's history were deposited in Spanish archives, which had been closed to Cuban colonial subjects. When an Academy of History was established in 1910, one of its first tasks was to send a team of academics to Spain, where they spent several years sifting through early material; and a collection of documents covering the period 1493–1512 was eventually published in 1929.[154]

Cuba's historiography has been complicated by the fact that from the 1850s onwards, US historians have taken a particular interest in the island's

238 INTELLECTUAL DISCOURSES OF POPULAR NATIONALISM

history. During the twentieth century, some Cuban historians probably benefited from contact with their US colleagues and access to US research facilities. However, Louis A. Pérez, Jr has argued that the main consequence of US involvement was that Cuban historians wrote a revisionist response to the imperialistic historiography coming from the United States *before* they had established a body of national history that warranted revision. He wrote:

> Devoted to the nineteenth-century ideal of Cuba Libre . . . [n]ational mythmakers rejected the republic, perceiving in the entity of state only a caricature of sovereignty and a betrayal of the ideals of independence. In repudiating the organic foundations of state, specifically the Constitution of 1901 and the . . . Platt Amendment, revisionist writers withheld from the republic the historiographical corroboration necessary to underwrite its claim of legitimacy.[155]

Pérez has analysed one very specific instance of how US interest in the writing of Cuba's history for its own political purposes shaped the development of Cubans' thinking about their own history.[156] In 1927, the Berkeley professor Charles E. Chapman published *A History of the Cuban Republic*, which became the standard text on Cuba for a generation of students. This book was commissioned by General Enoch Crowder, who, in 1921, had been appointed Special Representative of the President in Cuba, with instructions to eliminate corruption from Cuban government. When the US and Cuba upgraded their diplomatic missions to embassy status in 1923, Crowder stayed on as the first US ambassador, but rapidly found that he was losing influence with President Alfredo Zayas, who dismissed Crowder's 'Honest Cabinet' in June 1923. Crowder decided that a history of Cuba publicizing the degree of corruption and mismanagement in Cuban government affairs might help to generate support for his reform proposals. He duly approached the Carnegie Foundation in late 1923, and received a grant of $4,000. Although there is ample evidence that Professor Chapman resisted embassy pressure to represent all US administrative practice as wholly virtuous and all Cuban attempts at self-government as doomed to degenerate into vice, the final version of his book, which neglected to acknowledge the role played by Crowder in its instigation, turned out to be well-suited to Crowder's original intention. Although Chapman denied that the Spanish character was innately ungovernable or that Cuba was 'hopeless politically', his failure to make any structural connection between the persistence of administrative corruption and the role of the USA in limiting the possibility for meaningful politics in Cuba meant that the general impression given was that Cubans – rather like their fellow Spanish Americans – ultimately needed to be saved from themselves.[157]

It was against this kind of negative stereotyping of their country that younger Cuban historians began to react in the 1920s and 1930s. In 1940 a generation of revisionists led by Emilio Roig de Leuchsenring organized the

Cuban Society for Historical and International Studies as an alternative to
the Academy of History. As discussed in Chapter 5, their works were
dominated by anti-imperialism. Historical revisionism was encouraged by
Batista's first government (1940–44), which found the precepts of revisionist
history to its political advantage. His government funded the construction
of a building specially designed to house Cuba's national archives, which
had previously led a peripatetic existence around various sites in Havana.[158]
Batista also chaired the inaugural session of the Second National Congress
of History, held in 1943, an event that revealed how closely the Cuban
Society for Historical Studies had become tied in with his government. Roig
de Leuchsenring's opening speech, 'La cubanidad en los congresos nacionales de historia' ['*Cubanidad* in the national congresses of history'], took as
its main theme Cuba's contribution to democracy. In the midst of the
Second World War, he noted, with Cuba on the side of the Allies, this was
an opportune moment to dwell on Cuba's two centuries of struggle, which
he said had been conducted in the name of democracy.[159] Roig de Leuchsenring also went out of his way to emphasize that he and his colleagues
were not 'puffed up with useless knowledge and isolated in the unreal world
of speculation and dreams',[160] and that they were only too well aware of the
need not to 'criminally cut themselves off in the ivory tower of their literary,
artistic or scientific speculations'.[161] The Final Act of the congress affirmed
that 'Cuba is one of the nations of the Americas which struggles for
democracy, and aspires for democracy to be established throughout the
world.'[162]

The subsequent populist governments of the *auténticos* (1944–52), which
were weak, corrupt and acquiescent in US control of Cuba, similarly
encouraged historical revisionism as a means of bolstering their feeble
claims to be nationalist governments defending Cuban sovereignty. The
Cuban Society for Historical Studies held annual congresses until 1952
during which it passed resolutions on historical matters that had direct
implications for the stimulation of nationalist sentiment. For example, in
1943 the historians voted to change the name of the Spanish-American War
to the Spanish-Cuban-American War, an act that was subsequently approved
by the Cuban legislature.[163] In 1952 the Final Acts of the Tenth National
Congress of History declared that the war in 1898 had been won by Cuban
arms and therefore should not be regarded as a gift from the United States;
they decreed that the 'Hispanic' period was to be renamed the 'colonial
period'; and they denounced US interference with Cuban freedom from
the Platt Amendment up to 1952.[164] When the Academy of History published its ten-volume *Historia de la nación cubana* (1952), with a state
contribution towards the cost of publication and edited by the conservative
historian Ramiro Guerra y Sánchez (1880–1970), it included the work of a
few revisionists.[165]

Pérez has argued persuasively that the revisionists' reduction of Cuban history to anti-imperialism and the corresponding absence of good historiography on the republican period suited the desire of the post-1959 revolutionary government to represent it as 'a vice-laden age in which oppression, corruption, and exploitation flourished under the enforced sanction of the United States'.[166] Revisionism was adopted enthusiastically by the revolutionaries: revisionist works were reprinted, and their major themes – 'imperialism, neo-colonialism and the pseudo-republic' – became part of the rhetoric of the revolution. Cuba's history has officially been represented since the 1959 revolution as a continuous struggle for 'true' independence, starting with the first independence war – the Ten Years' War (1868–78), followed by the Independence War (1895–98), the 1933 revolution and finally, the 1959 revolution.

Conclusion

Tulio Halperín Donghi has argued that in the 1960s the literati abandoned history out of hope (that Latin America could escape from the weight of its past and that cultural liberation would ultimately lead to political freedom), and the social scientists did so out of despair (a sense that Latin America was trapped by its history and only a complete break with the past could achieve emancipation).[167] After the 1959 Cuban revolution, many Spanish American intellectuals, partly influenced by their readings of Stalin, who was still the main source of Marxist ideas (his *Short Course on the History of the Communist Party of the Soviet Union* [1938] was 'almost obligatory' in Argentina),[168] became caught up in a crude Marxist reductionism. This was a decade when belief in the possibility of revolution led many Spanish American intellectuals to give priority to politics and suppress the past in what has been referred to as a permanent 'flight towards the future'.[169] At the same time, history was also under threat from those who claimed that Spanish America's past could be captured only through literature.

The claim that Latin America's history was fiction was most famously made in Alejo Carpentier's prologue to his novel about the Haitian slave revolt of 1791, *El reino de este mundo* [*The Kingdom of This World*] (1949). Carpentier began by emphasizing that his work of fiction was founded on historical accuracy: 'the tale that is going to unfold before you was based on extremely rigorous documentation, which not only respects the historical truth of events, names of characters (including secondary ones), places and even streets, but also conceals beneath its apparent timelessness a highly detailed compilation of dates and chronologies'.[170] The prologue concluded, however, with the question, 'But what is the history of America if not a chronicle of the marvellous real?'[171] Thus Carpentier equated history

with fiction (a position that is distinct from the more usual observations that
history resembles fiction, can provide a basis for it, is analogous to it, has
fictional qualities, or indeed that literature itself has an alternative history
to tell). He thereby opened it up to the forces of invention and imagination.
González Echevarría has tellingly criticized Carpentier's nostalgia 'for that
elusive Golden Age when fable and history were one' and his desire 'to
isolate something . . . exclusively Latin American in his concept of the
"marvellous" '.[172] Carpentier evoked an allegedly special apprehension of
life peculiar to Latin America, which, he suggested, had escaped the self-
consciousness of the alienated European and was more inclined to faith,
thereby enabling Latin Americans 'to feel history not as a causal process
that can be analysed rationally . . . but as destiny' (a view that owed much to
Oswald Spengler).[173] González Echevarría raised the question: 'If the result
of historicity in Carpentier is ahistoricity, what of his avowed project to
rescue the origins and history of Latin America?'[174] During the 1960s, the
versions of Spanish American history that arguably had the most powerful
impact, especially abroad, were to be found not in history books but in
novels. The experimental literary style known as 'magical realism' became
transmuted into a methodology that was claimed to be more powerful than
history for decoding Latin American reality.

The idea disseminated internationally by the novelists who achieved
celebrity status during the 1960s was that fiction was the best way of writing
Spanish America's history. This new literary endeavour was qualitatively
different from earlier conceptions of poetry as the voice of those excluded
from history, or of the novel as a vehicle for evading censorship, both of
which preserved the idea of accumulated historical experience.[175] José
Donoso characterized the 1960s literary 'boom' as 'a series of books aspiring
to serve as shortcuts for reaching, as quickly as possible, a consciousness of
what is national in each of the countries'.[176] In one sense, many of these
novels represented a rejection of the search for essence that had dominated
the national character essays; for example, in his novel *La región más
transparente* [*Where the Air is Clear*] (1958) Carlos Fuentes wrote the following:

> The original lies in the impure, the mixed. Like us, like me, like Mexico. That is
> to say, the original assumes a mixing, a creation, not a purity previous to our
> experience. Rather than being born original, we come to be so: the origin is a
> creation. Mexico must attain its originality by looking forward; it won't find it by
> looking back.[177]

Paradoxically, however, given this rejection of history by many of the 'boom'
writers, as Halperín Donghi has argued, the success of the literary
'boom' was closely related to the conviction, both within and without the
region, that Spanish America's 'stormy history had entered into a phase of

resolution' – not only because of the hope afforded early in the decade by the Cuban revolution, but also because of the rapidity with which those dreams were punctured with the death of Che Guevara in 1967 and the rise of a 'modernized' version of military authoritarianism.[178]

The most famous novel of the literary 'boom', Gabriel García Márquez's *Cien años de soledad*, presented a cyclical view of history – a denial of any accumulation of collective experience and a return to the fables with which the history of the Americas began in the late fifteenth century. The novelists of the 1960s set up the opposition between official history (characterized by Eduardo Galeano as a 'display case where the system exhibits its old disguises')[179] and the 'real' history of Spanish America. In so doing, they ignored the fact that, by then, by no means all the history that was being written in Spanish America was official history.[180] The writers of the literary 'boom' exploded the myth of progress in Spanish American history and in doing so denied the value of any orthodox attempts to write history just at the time when professional historians were beginning to produce work that overcame earlier limitations. The novelists' linguistic and formalistic experimentation while treating historical themes was, Doris Sommer has argued, equivalent to 'a capitulation to the apparent chaos of Latin American history'.[181] The novels of the 'boom' represented the writers' sense of liberation from the shackles of having to be somehow 'typically' Spanish American in their works and, indeed, in the conduct of their lives. Linguistic and structural innovation enabled them to explore Spanish American reality without feeling constrained by it, as their nativist and socialist realist predecessors had been in the 1920s–40s. This was perceived as literature's chance to free itself from the constraints of history. But the 'boom' novels 'centred on the delusion that a certain total knowledge of Latin America must be sought through its literature'.[182] In this assertion of their own literary freedom, they imprisoned history within a set of stereotypes.

In the 1960s, language became reified and history was dismissed as a dangerous entrapment. This position was exemplified in Carlos Fuentes's essay *La nueva novela hispanoamericana* (1969), in which he argued that the long-established opposition between civilization and barbarism in Latin American culture could be transcended by the liberating force of imaginative language: 'Everything is language in Latin America: power and liberty, domination and hope. But if the language of barbarism desires to submit us to the lineal determinism of time, the language of the imagination desires to shatter that fate, freeing the simultaneous spaces of the real.'[183]

The extent to which history has been appropriated by culture in twentieth-century Spanish America was revealed more recently in Carlos Fuentes's response to the quincentenary of conquest in 1992. In a work of popular history, *The Buried Mirror*, which was based on a television series for the BBC, Fuentes proposed that Latin America's historical failure could be compensated for by its cultural success, arguing that 'few cultures in the world possess such continuity as those of Indo-Afro-Ibero America'.[184] Yet this myth of cultural continuity could be sustained only by denying that all the glories of Spanish colonization were the work of people who saw themselves as Spanish:

> From the catastrophe of the conquest, the Indoiberoamericans were born. We were, immediately, mestizos. . . . we built a new civilization, whose hubs were our great cities. . . . Cities with printing presses [and] universities . . . a century before any of this came into being in Anglo America.[185]

The historical evidence, so far as it can be ascertained, is that this 'new civilization' was created by people who saw themselves as Spaniards and whose allegiance was to the colonial power, until at least the mid-eighteenth century.[186] It was not until the late eighteenth century that a distinctively Spanish American consciousness can be identified. By his historical sleight of hand, Fuentes could uphold the claim that 'we have a good culture because we made it ourselves, and a bad politics and economics because, perhaps, they were made for us'.[187] This returns us to the problem that almost anything can be resolved by means of rhetoric. In a review of *The Buried Mirror*, Mike Gonzalez characterized the book's language as 'the marriage of civilization (precision) and barbarism (sensuality) in a rhetoric replete with metaphors and epiphanies' which 'fulfils a metropolitan expectation'.[188] Yet one of the major problems highlighted by the quincentenary of 1992 is that Spanish American cultures were still far from united: Fuentes himself opined, in the same article, that 'we, the modern Latin Americans, have behaved with as much cruelty or indifference toward the Indians as Columbus or Pizarro'.[189] As Magdalena Chocano has argued with respect to Peru, evasion of the past almost invariably leads to evasiveness about the present.[190]

The writing of Spanish American history has always posed dilemmas, and perhaps these are irresolvable. It may be that the pursuit of history is attractive only to a society that is comfortable with its present circumstances and confident about the future. In the absence of such relative security, 'the history of the past will seem a meaningless jumble of unrelated events'.[191] This is perhaps especially the case in less developed countries where the future often appears to be so unpromising. Renan observed as long ago as 1882 that an economical approach to historical truth has been a feature of all nation-building: 'Forgetting, I would even go so far as to say historical error, is a crucial factor in the creation of a nation.'[192] All creators of national identities have plundered the past for historical events and personages that could be represented in such a way as to stimulate popular pride and a sense of patriotic unity, while denying, ignoring or obscuring those that did not (although, as Benedict Anderson recently pointed out, there is always an implied consensus as to what should be forgotten, which itself becomes part of the national mythology.)[193] The underlying tension between what to commemorate and what to forget was particularly hard to resolve for nations that found themselves lagging behind in the process of industrialization: they needed both to celebrate their history in order to establish their identity and simultaneously to abandon their past in order to integrate into the modern world of scientific, technological and political rationality. But if history is written primarily as an adjunct to the creation of a myth of national identity, it will always tend towards one of two simplifications: either the past is everything (nostalgia) or the future is all (prophecy). As Halperín Donghi noted in a prologue to his *Historia contemporánea de América Latina* (probably the most widely read general history of the region among Spanish speakers), 'For Latin America, far more than for the more settled societies with a longer historical experience, the future will remain . . . an untrustworthy starting point for the study of history.'[194]

Conclusion

Much of the evidence presented in this book substantiates the view that the cumulative effect of Spanish American intellectuals' activity was to make them collectively accessories rather than advisers to the Prince. In those countries of the region where popular national identities have been consolidated with some degree of success, the main architects of this consolidation were state leaders: the Partido Revolucionario Institucional (PRI) from the 1930s to the 1950s, Perón (from 1946 to 1955), and Castro's government since 1959. As Castañeda notes, 'The great nationalist leaders of modern Latin America did not belong to the intellectual elite,'[1] and they were reluctant to concede any ground to intellectuals in their nation-building projects. These statesmen pursued their own designs for national integration, which were amalgams of bowdlerized ideas, often appropriated from intellectuals of different generations who were unlikely to have agreed either with each other or with the policies implemented. Thus, in Mexico, Vasconcelos, Ramos and Paz, all of whom were in their different ways opposed to cultural nationalism, found themselves acclaimed as the creators of its archetypes; in Argentina, Scalabrini Ortiz's works on economic nationalism had a significant influence on Peronism, but he despised the *gauchismo* of the Centenary Generation, which also became a stock-in-trade of Peronist vocabulary; and in Cuba, Martí was adopted as the 'intellectual author' of the revolution, but the commitment to freedom of expression he upheld was rarely accorded to his successors. Tensions often developed between the views of intellectuals and state leaders in Spanish America, but given the precarious conditions in which intellectuals worked, it was difficult for them to maintain a balance between culture and politics, and the former was almost invariably eclipsed by the latter. When intellectuals have secured public influence elsewhere in the world, it has usually been from an established institutional base that guaranteed the preservation of their status as intellectuals: a comparable degree of institutional security has been rare in Spanish America. As a result, Spanish American intellectuals were often obliged to choose between preserving their status as intellectuals or achieving a (usually minor) degree of political influence. In the quest for nationhood, it was the blueprints of the politicians, not the visions of the intellectuals, that prevailed. Indeed, many nationalist leaders deliberately shunned the work of intellectuals, preferring to promote alternative, more 'popular' media to articulate national identity: mural art in Mexico, radio in Perón's Argentina, film in both Mexico and Cuba.[2]

It is difficult to deny, therefore, that the modernizing state was 'a major producer' of national cultures in Spanish America,[3] or that political leaders manipulated the mythologies of national identity as a strategy to demobilize popular protest by means of nationalism's eternally postponed promise of a better future. Many intellectuals, especially during the 1940s and 1950s, proved reluctant to challenge this harnessing of culture to populist ends. Spanish American intellectuals defined themselves in terms set by the state, whether they supported or opposed it. It is an oversimplification to argue that they identified with the elites, as their critics allege, but neither should their own claims to be the voice of the people be accepted without qualification. Their self-proclaimed status as intellectuals usually resulted in their adopting an ambivalent attitude to both the elites and the masses. Likewise, many intellectuals remained uncertain about how far to support regimes of dubious legitimacy that were nevertheless pursuing at least some policies of national integration. Given the authoritarian, anti-intellectual bias of state structures in Spanish America, this failure to oppose was in practice equivalent to conformity and, in some cases, to collusion. While intellectuals made an important contribution to keeping the issues of *lo popular* and poverty in the public arena, the aggregate effect of their acquiescence in the displacing of culture by politics was to contribute to the continuation of an unrepresentative political culture where populist policies could thrive.

In this context, the idea of the Spanish American intellectual as national redeemer is best seen as an 'invented tradition', in the famous phrase of Hobsbawm and Ranger.[4] Like all invented traditions, this one built upon existing memories and perceptions; otherwise, it would never have captured anyone's imagination. But it was largely the creation of Spanish American intellectuals themselves during the first three decades of the twentieth century. Like other self-images fashioned by the intellectual sectors of society at different times and in other parts of the world, the invention of this 'tradition' should be understood as a strategy of resistance and an attempt to recuperate lost status. This is not to claim that what can retrospectively be identified as a self-legitimating role for intellectuals as forgers of popular national identities was intended as such at the time, nor is it to 'detract from the enormity of the task' of building national identities in Spanish America 'or the sincerity with which it was ... undertaken'.[5] But, by this stage, modernization had wrought irreversible changes in the socio-economic conditions that had enabled *caudillo–pensador* Simón Bolívar to govern Gran Colombia (1819–30), or *licenciado–político* Domingo Sarmiento to become President of Argentina (1868–74). Likewise, the apparently greater opportunities for intellectuals to participate in politics since Spanish American countries returned to constitutional government in the 1980s could not have arisen without a corresponding sea-change in socio-economic conditions. Momentarily, as it has transpired, in the aftermath of authoritarianism and unprecedented levels of corruption, the moral authority of the intellectual seemed potent and apposite. But both Vargas Llosa's presidential candidacy and President Raúl Alfonsín's appointment of Ernesto Sábato as head of a human rights commission became possible not only because of the changing political context, but precisely because the market had opened up a greater gap between culture and politics in Spanish America than had hitherto obtained. A 'from Sarmiento to Sábato' approach to the relationship between intellectuals and politics in Spanish America constitutes the perpetration of a myth rather than the writing of history.

And yet this, too, seems to tell only part of the story. Earlier in the twentieth century, especially during its first three decades, some Spanish American intellectuals sought to delineate and defend a public space where critical debate and opposition to encroaching state power could flourish. (One hesitates to apply Habermas's term 'public sphere' – which he defined as a part of civil society, interjacent between 'the intimate sphere' of the family, 'the private sphere' of the market, and the state[6] – across the region, although Hilda Sabato has made a convincing case for the three main elements of an expanded press, voluntary public associations and a culture of mobilization existing in late-nineteenth-century Buenos Aires.)[7] They attempted to create a space for critical debate above all in countries where the state most lacked legitimacy: Cuba and Peru. The intellectuals were not the only group trying to do this, of course; indeed, in both these cases it was precisely a coincidence of interests between intellectual projects of national redemption through revolution and worker/peasant militancy that enabled such opportunities for debate to exist. The careers of José Carlos Mariátegui and Julio Antonio Mella, among others, should give pause for thought to those who argue that intellectuals are invariably isolated from the 'people': intellectuals in both Peru and Cuba had extensive contacts with urban and rural popular organizations during the 1920s. The two national-popular movements were defeated (in Peru after the death of Mariátegui and the coup of 1930; in Cuba after the revolution of 1933 fell prey to US pressure on Batista), but both left a potent legacy. Mariátegui's radical vision of a nation incorporating *all* oppressed people, Indians and others, was ignored for several decades after the 1920s, but ultimately did prove inspirational to those who began to argue for recognition of a multicultural Peru.

The examples of Peru and Cuba in the 1920s lend support to Lewis Coser's idea that intellectuals tend to enjoy greater influence when political consensus is lacking.[8] This was also the case with the Argentine Centenary Generation, whose image of a national identity based on the *gaucho* as emblematic of liberty and an embryonic commitment to democracy proved potent in the context of the social upheaval caused by immigration. My main conclusion is that it was those who sought to maintain their role as independent, critical intellectuals committed to reasoned debate and enquiry whose ideas enjoyed lasting influence rather than those who adopted the political discourses of polemic and propaganda, whether at the service of the state or of an opposition party.

The evidence in this book suggests that neither modernist nor perennialist approaches are wholly convincing in explaining the development of nationalisms in Spanish America. Hobsbawm's argument that the region 'has remained largely immune to modern ethnic-cultural nationalism' is appropriate in one sense: during the twentieth century, there have been few instances of xenophobic nationalism dedicated to 'ethnic cleansing' in Spanish America (although Sendero Luminoso leaves room for doubt, as do the counter-insurgency campaigns of the Guatemalan military during the late 1960s and 1970s). Among the indigenous political organizations that were founded in the late 1980s and early 1990s, the majority were not separatist in intent, being instead geared more towards protecting indigenous identities within a nation-state. The basis of the Zapatistas' position, for example, was that indigenous identity should not preclude their being included within the Mexican nation and securing rights due to any other Mexican citizen. But this in itself reflects the fact that *indigenismo* had long been part of the discourse of Mexican popular national identity. Ethnic and cultural factors cannot be dismissed so readily. As illustrated in Chapter 4, they were prominent in debates about national identity in Mexico, Peru and Argentina from the early twentieth century onwards. In Cuba, although José Martí had posited an inclusive concept of *cubanidad* denying the importance of race and based on common values such as love of liberty and the dignity of man,[9] by the 1930s *afrocubanidad* was a prominent cultural movement and Fernando Ortiz was proposing a version of Cuban cultural *mestizaje*.[10] His most famous metaphor of national identity was 'Cuba is an *ajiaco*'.[11] An *ajiaco* is a typical Cuban stew seasoned with *ají* (chilli sauce) which originated with the Taino Indians and was added to, according to Ortiz, by Spaniards, Africans, Asians, French, and even 'the Anglo-Americans with their domestic appliances which simplified the cooking'.[12] Ortiz represented Cuba as: 'Mixture of cuisines, mixture of races, mixture of cultures. A thick broth of civilization bubbling away on the Caribbean stove.'[13] Even in Chile, where national identity remained closer to a civic model, emphasizing a democratic tradition and drawing its cultural strength from evocations of the landscape, attempts were made by middle-class intellectuals in the early twentieth century to create a bi-culturalist archetype, in part because of their opposition to immigration policies. Twentieth-century Spanish American nationalisms were not primarily 'civic' nationalisms based on political values.

As suggested in Chapter 1, the development of viable popular national identities in Spanish America was dependent upon *both* a state political project to incorporate the people (*l'institution politique*), *and* the creation, by intellectuals, of a shared culture commanding widespread popular acceptance (*l'institution imaginaire*). The varying success of national identity formation in Spanish American countries can be explained in relation to this hypothesis. The strongest bids to consolidate national identities in Spanish America during the twentieth century were made by regimes pursuing policies of incorporation along populist lines (Mexico and Argentina during the 1940s and 1950s). Of these two, Mexico was by far the more successful, partly because it could combine a civic component (drawn from the mythology of the revolution and its 'institutionalization' of social justice) with an ethnic one (the indigenous heritage and *mestizaje*). Florencia Mallon has argued that the Mexican post-revolutionary state 'emerged as hegemonic because it incorporated a part of the popular agenda'.[14] Mexico's official twentieth-century nationalism was founded on a revolutionary rhetoric that incorporated the ideology of *mestizaje* and was galvanized by proximity to the United States, which meant that the imperialist power played the role of 'other' for Mexico to a degree that it did not for any other Spanish American country. Mexican nationalism flourished because both its civic and its ethnic components bore a credible relationship to political realities.

The creation of this Mexican identity was quite clearly driven and controlled by the state. In the 1920s, intellectuals mistakenly believed that they could enjoy a degree of influence on nation-building comparable to that of the *philosophes* in eighteenth-century France. They did not at this stage envisage the need to create a role for themselves as mediators between the state and the masses; it briefly seemed that being an intellectual who was against the landed oligarchy, in favour of social justice for the masses, and a servant of the state were one and the same thing. It soon transpired, however, that while the post-revolutionary regime was anti-oligarchy, it was also hostile to independent-minded intellectuals, who were sharply brought up against the extent of their misjudgement when they witnessed the official sabotaging of Vasconcelos's election campaign of 1928. By that time, the initiative in creating a national identity was firmly in the hands of the state, which selectively sponsored particularistic visions of national identity put forward by artists, anthropologists and film-makers, but offered little or no opening to any intellectuals who advanced a fundamental critique of cultural nationalism. It was no coincidence that the post-revolutionary Mexican government quickly co-opted anthropologists to its nation-building project: anthropology tends to be a fragmentary discipline, in this case, facilitating the elaboration of a national culture 'by implication (through case studies)',[15] thereby avoiding the need to recognize the variety of cultures within the national territory.

The 1930s saw the emergence of a generation of Mexican intellectuals who, like their earlier counterparts in other Spanish American countries, belatedly tried to create a role for themselves as architects of popular national identity. Unlike their counterparts, however, they based their versions of national identity not on cultural nationalism but on a critique of it. The difficulty they then confronted was that the government had already set the terms of the debate, and it became almost impossible to challenge the hegemonic discourse of the state. The Sonoran leaders had bowdlerized the ideas of a few Mexican intellectuals in the 1920s to create the founding myth of *mestizaje*, from which it became very difficult for subsequent generations to dissent, especially since the official position was always to cite Vasconcelos's idea of a cosmic race. By the mid-1940s, Mexican intellectuals found themselves obliged to choose between allegiance to the state or to the masses. They could contribute to the official elaboration of Mexican national culture so long as they stopped trying to incorporate any more genuinely popular or radical dimension into it. During the 1940s and 1950s, Mexican governments successfully ensured that the historians and philosophers who were co-opted to create the national imaginary were those who were content to reproduce a set of stereotypes which by their nature denied the possibility of any accumulation of knowledge about national reality. Those who dissented from the official version of *mexicanidad* had little impact on the forging of national identity; their calls for Mexicans to think about themselves in terms that might go beyond the bi-culturalist divide and the love–hate relationship with their northern neighbour have repeatedly been ignored. Although their activities were tolerated by the ruling party, they proved unable to change the vocabulary in which the debates about Mexican national identity were conducted. The Mexican *institution politique* proved sufficiently flexible to accommodate a 'republic of letters' operating within certain unspoken but well understood limits, from which it could draw at will to create the *institution imaginaire* of national identity. That this relationship was by no means insignificant to state leaders was revealed only too clearly after the massacre of 1968: the Echeverría government initially bent over backwards to regain the goodwill of the intellectual community.

Argentina's experience has been far more mixed, and provides a particularly telling example of how shifting relationships between the intellectuals and the state can affect the creation of nationhood. During the 1920s,

Argentina was deemed by intellectuals elsewhere in the region to enjoy a relatively secure national identity: Mariátegui noted that, in the 1920s, 'an Argentine nationality already exists, whereas there is still . . . no Peruvian nationality'.[16] Vasconcelos too believed that Argentina had created a strong sense of national identity despite its high levels of immigration.[17] At this stage, the Centenary Generation's version of a national culture based on the archetypal *gaucho* coexisted with the Unión Cívica Radical's political project of incorporation, which drew significantly on economic nationalism as a rallying cry. After the oligarchy resumed control of the state in 1930, the two new versions of Argentine nationalism that emerged – one right-wing, Catholic and *hispanista*, the other urging popular participation and anti-British imperialism – both defined themselves in opposition not only to *mitrismo* but also to *gauchismo*. Neither became hegemonic, and both were displaced when Perón harnessed the Argentine state behind his own vision of national identity, itself an eclectic mix of the Centenary Generation's archetype of the *mestizo gaucho*, the *forjistas*' anti-Britishness, and the right-wing nationalists' celebration of Hispanic culture. He wove all this together into a grand illusion of an authentic, tellurian Argentina – *gaucho* and yet also Hispanic – rising up to throw off the yoke of foreign and *porteño* imposition and exploitation. Perón's version of Argentine national identity was partially successful, not least because he introduced (or extended) a broad range of inclusionary social policies. Hobsbawm has noted: 'In Perón's army more than half the generals were sons of immigrants, indicating a readiness to assimilate and a speed of assimilation without parallel in the world outside Latin America.'[18] But Peronist nationalism failed to impose its populist blueprint fully, and alternative versions of a pro-Western Argentine identity (some derived from the *mitrista* cosmopolitan ideal, others from a more conservative, Catholic standpoint) continued to compete for control of the state during the 1960s and 1970s.[19] During and after Perón's first two governments, Argentine intellectuals found themselves almost completely marginalized from debates about national identity. The idea of intellectual independence never shed its association with anti-Peronism, which became synonymous in populist discourse with being an enemy of the people. The last attempt by a generation of Argentine intellectuals, the *Contorno* generation of the 1950s, to carve out a role for themselves as mediators of a popular national identity that was not shackled to Peronism failed, and was probably doomed from the start. Many intellectuals went into exile, especially during the military governments; of those who remained, only those prepared to accept the role of an ideologue enjoyed any significant degree of public influence. Elitist and popular versions of national identity coexist uneasily in Argentina to this day.

Cuba stands out among its Caribbean neighbours in having developed a comparatively strong sense of national identity, much of which is attributable to the revolutionary government, and one that is largely based on political values, even though ethno-cultural elements are certainly present. Again, it is revealing to trace the relationship between intellectuals and the state in achieving this. The Cuban people are unique in Spanish America in that, because of their late independence, they began to develop a sense of national identity before Cuba became a republic in 1902. Although no consensus had been established, the most influential vision of national identity to emerge before the second war of independence (1895–98) was Martí's idea of civic patriotism, elaborated in opposition to colonial rule. During the first two decades of the republic, however, Martí's ideas were largely ignored as liberal-dominated elites conducted debates about Cuban national identity almost exclusively around the extent to which Cuba should try to emulate the United States. This elite nationalism echoed the concerns of liberals in the immediate aftermath of independence in other Spanish American states. It was not until the 1920s that a generation of intellectuals emerged who began to elaborate a popular national identity in opposition to the increasingly corrupt and bankrupt Cuban state. As in Peru, for many of them this was linked to radical politics. When Martí's work was resurrected in the 1920s, his idea of civic patriotism was overshadowed by his anti-imperialist thought, which seemed more immediately relevant. Around the same time, Ortiz and others began to introduce an ethno-cultural component to Cuban national identity. It was under Batista, by proxy in the 1930s and as President in person from 1940 to 1944, that moderate versions of both these strands of Cuban nationalism received official sanction, as the state began to assert its own role in nation-building. Anti-imperialism was encouraged in the form of revisionist history by Emilio Roig de Leuchsenring and others; likewise, Ortiz was encouraged to produce his studies of *afrocubanidad*. At the same time, Martí was inscribed – both by officialdom and by its opponents – as the founding father of the nation, so that his words came to be perceived as the primary source of Cuban national identity. As happens in the work of many prolific writers, Martí ranged widely across several genres, from poetry to journalism to propaganda tracts, and support for a broad range of visions of Cuban national identity could be found among the many volumes of his collected works. This consolidation of Martí in the position of founding father did, however, retain the distinctive accent on political values – rather than ethnicity – that has characterized Cuban debates about national identity throughout the twentieth century. After the 1959 revolution, the government sustained this emphasis on the civic virtues of revolutionary struggle, anti-imperialism and social justice; it promoted a discourse in which race, at least as a political issue, to this day remains largely subsumed. It has been argued that the history of blacks in Cuba has been written as one component of the overall Cuban struggle for liberation, rather than as a history in its own right.[20] But it should not be forgotten that the Cuban post-revolutionary state has encouraged intellectuals to produce literary and sociological works exploring Cuba's cultural *mestizaje*, thereby discreetly fostering the ethno-cultural elements of nationalism while containing them within a limited cultural sphere. A lot of attention has been paid to the Castro government's unwillingness to tolerate intellectuals who were in any way critical of the revolutionary process; but arguably the regime's success in promoting a strong sense of national identity has been at least partly dependent upon its capacity to support an active, albeit restricted and circumspect, cultural community.

In Chile, the nineteenth-century elites were more successful than their counterparts elsewhere in the continent in establishing a nationalism based on civic values and the conviction that Chile was distinguished from its neighbours by a greater degree of democracy. A short-lived attempt early in the twentieth century to inject ethnicity into concepts of Chilean national identity had less impact than comparable initiatives in other Spanish American countries. One reason for this was that the Chilean oligarchy continued to maintain ideological hegemony even after it lost control of the state in the 1920s, and it succeeded in reasserting and disseminating the nineteenth-century conviction of Chile's political superiority by accommodating it within a myth of national decline. But the bi-culturalist element did not disappear entirely: Francisco Encina, one of the main creators of the dominant right-wing vision of national identity, called upon the supposed 'gothic' heritage elaborated by Palacios in order to reinforce his account of Diego Portales as the incarnation of the Chilean national soul. Later, in the 1940s, a new generation of Chilean intellectuals sought to make their mark on national identity by invoking the land as its emotional basis, rather than extolling ethnicity. The most successful version of this was Neruda's *Canto general* (1950), which celebrated the Chilean landscape within a history of the whole subcontinent. But although Neruda's evocation of an alternative, tellurian national identity had great popular resonance, it did not completely succeed in dislodging the conservative hold on national values. As happened in Chilean politics, those claiming to represent popular interests may have been the most visible, but behind the scenes the Chilean oligarchy retained the edge in the battle for cultural hegemony. The apparent victory of a popular vision of national identity created a vacuum of ideas to challenge the elite formula, which was reimposed with a vengeance by General Pinochet's regime.

In contrast to the Mexican state, Mallon has suggested, the Peruvian state has 'never stabilized precisely because it repeatedly repressed and marginalized popular cultures'.[21] After a brief flirtation with *indigenismo* in the early 1920s, when President Leguía was partially successful in bypassing intellectuals and, for a time, won support among part of the Indian community,

subsequent Peruvian regimes rejected integrationist policies, denying the
Indian a place in the Peruvian nation. This endured for nearly four decades
until the military assumed power with its own modernizing agenda in 1968
('a final and tardy attempt to hegemonize a national-democratic discourse'
which itself was to fail by the mid-1970s).[22] In this context, to claim that
González Prada, Haya de la Torre and Mariátegui were 'primarily responsible for creating Peru's populist nationalism' tells too simple a story.[23] Haya
de la Torre, who functioned more as an ideologue than as a critical
intellectual, settled for the compromises of populism and arguably thereby
helped to sustain the conditions that prevented the emergence of popular
nationalist movements until the 1970s. González Prada and Mariátegui both
sought a national identity that was popular rather than populist; their legacy
was powerful, but went virtually unrecognized for several decades. Mariátegui was one of the few Spanish American intellectuals who explicitly
committed himself to resist the displacing of culture by politics. It was not
until the 1980s that he came to be acclaimed as the founding father of a
project of Peruvian national identity based on political rather than cultural
values: 'a nation thought of in terms of a progressive, participatory social
democracy'.[24] This interpretation of Mariátegui was, of course, partly an
accommodation to the political mores of the 1980s: he was an advocate of
socialism, not social democracy, who saw not only civic rights but also
collective economic ownership as a necessary component of nationality.
Mariátegui's conception of national identity was primarily concerned with
political values (equality and solidarity) rather than ethnicity or culture: he
sought to subsume Peru's alleged 'racial question' into revolutionary politics. The conditions of the 1980s made it easier to view Mariátegui's efforts
to maintain a balance between political strategies for revolution and objective theoretical analysis of Peruvian reality in a different light: not as
evidence that he was ideologically unsound or uncommitted to practical
politics, as his contemporary enemies suggested, but as the consequence of
his belief that a critical intellectual input was both valuable in itself and an
important element in the revolutionary process. Mariátegui, who was so
often accused of being *europeizante* during his lifetime, finally came to be
hailed as an exponent of 'Ibero-America's intrinsic originality'.[25] But, after
decades of thinking about Peru in terms of an irreconcilable opposition
between *hispanismo* and *indigenismo*, it had become almost impossible to
return to his conception of a nation integrated by common political and
socio-economic values. Despite initiatives by intellectuals and others since
the early 1970s to emphasize ethnic and cultural plurality, Peru is still
fragmented along bi-culturalist lines and its identity as a nation is one of
the most unstable in the region.

A comparison with Brazil, where the relationship between the state
and intellectuals has been more reciprocal than in Spanish America, is

illuminating. Twentieth-century Brazilian intellectuals clearly did make influential contributions to the discourse on national identity. Not coincidentally, the state played a dominant role in the organization of Brazilian intellectual life. Daniel Pécaut argues that the Brazilian state never made its intellectuals feel excluded from their own society, even during its overtly authoritarian phases: both the Estado Nôvo (1937–45) and the military regime of 1964–85 tried to co-opt intellectuals.[26] Brazilian intellectuals identified with the state, sharing its self-definition of being distinct from and above society (the enduring influence of positivism was important in this). Unlike in Spanish America, it was not that the intellectuals approached the state; rather, things happened the other way around: 'The generation of 1925–1940 [did] not seek the helping hand of the state. The truth was far closer to the reverse. [This generation was] willing to come to the state's aid in order to construct society on a rational basis.'[27] The São Paulo modernists had already launched themselves into cultural prominence with Modern Art Week (1922), the Brazilwood Manifesto (1924) and the Anthropophagic Manifesto (1928), declaring their commitment to a Brazilian language and literature.[28] After the overthrow in 1930 of the Old Republic, intellectuals, politicians who supported Getúlio Vargas, and indeed many in the military shared the belief that the opportunity had arrived to create a new, modernizing elite committed to nationalism. Under the Estado Nôvo, the professions were given official status, from which point onwards the intellectual sectors of Brazilian society were endowed with specific rights and identities,[29] mainly as specialists in the social sciences (which were established in institutional form during the 1930s in Brazil, compared with the 1950s in Spanish America). In Brazil, the social sciences shaped the discourse in which debates about national identity were conducted. The ideology of 'racial democracy', which has been described as the most 'elaborate "solution"' in the Americas to 'the "problem" of racial and cultural pluralism', emerged from Gilberto Freyre's 1933 *Casa grande e senzala* [*The Masters and the Slaves*] to dominate discussion of Brazil's racial mix until it was challenged in the late 1960s.[30] Pécaut describes how the Brazilian intellectuals of 1925–40 were preoccupied not only by national identity but also by institution-building. They sought to dismantle the institutions of the Old Republic and found new institutions to 'organize the nation'. Their concept of national identity embraced not only cultural distinction but also civic pride. After 1930, the state gave them opportunities to serve in the construction of society on a rational basis. Two major new universities were created, the University of São Paulo in 1934 and the University of Brazil in 1937. The latter gradually came to displace the University of Rio de Janeiro, itself dating only from 1920, as the leading university in the capital city. It has been generally acknowledged that even under the Estado Nôvo, Vargas 'preserved a broad leeway of creative

freedom for intellectuals, even for those who worked for him directly'.[31] He
allowed room for intellectuals who were politically opposed to his means
but shared similar goals of nation-building. It was not necessary to become
an ideologue of authoritarianism or to put one's literary talent directly at
the service of official culture in order to participate in the broader project
of 'venturing . . . in search of authentic Brazil . . . struggling to impose
national themes . . . inventing Brazilian modes of expression'.[32] It seems
plausible to accept Roger Bastide's argument that Brazilian national consciousness was born in the early twentieth century 'as a mythical reality,
crafted by intellectuals'.[33] A cultural community devoted to the elaboration
of national identity was institutionalized in Brazil during the 1930s to an
extent that, with the partial exception of Mexico from 1946 until the early
1960s, never happened in Spanish America.

The relationship between the *institution politique* and the *institution imaginaire* highlights the importance of Spanish America's distinctive history of
nationhood. Whereas the idea of nation first took root in the region during
the early 1800s, it was not until almost a century later that the process of
incorporating the masses into national life began. In the cases both of those
European nations that embarked on nation-building in the late eighteenth
or early nineteenth centuries (for example, France, Russia and Germany)
and of the nations that emerged from decolonization after the Second
World War, the idea of nation developed in parallel with the consolidation
of a modern secular intellectual community. The *institution politique* of state-
building dovetailed with the intellectuals' project of creating the *institution
imaginaire* of a national culture. In Spanish America, by contrast, attempts
by twentieth-century intellectuals to elaborate a more inclusive, popular
nationalism were launched without the political consensus and state backing
such initiatives had enjoyed from the outset in France, Russia and many
former colonies in Africa, Asia and the non-Hispanic Caribbean. When
Spanish American states incorporated the ideas of intellectuals into their
nation-building projects, it was usually on the basis of terms set by the state
rather than by the intellectuals.

Since the return to elected rule in the 1980s, a new conception of the
state, related to the adoption of neo-liberal economic policies, has become
axiomatic in Spanish America. Reduction of the state apparatus (more
accurately, perhaps, of its direct involvement in economic enterprise) has
been the declared aim. Modernization is held to be more the preserve of
the free market than of the state. As the interventionist state lost its link
with the middle classes (or was reduced to reinforcing it by means of
repression) in the 1960s and 1970s, so also its symbiotic relationship with
the intellectuals was weakened. At the structural level, private funding once
again became a significant factor in intellectual life. This was manifested in
a variety of forms, ranging from the foundation in 1958 of the Di Tella

Institute in Buenos Aires by the sons of a prominent Argentine industrialist
to the proliferation since the 1960s of social science research bodies
financed by grants from US and European foundations and, indeed, the
Catholic Church. These institutions provided a refuge for intellectuals
excluded from universities subjected to military intervention, and after the
return to elected rule many have continued to offer an alternative to state
employment (although some of them have also received public funding).
These organizations often command resources that are far superior to those
available in public universities, and because of this they constitute a valuable, if still fragile, institutional basis for intellectual independence from the
state. Such opportunities have been enhanced by the fact that since the
1960s, there has emerged in the region what can be termed, at least in
relation to earlier decades, a mass market for books and magazines. From
the 1980s onwards, therefore, Spanish American intellectuals have experienced marked changes both in their conditions of work and in their
relationship to the state.

All this occurred in the context of the gathering sense of a worldwide
'crisis among intellectuals' and of a prevailing tendency towards 'the
recycling of knowledge in an academically or technically specialized guise'.[34]
Intellectuals in most countries have felt a sense of disorientation in the face
of the information revolution, the apparent lack of any plausible alternative
to free market capitalism after the collapse of Communism in the Soviet
Union and Eastern Europe, and an increasingly widespread consciousness
of the 'radical incoherence' underlying the role of universal intellectual.[35]
Many have come to accept Foucault's view that the intellectual could no
longer be perceived as the bearer of universal values, but was instead to play
a far more specific role as a specialist, whose interventions would be in local
struggles.[36] The idea that national identity could be debated in primarily
cultural terms also came under increasing scrutiny in the face of challenges
to state sovereignty posed by the global media, the international debt crises,
the drugs trade, and the development of a mass politics from below, based
on cross-border issues such as the environment, religion, ethnicity and
gender. José Joaquín Brunner, for example, has argued that although
national identity retained a strong cultural component, it was also shaped
by 'the economy and . . . the power of integration possessed by a society; . . .
its competitiveness and capacity for self-government; . . . the modernity of
its productive base and . . . its capacity to produce knowledge and incorporate [new] technologies'.[37] For Spanish American intellectuals, these changes
were compounded by their own local experiences of prolonged authoritarian rule, which for many had meant exile, and the subsequent restoration
of democratic procedure, which posed its own dilemmas.[38] In this context,
the tradition of the Spanish American intellectual as the repository of

national consciousness became much harder to sustain, although it has undoubtedly lingered on in residual form.

Despite all the changes that have undeniably taken place in the intellectual communities of Spanish America, many of the questions raised by a study of the period from the 1920s to the 1970s are still relevant to current debates about the role of the intellectual. The role of the state in Spanish American cultural life should not be underestimated even in the 1990s. The prospect of state power remains alluring for many intellectuals. As opportunities opened up under democratization for them to participate not only in ministries (still rare) but also political parties, academic institutes or the media, the autonomy of culture in Spanish America was still arguably undervalued by many of the intellectuals themselves. In Chile, Brunner observed:

> Above all, it is necessary to affirm the autonomy of our field and its institutions, its values, methods and procedures. It is worrying to see how many of us are slipping back again into the old conception of culture as the business of the state and its policies. We very quickly began to dream of ministries and bureaus of culture, with public subsidies . . . and bureaucracies, and the possibility of acting as advisers to the Prince or as agents of power.[39]

Only by defending cultural autonomy, he argued, could intellectuals preserve the necessary basis from which to 'offer opportunities for criticism, debate, exploration and creation'.[40]

In Mexico, Sergio Zermeño has described how intellectuals 'put themselves at the service' of the political elite (the '*núcleo duro*', or hard core) during the 1980s 'in exchange for only limited influence but much personal prestige'.[41] Mexican intellectuals were 'made into celebrities by constant publicity in the press and on television',[42] especially after the presidential elections of 1988, in which the PRI's victory was widely suspected to have been fraudulent. The incoming President, Carlos Salinas, 'threw open the doors of the National Palace and invited all and sundry to negotiations. . . . Some intellectuals were made not only the object of publicity but also its very promoters, hosting popular television shows or receiving generous government support for their prestigious magazines or specially created newspapers.'[43] A neat illustration of the continuing ritual dance between intellectuals and the state in Mexico is the following story about pre-election bargaining over the tax status of authors. In November 1993, Salinas invited famous writers to his official residence at Los Pinos in order to reassure them of the restoration of full tax exemption on their royalties in 1994. Tax exemption for authors is traditional in Mexico, but in 1989 the new government, full of technocratic zeal, had decided to tighten up on laws that enabled advertising copywriters to receive 'royalties' rather than taxable salaries for their commercials. The finance ministry announced that only authors of book-length fiction were eligible for tax exemption, but writers were successful in convincing the Supreme Court that it was iniquitous to discriminate against academic texts. The government somewhat mischievously responded that, in that case, all writers would henceforth be subject to taxation. This was a piece of audacity it came to regret, as authors set to work to demonstrate that the power of the pen was not yet wholly redundant, producing a series of articles pleading their case in the national press. Despite a partial concession from the government early in 1993, which increased the amount a writer could earn before taxation, the writers pursued their campaign vigorously, resulting in government capitulation at Los Pinos. The finance ministry did succeed, however, in ruling out advertising.[44]

Although democratization has brought new opportunities for critical intellectuals to intervene in national debates, official (and unofficial) sanctions continue to operate against their influence. During the 1980s, greater pressure on resources because of increased student numbers combined with the drastic retrenchment induced by debt crises, exacerbated an already adverse situation in Spanish American universities. Within the space of a couple of years during the early 1980s, the annual salary of a full-time lecturer fell by over 50 per cent to around US$8,000–10,000;[45] a few years later, there was a mini-scandal among the Mexican intelligentsia when it was revealed that teachers and researchers at the Universidad Nacional Autónoma de México were earning well under half the salary of a Mexico City bus driver.[46] The combination of economic and ideological pressures meant that the possibility of dissent was again reduced: 'Intellectuals find themselves obliged, frequently more for structural than vocational reasons, to qualify their criticisms if not to silence them altogether.'[47] In the early 1990s, the Rector of the University of Buenos Aires reiterated the need for 'a modern, scientific, innovatory university' to provide a secure institutional base for an intellectual community.[48] In various ominous ways, the elected governments have maintained the bias against critical discourse that characterized intellectual life in the region from the 1920s to the 1960s. For most of the twentieth century, Spanish American intellectuals have functioned in the shadow of the state.

Notes

Introduction

1. Régis Debray, *Teachers, Writers, Celebrities: The Intellectuals of Modern France*, trans. David Macey, NLB and Verso, London 1981, p. 2.
2. Jorge Castañeda is probably the best-known recent exponent of this approach: see his *Utopia Unarmed: The Latin American Left after the Cold War*, Knopf, New York 1993, Chapter 6, quotation at p. 177. He traces a tradition dating back nearly five centuries to Fr. Bartolomé de Las Casas and his defence of the Indians in 1552. Most studies along these lines concentrate on the post-independence period, when cultural debates began to be conducted in explicitly national terms: the leading examples are Jean Franco, *The Modern Culture of Latin America: Society and the Artist*, Pall Mall Press, London 1967; and Martin Stabb, *In Quest of Identity*, University of North Carolina Press, Carolina 1967. In earlier, pioneering reviews of Latin American cultural history, the identity theme is notably absent: see Pedro Henríquez Ureña, *A Concise History of Latin American Culture* [1947], trans. Gilbert Chase, Pall Mall Press, London 1966; and Mariano Picón-Salas, *A Cultural History of Spanish America from Conquest to Independence* [1944], trans. Irving Leonard, University of California Press, Berkeley 1962. Leopoldo Zea, *The Latin American Mind* [1949], trans. James H. Abbott and Lowell Dunham, University of Oklahoma Press, Norman 1963, which concentrates on the nineteenth century, discusses the issues in terms of mental emancipation rather than a quest for identity, thereby lending a markedly different emphasis.
3. See Juan Marsal, ed., *El intelectual latinoamericano: un simposio sobre sociología de los intelectuales*, Editorial del Instituto, Buenos Aires 1970, especially Gloria Cucullú, 'El estereotipo del "intelectual latinoamericano": su relación con los cambios económicos y sociales', pp. 73–106. Perhaps the most typical example of the argument she wishes to disprove is William Stokes, 'The Drag of the "Pensadores"', in J. W. Higgins and Helmut Schoeck, eds, *Foreign Aid Re-examined*, Public Affairs Press, Washington, DC 1958.
4. José Donoso, 'Ithaca: The Impossible Return', in Doris Meyer, ed., *Lives on the Line: The Testimony of Contemporary Latin American Authors*, University of California Press, Berkeley and Los Angeles 1988 pp. 181–95, (p. 187).
5. The term 'civil society', referring to 'the idea of institutional and ideological

pluralism, which prevents the establishment of monopoly of power and truth',
began to acquire positive connotations among the Latin American Left during
the 1970s, after decades during which the classic Marxist view of civil society as
merely another mechanism of mystification by which the bourgeoisie was able
to sustain its dominance had prevailed. For a definition, see Ernest Gellner,
Conditions of Liberty: Civil Society and Its Rivals [1994], Penguin, Harmondsworth 1996, p. 3. For further discussion of the concept of 'civil society', see
Chapter 1.
6. Carlos Fuentes, interview, in Castañeda, *Utopia Unarmed*, p. 182. In this quotation, Fuentes evidently attaches a positive value to civil society.
7. César Graña, 'La identidad cultural como invento cultural', in Marsal, ed., *El
intelectual latinoamericano*, p. 70. For an analysis of Mexico, see Roger Bartra, *The
Cage of Melancholy: Identity and Metamorphosis in the Mexican Character*, trans.
Christopher Hall, Rutgers University Press, New Brunswick, NJ 1992.
8. Graña, 'La identidad cultural', pp. 70 and 58.
9. Ibid., p. 67.
10. Ibid., p. 58.
11. Eduardo Galeano, 'Defensa de la palabra' [1976], in *El descubrimiento de América
que todavía no fue y otros ensayos*, Alfadil Ediciones, Caracas 1991, pp. 7–21, p. 18.
12. 'Modernity' and 'modernization', like 'civil society', are highly debated terms,
primarily because of the difficulties involved in defining what is meant by
'modern' (see Bruno Latour, *We Have Never been Modern* [1991], trans. Cath-
erine Porter, Harvester Wheatsheaf, New York 1993). There is the further
difficulty, particularly with respect to Spanish America, that the 'modernization
theory' developed by US social scientists in the late 1950s was based on the
assumption that modernization was synonymous with ever-increasing benefits
for any society (progress). Many people would, of course, dispute that modernization, particularly as effected by capitalism, has improved life for many of
those who have experienced it. The term as used in this book is not intended
to carry such connotations. Here, it serves as a brief way of referring to the
development of capitalism in Spanish America, with all the accompanying
changes such as industrialization, urbanization, the introduction of technology,
and the growth of bureaucracy. This process is conventionally dated among
historians of the region as beginning in the 1870s.
13. Alain Touraine, in Silvia Sigal, 'América Latina y sus intelectuales: conversación
con Alain Touraine', *Crítica y Utopía* (Buenos Aires), no. 13, December 1985,
pp. 25–38, p. 26.
14. José Joaquín Brunner, *América Latina: cultura y modernidad*, Editorial Grijalbo,
Mexico City 1992, p. 59.
15. Saúl Yurkievich, *A través de la trama*, Muchnik Editores, Barcelona 1984;
Magdalena García-Pinto, 'La identidad cultural de la vanguardia en Latinoamérica', in Saúl Yurkievich, ed., *Identidad cultural de Iberoamérica en su literatura*,
Alhambra, Madrid 1986, pp. 102–11; Hugo Verani, ed., *Las vanguardias literarias
en Hispanoamérica: manifiestos, proclamas y otros escritos*, Fondo de Cultura Económica, Mexico City, 2nd edn, 1990; and Vicky Unruh, *Latin American Vanguards:
The Art of Contentious Encounters*, University of California Press, Berkeley 1994.
16. Beatriz Sarlo, *Una modernidad periférica: Buenos Aires 1920 y 1930*, Ediciones
Nueva Visión, Buenos Aires 1988. See also Néstor García Canclini, *Culturas

híbridas: estrategias para entrar y salir de la modernidad, Editorial Sudamericana, Buenos Aires 1992.

17. Nelly Richard, 'Latinoamérica y la postmodernidad', *Revista de Cultura Crítica* (Santiago), vol. 2, no. 3 (April 1991), pp. 15–19, p. 17. For a useful summary of debates about the applicability of postmodernist ideas to Latin America, see John Beverley, Michael Aronna, and José Oviedo, *The Postmodernism Debate in Latin America*, Duke University Press, Durham, NC and London 1995.

18. See Angel Rama, *La ciudad letrada*, Ediciones del Norte, Hanover, NH 1984, especially pp. 71–135; and José Luis Romero, *Latinoamérica: las ciudades y las ideas*, Siglo XXI, Buenos Aires and Mexico City, 4th edn, 1986, especially pp. 247–389.

19. Laurence Whitehead, 'State Organization in Latin America since 1930', in Leslie Bethell, ed., *Cambridge History of Latin America*, vol. VI, part 2, Cambridge University Press, Cambridge 1995, pp. 3–95, p. 90. The term 'modernizing' is used both in Whitehead and here without the ideological connotations of US modernization theory; see note 12.

20. Antonio Gramsci, *Selections from the Prison Notebooks*, ed. and trans. Quintin Hoare and Geoffrey Nowell Smith, Lawrence & Wishart, London 1971, p. 260.

21. Pedro Henríquez Ureña, *Historia de la cultura en la América hispánica*, Fondo de Cultura Económica, Mexico 1947, p. 119.

22. This discussion is obviously based on ideal types. In practice, there were many who fulfilled a role much closer to that of the *pensador* than 'the intellectual' until after the Second World War.

23. Enrique Krauze, *Caudillos culturales en la Revolución Mexicana*, Editorial Siglo XXI, Mexico City 1985.

24. A periodization along these lines is increasingly becoming accepted. See Richard Morse, 'The Multiverse of Latin American Identity, *c.* 1920–*c.*1970', in Leslie Bethell, ed., *Cambridge History of Latin America*, vol. X, *Latin America since 1930: Ideas, Culture and Society*, Cambridge University Press, Cambridge 1995, pp. 1–127. Martin Stabb identifies the emergence of what he refers to as the 'new Spanish American essay' in the 1960s: see *The Dissenting Voice: The New Essay of Spanish America, 1960–1985*, University of Texas Press, Austin 1994.

25. A case could always be made for the inclusion of other countries, particularly Colombia, Venezuela and Uruguay, the intellectual traditions of which are not analysed in depth here, although individual intellectuals from all three countries are discussed.

26. See especially Gerald Martin, *Journeys through the Labyrinth*, Verso, London 1989; and David Treece and Mike Gonzalez, *The Gathering of Voices: The Twentieth-century Poetry of Latin America*, Verso, London 1992.

Chapter 1

1. Anthony D. Smith, *National Identity*, Penguin Books, Harmondsworth 1991, p. 40.

2. Ernest Gellner, *Nations and Nationalism*, Blackwell, Oxford 1983, p. 135.

3. Hugh Seton-Watson, *Nations and States: An Enquiry into the Origins of Nations and the Politics of Nationalism*, Westview Press, Boulder, CO 1977, Chapter 5, 'European Nations Overseas', pp. 193–237. This book was noteworthy at the time for drawing a distinction between 'old, continuous nations' and 'nations of design'. Despite its title, however, it was a largely descriptive work, at least with reference to the Americas. Seton-Watson divided the nations of Spanish America into four categories, on the basis of racial differences. Thus there were those nations 'overwhelmingly of European stock' (Argentina, Uruguay, Chile); those where Indians and people of mixed race were in the majority (Ecuador, Peru, Bolivia and Paraguay); those with 'a large element of African origin' (the Caribbean islands, Venezuela and 'some of the Central American states); and Mexico, which was 'a unique case'. He acknowledged that neither Colombia nor Costa Rica fitted into this schema (pp. 220–1), which overall did not add significantly to an understanding of nationalism in Spanish America.

4. For examples, see Hans Kohn, *The Age of Nationalism: The First Era of Global History*, Greenwood Press, Westport, CO 1962, p. 156, where Mexico is given as another instance of the tendency to monolithic regimes that he identifies in Africa and Asia; or Peter Alter, *Nationalism* [1985], Edward Arnold, London, 2nd edn, 1994, pp. 113–14, where Latin America is cited as exemplary of a general trend in underdeveloped countries towards the manipulation of nationalism 'to defuse domestic tension'.

5. Anthony D. Smith, *Nations and Nationalism in a Global Era*, Polity Press, Cambridge 1995, p. 42.

6. Anthony D. Smith, seminar, University College London, 8 February 1995. Smith's main distinction is between 'civic-territorial' and 'ethnic-genealogical' nations. For a discussion of these types, see his *The Ethnic Origins of Nations*, Blackwell, Oxford 1986, Chapter 6, especially pp. 134–52.

7. Until the 1970s, dominant versions of Peruvian national identity were based on denial, not incorporation, of the pre-modern ethnic heritage of the Incas.

8. Smith, *National Identity*, p. 95.

9. For a comparative study of England, France, Germany, Russia and the United States, see Liah Greenfeld, *Nationalism: Five Roads to Modernity*, Harvard University Press, Cambridge, MA and London 1992.

10. Weber's views can be found in *From Max Weber: Essays in Sociology*, H. H. Gerth and C. Wright Mills, eds, Routledge and Kegan Paul, London 1948, especially pp. 371–2. For other general works in this tradition, see Karl Mannheim, *Essays on the Sociology of Culture*, Routledge and Kegan Paul, London 1956; Lewis Coser, *Men of Ideas: A Sociologist's View*, Free Press, Collier-Macmillan, New York 1965; Edward Shils, *The Intellectuals and the Powers and Other Essays*, University of Chicago Press, Chicago and London 1972; and Alvin Gouldner, *The Future of the Intellectuals and the Rise of the New Class*, Macmillan, London 1979.

11. Gramsci, *Prison Notebooks*, especially 'The Intellectuals', pp. 5–23.

12. See Raymond Williams, *Culture and Society 1780–1950*, Chatto and Windus, London 1958, and *Marxism and Literature*, Oxford University Press, Oxford and New York 1977; Pierre Bourdieu, *Distinction: A Social Critique of the Judgement of Taste* [1979], trans. Richard Nice, Routledge and Kegan Paul, London 1984; Michel Foucault, *Power/Knowledge: Selected Interviews and Writings 1972–77*, ed. and trans. Colin Gordon, Harvester Press, Brighton 1980.

13. Arnaldo Córdova, 'Gramsci y la izquierda mexicana', *La Ciudad Futura* (Buenos Aires), no. 6, August 1987, supplement, 'Gramsci en América Latina', p. 14.
14. For an overview of Gramsci's influence in Latin America, see José Aricó, *La cola del diablo: itinerario de Gramsci en América Latina*, Puntosur, Buenos Aires 1988. For an early study of Latin American intellectuals that adopted a Gramscian approach, see Marsal, *El intelectual latinoamericano*.
15. Aricó, *La cola*, pp. 23–4.
16. Ibid., p. 120.
17. Ibid.
18. Gramsci, *Prison Notebooks*, p. 12.
19. For example Morse, 'The Multiverse'.
20. Gramsci, *Prison Notebooks*, p. 366. See also pp. 407–9.
21. For his discussion of the different historical formations of 'advanced' and 'peripheral' capitalist states, see Antonio Gramsci, *Pre-prison Writings*, ed. Richard Bellamy, trans. Virginia Cox, Cambridge University Press, Cambridge 1994, pp. 297–9. On Western and Eastern states, see p. 17.
22. See John Keane, ed., *Civil Society and the State: New European Perspectives*, Verso, London 1988; and Krishnan Kumar, 'Civil Society: An Inquiry into the Usefulness of an Historical Term', *British Journal of Sociology*, 44:3 (September 1993), pp. 375–95. For more recent thinking, see John A. Hall, ed., *Civil Society: Theory, History, Comparison*, Polity Press, Cambridge 1995.
23. Gellner, *Conditions of Liberty*, p. 56.
24. Ibid., p. 1.
25. Ibid.
26. Maxine Molyneux, 'Citizenship and social policy', paper presented at a workshop on social policy, Institute of Latin American Studies, University of London, 1998, p. 6.
27. Gramsci, *Prison Notebooks*, p. 12.
28. Ibid., p. 263. At yet another time, Gramsci represented civil society and the state as 'one and the same' (ibid., p. 160).
29. Ibid., p. 52.
30. Ibid., p. 238.
31. Gellner, *Conditions of Liberty*, pp. 73–8.
32. Gramsci, *Prison Notebooks*, pp. 8 and 9.
33. Ibid., p. 9.
34. Ibid.
35. Ibid., p. 12.
36. Ibid., pp. 7–8.
37. Ibid., p. 9.
38. Ibid., pp. 7 and 9.
39. Aricó, *La còla*, p. 102.
40. See Louis Althusser, *For Marx* [1965], trans. Ben Brewster, Verso, London 1990, n. 23, pp. 105–6. Original emphases.
41. Oscar Terán, *Nuestros años sesentas: la formación de la nueva izquierda intelectual en la Argentina 1956–1966*, Editores Puntosur, Buenos Aires 1991, p. 14.
42. Oscar Landi, in Adolfo Canitrot *et al.*, 'Intelectuales y política en Argentina', *Debates en la sociedad y la cultura* (Buenos Aires), Year 2, no. 4 (October–November 1985), pp. 4–8, p. 4.

43. Gabriel García Márquez, interviewed by Jorge Castañeda, in *Utopia Unarmed*, p. 185.

44. Gramsci, *Prison Notebooks*, p. 5.

45. Ibid. However, it is not always easy to distinguish in practice between a 'traditional' intellectual who, while not acknowledging his role in propping up the bourgeoisie, fulfils it none the less, and an 'organic' intellectual of the bourgeoisie who '[organizes] a new culture' to perpetuate bourgeois hegemony.

46. Ibid., p. 10.

47. Ibid., 'The Intellectuals', pp. 5–23 and 'On Education', pp. 26–43; Antonio Gramsci, *Quaderni del carcere*, Edizione critica del'Istituto Gramsci, Einaudi, Turin 1975, vol. III, 'Per la storia degli intellettuali', pp. 1513–51.

48. Gramsci, *Prison Notebooks*, pp. 10 and 40.

49. Ibid., pp. 29, 31 and 30.

50. Ibid., p. 43.

51. Ibid., p. 9.

52. Ibid., p. 6.

53. Luis Emilio Recabarren, '¿ Cómo se realizará el socialismo?' in his *El pensamiento de Luis Emilio Recabarren*, vol. 1, Editorial Austral, Santiago 1971, pp. 49–75, p. 72.

54. Mario Benedetti, 'Las prioridades del escritor', in Benedetti, *El escritor latino-americano y la revolución posible*, Editorial Nueva Imagen, Buenos Aires 1987, pp. 61–82, p. 62.

55. Gramsci, *Prison Notebooks*, p. 14.

56. Ibid., p. 15.

57. For more detailed discussion, see Chapter 6.

58. Castañeda, *Utopia Unarmed*, p. 273.

59. Ibid., p. 276.

60. Victor Alba, *Nationalists without Nations: The Oligarchy versus the People in Latin America*, Praeger, New York 1968, especially pp. 101–5 and 149–60; quotation at p. 105.

61. Martin, *Journeys*, p. 82.

62. Castañeda, *Utopia Unarmed*, pp. 282–5.

63. Shils, *The Intellectuals*, p. 3.

64. James D. Cockcroft, *Intellectual Precursors of the Mexican Revolution, 1900–1913*, University of Texas Press, Austin and London 1968, p. 3.

65. Francisco Madero, *La sucesión presidencial en 1910*, facsimile edn, Ediciones de la Secretaría de Hacienda, Mexico City 1960.

66. Beatriz Sarlo, 'El intelectual socialista', *La Ciudad Futura*, no. 30/31, December 1991–February 1992, p. 28.

67. Mario Vargas Llosa, *José María Arguedas, entre sapos y halcones*, Ediciones cultura hispánica del Centro Iberoamericano de Cooperación, Madrid 1978, p. 23.

68. Daniel Cosío Villegas, 'L'intellectuel mexicain et la politique', in GRAL Institut d'Études Mexicaines-Perpignan, *Intellectuels et état au Mexique au xxe siècle*, Éditions du CNRS, Paris 1979, pp. 9–17, p. 13.

69. Julio Ortega, 'Sobre el discurso político de Octavio Paz', *Socialismo y Participación* (Lima), no. 33, March 1986, pp. 89–95, p. 89.

70. On the Padilla affair, see Lourdes Casal, *El caso Padilla: literatura y revolución en Cuba*, Ediciones Universal, Miami 1971.

71. Fidel Castro, speech to the Primer Congreso Nacional de Educación y Cultura, cited in Roberto Fernández Retamar, 'Calibán' [1971], in *Para el perfil definitivo del hombre*, Editorial Letras Cubanas, Havana, 1985, pp. 219–89, p. 279, n. 168.

72. Carlos Fuentes, *Myself with Others: Selected Essays*, Pan Books, London 1989, p. 20.

73. Octavio Paz, cited in Julio Scherer García, *Los presidentes*, Editorial Grijalbo, Mexico City 1986, p. 83.

74. Pierre Bourdieu, *Homo academicus* [1984], trans. Peter Collier, Polity Press, Cambridge 1988.

75. Ibid., p. 79.

76. Mario Vargas Llosa, 'El papel del intelectual en los movimientos de liberación nacional' [1966], in his *Contra viento y marea*, Seix Barral, Barcelona, 2 vols, 1986, vol. I, p. 105.

77. Beatriz Sarlo, in Carlos Altamirano and Beatriz Sarlo, *Literatura/sociedad*, Librería Hachette, Buenos Aires, 1983, p. 86.

78. Carlos Pérez, interviewed by Francesco Chioldi, in 'La no identidad latino-americana: una visión peregrina', *Revista de Crítica Cultural*, vol. II, no. 3 (April 1991), pp. 28–32, p. 28.

79. Jean Baudrillard, cited in Mike Gane, ed., *Baudrillard Live: Selected Interviews*, Routledge, London and New York 1993, p. 73.

80. Alain Touraine, *La parole et le sang: politique et société en Amérique Latine*, Editions Odile Jacob, Paris 1988, p. 138.

81. Ibid., pp. 138–9.

82. Pablo Macera, *Trabajos de historia: Teoría – Tomo I* [1977], G. Herrera Editores, Lima, 2nd edn, 1988, p. 96.

83. Baudrillard, in Gane, *Baudrillard Live*, p. 77.

84. Aricó, *La cola*, p. 121. See also Liliana de Riz and Emilio de Ipola, 'Acerca de la hegemonía como producción histórica (Apuntes para un debate sobre las alternativas políticas en América Latina)', in Julio Labastida Martín del Campo, ed., *Hegemonía y alternativas políticas en América Latina*, Siglo XXI, Mexico City 1985, pp. 45–70, especially pp. 60–1.

85. For a useful discussion of these issues, see Jean-François Sirinelli, 'The Concept of an Intellectual Generation', in Jeremy Jennings, ed., *Intellectuals in Twentieth-century France: Mandarins and Samurais*, Macmillan, London 1993, pp. 82–93.

86. Enrique Krauze, 'Los temples de la cultura', in Roderic A. Camp, Charles A. Hale and Josefina Zoraída Vásquez, eds, *Los intelectuales y el poder en México*, El Colegio de México/UCLA Latin American Center Publications, Mexico City 1991, pp. 583–605, p. 584. Angel Rama estimated that in 1900 there were perhaps one hundred writers in Buenos Aires, then the cultural capital of the region, out of a population of 1 million (*La ciudad letrada*, p. 157).

87. This is in effect the field studied by José Joaquín Brunner in reference to Chile, although his typology of intellectuals is more nuanced. See José Joaquín Brunner, *Los intelectuales: esbozos y antecedentes para la constitución del campo de estudios*, 2 vols, FLACSO, Documento de Trabajo, no. 135, Santiago, March 1982.

88. Alan Knight, 'Intellectuals in the Mexican Revolution', in Camp *et al.*, *Los intelectuales y el poder*, pp. 141–72, pp. 141 and 143.

89. Ibid., p. 143.

90. Florencia Mallon, *Peasant and Nation: The Making of Postcolonial Mexico and Peru*, University of California Press, Berkeley and London 1995, p. 12.

91. Mallon, *Peasant and Nation*; Knight, 'Intellectuals'; and Mary Kay Vaughan, *Cultural Politics in Revolution: Teachers, Peasants, and Schools in Mexico, 1930–1940*, University of Arizona Press, Tucson 1997.

92. The phrase 'historical embeddedness' comes from Anthony Smith, currently the leading exponent of a carefully moderated version of this position. See his *Nations and Nationalism in a Global Era*, p. viii; and *National Identity*. The modernist view can be found in Gellner, *Nations and Nationalism*, and in his posthumously published essay *Nationalism*, Weidenfeld and Nicolson, London 1997; Eric Hobsbawm, *Nations and Nationalism since 1870*, Cambridge University Press, Cambridge, 2nd edn, 1992; and Eric Hobsbawm and Terence Ranger, eds, *The Invention of Tradition*, Canto edn, Cambridge University Press, Cambridge 1992.

93. Smith, *Nations and Nationalism*, p. 36.

94. Eric J. Hobsbawm, 'Nationalism and Nationality in Latin America', in Bouda Etemad, Jean Baton and Thomas David, eds, *Pour une histoire économique et sociale internationale: mélanges offerts à Paul Bairoch*, Éditions Passé Présent, Geneva, 1995, pp. 313–23, p. 313.

95. John J. Johnson, 'Foreword', in Arthur P. Whitaker and David C. Jordan, *Nationalism in Contemporary Latin America*, Free Press, New York, and Collier-Macmillan Ltd, London 1966, p. v.

96. Arthur P. Whitaker, *Nationalism in Latin America, Past and Present*, University of Florida Press, Gainesville 1962, p. 14. See also Gerhard Masur, *Nationalism in Latin America: Diversity and Unity*, Macmillan, New York 1966. In similar vein, although published a decade later, was Robert Swansborough's pioneering account of economic nationalism in Latin America: *The Embattled Colossus: Economic Nationalism and United States Investors in Latin America*, University Presses of Florida, Gainesville 1976. In addition, there is the far more overtly anti-Communist interpretation by Victor Alba, *Nationalists without Nations*.

97. Whitaker, *Nationalism*, pp. 20–3.

98. Ibid., p. 16.

99. Ibid., pp. 76–7.

100. Masur, *Nationalism*, pp. 250–1.

101. Claudio Veliz, 'Centralism and Nationalism in Latin America', in Howard J. Wiarda, ed., *Politics and Social Change in Latin America: The Distinct Tradition*, University of Massachusetts Press, Amherst 1974, pp. 181–95, pp. 194 and 192.

102. See David Brading, *The Origins of Mexican Nationalism*, Cambridge University Press, Cambridge 1985; and Richard M. Morse, *New World Soundings: Culture and Ideology in the Americas*, Johns Hopkins University Press, Baltimore and London 1989, p. 110. Benedict Anderson is an exception in arguing that the independence movements were nationalist in character: see the discussion below.

103. John Lynch, in Leslie Bethell, ed., *Argentina since Independence*, Cambridge University Press, Cambridge 1993, p. 41.

104. Morse, *New World Soundings*, p. 114.
105. Hobsbawm, 'Nationalism'.
106. Ibid., p. 314.
107. Ibid., p. 317.
108. Ibid.
109. Ibid., p. 318.
110. Ibid., p. 319.
111. Ibid., p. 313.
112. Ibid., p. 320.
113. Smith, *Nations and Nationalism*, p. 40.
114. Mario Góngora has argued that 'Chilean nationality has been formed by a state which anteceded it, in which respect it is like Argentina, and different from Mexico and Peru, where great indigenous cultures prefigured the Vice-Royalties and the Republics.' *Ensayo histórico sobre la noción del Estado en Chile en los siglos xix y xx*, Ediciones La Ciudad, Santiago 1981, p. 11.
115. See Shirley Brice Heath, *Telling Tongues: Language Policy in Mexico – Colony to Nation*, Teachers College Press, Columbia 1972, Chapter 1; and Jacques Lafaye, 'Literature and Intellectual Life in Colonial Spanish America', in Leslie Bethell, ed., *Cambridge History of Latin America*, vol. II, Cambridge University Press, Cambridge 1984, pp. 663–704.
116. See Richard Morse, 'Language in America', in his *New World Soundings*, pp. 11–60.
117. Ricardo Palma, *Tradiciones peruanas*, selected by Pamela Francis, Pergamon, Oxford 1966, p. xi.
118. Américo Castro, *La peculiaridad lingüística rioplatense*, Taurus, Madrid, 2nd edn, 1961; Jorge Luis Borges and José E. Clemente, *El lenguaje de Buenos Aires*, Emecé Editores, Buenos Aires, 3rd edn, 1968.
119. In Peru, the pioneering work was Juan de Arona, *Diccionario de peruanismos: ensayo filológico*, Lima 1883; the standard reference work for several decades was Pedro Benvenutto Murrieta, *El lenguaje peruano*, Talleres de Sanmartí y Cía, Lima 1936; see also Ricardo Palma, *Neologismos y americanismos*, Imprenta y Librería de Carlos Prince, Lima 1896 and *Papeletas lexicográficas*, Imprenta La Industria, Lima 1903. In Cuba, Fernando Ortiz compiled a *Catauro de cubanismos* [1923], Editorial de Ciencias Sociales, Havana 1985; *catauro* was itself a distinctively Cuban word for 'dictionary'. For Argentina, see Tobías Garzón, *Diccionario argentino*, Comisión Nacional del Centenario de la Revolución de Mayo, Universidad Nacional de Córdoba, Imprenta de Borras y Mestres, 1910. On Chile, see Zorobabel Rodríguez, *Diccionario de chilenismos* [1875], facsimile edn, Ediciones Universitarios de Valparaíso, Universidad Católica de Valparaíso, 1979. Less of this type of work was done in Mexico because of the disruption caused by the revolution.
120. Smith, *Nations and Nationalism*, p. 38.
121. Morse, 'The Multiverse', p. 2. Morse's comments are directed explicitly against Nicholas Canny and Anthony Pagden's edited collection, *Colonial Identity in the Atlantic World, 1500–1800*, Princeton University Press, Princeton, 1988; they are also applicable to Benedict Anderson's emphasis on literacy and literati in the creation of national identities.
122. Morse, 'The Multiverse', p. 3.

123. Benedict Anderson, *Imagined Communities: Reflections on the Origins and Spread of Nationalism*, Verso, London and New York 1983 and revised edn, 1991.

124. Mary Fulbrook, 'Introduction: States, Nations, and the Development of Europe', in Mary Fulbrook, ed., *National Histories and European History*, UCL Press, London 1993, pp. 1–20, p. 5.

125. Anderson, *Imagined Communities*, p. 52. For the argument that the independence movements were not in any significant sense 'nationalist', see John Lynch, *Spanish American Revolutions, 1808–1826* [1973], W. W. Norton, New York, 2nd edn, 1986; and David Brading, 'Classical Republicanism and Creole Patriotism: Simón Bolívar (1783–1830) and the Spanish American Revolution', Centre of Latin American Studies, University of Cambridge, Cambridge 1983.

126. Simon Collier, 'Nationality, Nationalism, and Supranationalism in the Writings of Símon Bolívar', *Hispanic American Historical Review*, 63:1, 1983, pp. 37–64, pp. 38 and 39.

127. Lynch, *Spanish American Revolutions*, p. 25.

128. Collier, 'Nationality', pp. 42–3.

129. Anderson, *Imagined Communities*, p. 65.

130. *El periquillo sarniento* [*The Itching Parrot*] was the first novel to be published in the region partly because of Spanish censorship laws; and partly because of the lack of an autonomous intellectual community to produce works of creative literature: most intellectual functions under the colonial regime were performed by clerics or lawyers and those literary energies which did break free were channelled into poetry.

131. Anthony Pagden, 'Identity formation in Spanish America', in Canny and Pagden, *Colonial Identity*, pp. 51–93.

132. Jorge Cañizares Esguerra, 'Nation and Nature: Natural History and the Fashioning of Creole National Identity in Late Colonial Spanish America', paper delivered to XX LASA Congress, Guadalajara, April, 1997. See also Thomas F. Glick, 'Science and Independence in Latin America (with Special Reference to New Granada)', *Hispanic American Historical Review*, 71:2 (May 1991), pp. 307–34.

133. William Rowe and Vivien Schelling, *Memory and Modernity: Popular Culture in Latin America*, Verso, London 1991, p. 204. See also Doris Sommer, *Foundational Fictions: The National Romances of Latin America*, University of California Press, Berkeley 1991; and Martin, *Journeys*.

134. Collier, 'Nationality', p. 39.

135. Louis Panabière, 'Les intellectuels et l'état au Mexique (1930–1940) – Le cas de dissidence des *Contemporáneos*', in GRAL Institut, *Intellectuels et état au Mexique*, pp. 77–112, pp. 77–8.

136. Walker Connor, 'A Nation is a Nation, is a State, is an Ethnic Group is a . . .', *Ethnic and Racial Studies*, 1:4 (October 1978), pp. 377–400.

137. Alfred Stepan, *The State and Society: Peru in Comparative Perspective*, Princeton University Press, Princeton, NJ 1978, p. xi.

138. John D. Martz and David J. Myers, 'Understanding Latin American Politics: Analytic Models and Intellectual Traditions', in Howard J. Wiarda, ed., *Politics and Social Change in Latin America: Still a Distinct Tradition?*, Westview Press, Boulder, CO 1992, pp. 255–78, p. 272.

139. Juan José Hernández Arregui, *La formación de la conciencia nacional, 1930–1960*, Ediciones Hachea, Buenos Aires 1960, pp. 149–50.
140. Guillermo O'Donnell, 'On the State, Democratization and Some Conceptual Problems: A Latin American View with Glances at Some Postcommunist Countries', *World Development*, 21:8 (1993), pp. 1,355–69, p. 1,356.
141. Ibid., p. 1,360.
142. Theda Skocpol, 'Bringing the State Back In: Strategies of Analysis in Current Research', in Peter Evans, Dietrich Rueschemeyer and Theda Skocpol, eds, *Bringing the State Back In*, Cambridge University Press, Cambridge 1985, pp. 3–37, p. 21.
143. Ibid., p. 14.
144. On Mexico, see Alan Knight, 'State Power and Political Stability in Mexico', in Neil Harvey, ed., *Mexico: Dilemmas of Transition*, British Academic Press for the Institute of Latin American Studies, University of London, London and New York 1993, pp. 29–63.

Chapter 2

Parts of an earlier version of this chapter appeared in Nicola Miller, 'Intellectuals and the State in Spanish America: A Comparative Perspective', in Will Fowler, ed., *Ideologues and Ideologies in Latin America*, Greenwood Press, Westport, CO, and London 1997, pp. 45–64.

1. Gabriel García Márquez interviewed by Castañeda, in *Utopia Unarmed*, p. 196.
2. Mario Vargas Llosa, 'El intelectual barato' [1979], in his *Contra viento y marea*, vol. II, pp. 143–55, p. 144.
3. Belaúnde offered Vargas Llosa ambassadorships in London and Washington, the Ministry of Education, the Ministry of Foreign Relations and even the position of Prime Minister.
4. On the revisionist historiography of the 1970s, which questioned the traditional – and also the official – interpretation of the Mexican revolution as a popular agrarian uprising, see David C. Bailey, 'Revisionism and the Recent History of the Mexican Revolution', *Hispanic American Historical Review*, 58:1, 1978, pp. 62–79. For a further discussion of the character of the Revolution, see Alan Knight, 'The Mexican Revolution: Bourgeois? Nationalist? Or just a "Great Rebellion"?', *Bulletin of Latin American Research*, 4:2, 1985, pp. 1–37.
5. Pierre Bourdieu, *Distinction: A Social Critique of the Judgement of Taste*, trans. Richard Nice, Routledge and Kegan Paul, London 1984, pp. 114–15.
6. See David R. Maciel, 'Los orígenes de la cultura oficial en México: los intelectuales y el estado en la república restaurada', in Camp *et al.*, *Los intelectuales y el poder*, pp. 569–82.
7. Cosío Villegas, 'L'intellectuel mexicain et la politique', p. 12.
8. Cockcroft, *Intellectual Precursors*, p. 45.
9. Luis Cabrera, 'El Partido Científico', cited in Gabriella de Beer, *Luis Cabrera: un intelectual de la Revolución Mexicana*, trans. Ismael Pizarro and Mercedes Pizarro, Fondo de Cultura Económica, Mexico City 1984, p. 45. Cabrera went

on to become an adviser to Venustiano Carranza during the revolution, drafting his decrees on labour and agrarianism.

10. Mary Kay Vaughan, *The State, Education, and Social Class in Mexico, 1880–1928*, Northern Illinois University Press, DeKalb 1982, p. 240.
11. Cockcroft, *Intellectual Precursors*, p. 233.
12. Knight summarizes the arguments in 'Intellectuals', pp. 143–4.
13. Over half of the exiles from the Carranza government were intellectuals, including Ricardo Flores Magón, who had left in late 1911 and ended his days in a Kansas prison, Pedro Henríquez Ureña (from 1914), and Alfonso Reyes, who did not return permanently until 1938. One of the few who remained was Antonio Caso, who continued to hold his classes in philosophy throughout the conflict. See Henry C. Schmidt, 'Power and Sensibility: Towards a Typology of Mexican Intellectuals and Intellectual Life, 1910–1920', in Camp *et al.*, *Los intelectuales y el poder*, pp. 173–88, p. 185, n. 53.
14. Knight, 'Intellectuals', p. 167.
15. One notable exception was Luis Cabrera.
16. Knight, 'Intellectuals', p. 142.
17. Alan Knight, *The Mexican Revolution*, Cambridge University Press, Cambridge 1986, vol. 2, pp. 473–5. Compare the far greater contribution of men of letters to the constitutions of 1824 and 1857. See Jaime E. Rodríguez O., 'Intellectuals and the Mexican Constitution of 1824', in Camp *et al.*, *Los intelectuales y el poder*, pp. 63–74.
18. Knight, *Mexican Revolution*, vol. 2, pp. 475 and 292.
19. José Vasconcelos, 'Intelectuales y políticos', *Memorias*, Fondo de Cultura Económica, Mexico City 1982, vol. I, p. 840.
20. The 'Sonoran state' was named in reference to the fact that the leaders who controlled the central Mexican state from 1920 until Lázaro Cárdenas (from Michoacán) assumed the presidency in 1934 were all from the northern state of Sonora.
21. Jean Meyer, 'Revolution and Reconstruction in the 1920s', in Leslie Bethell, ed., *Mexico since Independence*, Cambridge University Press, Cambridge 1991, pp. 201–40, p. 203.
22. Intellectuals were more than willing to play their part. In 1921, for example, Daniel Cosío Villegas organized a congress of students which promoted recognition of Obregón's government by an international cultural elite. Gabriel Zaid, *De los libros al poder*, Editorial Grijalbo, Mexico City 1988, p. 67.
23. Knight, *Mexican Revolution*, vol. 2, pp. 290–4 and 297. Gabriella de Beer, *José Vasconcelos and His World*, Las Americas Publishing Company, New York 1966, pp. 102–4.
24. De Beer, *Vasconcelos and His World*, pp. 102–4.
25. Christopher Domínguez Michael, 'Prólogo', in José Vasconcelos, *Obra selecta*, Biblioteca Ayacucho, Caracas 1992, pp. xxvii–xxviii.
26. Domínguez Michael, 'Prólogo', p. xxviii.
27. Vasconcelos, *Memorias*, vol. I, p. 945.
28. Under Porfirio Díaz, 'national' public education initiatives had in practice been restricted to the capital. Carranza, who believed that public education should be in the hands of the municipalities, as it was in the United States, closed the

Ministry of Public Instruction, which was formally abolished in the 1917 constitution.

29. Domínguez Michael, 'Prólogo', p. xxxii.

30. Meyer, 'Revolution and Reconstruction', p. 208. The budget was drastically cut after Vasconcelos had tendered his resignation (which was rejected) in protest at the assassination in January 1924 of Senator Field Jurado, an opponent of the Bucareli accords by which the United States and Mexico established a mechanism for resolving their disputes over property after the nationalization clauses in the constitution of 1917. Claude Fell, *José Vasconcelos: los años del águila (1920–1925)*, UNAM, Mexico City 1989, p. 667.

31. Vasconcelos, 'El desastre', in *Obra selecta*, pp. 254–72, p. 256.

32. Ibid., p. 257.

33. José Joaquín Blanco, *Se llamaba Vasconcelos: una evocación crítica*, Fondo de Cultura Económica, Mexico City 1977, p. 106.

34. Domínguez Michael, 'Prólogo', p. xxxiii.

35. Vasconcelos, 'Discurso en la Universidad' [1920], in *Obra selecta*, pp. 41–5, pp. 43 and 44.

36. Ibid., p. 44.

37. Ibid.

38. Meyer, 'Revolution and Reconstruction', p. 207. Vasconcelos himself noted, 'when I left the ministry the enemies of reading triumphed'. See his account of his time at SEP in *Indología: una interpretación de la cultura Ibero-Americana*, Agencia Mundial de Librería, Paris 1927, pp. 159–90, quotation at p. 168.

39. Octavio Paz, 'La ilusiones y las convicciones' [1976], in *El ogro filantrópico: historia y política 1971–1978*, Editorial Seix Barral, Barcelona 1979, p. 73.

40. *Ulises criollo* was the title of the first volume of Vasconcelos's memoirs.

41. Vaughan, *The State*, p. 265.

42. Domínguez Michael, 'Prólogo', p. xxxiii.

43. Blanco, *Se llamaba Vasconcelos*, p. 100.

44. Carlos Monsiváis, 'Diego Rivera: creador de públicos', *Historias* (Mexico City), no. 13, April–June 1986, pp. 117–27, p. 120.

45. Monsiváis, 'Diego Rivera', p. 121.

46. Carlos Monsiváis, *De que se ríe el licenciado (una crónica de los 40)*, Colección Práctica de vuelo, Delegación Venustiano Carranza del Departamento del Distrito Federal, Mexico City 1984, p. 17.

47. Carlos Monsiváis, 'L'état et les intellectuels au Mexique', in GRAL Institut d'Études Mexicaines–Perpignan, *Champs de pouvoir et de savoir au Mexique*, Éditions de CNRS, Paris 1982, pp. 83–107, p. 93.

48. Jean Meyer, 'Introduction', in GRAL Institut, *Intellectuels et état au Mexique*, p. 7.

49. Panabière, 'Les intellectuels et l'état au Mexique', p. 86, my emphasis.

50. For this group's view of culture, see Samuel Ramos, 'La cultura criolla', in *Contemporáneos*, nos. 38–9, July–August 1931, pp. 61–82; on government harassment of them, see Octavio Paz, 'Vuelta a *El laberinto de la soledad*', in *El ogro filantrópico*, p. 29.

51. Lázaro Cárdenas, 'Mensaje del Presidente de la República a los universitarios', 21 March 1935, in *Palabras y documentos públicos de Lázaro Cárdenas (1928–1970). Vol. I: 1928–1940*, Siglo Veintiuno Editores, Mexico City 1978, pp. 150–2, p. 151.

52. Vaughan, *Cultural Politics in Revolution*, p. 7.

53. Vasconcelos, 'Discurso en la Universidad', p. 44.

54. Fell, *José Vasconcelos*, p. 665.

55. Jesús Silva Herzog, *Una historia de la Universidad de México y sus problemas*, Siglo Veintiuno, Mexico City 1974, pp. 18–19.

56. Francisco López Cámara, 'La UNAM en la política mexicana', *Revista Universidad de México*, September 1992, pp. 19–23, p. 20; and Daniel C. Levy, *University and Government in Mexico: Autonomy in an Authoritarian System*, Praeger, NY 1980, p. 26. Vasconcelos himself argued (perhaps unsurprisingly) that the granting of university autonomy eroded his student support base: 'The students, distracted by their new toy of a university in which exams had been abolished and students nominated and removed their lecturers at will, largely abandoned electioneering activities.' *Memorias*, vol. II, p. 855.

57. Cárdenas, 'Mensaje del Presidente de la República a los universitarios', pp. 151–2.

58. Daniel Cosío Villegas, 'Un poco de historia', *Historia mexicana*, vol. XXV:4 (no. 100), April–June 1976, pp. 505–29, p. 518.

59. See T. G. Powell, 'Mexico', in Mark Falcoff and Fredrick B. Pike, eds, *The Spanish Civil War, 1936–9: American Hemispheric Perspectives*, University of Nebraska Press, Lincoln 1982, pp. 49–99.

60. Miguel Alemán, *Programa educativo del Lic. Miguel Alemán, Presidente de los Estados Unidos Mexicanos y diez discursos sobre educación*, Edición del Departamento de Publicidad y Propaganda, Mexico City 1947, p. xi.

61. Zaid, *De los libros al poder*, p. 25.

62. Ibid., p. 149.

63. Jean Meyer, 'Introduction', in GRAL, *Intellectuels et état au Mexique*, p. 5.

64. Enrique Krauze, 'Los temples de la cultura', in Camp *et al.*, *Los intelectuales y el poder*, pp. 583–605, pp. 595 and 597.

65. Xavier Rodríguez Ledesma, 'El poder como espejo de los intelectuales', *Revista Mexicana de Ciencias Políticas y Sociales*, XXXIX:158, October–December 1994, pp. 67–91, p. 79.

66. Enrique Krauze, 'La comedia mexicana de Carlos Fuentes', in his *Textos heréticos*, Editorial Grijalbo, Mexico City 1992, pp. 31–57, p. 45.

67. Krauze, *Textos heréticos*, p. 22.

68. Rodríguez Ledesma, 'El poder como espejo' p. 87.

69. Ibid., p. 90.

70. Roderic Camp, *Intellectuals and the State in Twentieth-century Mexico*, University of Texas Press, Austin 1985, p. 231. Camp's definition of an intellectual is far broader than mine, including virtually everybody who has received higher education, which reinforces rather than detracts from this point.

71. Oscar Landi *et al.*, 'Intelectuales y política en Argentina', *Debates en la sociedad y la cultura*, vol. 2, no. 4, October–November 1985, pp. 4–8, p. 4.

72. Silvia Sigal, *Intelectuales y poder en la década del sesenta*, Puntosur Editores, Buenos Aires 1991, p. 61.

73. Yrigoyen did send in the troops briefly during the struggle for university reform, but this was fundamentally a manoeuvre designed to appease the Right. His government subsequently granted student demands. See the discussion on pages 56–7.

74. In 1896, one of the two main newspapers, *La Prensa*, sold 58,000 copies in Buenos Aires but only 16,000 in the provinces. In 1913, it sold 70,000 in the capital city and 160,000 throughout the rest of Argentina. Jesús Méndez, 'Argentine Intellectuals in the Twentieth Century, 1900–1943', PhD thesis, University of Texas at Austin 1980, p. 90.

75. David Viñas, *Apogeo de la oligarquía: literatura argentina y realidad política*, Ediciones Siglo Veinte, Buenos Aires 1975, p. 125. See also Méndez, 'Argentine Intellectuals', Chapter 1.

76. Méndez, 'Argentine Intellectuals', pp. 102–3.

77. This account draws substantially on Juan Carlos Portantiero, *Estudiantes y política en América Latina 1918–1938*, Siglo XXI, Mexico City, 2nd edn, 1987, pp. 30–57.

78. Ibid., p. 85.

79. Tulio Halperín Donghi, *Historia de la Universidad de Buenos Aires*, Eudeba, Buenos Aires 1962, p. 134.

80. Hipólito Yrigoyen, *Mi vida y mi doctrina*, Editorial Raigal, Buenos Aires 1957, p. 68.

81. *PEN Club – noticiero mensual*, no. 5, September 1930, cited in Méndez, 'Argentine Intellectuals', p. 273.

82. Méndez, 'Argentine Intellectuals', Chapter 5.

83. Arturo Armada, 'Perón: intelectuales, militantes y herbívoros', *Unidos* (Buenos Aires), no. 13, December 1986, pp. 45–65, p. 55.

84. Eva Perón, *Historia del peronismo*, Editorial Freeland, Buenos Aires 1971, pp. 16 and 10.

85. Juan Domingo Perón, 'La cultura', no publisher given, Buenos Aires 1948, p. 5.

86. Ibid., p. 5.

87. Juan Domingo Perón, 'Speech to the Intellectuals', no publisher given, Buenos Aires November 1947, p. 12.

88. Eva Perón, *Historia del peronismo*, p. 179.

89. Ibid., p. 27 (original emphases).

90. Ibid., pp. 42–3 (original emphasis).

91. *Plano quinquenal del general Perón (1953–7)*, no publisher, Buenos Aires, no date, c. 1952, pp. 5–6.

92. Ibid., p. 7.

93. Eva Perón, *Historia del peronismo*, p. 42. There is no knowledge about Lycurgus which can reliably be accepted as accurate. Even his dates are in dispute, varying between 950 and 650 B.C. Modern historical opinion is that Lycurgus was a legendary figure to whom all the major characteristics of Spartan life and politics were retrospectively attributed. I am grateful to Hans van Wees for this information.

94. Pedro Santos Martínez, *La nueva Argentina 1946–55*, vol. I, Ediciones La Bastilla, Buenos Aires 1976, p. 188.

95. The main examples of direct repression against the intellectual community were as follows. On VJ day, a student, Enrique Blaisten, was killed by gunfire from the Peronist-run Secretaría de Informaciones. In 1950 Communist student leader Jorge Calvo was assassinated, and the following year chemistry student Ernesto Mario Bravo was arrested and allegedly tortured (Richard J. Walter, *Student Politics in Argentina: The University Reform and Its Effects, 1918–64*, Basic Books, New York and London 1968, p. 141). Other student leaders who

supported a strike by railway workers in 1950 and 1951 were tortured while in detention (William H. Katra, *Contorno: Literary Engagement in Post-Peronist Argentina*, Associated University Presses, London and Toronto 1988, p. 22). In the 1953–54 demonstrations against Perón, several intellectuals were imprisoned, including Roberto Giusti, José Luis Romero, Francisco Romero and, most famously, Victoria Ocampo (see note 118 below). Terán, *Nuestros años sesentas*, p. 35.

96. Arthur P. Whitaker, *The United States and Argentina*, Harvard University Press, Cambridge, MA 1954, p. 153.

97. Carlos Mangone and Jorge A. Warley, *Universidad y peronismo (1946–1955)*, Centro Editor de América Latina, Buenos Aires 1984, p. 35.

98. Terán, *Nuestros años sesentas*, p. 37.

99. Katra, *Contorno*, p. 69.

100. Juan Domingo Perón, *La cultura a través del pensamiento de Perón*, Presidencia de la Nación, Subsecretaría de Información, Buenos Aires 1954, p. 11.

101. Perón, 'La cultura', p. 4.

102. Santos Martínez, *La nueva Argentina*, vol. I, p. 186.

103. Ministerio de Educación, Subsecretaría de Cultura, *Anteproyecto de Estatuto del Trabajador Intelectual*, Buenos Aires July 1949.

104. Martin S. Stabb, 'Argentine Letters and the *Peronato*: An Overview', *Journal of Inter-American Studies*, XIII:3–4 (July–October 1971), pp. 434–55, p. 438.

105. *Plano quinquenal*, p. 10.

106. Norberto Galasso, *Vida de Scalabrini Ortiz*, Ediciones del Mar Dulce, Buenos Aires 1970, p. 432.

107. Raúl Scalabrini Ortiz, 'Los enemigos del pueblo argentino' [1948], in his *Yrigoyen y Perón*, Editorial Plus Ultra, Buenos Aires 1972, pp. 23–8.

108. Raúl Scalabrini Ortiz, *Los ferrocarriles deben ser del pueblo argentino*, Editorial Reconquista, Buenos Aires 1946.

109. Tulio Halperín Donghi, 'El revisionismo histórico como visión decadentista de la historia argentina', *Punto de Vista* (Buenos Aires), no. 23 (April 1985), pp. 9–17, p. 13.

110. Galasso, *Vida de Scalabrini Ortiz*, pp. 432, 442–3, 455–7 and 462.

111. Ibid., p. 457.

112. Perón, letter to Scalabrini Ortiz, Ciudad Trujillo, 18 March 1958, in Juan Domingo Perón, *Correspondencia*, Ediciones Corregidor, Buenos Aires, 2 vols, 1983, vol. II, pp. 38–42, p. 41.

113. Perón, letter to Scalabrini Ortiz, Caracas, 31 December 1957, in *Correspondencia*, vol. I, pp. 50–2, p. 51.

114. Perón to Scalabrini Ortiz, 18 March 1958, p. 40.

115. Norberto Galasso, *Manuel Ugarte: un argentino 'maldito'*, Ediciones del Pensamiento Nacional, Buenos Aires 1981, p. 111.

116. Ibid., p. 113.

117. Ibid., p. 116.

118. Ocampo was one of perhaps 1,000 people arrested after a bomb attack on Perón in 1953. Following a brief period in jail, she was released after a special appeal from Gabriela Mistral. John King, *Sur: A Study of the Argentine Literary Journal and Its Role in the Development of a Culture, 1931–1970*, Cambridge University Press, Cambridge 1986, pp. 130 and 148.

119. Juan José Sebreli and Dalmiro Sáenz, '¿Existió una cultura Peronista?', *La Maga* (Buenos Aires), I:31, 12 August 1992, pp. 2–4.

120. Terán, *Nuestros años sesentas*, p. 36.

121. For a detailed account, see Sigal, *Intelectuales y poder*, pp. 158–71.

122. Arturo Frondizi, *Industria Argentina y desarrollo nacional*, Ediciones Qué, Buenos Aires 1957, p. 114. See also Celia Szusterman, *Frondizi and the Politics of Developmentalism in Argentina, 1955–62*, Macmillan, Basingstoke 1993.

123. Sigal, *Intelectuales y poder*, pp. 160–1.

124. José María Arguedas, *El sexto*, Editorial Horizonte, Lima 1969.

125. For the former interpretation, see Peter F. Klarén, 'The Origins of Modern Peru, 1880–1930', in Leslie Bethell, ed., *Cambridge History of Latin America*, vol. V, Cambridge University Press, Cambridge 1986, pp. 587–640; for the latter, see Steve Stein, *Populism in Peru*, University of Wisconsin Press, Madison 1980, Chapter 3. See also the bibliography, 'Peru 1930–60', in Leslie Bethell, ed., *Cambridge History of Latin America*, vol. VIII, Cambridge University Press, Cambridge 1991, p. 828.

126. Julio Ortega, *Cultura y modernización en la Lima del 900*, Centro de Estudios para el Desarrollo y la Participación, Lima 1986, p. 78.

127. Manuel Burga and Alberto Flores Galindo, *Apogeo y crisis de la república aristocrática*, Ediciones Rikchay Perú, Lima, 3rd edn, 1984, p. 161.

128. Jorge Cornejo Pilar, *Intelectuales, artistas y Estado en el Perú del siglo XX*, Universidad de Lima, Cuadernos de Historia, no. XVII, 1993, p. 57.

129. Ibid., p. 56.

130. Ortega, *Cultura y modernización*, p. 83.

131. For a discussion of the conflicting versions of this much-disputed event, see Phyllis W. Rodríguez-Peralta, *José Santos Chocano*, Twayne Publishers, New York 1970, pp. 37–40.

132. Alberto Flores Galindo, *La agonía de Mariátegui*, Editorial Revolución, Madrid 1991, p. 91.

133. Cornejo Pilar, *Intelectuales, artistas y Estado*, p. 66.

134. Harry E. Vanden, *National Marxism in Latin America: José Carlos Mariátegui's Thought and Politics*, Lynne Rienner, Boulder, CO 1986, p. 118.

135. Jesús Chavarría, *José Carlos Mariátegui and the Rise of Modern Peru, 1890–1930*, University of New Mexico Press, Albuquerque 1979, p. 62.

136. Ibid., pp. 63–4.

137. Flores Galindo, *La agonía*, pp. 29–30.

138. Chavarría, *Mariátegui*, p. 97.

139. See Mariátegui, 'La Reforma Universitaria', in his *Siete ensayos de interpretación de la realidad peruana*, vol. 2 of his *Obras completas*, Empresa Editora Amauta, Lima, 18th edn, 1970, pp. 122–61; also Jeffrey Klaiber, 'The Popular Universities and the Origins of *Aprismo*, 1921–1924', *Hispanic American Historical Review*, 55:4 (November 1975), pp. 693–715.

140. Jorge Basadre, *Historia de la República del Perú, 1822–1933*, vol. 15, Editorial Universitaria, Lima 1970, p. 121.

141. Cornejo Pilar, *Intelectuales, artistas y Estado*, p. 105.

142. Mario Vargas Llosa's autobiography devotes about half the text to an account of his campaign for the presidency: see Mario Vargas Llosa, *A Fish in the Water*, trans. Helen Lane, Faber and Faber, London 1994.

143. Geoffrey Bertram, 'Peru, 1930–60', in Leslie Bethell, ed., *Cambridge History of Latin America*, Cambridge University Press, Cambridge 1991, vol. VIII, p. 448.

144. José Martí, 'Carta a Carmen Miyares de Mantilla y a sus hijos', 28 April 1895, in *Obras escogidas* (hereafter *OE*), Centro de Estudios Martianos, Editora Política, Havana, 3 vols 1978–81, vol. III, pp. 548–51, p. 548.

145. Martí, 'Lectura en Steck Hall', speech to Cuban exiles in New York [1880], in *OE*, vol. I, pp. 140–71, p. 151.

146. See Louis A. Pérez, Jr, *José Martí in the United States: The Florida Experience*, Arizona State University, Tempe 1995, especially Chapters vi and vii.

147. Laurie Johnston, '*Por la escuela cubana en Cuba Libre*: Themes in the History of Primary and Secondary Education in Cuba, 1899–1958', unpublished PhD thesis, University of London, 1996.

148. 'El ABC al pueblo cubano, manifiesto-programa' [1932], in Hortensia Pichardo, *Documentos para la historia de Cuba*, Editorial de Ciencias Sociales, Havana, 4 vols 1978, vol. III, pp. 532–64.

149. Virgilio Piñera, 'Notas sobre la vieja y la nueva generación', *La Gaceta de Cuba*, no. 2, 1 May 1962, pp. 2–3.

150. Julio Antonio Mella, 'El Congreso Nacional de Estudiantes', 1923, in *Documentos y artículos*, Editorial de Ciencias Sociales, Instituto Cubano del Libro, Havana 1975, pp. 57–8. For a useful overview of the Cuban student movement, with key documents reprinted, see Olga Cabrera and Carmen Almodóvar, *Las luchas estudiantiles universitarias 1923–1934*, Editorial de Ciencias Sociales, Havana 1975.

151. 'Al pueblo de Cuba, Manifiesto de los Estudiantes Universitarios', in Pichardo, *Documentos*, vol. III, pp. 481–4, p. 483.

152. Jules R. Benjamin, 'The *Machadato* and Cuban Nationalism, 1928–1932', *Hispanic American Historical Review*, 55:1 (February 1975), pp. 66–91, p. 74.

153. 'La Protesta de los trece', in Pichardo, *Documentos*, vol. III, pp. 116–17.

154. Fabio Grobart, cited in Ana Núñez Machín, *Rubén Martínez Villena*, UNEAC, Havana 1971, p. 176.

155. Louis A. Pérez Jr, *Cuba Under the Platt Amendment, 1902–34*, University of Pittsburgh Press, Pittsburgh, PA 1986, p. 332.

156. The Platt Amendment was a clause inserted into the Cuban constitution (1902) stating: 'That the government of Cuba consents that the United States may exercise the right to intervene for the preservation of Cuban independence, the maintenance of a government adequate for the protection of life, property, and individual liberty, and for discharging the obligations with respect to Cuba imposed by the Treaty of Paris on the United States, now to be assumed and undertaken by the government of Cuba.' Cited in Robert F. Smith, *What Happened in Cuba? A Documentary History*, Twayne Publishers, New York 1963, pp. 125–6.

157. Johnston, '*Por la escuela cubana*', p. 182.

158. Ibid., p. 179.

159. José Rodríguez Feo, 'Cultura y moral', insert in *Ciclón* (Havana), I(6), November 1955.

160. Piñera, 'Notas', p. 2.

161. Roberto González Echevarría, 'Criticism and Literature in Revolutionary Cuba', *Cuban Studies*, 11:1, January 1981, pp. 1–17, p. 5.

278 NOTES TO PAGES 75-9

NOTES TO PAGES 75-9

162. 'Una posición' (editorial), *Lunes de Revolución* (Havana), 23 March 1959, p. 2.
163. Onelio Jorge Cardoso, 'To Be a Writer in "Old" Cuba', in Irwin Silber, ed., *Voices of National Liberation: The Revolutionary Ideology of the 'Third World' as Expressed by Intellectuals and Artists at the Cultural Congress of Havana, January 1968*, Central Book Co., New York 1970, p. 69.
164. Ambrosio Fornet, 'We are not Guardians of an Already Burning Fire ... But Incendiaries – Creators of a New Fire', in Silber, *Voices*, pp. 211–15, p. 212.
165. Carlos Franqui, *Family Portrait with Fidel*, trans. Alfred MacAdam, Jonathan Cape, London 1983, especially pp. 9, 68–9 and 99–101.
166. Fidel Castro, 'Palabras a los intelectuales', in María Guerra and Ezéquiel Maldonado, *El compromiso del intelectual*, Editorial Nuestro Tiempo, Mexico City 1979, pp. 69–87, p. 74. For an outline of the Padilla affair, see Chapter 1.
167. See Lisandro Otero, 'Notas sobre la funcionalidad de la cultura', *Casa de las Américas* (Havana), September–October 1971, no. 68, p. 94; and Raúl Roa, 'Los intelectuales y la revolución', 1975, in Guerra and Maldonado, *El compromiso*, pp. 63–8.
168. Bernardo Subercaseaux, *Fin de siglo: la época de Balmaceda. Modernización y cultura en Chile*, Editorial Aconcagua, Santiago 1988, pp. 53–67.
169. See ibid., pp. 26–52 for an analysis of four alternative explanations of the events of 1891. See also Harold Blakemore, 'The Chilean Revolution of 1891 and Its Historiography', *Hispanic American Historical Review*, XLV:3, 1965, pp. 393–421.
170. Mario Góngora, *Ensayo histórico sobre la noción de Estado en Chile en los siglos XIX y XX*, Ediciones La Ciudad, Santiago 1981.
171. Subercaseaux, *Fin de siglo*, pp. 55–6.
172. Andrés Bello, 'Discurso pronunciado en la instalación de la Universidad de Chile, el setiembre de 1843', in Pedro Grases, ed., *Antología de Andrés Bello*, Editorial Kapelusz Venezolana, Caracas 1964, pp. 95–109, p. 104.
173. Iván Jaksić and Sol Serrano, 'In the Service of the Nation: The Establishment and Consolidation of the University of Chile, 1842–79', *Hispanic American Historical Review*, 70:1 (February 1990), pp. 139–71.
174. Alicia Barrios and José Joaquín Brunner, *La sociología en Chile*, FLACSO, Santiago 1988.
175. Luis Durand, *Don Arturo*, Editorial Zig-Zag, Santiago 1952, pp. 50–3.
176. Ricardo Donoso, *Alessandri: agitador y demoledor*, Fondo de Cultura Económica, Mexico City 1952, p. 247.
177. Arturo Alessandri Palma, 'Mensaje presidencial al Congreso Nacional', 1 June 1921, in René León Echaiz, ed., *Pensamiento de Alessandri*, Editorial Nacional Gabriela Mistral, Santiago 1974, p. 105.
178. Durand, *Don Arturo*, p. 181.
179. A. Alessandri Palma, 'Discurso ... pronunciado en la Convención Liberal de Santiago el 25 de Abril de 1920 y que constituye su programa de Gobierno', *El presidente Alessandri a través de sus discursos*, Biblioteca América, Imprenta Gutenberg, Santiago 1926, pp. 7–32, p. 18.
180. Ibid., p. 8.
181. Frank Bonilla and Myron Glazer, *Student Politics in Chile*, Basic Books, New York 1970, p. 43.
182. Federación de Estudiantes Chilenos, 'Manifiesto pro reforma universitaria'

(1922), in Juan Carlos Portantiero, *Estudiantes y política en América Latina 1918–1938*, Siglo Veintiuno, Mexico and Argentina, 2nd edn, 1987, pp. 188 and 172.

183. Jeffrey M. Puryear, *Thinking Politics: Intellectuals and Democracy in Chile, 1973–1988*, Johns Hopkins University Press, Baltimore and London 1994, pp. 13–14.

184. Aníbal Ponce, 'Estado y gran empresa: de la precrisis hasta el gobierno de Jorge Alessandri', *Colección Estudios CIEPLAN* (Santiago), no. 16 (1985), pp. 5–40, p. 33.

185. Interview with Eugenio Tironi, cited in Jeffrey Puryear, *Thinking Politics*, p. 23.

186. Supplement to *Aurora de Chile* (Santiago), 3:6, 23 October 1938, p. 1.

187. Editorial, 'La unificación de trabajo cultural del Estado', in *Aurora de Chile*, vol. 4:6, 6 May 1939, p. 3.

188. Alberto Cabero, *Recuerdos de don Pedro Aguirre Cerda*, Nascimento, Santiago 1948, p. 349.

189. Volodia Teitelboim, *Neruda* [1984], Ediciones Bat, Santiago, 4th revised edn, 1991, pp. 259–60.

190. Ibid., p. 260.

191. Ibid., p. 268.

192. Ibid., p. 248.

193. Ibid. pp. 307–8. Echoing Zola, Neruda's speech consisted of thirteen specific accusations. It was later published as a pamphlet entitled *Yo acuso*. For a fuller discussion of the influence of the Dreyfus affair in Spanish America, see Chapter 3.

194. Gabriel González Videla, *Memorias*, Editora Nacional Gabriela Mistral, Santiago 1975, 2 vols, vol. I, p. 761.

195. José Joaquín Brunner, 'La intelligentsia: escenarios institucionales y universos ideológicos', *Proposiciones* (Santiago), 18 (1990), pp. 180–91, p. 181.

196. Gellner, *Nations and Nationalism*.

197. William Cameron Townsend, *Lázaro Cárdenas: Mexican Democrat*, George Wahr Publishing Company, Ann Arbor 1952, p. 63.

198. Among the most famous examples were Domingo Sarmiento in Argentina, Valentín Letelier in Chile, Justo Sierra in Mexico, and Francisco García Calderón in Peru.

199. Rómulo Gallegos, resignation as Senator of Estado Apure (no title), [*Repertorio Americano*, 15 August 1931], in his *Una posición en la vida*, Ediciones Humanismo, Mexico City 1954, pp. 110–11.

200. Rómulo Betancourt, *Venezuela: política y petróleo* [1956], Monte Avila Editores, Caracas 1986.

201. Robert J. Alexander, *Rómulo Betancourt and the Transformation of Venezuela*, Transaction Books, New Brunswick, NJ 1982, p. 164.

202. Ibid., pp. 203–4.

203. Ibid., p. 316.

204. Ibid., p. 646.

205. Harrison S. Howard, *Rómulo Gallegos y la revolución burguesa de Venezuela*, Monte Avila Editores, Caracas 1976, p. 294.

206. Gallegos, *Una posición en la vida*, especially 'Necesidad de valores culturales', pp. 82–109.

207. Gallegos, 'No prostituyas la dignidad intelectual', lecture given at UNAM, 30 November 1949, in *Una posición en la vida*, pp. 451–76.
208. Alexander, *Rómulo Betancourt*, p. 316.
209. Edwards wrote about his experiences in *Persona Non Grata: An Envoy in Castro's Cuba* [1973], trans. Colin Harding, Bodley Head, London 1977.
210. Reyes joined the Mexican diplomatic service in 1920. He was posted as ambassador to France in 1924, Spain in 1926, Argentina in 1927–29, Brazil in 1930–36 and Argentina again in 1936–37. Roderic Camp, *Mexican Political Biographies, 1884–1935*, University of Texas Press, Austin 1991.
211. Alfonso Reyes, 'A vuelta de correo', in his *Vocación de América (Antología)*, Fondo de Cultura Económica, Mexico City 1989, pp. 240–58, p. 241.
212. Cosío Villegas, 'Un poco de historia' pp. 509–10.
213. Fernando Benítez, *Lázaro Cárdenas y la Revolución Mexicana*, Fondo de Cultura Económica, Mexico City 1978.
214. John A. Britton, *Educación y radicalismo en México*, 2 vols, Secretaría de Educación Pública, Dirección General de Divulgación, Mexico City 1976, vol. I, pp. 73–4.
215. The main names associated with the journal *Contemporáneos* (1928–31) were those of Jaime Torres Bodet, Carlos Pellicer, José Gorostiza, Salvador Novo, Xavier Villaurrutia and Jorge Cuesta. Of those, José Gorostiza (1901–73) pursued a diplomatic career from 1937 onwards, was Under-secretary of Foreign Relations from 1953 to 1958 and again from 1958 to 1964, and briefly served as Secretary of Foreign Relations in 1964. Jaime Torres Bodet (1902–74) joined the foreign service in 1929, served as Cárdenas's Under-secretary of Foreign Relations, from 1938 to 1940, and Secretary of Foreign Relations, from 1946 to 1948, before becoming Secretary-General of UNESCO, from 1953 to 1958. Camp, *Mexican Political Biographies*. The others found positions in the national bureaucracy.
216. See the discussion in Chapter 3.
217. A friend of his father, Francisco Castillo Najera, became Secretary of Foreign Relations in the government of Avila Camacho. Fernando Vizcaino, *Biografía política de Octavio Paz o La razón ardiente*, Editorial Algazara, Málaga 1993, p. 83.
218. Apart from the activities of left-wing intellectuals in the journals *El Espectador* and *Política* during the early 1960s, intellectuals established a political organization called the Movement for National Liberation (MLN) in 1961, calling upon the Mexican government to address the 'true' goals of the revolution, specifically, democracy and national independence. Within two years, the movement had become divided over the issue of electoral participation, and the intellectuals resigned. See Gabriel Careaga, *Los intelectuales y la política en México*, Editorial Extemporáneos, Mexico City 1971, pp. 75–101.
219. Vizcaino, *Biografía política de Octavio Paz*, pp. 118–19.
220. Daniel Cosío Villegas, *Memorias*, Editorial Joaquín Mortiz, Mexico City 1976, p. 109.
221. Krauze, *Textos heréticos*, p. 116. With some validity, Krauze sees this as a lost opportunity to establish 'a broad civic front'. See also John Skirius, *José Vasconcelos y la cruzada de 1929*, Siglo XXI, Mexico City 1978.
222. Meyer, 'Revolution and Reconstruction', in Bethell, *Mexico since Independence*, p. 215.
223. De Beer, *José Vasconcelos and His World*, pp. 252–3.

224. *Conferencia del excmo. señor presidente de la nación argentina Gral. Juan Perón pronunciada en el acto de clausura del primer congreso nacional de filosofía*, Mendoza, 9 April 1949.

225. 'History Will Absolve Me', in Fidel Castro/Régis Debray, *On Trial*, Lorrimer Publishing, London 1968, pp. 33, 42 and 62–5. I am grateful to Walter Little for drawing this point to my attention.

226. 'The Mexican Constitution of 1917', article 73, clause 25, in Russell H. Fitzgibbon, ed., *The Constitutions of the Americas*, University of Chicago Press, Chicago 1948, p. 527. Both Chile's constitution of 1925 (article 10, clause 7) and Peru's of 1933 (article 71) assert state control over public education, although neither mentions culture specifically. Ibid., pp. 141 and 674.

227. 'Constitución política de 1920', in José Pareja Paz-Soldán, *Las constituciones del Perú*, Ediciones Cultura Hispánica, Madrid 1954, pp. 743–78, title 1, article 4, p. 745 and title 4, article 53, p. 751.

228. 'Constitución política de 1933', in Paz-Soldán, *Las constituciones del Perú*, pp. 783–824, title 3 on Education, p. 793.

229. 'Constitución de la República de Cuba' (1940), in Pichardo, *Documentos*, vol. IV, part 2, pp. 329–418, p. 340.

230. Santos Martínez, *La nueva Argentina*, vol. I, p. 205.

231. Ezéquiel Martínez Estrada, *X-Ray of the Pampa* [1933], trans. Alain Swietlicki, University of Texas Press, Austin and London 1971, pp. 285–6.

232. Joseph Maier and Richard W. Weatherhead, eds, *The Latin American University*, University of New Mexico Press, Albuquerque 1979, p. 6.

233. Néstor García Canclini, *Culturas híbridas: estrategias para entrar y salir de la modernidad*, Editorial Sudamericana, Buenos Aires 1992, p. 72.

234. Castañeda, *Utopia Unarmed*, p. 175.

235. Orlando Albornoz, *Education and Society in Latin America*, Macmillan/St Antony's, Basingstoke 1993, p. 13.

236. In Argentina, for example, university attendance more than quadrupled from 3,000 in 1900 to 14,000 in 1918. David Rock, 'From the First World War to 1930', in Leslie Bethell, ed., *Argentina since Independence*, Cambridge University Press, Cambridge 1993, pp. 139–72, p. 152. In Peru, numbers nearly doubled during the corresponding period, from 991 in 1902 to 1,741 in 1920, according to the Ministry of Trade and Commerce, cited in José Deustua and José Luis Reñique, *Intelectuales, indigenismo y descentralismo en el Perú, 1897–1931*, Centro de Estudios Rurales Andino 'Bartolomé de Las Casas', Cuzco 1984, p. 7.

237. Halperín Donghi, *Historia de la Universidad de Buenos Aires*, pp. 133–4. See also Portantiero, *Estudiantes y política*; and Rock, 'From the First World War to 1930', p. 151.

238. José Luis Romero, 'University Reform', in Maier and Weatherhead, eds, *The Latin American University*, p. 139.

239. Francisco López Cámara, 'La UNAM en la política mexicana', *Revista Universidad de México* (September 1992), pp. 19–23, p. 20; and Daniel C. Levy, *University and Government in Mexico: Autonomy in an Authoritarian System*, Praeger, New York 1980, p. 26.

240. Rock, 'From the First World War to 1930'; Daniel Levy, *Higher Education and the State in Latin America: Private Challenges to Public Dominance*, University of Chicago Press, Chicago 1986.

241. Romero, 'University Reform', p. 136.
242. Alfredo Palacios, cited in Mariátegui, 'La reforma universitaria', *Siete ensayos*, p. 142.
243. Daniel C. Levy, *Higher Education and the State in Latin America: Private Challenges to Public Dominance*, University of Chicago Press, Chicago and London 1986, p. 48.
244. In Cuba, the Universidad Popular José Martí, founded in 1923, was closed by Machado in 1927. Mexico's Universidad Popular, which antedated the reform and had been founded by members of the Ateneo in 1913, closed down in 1922, apparently due to lack of funds. (Vasconcelos was notably parsimonious not only with the Popular University but also with the National University, arguing that resources should be concentrated on elementary education.) It was replaced by an extension department at the University of Mexico, directed by Pedro Henríquez Ureña. In Peru, the Universidad Popular lasted just three years, from 1921 until it was closed in 1924. Chile's Federation of Students had begun a night school for workers as early as 1910, which evolved into the Universidad Popular José Victorino Lastarria from 1918 to 1927. In Argentina, a popular university operated briefly in 1917, but had little impact; despite the proclamations of student congresses, 'no notable popular centre resulted from the Córdoba movement'. Jeffrey L. Klaiber, 'The Popular Universities and the Origins of Aprismo, 1921–1924', *Hispanic American Historical Review*, no. 4, November 1975, pp. 693–715, p. 695.
245. Carlos M. Vilas, 'Sobre cierta inter*Petras*ción de la intelectualidad latinoamericana', *Nueva Sociedad* (Caracas), no. 107 (May–June 1990), pp. 121–30, p. 123.
246. Roger Bartra, 'Luis Villoro piensa en México', *La Gaceta del Fondo de Cultura Económica* (Mexico City), no. 301, January 1996, pp. 47–9.
247. Ricardo Piglia, 'Los pensadores ventrílocuos', in Raquel Ángel, ed., *Rebeldes y domesticados: los intelectuales frente al poder*, Ediciones El Cielo por Asalto, Buenos Aires 1992, pp. 27–35, p. 29.

Chapter 3

1. Alain Touraine has argued that in Latin America, where 'social demands are far greater than the capacity of the system to articulate them, the role of the *go between* is enhanced'. Silvia Sigal, 'América Latina y sus intelectuales: conversación con Alain Touraine', *Crítica y utopía* (Buenos Aires), no. 13, December 1985, pp. 25–38, p. 28.
2. John M. Kirk, in Christopher Abel and Nissa Torrents, eds, *José Martí: Revolutionary Democrat*, Athlone Press, London 1986, pp. 108–23. Kirk's view is based on his interpretation of Martí's 1893 article 'A la raiz' as a self-definition, citing 'The true man goes to the root of things. No man should call himself a radical unless he sees things in depth.' Kirk then equates Martí's idea of 'a true radical' with 'an intellectual', although Martí's article does not mention intellectuals in any terms, and instead is a plea for all Cubans to realize where their main problem lay, namely in the lack of their own nation. See 'A la raiz', *OE*, vol. III, pp. 268–71.

3. Juan Valera, 'Carta-prólogo' [1896], in Rubén Darío, *Azul*, Editorial Espasa-Calpe, Madrid, 14th edn, 1966, pp. 9–25, p. 25.

4. See Keith Ellis, *Critical Approaches to Rubén Darío*, University of Toronto Press, Toronto 1974, especially pp. 25–45, for a summary of earlier debates; and Iris M. Zavala, *Colonialism and Culture: Hispanic Modernisms and the Social Imaginary*, Indiana University Press, Bloomington and Indianapolis 1992.

5. For example, see Luis Alberto Sánchez, *Balance y liquidación del novecientos*, Editorial Ercilla, Santiago 1941.

6. Rubén Darío, *Escritos inéditos de Rubén Darío (recogidos de periódicos de Buenos Aires y anotados por E. K. Mapes)*, Instituto de las Españas, New York 1938, p. 68.

7. The Chilean positivist Valentín Letelier referred to the need to 'create a highly select class of intellectuals', in his *Filosofía de la educación*, Imprenta Cervantes, Santiago [1892], 2nd edn 1912, p. 538; cited in José Joaquín Brunner, *Los intelectuales: esbozos y antecedentes para la constitución del campo de estudios*, FLACSO working paper, no. 135, Santiago March 1982, p. 3.

8. Rodó wrote: 'I should like this work of mine to be the starting point for a propaganda campaign that will continue to spread among America's intellectuals'. 'América', *El Cojo Ilustrado* (Caracas), IX, 15 August 1900, p. 526, cited in Stabb, *In Quest of Identity*, p. 38.

9. Carlos Vaz Ferreira, *Lógica viva. Moral para intelectuales* [1909], Biblioteca Ayacucho, Caracas 1979.

10. Rubén Darío, *Autobiografía* [1912], Editorial Universitaria, Buenos Aires 1968. See p. 76 ('both of them true intellectuals') and p. 118 ('some intellectuals').

11. The Alsatian Jew Captain Alfred Dreyfus was court-martialled for treason in December 1894 and sentenced to life imprisonment. After evidence surfaced suggesting that an injustice had been done, the Dreyfus family's campaign for his release was set alight by the publication of Émile Zola's open letter to the President, 'J'accuse' (1 January 1898), denouncing militarism, clericalism and anti-Semitism, and challenging the authorities to prosecute the author for his temerity. Zola's letter was accompanied by a petition from a group of writers and academics, which was christened by the newspaper editor Georges Clemenceau as the 'Manifesto of the Intellectuals'. Zola was duly tried and sentenced to a year in prison, but fled to England. Eventually, in 1906, Dreyfus was publicly rehabilitated. See Émile Zola, *The Dreyfus Affair: 'J'accuse' and Other Writings*, ed. Alain Pagès, Yale University Press, New Haven and London 1996.

12. Eric Cahm, *The Dreyfus Affair in French Society and Politics*, Longman, London and New York 1996, p. 70.

13. As late as the 1920s, Argentine intellectuals were still analysing events such as the Russian revolution and the Sacco and Vanzetti affair with reference to Dreyfus. See Leticia Prislei, 'Itinerario intelectual y político de los maestro-ciudadanos (Del fin del siglo a la década del '20)', *Entrepasados (Revista de Historia)* (Buenos Aires), II:2 (beginning of 1992 [*sic*]), pp. 41–59.

14. Douglas Johnson, *France and the Dreyfus Affair*, Walker and Co., New York 1966, p. 212. See also Christophe Charle, *Naissance del 'intellectuels': 1880–1900*, Éditions du Minuit, Paris 1990.

15. Johnson, *France and the Dreyfus Affair*, p. 224.

16. Francis Mulhearn, '"Teachers, Writers, Celebrities": Intelligentsias and Their Histories', *New Left Review*, no. 126 (1981), pp. 43–59, p. 50.

17. Ibid., p. 54.

18. Antenor Orrego, 'Palabras prologales' to Alcides Spelucín's *El libro de la nave dorada*, in *Amauta* (Lima), no. 1, September 1926, p. 36.

19. Manuel Gálvez, *La Argentina en nuestros libros*, Editorial Ercilla, Santiago 1935, p. 30.

20. Manuel Gálvez, *Recuerdos de la vida literaria, I: Amigos y maestros de mi juventud*, Librería Hachette, Buenos Aires 1961, p. 36.

21. Domingo Faustino Sarmiento, *Mi defensa* [1843], in Armando Donoso, ed., *Sarmiento en el destierro*, Editora M. Gleizer, Buenos Aires 1927, pp. 153–81, p. 157.

22. Ibid., p. 166.

23. Ibid., p. 157.

24. Ibid., pp. 164 and 165.

25. Tulio Halperín Donghi, *El espejo de la historia*, Editorial Sudamericana, Buenos Aires 1987, p. 58.

26. Víctor Pérez Petit, *Rodó: su vida – su obra* [1918], Claudio García y Cía, Montevideo 1967, p. 53.

27. Mario Benedetti, *Genio y figura de José Enrique Rodó*, Editorial Universitaria de Buenos Aires 1966, pp. 15–16 and 20.

28. Pérez Petit states that Rodó left the university because his nerves could not withstand examinations. *Rodó*, p. 61. Alberto Zum Felde confirms this but also notes that he was 'distracted by reading matter unrelated to his studies, and at odds with chemistry, logic and mathematics'. *Proceso intelectual del Uruguay y crítica de su literatura*, Editorial Claridad, Montevideo 1941, p. 225.

29. José Enrique Rodó, *Motivos de Proteo: nuevos motivos de Proteo*, Editorial Porrúa, Mexico City 1969, no. lxxv, p. 91 (original emphasis).

30. Milton E. Vanger, *José Batlle y Ordóñez of Uruguay: The Creator of His Times 1902–1907*, Harvard University Press, Cambridge, MA 1963, p. 21.

31. Rodó, fragment of a letter to Juan Francisco Piquet, April 1910, in José Enrique Rodó, *Obras completas*, ed. Emir Rodríguez Monegal, Editorial Aguilar, Madrid 1957, p. 1,284.

32. Pérez Petit, *Rodó*, p. 245.

33. Zum Felde, *Proceso intelectual*, p. 231.

34. Rodó, letter of 1916, cited in Jorge A. Silva Cencio, *Rodó y la legislación social*, Biblioteca de Marcha, Montevideo 1973, p. 39.

35. José Martí, 'The New School' [1883], in Philip Foner, ed., *José Martí On Education: Articles on Educational Theory and Pedagogy*, trans. Elinor Randall, Monthly Review Press, New York 1979, p. 98.

36. 'Look at Oscar Wilde! He doesn't dress like the rest of us, but in a completely different way. And his choice of clothes makes all too clear the flaw in his message, namely that he creates nothing new, because he feels unable to do so, but merely reworks the old.' José Martí, '¡Ved a Oscar Wilde!' [1882], *OE*, vol. I, pp. 246–54, p. 248.

37. Ibid., p. 254.

38. José Martí, 'Joaquín Tejada' [1894], in *OE*, vol. III, pp. 419–21, p. 419.

39. José Martí, 'La exhibición de pinturas de Iruso Vereschagin' [1889], *OE*, vol. II, pp. 325–35, p. 329.

40. José Martí, 'Francisco Sellen' [1890], *OE*, vol. II, pp. 506–18, p. 506.

41. José Martí, 'La última página' of his review for children, *La edad de oro* [1889], *OE*, vol. II, pp. 362–3.
42. José Martí, 'Ni será escritor' [1881], *OE*, vol. I, pp. 194–5.
43. José Martí, 'El poema de Niagara' [1882], *OE*, vol. I, pp. 229–45, p. 237.
44. José Enrique Rodó, draft letter to Rafael Altamira, 1900, in *Obras completas*, p. 1,286.
45. Pérez Petit, *Rodó*, p. 71.
46. Silva Cencio, *Rodó y la legislación social*, pp. 44–54.
47. José Enrique Rodó, *El mirador de Próspero*, José María Serrano Editor, Montevideo 1913, p. 342.
48. Silva Cencio, *Rodó y la legislación social*, p. 44.
49. Rubén Darío, 'La producción intelectual latinoamericano' [Paris, July 1913], in Pedro Luis Barcia, ed., *Escritos dispersos de Rubén Darío*, vol. I, Universidad Nacional de La Plata, La Plata 1968, pp. 344–8, p. 348.
50. Rubén Darío, *Obras completas*, ed. Sanmiguel Raimúndez and Emilio Gasco Contell, Editorial Afrodísio Aguado, Madrid 1950–55, vol. II, p. 505.
51. *La vida de Rubén Darío escrita por él mismo* was originally published in instalments in the Argentine magazine *Caras y Caretas* (Buenos Aires 1912).
52. Rubén Darío, *Historia de mis libros*, Editorial Nueva Nicaragua, Managua 1988, p. 57. This originally appeared as three articles in the daily newspaper *La Nación* (Buenos Aires).
53. Darío, *Historia de mis libros*, p. 61. Andrés Bello, 'La agricultura de la zona torrida' [1826], in Grases, *Antología*, pp. 48–58.
54. Ángel Rama, *Rubén Darío y el modernismo*, Ediciones de la Biblioteca, Universidad Central de Venezuela, Caracas 1970, p. 9.
55. Juan Ramón Jiménez to Rubén Darío, 1902 (no exact date), in Alberto Ghiraldo, *El archivo de Rubén Darío*, Editorial Losada, Buenos Aires 1943, pp. 16–18, p. 16.
56. Darío, *Autobiografía*, p. 76.
57. Enrique Anderson Imbert, *La originalidad de Rubén Darío*, Centro Editor de América Latina, Buenos Aires 1967, pp. 24–5.
58. Darío, *Autobiografía*, p. 23.
59. Rubén Darío, 'Palabras liminares', *Prosas profanas* [1896], Espasa-Calpe, Madrid, 6th edn, 1967, pp. 9–12, p. 10. I am very grateful to Dr Fernando Cervantes for his help in translating this passage.
60. Darío, *Autobiografía*, p. 113.
61. Gabriela Mistral, letter of 1916, cited in Bernardo Subercaseaux, 'Gabriela Mistral: espiritualismo y canciones de cuna', in *Historia, literatura y sociedad: ensayos de hermenéutica cultural*, Ediciones documentas, Santiago 1991, pp. 57–83, p. 61.
62. D'Halmar had been baptized Augusto Goemine Thomson.
63. Gonzalo Vial, *Historia de Chile (1891–1973)*, vol. 1, Editorial Santillana del Pacífico, Santiago 1987, p. 262.
64. Ibid., p. 263. Later, the fact that D'Halmar lived for many years in Spain, where his work was published, had a great impact on subsequent generations, for whom he was a 'literary hero' who had ventured forth from Chile to conquer distant shores. Fernando Alegría (b. 1918) cited in Juan Andrés Piña, *Conversaciones con la narrativa chilena*, Editorial Los Andes, Santiago 1991, pp. 18–19.

65. José Martí, 'Persona y patria' [1893], *OE*, vol. III, pp. 203–7, p. 204.
66. Darío, 'Palabras liminares', p. 9.
67. *Amauta*, no. 3, November 1926, p. 7.
68. Rodó, *Motivos de Proteo*, no. lxxv, p. 91.
69. José Martí, 'Nuestra América' [1891], *OE*, vol. II, pp. 519–27, p. 521.
70. José Martí, Prologue to *Versos libres* [1882], *OE*, vol. I, p. 301.
71. Rodó, 'Bolívar', n.d., in *El mirador*, pp. 105–42, p. 115. Original ellipsis.
72. Darío, 'Los "Versos libres"' [Paris, June 1913], in Barcia, *Escritos dispersos de Rubén Darío*, pp. 334–9, p. 339.
73. Julio Ortega, *Cultura y modernización en la Lima del 900*, Centro de Estudios para el Desarrollo y la Participación, Lima 1986, pp. 71–2.
74. Manuel González Prada, 'El intelectual y el obrero', in Bruno Podestà, ed., *Pensamiento político de González Prada*, Universidad del Pacífico, Lima, 2nd edn, 1983, pp. 79–86.
75. Rubén Darío, 'El ejemplo de Zola', *Opiniones*, Librería de Fernando Fe, Madrid 1961, pp. 7–22, p. 9.
76. Darío, 'El ejemplo de Zola', pp. 21 and 22.
77. Describing the Ateneo group which gathered around him in Buenos Aires, Darío wrote of 'our souls of fighters and *rêveurs*'. Darío, *Autobiografía*, p. 121.
78. Gordon Brotherston points out that Darío's famous assertion that God was on the side of Spanish America (in his sonnet 'A Roosevelt' in *Cantos de vida y esperanza* [1905]), is contradicted by the pro-US sentiments expressed in 'Salutación al águila' (1906). See the introduction to J. E. Rodó, *Ariel*, ed. Gordon Brotherston, Cambridge University Press, Cambridge 1967, p. 12. (All subsequent references to *Ariel* are to this edition, unless otherwise stated.) Other examples of Darío's political poetry are *Canto épico a las glorias de Chile* (1887); *Canto a la Argentina* (1914); and various poems in *El canto errante* (1907).
79. Darío, 'El ejemplo de Zola', pp. 18–19.
80. Halperín Donghi, *El espejo de la historia*, p. 61.
81. Michael Foot, *Aneurin Bevan*, vol. 1, Paladin, St Albans 1975, p. 195. Bevan interpreted Rodó in a way diametrically opposite to the way that the Uruguayan was received in Spanish America. Whereas Spanish Americans argued that Rodó's point was that spiritual emancipation was the prerequisite to economic well-being, Bevan found in Rodó support for his own belief that ' "freedom is the by-product of economic surplus" '. Foot links this to the following passage in *Ariel*: 'Without the achievement of a reasonable level of material well-being, the reign of the spirit cannot be realised in human societies' (Rodó, *Ariel*, p. 88).
82. Rodó, *Ariel*, pp. 61 and 62.
83. Rodó, *El mirador*, pp. 43 and 47.
84. Rodó, *Ariel*, p. 62; see also pp. 53–5.
85. Ibid., p. 65.
86. Ibid., pp. 62–5.
87. Cited in Pérez Petit, *Rodó*, p. 177.
88. Rodó, *El mirador*, p. 342.
89. José Enrique Rodó, *Artigas* [1915], facsimile edn, Homenaje de la Facultad de Humanidades y Ciencias, Montevideo 1950, p. 6. In this essay, Rodó raises ideas

that are comparable to those discussed by Ricardo Rojas in *La argentinidad* (1916). See my discussion in Chapter 4, pp. 167–9.

90. There are numerous references to action throughout the texts. See, for example, in *Ariel*: 'as you prepare yourselves to breathe the fresh air of action', p. 23; 'we cannot imagine any spectacle more likely to capture the *pensador*'s interest and the artist's enthusiasm than that of an entire generation marching towards the future, trembling with impatience to go into action', p. 24; and other passages on pp. 26 and 31. See also *Motivos de Proteo*, nos. x, xix, xxxii.

91. José Enrique Rodó, letter to Miguel de Unamuno, 20 March 1904, in *Obras completas*, pp. 1,393–4.

92. Rodó, *Motivos de Proteo*, p. 19.

93. Rodó, *Ariel*, p. 103.

94. Rodó, *El mirador*, p. 15.

95. Roberto González Echevarría, *The Voice of the Masters: Writing and Authority in Modern Latin American Literature*, University of Texas Press, Austin 1985, p. 27. Rodó, *Ariel*, p. 102.

96. González Echevarría, *Voice of the Masters*, p. 21.

97. Julio Ortega, *Luis Rafael Sánchez: teoría y práctica del discurso popular*, Centre for Latin American Cultural Studies, King's College, London, Research Paper no. 1, 1989, p. 11.

98. José Enrique Rodó, 'El centenario de Chile', 17 September 1910, in *El mirador*, pp. 158–65, p. 158. See also 'A Anatole France', speech at official banquet held for Anatole France's visit to Montevideo, 16 July 1909, in *El mirador*, pp. 175–80, when Rodó also speaks in the name of his people.

99. José Enrique Rodó, 'Rumbos nuevos' [1910], in *El mirador*, pp. 31–53, p. 49.

100. Ibid., p. 48.

101. Rodó, *El mirador*, p. 14.

102. Ibid., p. 334.

103. José Enrique Rodó, 'La prensa de Montevideo', speech at the inauguration of the Círculo de la Prensa, Montevideo, 14 April 1909, in *El mirador*, pp. 331–43, p. 332.

104. Benedetti, *Genio y figura*, p. 36 (original emphasis).

105. Pérez Petit, *Rodó*, p. 246.

106. José Enrique Rodó, Letter to Juan Piquet, 6 March 1904, in *Obras completas*, pp. 1,343–4; and Pérez Petit, *Rodó*, p. 248.

107. José Enrique Rodó, draft of a letter to Baldomero Sanín Cano, in *Obras completas*, p. 1,299.

108. Pérez Petit, *Rodó*, p. 355.

109. Zum Felde, *Proceso intelectual*, p. 223. See also Pérez Petit, *Rodó*, pp. 462–3.

110. Silva Cencio, *Rodó y la legislación social*, p. 29.

111. Rodó, *Ariel*, p. 38.

112. Rodó, *Ariel*, p. 55. See Carlos Fuentes, 'Prologue', in Rodó, *Ariel*, trans. Margaret Sayers Peden, University of Texas Press, Austin 1988, pp. 14–28, p. 27.

113. Leading examples are José Martí, 'Con todos y para el bien de todos' [1891], *OE*, vol. III, pp. 16–27; 'La oración de Tampa y Cayo Hueso', and 'En los talleres' [1892], in ibid., pp. 65–78 and 116–18.

114. See, for example, chapters I and II of Domingo Faustino Sarmiento, *Facundo: civilización o barbarie*, Alianza Editorial, Madrid 1970.

115. Pedro Henríquez Ureña, *Literary Currents in Hispanic America*, Harvard University Press, Cambridge, MA 1946, p. 173.
116. José Martí, 'Carta a Manuel Mercado' [1878], in *OE*, vol. I, pp. 121–5, p. 124.
117. José Martí, 'Discurso en conmemoración del 10 de octubre' [1889], *OE*, vol. II, pp. 438–48, p. 439.
118. José Martí, 'Francisco Sellen' [1890], *OE*, vol. II, pp. 506–18, p. 506.
119. José Martí, 'Carta a Serafín Bello' [1892], *OE*, vol. III, pp. 59–60, p. 59.
120. Martí, 'Carta a Carmen Miyares', p. 542.
121. Juan Marinello, cited in Antoni Kapcia, 'Cuban populism and the birth of the myth of Martí', in Abel and Torrents, *José Martí*, pp. 32–64, p. 45.
122. See José Ingenieros, *Los tiempos nuevos: reflexiones optimistas sobre la guerra y la revolución*, Ediciones M. Gleizer, Buenos Aires 1921, p. 9.
123. Anatole France and Henri Barbusse, 'A los intelectuales y estudiantes de la América Latina', *Nosotros* (Buenos Aires), vol. XV, no. 141 (February 1921), pp. 224–6, p. 226.
124. José Aricó, '1917 y América Latina', *La Ciudad Futura*, no. 30–1 (December 1991–February 1992), pp. 14–16, p. 14.
125. Julio Antonio Mella, 'Intelectuales y tartufos' [1924], in his *Documentos y artículos*, Editorial de Ciencias Sociales, Instituto Cubano del Libro, Havana 1975, pp. 88–91. For the Rodó quotation Mella echoes, see p. 109 above.
126. Julio Antonio Mella, 'Los falsos maestros y discípulos' [1924], in *Documentos y artículos*, pp. 118–20.
127. Julio Antonio Mella, 'Todo tiempo futuro tiene que ser mejor' [1923], in *Documentos y artículos*, pp. 77–9, p. 79.
128. Julio Antonio Mella, 'El nuevo curso de la Universidad Popular' [1924], in *Documentos y artículos*, pp. 126–7, p. 127.
129. Julio Antonio Mella, 'Víctor Raúl Haya de la Torre' [1923], in *Documentos y artículos*, pp. 76–7.
130. Mella, 'Todo tiempo futuro tiene que ser mejor', p. 78.
131. Julio Antonio Mella, 'A los alumnos de la Universidad Popular y al pueblo de Cuba' [1924], in *Documentos y artículos*, p. 101. See also 'Declaración de principios de la Federación de Estudiantes de Cuba' [1924], in *Documentos y artículos*, pp. 102–5, where he wrote: 'only by means of a complete command of culture will men be able to emancipate themselves' (p. 104).
132. Julio Antonio Mella, 'Intelectuales y tartufos', in *Documentos y artículos*, p. 89.
133. Julio Antonio Mella, 'Carta a Gustavo Aldereguía' [Mexico, 1926], in *Documentos y artículos*, pp. 258–60, p. 259.
134. Julio Antonio Mella, ' "La libertad sindical en México" de Vicente Lombardo Toledano' [1927], in *Documentos y artículos*, pp. 294–6.
135. Julio Antonio Mella, '¿Qué es el ARPA [*sic*]?' [1928], in *Documentos y artículos*, pp. 370–403, p. 382.
136. Julio Antonio Mella, 'Nuestras enfermedades infantiles' [1928], in *Documentos y artículos*, pp. 424–8, pp. 425–6.
137. Mella, 'Nuestras enfermedades infantiles', p. 426.
138. Rubén Martínez Villena, cited in Roa, 'Una semilla en un surco de fuego' [1936] in Rubén Martínez Villena, *La pupila insomne*, Biblioteca Básica de Cultura Cubana, Havana 1977, pp. 58–9.
139. France and Barbusse, 'A los intelectuales'. Lunacharsky's 'Los intelectuales

frente a la revolución mundial' was published in several leading Spanish American journals in 1921, for example, *Revista de Filosofía* (Buenos Aires), vol. VII, no. 6 (November 1921), p. 476.

140. José Carlos Mariátegui, 'Henri Barbusse' [1925], in *Ensayos escogidos*, Patronato del libro peruano, Lima 1956, pp. 91–4, pp. 93–4. See also 'La revolución y la inteligencia: el grupo "Clarté"' [1925], in ibid., pp. 85–90.

141. Mariátegui, 'La revolución y la inteligencia', p. 89.

142. José Carlos Mariátegui, 'El proceso a la literatura francesa contemporánea' [n.d., between July 1928 and June 1929], in *Defensa del marxismo*, vol. 5 of *Obras completas*, Empresa Editora Amauta, Lima 1969, pp. 117–26, p. 126.

143. Harry E. Vanden, *National Marxism in Latin America: José Carlos Mariátegui's Thought and Politics*, Lynne Rienner, Boulder, CO 1986, p. 8.

144. Mariátegui, 'El proceso', pp. 122–3.

145. Mariátegui, 'La revolución y la inteligencia', p. 87.

146. Ibid., p. 125.

147. Mariátegui to Samuel Glusberg, 10 January 1928, in José Carlos Mariátegui, *Correspondencia (1915–1930)*, ed. Antonio Melis, 2 vols, Empresa Editora Amauta, Lima 1984, vol. I, pp. 330–2, p. 332.

148. Alberto Flores Galindo, *La agonía de Mariátegui*, Editorial Revolución, Madrid 1991, p. 88.

149. Mariátegui, letter to Eudocio Ravines, 31 December 1928, *Correspondencia*, vol. I, pp. 490–2, p. 491.

150. Mariátegui, *Correspondencia*, vol. I, pp. 221 and 293.

151. Mariátegui expressed this view in a book review, *Variedades*, Lima, XXV:1136, 11 December 1919, pp. 4–5, cited in *Correspondencia*, vol. I, p. xxv.

152. Mariátegui to Samuel Glusberg, 30 April 1927, in *Correspondencia*, vol. I, pp. 273–4, p. 273.

153. Flores Galindo, *La agonía*, p. 102.

154. Mariátegui, 'Presentación de "Amauta"', *Amauta*, no. 1 (September 1926), p. 1.

155. Ibid.

156. Mariátegui, letter to Celestino Manchego Muñoz, Minister of the Interior, 6 December 1927, in *Correspondencia*, vol. I, p. 316.

157. Flores Galindo, *La agonía*, p. 92, referring to an article by the Uruguayan critic Alberto Zum Felde.

158. Ibid., p. 32.

159. Mariátegui, *Correspondencia*, vol. I, pp. 293–4.

160. Flores Galindo, *La agonía*, pp. 32–6.

161. Ibid., p. 42.

162. Ibid., pp. 144–5.

163. 'De José Carlos Mariátegui a Eudocio Ravines', 31 December 1928, in *Correspondencia*, vol. I, pp. 490–2, pp. 490 and 491.

164. Víctor Raúl Haya de la Torre, letter to César Mendoza, Berlin, 22 September 1929, in *Obras completas*, Editorial Juan Mejía Baca, Lima 1976, vol. V, pp. 250–6, p. 253.

165. Flores Galindo, *La agonía*, p. 28. Luis Alberto Sánchez, *Haya de la Torre o el político: crónica de una vida sin tregua* [1934], Ediciones Ercilla, Santiago, 2nd edn, 1936.

166. Julien Benda, *The Treason of the Intellectuals* [1928], trans. Richard Aldington, Norton and Co., New York 1969.

167. César Vallejo, 'El pensamiento revolucionario' [1929], in his *La cultura peruana (Crónicas)*, ed. Enrique Ballón Aguirre, Mosca Azul Editores, Lima 1987, p. 168.

168. César Vallejo, *Contra el secreto profesional*, Mosca Azul Editores, Lima 1973, p. 75.

169. César Vallejo, 'Los artistas ante la política' [1927], in *La cultura peruana*, p. 119.

170. Ibid., p. 121.

171. César Vallejo, 'La responsabilidad del escritor' (speech to the Second International Congress of Writers for the Defence of Culture, July 1937), in *La cultura peruana*, p. 234.

172. César Vallejo, 'Ejecutoria del arte socialista', in Vallejo, *El arte y la revolución*, vol. II of *Obras completas*, Mosca Azul Editores, Lima 1973, pp. 28–9. p. 28.

173. César Vallejo, 'El caso Maiakovski', in his *El arte y la revolución*, pp. 104–10, p. 109.

174. César Vallejo, 'Literatura proletaria' [Paris, August 1928], in *La cultura peruana*, p. 128.

175. See special edition (*Defensa de la inteligencia*) of *Sur* (Buenos Aires), vol. VIII, July 1938.

176. See José Ortega y Gasset, 'Ni vitalismo ni racionalismo' [1924], in *Obras completas*, vol. III, Editorial Revista de Occidente, Madrid, 5th edn, 1957, pp. 270–80.

177. Ortega visited Argentina in 1916 and 1928, and fled there in 1939 as a refugee. For a useful discussion of his influence in Spanish America, see Tzvi Medin, *Ortega y Gasset en la cultura hispanoamericana*, Fondo de Cultura Económica, Mexico City 1994.

178. Pablo Neruda, *Confieso que he vivido: memorias*, Editorial Seix Barral, Barcelona 1974, p. 14.

179. Ibid., pp. 21–2.

180. Ibid., p. 236.

181. Ibid., p. 242.

182. Nydia Lamarque, 'La vida heroica de Rosa Luxemburgo', *Amauta*, no. 28, January 1930, pp. 9–15, pp. 9 and 14.

183. José Donoso, *The Boom in Spanish American Literature: A Personal History*, trans. Gregory Kolovakos, Columbia University Press, New York 1977, p. 21.

184. Antonio Skármeta, 'A Generation on the Move', in Doris Meyer, *Lives on the Line: The Testimony of Contemporary Latin American Authors*, University of California Press, Berkeley and Los Angeles 1988, pp. 250–64, pp. 252–3.

185. María Guerra and Ezéquiel Maldonado, eds, *El compromiso del intelectual*, Editorial Nuestro Tiempo, Mexico 1979, p. 25.

186. Roque Dalton, 'La responsabilidad del intelectual con su pueblo', 1969, in ibid., pp. 222–6, p. 223. Original emphasis.

187. Frantz Fanon, *The Wretched of the Earth*, trans. Constance Farrington, Penguin, Harmondsworth 1967.

188. See the account by 'the valient little Sartre' himself, Mario Vargas Llosa, in *Contra viento y marea*, especially vol. I, which was originally published as *Entre Sartre y Camus* (1981). Also, Octavio Paz, 'Memento: J. P. Sartre', in his *Hombres en su siglo y otros ensayos*, Editorial Seix Barral, Barcelona 1984, pp. 11–25.

189. Adolfo Canitrot, in 'Intelectuales y política en Argentina', *Debates* (Buenos Aires), vol. 2, no. 4, October–November 1985, pp. 4–8, p. 8.

190. Mario Vargas Llosa, 'Los otros contra Sartre' [June 1964], in his *Contra viento y marea*, vol. I, p. 45.

191. Oscar Terán, 'Los intelectuales frente a la política', *Punto de Vista*, no. 42 (April 1992), pp. 42–8, p. 48.

192. Régis Debray's first influential article was 'El castrismo: La Gran Marcha en América Latina', first published in *Pasado y Presente*, the major left-wing journal from Córdoba, Argentina, in 1965.

193. Régis Debray, *Revolution in the Revolution*, trans. Bobbye Ortiz, Monthly Review Press, New York and London 1967. The average print run in Spanish America for new literary or political texts was only 1,000–2,000 even in the mid-1960s.

194. Ibid., p. 112. Here, Debray cites Amilcar Cabral.

195. Ibid., p. 21.

196. Vargas Llosa, 'Homenaje a Javier Heraud' [Paris, 19 May 1963], in his *Contra viento y marea*, vol. I, pp. 42–3, p. 42.

197. Régis Debray, 'Le rôle de l'intellectuel', in *Essais sur l'Amérique latine*, François Maspero, Paris 1967, pp. 185–7, p. 185.

198. Mario Benedetti, *El escritor latinoamericano y la revolución posible*, Editorial Nueva Imagen, Argentina 1987, pp. 77–8.

199. Tomás Moulián, cited in 'Los intelectuales han muerto (¡Vivan los intelectuales!', *Página Abierta* (Santiago), no. 74, 31 August to 13 September 1992, pp. 18–20, p. 18.

200. Aricó, *La cola del diablo*, p. 24.

201. See Vargas Llosa's statement of support for the Peruvian Movement of the Revolutionary Left (MIR): 'Toma de posición', Paris, 22 July 1965, in his *Contra viento y marea*, vol. I, pp. 91–2.

202. For a typical example, see Carlos Fuentes, 'Gabriel García Márquez and the Invention of America', in *Myself with Others: Selected Essays*, Pan Books, London 1988, pp. 180–95.

203. Julio Cortázar, 'América Latina y sus escritores', in *Argentina: años de alambradas culturales*, Muchnik, Barcelona 1984, pp. 76–7, p. 77.

204. Benedetti, *El escritor*, p. 81.

205. See Octavio Paz, 'Vuelta a *El laberinto de la soledad*', in *El ogro filantrópico*, p. 20. This is undoubtedly the role that Paz wished to play, although he considered the term 'intellectual' itself synonymous with 'ideologue' (see, for example, 'Propósito', *El ogro filantrópico*, pp. 7–14, p. 12) and preferred to describe himself as 'a writer' ('Suma y sigue', *El ogro filantrópico*, p. 333).

206. Paz, *El ogro filantrópico*, p. 34.

207. Ibid., p. 333.

208. Ibid., p. 34.

209. Ibid., p. 9.

210. Octavio Paz, *Tiempo nublado*, Editorial Seix Barral, Barcelona 1983, p. 7.

211. Paz, *El ogro filantrópico*, p. 89.

212. Ibid., p. 86.

213. Paz, *Tiempo nublado*, p. 129.

214. Paz, *El ogro filantrópico*, p. 100.

215. Stabb, *In Quest of Identity*, p. 5.

216. Paz, *El ogro filantrópico*, pp. 34–5.

217. Zygmunt Bauman, *Legislators and Interpreters: On Modernity, Post-modernity and Intellectuals*, Cornell University Press, Ithaca, NY 1987.

218. Roa, 'Una semilla en un surco de fuego', p. 7.

219. Julio Antonio Mella, 'Glosas al pensamiento de José Martí: un libro que debe escribirse' [no date, ?1926], in his *Documentos y artículos*, pp. 267-74, p. 269.

220. Sergio Luiz Prado Bellei, 'Brazilian Culture in the Frontier', *Bulletin of Latin American Research*, 14:1 (January 1995), pp. 47-61, p. 60. He draws substantially on the work of Roberto Schwarz; see Schwarz, *Misplaced Ideas*, Verso, London 1992, especially pp. 6-7.

221. Touraine, cited in Sigal, 'América Latina y sus intelectuales', p. 26.

222. Rama, *La ciudad letrada*, p. 110.

223. Rodó, 'Rumbos nuevos', *Obras completas*, pp. 497-507, p. 507.

224. Anonymous source from a sociological survey, cited in Alicia Barrios and José Joaquín Brunner, *La sociología en Chile: instituciones y practicantes*, FLACSO, Santiago 1988, pp. 51-2.

225. Sigal, *Intelectuales y poder*, p. 13.

Chapter 4

1. Simón Bolívar, 'The Angostura Address' [1819], in *Bolívar: His Basic Thoughts*, Presidency of the Republic of Venezuela, Caracas 1981, p. 92.

2. Tulio Halperín Donghi, *The Aftermath of Revolution in Latin America*, trans. Josephine de Bunsen, Harper and Row, New York 1973, p. 30.

3. See pp. 104-5 above.

4. Florencia Mallon, 'Indian Communities, Political Cultures, and the State in Latin America, 1780-1990', *Journal of Latin American Studies*, vol. 24, Quincentenary Supplement, 1992, pp. 35-54, p. 35.

5. Alan Knight, 'Racism, Revolution, and *Indigenismo*: Mexico, 1910-1940', in Richard Graham, ed., *The Idea of Race in Latin America, 1870-1940*, University of Texas Press, Austin 1990, pp. 71-113; Mallon, 'Indian Communities'.

6. Luis Villoro, *Los grandes momentos del indigenismo en México*, El Colegio de México, Mexico City 1950, pp. 234-5.

7. Ibid., pp. 189 and 193.

8. Manuel Gamio, *Forjando patria* [1916], Editorial Porrúa, Mexico City 1982, p. 29.

9. David Brading, 'Manuel Gamio and Official Indigenismo in Mexico', *Bulletin of Latin American Research*, 7:1 (1988), pp. 75-89.

10. Gamio, *Forjando patria*, p. 77.

11. Ibid., p. 183.

12. Ibid.

13. Ángeles González Gamio, *Manuel Gamio: una lucha sin final*, UNAM, Mexico City 1987, p. 47.

14. The story was recalled by Miguel León Portillo, cited in González Gamio, *Manuel Gamio*, p. 124.

15. Manuel Gamio, 'The Population of the Valley of Teotihuacán: Introduction, Synthesis and Conclusions', PhD thesis (University of Colombia), Secretaría de Agricultura y Fomento, Mexico City 1922.

16. Manuel Gamio, letter of 29 June 1942, cited in González Gamio, *Manuel Gamio*, p. 131.

17. Manuel Gamio, 'Informe confidencial relativo a la candidatura del General Calles', 20 May 1924, in Plutarco Elías Calles, *Correspondencia personal 1919–1945*, Fondo de Cultura Económica, Mexico City 1991, p. 327.
18. González Gamio, *Manuel Gamio*, p. 79.
19. Ibid., pp. 79–82.
20. Ibid., p. 86.
21. In Manuel Gamio, *Consideraciones sobre el problema indígena*, Instituto Indigenista Interamericano, Mexico City 1966, pp. 237–9.
22. González Gamio, *Manuel Gamio*, p. 108.
23. Luis González, *Historia de la Revolución Mexicana, Vol. 15, 1934–40: Los días del presidente Cárdenas*, El Colegio de México, Mexico City 1981, p. 126.
24. Panabière, 'Les intellectuels et l'état au Mexique', p. 86.
25. José Vasconcelos, *La raza cósmica* [1925], Espasa-Calpe Mexicana, Mexico City, 3rd edn, 1966, pp. 50–1.
26. Ibid., pp. 23–4.
27. Ibid., pp. 27 and 30.
28. Ibid., p. 36.
29. Mariátegui, *Siete ensayos*, p. 340.
30. José Vasconcelos, 'Carta a "T"', 24 November 1934, in *Cartas políticas de José Vasconcelos (primera serie 1924–1936)*, ed. Alfonso Taracena, Editora Librera, Mexico City 1959, p. 146.
31. José Vasconcelos, extract from *Indología*, p. 9.
32. Ibid., p. 27.
33. José Vasconcelos, 'Inauguración de una escuela en La Ceiba', in *Discursos: 1920–1950*, Ediciones Botas, Mexico City, p. 10.
34. Vasconcelos, 'Prólogo a la segunda edición' [1945], in *La raza cósmica*, pp. 11–12.
35. José Vasconcelos, 'Advertencia', *Memorias*, vol. I, p. 6.
36. Daniel Cosío Villegas, *Memorias*, Editorial Joaquín Mortiz, Mexico City 1976, pp. 90–1.
37. Vasconcelos, *La raza cósmica*, p. 25.
38. Ibid.; Lázaro Cárdenas, *Palabras y documentos políticos, vol. I, 1928–40*, Siglo Veintiuno, Mexico City 1978, p. 403.
39. Vasconcelos, *La raza cósmica*, p. 20.
40. Henry C. Schmidt, *The Roots of Lo Mexicano: Self and Society in Mexican Thought, 1900–1934*, Texas A&M University Press, College Station and London 1978, p. 164.
41. 'El "abandono de la cultura" en Mexico' is the title of a chapter in Samuel Ramos, *El perfil del hombre y la cultura en México*, Editorial Pedro Robredo, Mexico City, 2nd edn, 1938, pp. 132–41.
42. See Samuel Ramos, 'El pecado original de la Universidad Mexicana' [1925], in *Obras completas* (3 vols) [hereafter *OC*], UNAM, Mexico City, vol. I (1975), pp. 234–6; and 'Incipit vita nuova' [1925] in *OC*, vol. I, pp. 246–7.
43. Samuel Ramos, 'El evangelio de la inteligencia' [1925], in *OC*, vol. I, pp. 243–4.
44. Samuel Ramos, 'A guisa de prólogo' [1925], *OC*, vol. I, pp. 255–9.
45. Samuel Ramos, 'El ocaso de Ariel' [1925], *OC*, vol. I, pp. 252–4, p. 252.
46. Ibid., p. 254.

47. Samuel Ramos, 'Antonio Caso' [1927], in *OC*, vol. I, pp. 58–69.

48. Antonio Caso, 'Ramos y yo: un ensayo de valoración personal' [1927], in his *Obras completas*, vol. I, *Polémicas*, UNAM, Mexico City 1971, pp. 142–57.

49. Ramos, 'Antonio Caso', p. 63.

50. Ibid., p. 65.

51. Ibid., p. 66.

52. Ibid., p. 65.

53. Caso, 'Ramos y yo', pp. 143 and 157.

54. Ibid., p. 145.

55. Ibid., p. 146.

56. Ibid., p. 155.

57. Ramos, 'Antonio Caso', p. 66. See also Samuel Ramos, 'Mi experiencia pragmatista' [1928], *OC*, vol. I, pp. 79–85.

58. Enrique Krauze, 'Intelectuales y cultura', in Jean Meyer, *Historia de la revolución mexicana, vol. 11, Estado y sociedad con Calles*, El Colegio de México, Mexico City, 1977, pp. 315–19, p. 319.

59. Meyer, *Historia de la revolución mexicana*, p. 343.

60. Calles, letter to Abelardo L. Rodríguez, President, 27 April 1933, in *Correspondencia personal, 1919–1945*, Fondo de Cultura Económica, Mexico City 1991, pp. 275–6, p. 276.

61. Ibid.

62. Meyer, *Historia de la revolución mexicana*, p. 344.

63. Vicente de P. Cano, 'Las misiones culturales del PNR', *El Nacional*, 30 June 1930, cited in Schmidt, *Roots*, pp. 104–5 (Schmidt's translation).

64. See note 41.

65. Schmidt, *Roots*, p. 140.

66. Ibid., p. 157.

67. Samuel Ramos, '20 años de pintura en México' [1940], in *OC*, vol. III, pp. 71–4, p. 72.

68. Ramos, *El perfil*, p. 38.

69. Ibid.

70. Ibid.

71. Ibid., p. 40.

72. Ibid., p. 101.

73. Ibid., p. 137. Original ellipsis.

74. Ibid., p. 154.

75. Ibid. p. 71.

76. Ibid., p. 72.

77. Ibid.

78. Ibid., pp. 72–3.

79. Ibid., p. 71.

80. Ibid., p. 73.

81. Ibid., p. 39.

82. Ibid., p. 36.

83. Ibid., p. 28.

84. Ibid., p. 85.

85. Ibid., p. 77.

86. Ibid., p. 47.

87. Schmidt, *Roots*, p. xi. As Schmidt argues, most of Ramos's themes had been anticipated for at least two decades.
88. Octavio Paz, *El laberinto de la soledad* [1950], Fondo de Cultura Económica, Mexico City, 2nd edn, 1959, pp. 42, 26 and 52.
89. Paz, *El laberinto*, pp. 173–4.
90. Paz, 'Vuelta a *El laberinto de la soledad*', p. 20.
91. Ibid., p. 17.
92. Octavio Paz, interview in New Delhi, 13 November 1968, in Fernando Vizcaino, *Biografía política de Octavio Paz o La razón ardiente*, Editorial Algazara, Málaga 1993, pp. 125–8, p. 128.
93. This generation included Manuel Gómez Morín, Vicente Lombardo Toledano, Jesús Silva Herzog, Narciso Bassols, Daniel Cosío Villegas, Manuel Gamio and Ignacio Chávez. Enrique Krauze, 'Los temples de la cultura', in Camp *et al.*, *Los intelectuales y el poder*, pp. 583–605, p. 585.
94. Enrique Krauze, *Caudillos culturales en la Revolución Mexicana*, Editorial Siglo XXI, Mexico City 1985, pp. 154–5.
95. Henry Schmidt notes: 'Jesús S. Soto called for a comparative study of the ideology of the twenties and in effect issued a plea for the history of ideas in Mexico'; Manuel Gómez Morín 'wanted a criticism that would offer the Mexican standards for distinguishing between the national and the foreign basis of culture'. Schmidt, *Roots*, p. 107.
96. Fredrick B. Pike, 'The Problem of Identity and National Destiny in Peru and Argentina', in Fredrick B. Pike, ed., *Latin American History: Select Problems*, Harcourt, Brace and World, New York 1969, pp. 173–87. On the question of national consciousness among the Indians, see Mallon, *Peasant and Nation*.
97. Manuel González Prada, 'Nuestros indios' [1904], in his *Pensamiento político de González Prada*, ed. Bruno Podestà, Universidad del Pacífico, Lima 1983, p. 78.
98. Mallon, 'Indian Communities', p. 37.
99. Mariátegui, *Siete ensayos*; Víctor Andrés Belaúnde, *La realidad nacional*, publisher unknown, Lima, 3rd edn, 1964.
100. José Carlos Mariátegui, 'El indigenismo en la literatura nacional' [21 January, 28 January and 4 February 1927], reproduced in Manuel Aquézolo Castro, ed., *La polémica del indigenismo*, Mosca Azul Editores, Lima 1976, pp. 31–9. These articles were later incorporated into *Siete ensayos*.
101. José Ángel Escalante, 'Nosotros, los indios . . .' [3 February 1927], in Aquézolo Castro, *La polémica*, pp. 39–55.
102. Ibid. Escalante later became Minister of Justice.
103. Ibid., p. 48.
104. Ibid., p. 50.
105. Ibid., p. 52.
106. José Ángel Escalante, 'Literatura indigenista' [4 March 1927], in Aquézolo Castro, *La polémica*, pp. 57–9.
107. José Deustua and José Luis Reñique, *Intelectuales, indigenismo y descentralismo en el Perú 1897–1931*, Centro de Estudios Rurales Andinos 'Bartolomé de Las Casas', Cuzco 1984, p. 90.
108. Luis Alberto Sánchez, 'Batiburrillo indigenista' [18 February 1927], in Aquézolo Castro, *La polémica*, pp. 69–73, p. 70.

109. José Carlos Mariátegui, 'Intermezzo polémico' [25 February 1927], in Aquézolo Castro, *La polémica*, pp. 73–7, p. 73.
110. Ibid., p. 74.
111. Ibid., p. 77.
112. Luis Alberto Sánchez, 'Respuesta a José Carlos Mariátegui' [4 March 1927], in Aquézolo Castro, *La polémica*, pp. 77–81, p. 77.
113. Ibid.
114. Ibid., p. 78.
115. Luis Alberto Sánchez, 'Punto final con José Carlos Mariátegui', *Amauta*, 7 March 1927, in Aquézolo Castro, *La polémica*, pp. 86–91, p. 88.
116. José Carlos Mariátegui, 'Réplica a Luis Alberto Sánchez' [11 March 1927], in Aquézolo Castro, *La polémica*, pp. 81–5, p. 82.
117. José Carlos Mariátegui, 'Polémica finita' [27 April 1927], in Aquézolo Castro, *La polémica*, pp. 91–3.
118. Mariátegui, *Siete ensayos*, pp. 278 and 275.
119. Belaúnde, *La realidad nacional*, p. 1.
120. Ibid., pp. 14–15.
121. Belaúnde, 'Prólogo a la segunda edicion' [1945], in *La realidad nacional*, pp. xiv–xv.
122. Belaúnde, *La realidad nacional*, p. 2.
123. Ibid., p. 44.
124. Mariátegui, *Siete ensayos*, p. 39.
125. Ibid., pp. 35–6.
126. Mariátegui, 'El problema de las razas en la América Latina', *Obras completas*, vol. 13, *Ideología y política*, Empresa Editora Amauta, Lima 1969, pp. 21–86, p. 22. See also *Siete ensayos*, p. 40.
127. Ibid., p. 27.
128. Ibid., p. 21.
129. Ofelia Schutte, *Cultural Identity and Social Liberation in Latin American Thought*, State University of New York Press, Albany 1993, pp. 64–5.
130. Mariátegui, *Siete ensayos*, p. 55 and p. 78, n. 15.
131. Ibid., pp. 83–5.
132. Ibid., p. 43.
133. Mariátegui, 'El problema de las razas', p. 81.
134. Mariátegui, 'La nueva cruzada pro indígena', *Amauta*, Lima, January 1927, no.5, in Aquézolo Castro, *La polémica*, pp. 52–5, p. 54.
135. Mariátegui, 'El problema de las razas', p. 25.
136. Ibid., p. 37.
137. Luis Alberto Sánchez, 'Punto final con José Carlos Mariátegui' [7 March 1927], in Aquézolo Castro, *La polémica*, pp. 86–91, p. 88.
138. Belaúnde, *La realidad nacional*, pp. 30–1.
139. Ibid., p. 30.
140. Ibid., p. 31.
141. Ibid.
142. Mariátegui, 'Réplica', p. 83.
143. Mariátegui, *Siete ensayos*, p. 332.
144. José Carlos Mariátegui, 'El problema primaria del Perú', in his *Peruanicemos al Perú*, vol. II of *Obras completas*, Empresa Editora Amauta, Lima 1975, p. 30.

145. Belaúnde, *La realidad nacional*, p. 31.
146. Manuel Burga and Alberto Flores Galindo, *Apogeo y crisis de la república aristocrá-tica*, Ediciones Rikchay Peru, Lima, 3rd edn, 1984, p. 12.
147. Lima's population increased from 200,000 in 1920 to 300,000 in 1930. Burga and Flores Galindo, *Apogeo y crisis*, p. 12.
148. Mariátegui, *Siete ensayos*, p. 48.
149. Mariátegui, 'Intermezzo', p. 76.
150. Mariátegui, 'La nueva cruzada pro indígena', p. 54.
151. For further discussion, see Chapter 5.
152. Mariátegui, 'Réplica', p. 84.
153. Mariátegui, 'El problema de las razas', p. 30.
154. Ibid., p. 31.
155. Ibid., p. 45.
156. Mariátegui, *Siete ensayos*, p. 343.
157. Ibid., pp. 340–1.
158. Sánchez, 'Respuesta', p. 81.
159. Mariátegui, 'Réplica', p. 222.
160. Mariátegui, 'Intermezzo', p. 76.
161. Luis Alberto Sánchez, 'Más sobre lo mismo' [25 March 1927]; in Aquézolo Castro, *La polémica*, pp. 94–6, p. 96.
162. Luis Alberto Sánchez, 'Colofón a *Tempestad en los Andes*' [1927], in Aquézolo Castro, *La polémica*, pp. 140–6, p. 143.
163. Belaúnde, *La realidad nacional*, pp. 60–3, quotation on p. 61.
164. Mariátegui, 'La nueva cruzada pro indígena', p. 54.
165. Mariátegui, 'César Vallejo', in *Siete ensayos*, pp. 311–12.
166. Mariátegui, *Siete ensayos*, p. 336.
167. Geoffrey Bertram, 'Peru, 1930–60', in Leslie Bethell, ed., *Cambridge History of Latin America*, vol. VIII, Cambridge University Press, Cambridge 1991, pp. 385–449, p. 394.
168. Alejandro Marroquín, cited in Ruth E. Arboleyda and Luis Vásquez León, *Mariátegui y el indigenismo revolucionario peruano*, Instituto Nacional de Antropología e Historia, Mexico City 1979, p. 7.
169. Mario Vargas Llosa, *José María Arguedas entre sapos y halcones*, Ediciones cultura hispánica del Centro Iberoamericano de Cooperación, Madrid 1978, p. 24.
170. Ibid., p. 32.
171. Ibid., p. 24.
172. Mario Vargas Llosa, 'El intelectual barato' [1979] and 'Entre tocayos' [1984], in his *Contra viento y marea*, vol. II, pp. 143–55 and pp. 408–17.
173. Flores Galindo, 'La imagen', p. 79.
174. Figures from Aline Helg, 'Race in Argentina and Cuba, 1880–1930, Theory, Policies, and Popular Reaction', in Graham, *The Idea of Race*, pp. 37–69, p. 43. See also George Reid Andrews, *The Afro-Argentines of Buenos Aires, 1800–1900*, University of Wisconsin Press, Madison 1980.
175. Figures vary slightly. Those given here are taken from Alastair Hennessy, 'Argentines, Anglo-Argentines and Others', in Alastair Hennessy and John King, eds, *The Land that England Lost*, British Academic Press, London 1992, pp. 9–48, p. 9. Data on Bolivians and Uruguayans is from Carl Solberg,

Immigration and Nationalism in Argentina and Chile, 1890–1914, University of Texas Press, Austin and London 1970, p. 38.

176. Tulio Halperín Donghi, review of *Cambridge History of Latin America*, vol. X, in *Journal of Latin American Studies*, 29:1 (February 1997), pp. 223–4, p. 223.

177. José Ingenieros, 'La formación de una raza argentina', *Revista de Filosofía* (Buenos Aires), vol. I, 1915.

178. Eduardo José Cárdenas and Carlos Manuel Payá, *El primer nacionalismo argentino en Manuel Gálvez y Ricardo Rojas*, Editorial A. Peña Lillo, Buenos Aires 1978.

179. José Ramos Mejía (1849–1914), *Las multitudes argentinas* [1899], Talleres gráficos argentinos L. J. Rosso, Buenos Aires 1934, p. 262. See also Ricardo Rojas, *La restauración nacionalista: crítica de la educación Argentina y bases para una reforma en el estudio de las humanidades modernas* [1909], Editorial A. Peña Lillo, Buenos Aires 1971.

180. Hennessy, 'Argentines', p. 33.

181. Manuel Gálvez, *Recuerdos de la vida literaria, vol. I: Amigos y maestros de mi juventud* [1944], Librería Hachette, Buenos Aires 1961, Chapter xviii ('Desencuentros con Lugones').

182. Myron I. Lichtblau, *Manuel Gálvez*, Twayne Publishers, New York 1972, p. 7.

183. Noé Jitrik, *Leopoldo Lugones, mito nacional*, Editorial Palestra, Buenos Aires 1960, p. 8.

184. Gálvez, *Amigos y maestros*, pp. 36–7.

185. Ibid.

186. Ibid., p. 43.

187. David Rock, *Authoritarian Argentina: The Nationalist Movement, Its History and Its Impact*, University of California Press, Berkeley 1993, p. 49.

188. Nicolás Shumway, *The Invention of Argentina*, University of California Press, Berkeley 1991, p. 214.

189. Manuel Gálvez, *El solar de la raza*, Editorial La Facultad, Buenos Aires, 5th edn, 1930, p. 15.

190. Manuel Gálvez, *El diario de Gabriel Quiroga: opiniones sobre la vida argentina*, Arnoldo Moen and Hno. Editores, Buenos Aires 1910, p. 32.

191. Rock, *Authoritarian Argentina*, p. 42.

192. Gálvez, *El solar de la raza*, p. 9.

193. Ibid., pp. 9–10.

194. Ibid., pp. 17–18.

195. Ricardo Rojas, *Blasón de plata*, Martín-García Editores, Buenos Aires 1912, p. 117; Gálvez, *El diario de Gabriel Quiroga*, p. 117.

196. Juan José Hernández Arregui argues that they had an attitude of 'national consciousness, without any love for the people'. *La formación de la conciencia nacional, 1930–1960*, Ediciones Hachea, Buenos Aires 1964, p. 19.

197. The articles are reproduced in Ricardo Rojas, *Cosmópolis*, Garnier Hermanos Libreros-Editores, Paris 1908, p. 21.

198. Rojas, *Cosmópolis*, pp. 18 and 29.

199. Ricardo Rojas, *Eurindia: ensayo de estética sobre las culturas americanas* [1924], Editorial Losada, Buenos Aires 1951, pp. 11–12.

200. Ibid., p. 21.

201. Rojas, *Blasón de plata*, p. 16.

202. Earl T. Glauert, 'Ricardo Rojas and the Emergence of Argentine Cultural

Nationalism', *Hispanic American Historical Review*, 43:1 (February 1963), pp. 1–13, p. 3.

203. Rojas, *Blasón de plata*, pp. 247 and 164.
204. Ibid., p. 230.
205. Fredrick B. Pike, 'The Problem of Identity', p. 186.
206. Rojas, *Blasón de plata*, p. 173.
207. Ibid., p. 187.
208. Ibid., p. 243.
209. Ricardo Rojas, *La argentinidad: ensayo histórico sobre nuestra conciencia nacional en la gesta de emancipación 1810–1816*, Editorial 'La Facultad' de Juan Roldán, Buenos Aires 1916.
210. Ibid., p. 10.
211. Ibid., p. 3.
212. Ibid., p. 8.
213. Ibid., p. 50.
214. Ibid., pp. 407 and 23.
215. Rojas, *Eurindia*, p. 260.
216. Ibid., p. 21.
217. See Stephen E. Lewis, 'Myth and the History of Chile's Araucanians', *Radical History*, 58 (Winter 1994), pp. 113–41.
218. Rojas published a collection of Quechua hymns and prayers, insisting that they were part of the Argentine oral tradition: see his *Himnos quichuas*, Instituto de Literatura Argentina, Universidad de Buenos Aires, 1937.
219. My thanks go to Dr Rick Halpern for information about US cowboys.
220. Shumway, *Invention of Argentina*, p. 258. Lucio Mansilla's essay has recently been translated as *A Visit to the Ranquel Indians*, trans. Eva Gillies, University of Nebraska Press, Lincoln 1997.
221. Manuel Gálvez, *El diario de Gabriel Quiriga*, Arnoldo Moen y Hno. Editores, Buenos Aires 1910, pp. 167–72; and Ricardo Rojas, *Historia de la literatura argentina*, vol. II, *Los gauchescos, part II*, [1917], Editorial Guillermo Kraft, Buenos Aires 1960, pp. 549–65. See also Richard W. Slatta, 'The Gaucho in Argentina's Quest for National Identity', in David J. Weber and Jane M. Rausch, *Where Cultures Meet: Frontiers in Latin American History*, SR Books, Wilmington 1994, pp. 151–64.
222. Solberg, *Immigration*, p. 155.
223. Lugones, *El payador*, in *Obras en prosa*, Editorial Aguilar, Mexico City 1962, pp. 1,079–345, p. 1,083.
224. Ibid., p. 1,245.
225. Ibid., pp. 1,256–7.
226. Ibid., p. 1,255.
227. Ibid., p. 1,344.
228. Ibid., pp. 1,137–8.
229. Gálvez, *El diario de Gabriel Quiroga*, p. 114.
230. Alfonso Reyes, *Vocación de América (Antología)*, Fondo de Cultura Económica, Mexico City 1989, p. 182.
231. Solberg, *Immigration*, p. 170. Jitrik made the case for this interpretation of Lugones in *Leopoldo Lugones*, pp. 20–1.
232. The ideas of Karl Krause (1781–1832), a follower of Kant, were not influential

for long in his native Germany, but appealed strongly to a minority of mid-nineteenth-century Spanish intellectuals, led by Julián Sanz del Río (1814–69), who launched Krausism in Madrid in 1854. As 'a version of the Kantian notion of religion within the limits of reason alone', emphasizing the holistic development of both the individual and the community, the importance of social solidarity and humanitarianism, Krausism attracted those thinkers in Spain and, later, Spanish America 'who sought a rational, humane and socially just alternative to the doctrines of the Church'. See Rockwell Gray, *The Imperative of Modernity: An Intellectual Biography of José Ortega y Gasset*, University of California Press, Berkeley 1989, pp. 43–8, p. 47.

233. Hipólito Yrigoyen, *Mi vida y mi doctrina*, Editorial Raigal, Buenos Aires 1957, pp. 124 and 123.
234. Rock, *Authoritarian Argentina*, pp. 62–3.
235. Slatta, 'The Gaucho', p. 160.
236. Aline Helg, *Our Rightful Share: The Afro-Cuban Struggle for Equality, 1886–1912*, University of North Carolina Press, Chapel Hill and London 1995, p. 247.
237. Lugones, *El payador*, p. 1,134.
238. Charles Hale, 'Political and social ideas, 1870–1930', in Leslie Bethell, ed., *Cambridge History of Latin America*, vol. V, Cambridge University Press, Cambridge 1986, pp. 367–441, p. 274. See Rodó, *Ariel*, p. 72.

Chapter 5

1. Carlos Monsiváis, *Amor perdido*, Ediciones Era, Mexico City 1977, p. 99.
2. The relevant part of President Monroe's speech read as follows: 'It is impossible that the allied powers should extend their political system to any portion of either continent [of the Americas] without endangering our peace and happiness; nor can anyone believe that our southern brethren, if left to themselves, would adopt it of their own accord. It is equally impossible, therefore, that we should behold such interposition, in any form, with indifference.' 'Annual Message to the United States Congress', 2 December 1823, in James Gantenbein, ed., *The Evolution of Our Latin American Policy: A Documentary Record*, Columbia University Press, New York 1950, pp. 323–5, p. 325.
3. Juan Bautista Alberdi, *La unidad de América Latina: memoria* [1844], Granica Editor, Buenos Aires 1974. See also Alfredo L. Palacios, *La comunidad iberoamericana: Bolívar y Alberdi*, Editor Abeledo-Perrot, Buenos Aires 1959.
4. R. W. Emerson, 'The American Scholar', oration before the Phi Beta Kappa Society, at Cambridge, MA, 31 August 1837, in *Essays and Lectures*, Library of America, New York 1983, pp. 51–71. The earliest and clearest statement in Spanish America was Andrés Bello's 'Autonomía cultural de América' [1838], in Carlos Ripoll, *Conciencia intelectual de América: antología del ensayo hispanoamericano (1836–1959)*, Las Américas Publishing, New York 1966, pp. 44–50.
5. Francisco Bilbao, 'El evangelio americano' [1864], in his *Obras completas*, Imprenta de Buenos Aires, 1865, vol. II, pp. 311–444, p. 400.
6. Ibid., p. 401.
7. See, for example, Oscar Terán, 'El primer antimperialismo latinamericano',

Punto de Vista (Buenos Aires), Year IV, no. 12, July–October 1981, pp. 3–11, p. 8.

8. José Enrique Rodó, insert into *El Día* (Montevideo), 23 January 1900, cited in *Obras completas*, pp. 194–5.

9. José Enrique Rodó, *Ariel*, ed. Gordon Brotherston, Cambridge University Press, Cambridge 1967, pp. 69–70. All references are to this edition unless otherwise stated.

10. Ibid., p. 91.

11. Brotherston, 'Introduction', in Rodó, *Ariel*, p. 10.

12. Fuentes, 'Prologue', in Rodó, *Ariel*, trans. Sayers Peden, p. 14.

13. Rodó, *Ariel*, p. 69.

14. Ibid., pp. 81–2.

15. Rodó, *El mirador*, p. 177.

16. Terán, 'El primer antimperialismo', p. 6.

17. Gustave Le Bon, *The Psychology of Socialism*, T. Fisher Unwin, London 1899, pp. 193–8.

18. Rodó, *Ariel*, p. 71. Original emphasis.

19. José Enrique Rodó, 'El americanismo literario' [1895], in Arturo Ardao, ed., *Rodó: su americanismo*, Biblioteca de Marcha, Montevideo 1970, pp. 45–63, p. 47.

20. José Enrique Rodó, 'Imitación y originalidad en la literatura hispanoamericana' [1907], in Ardao, *Rodó*, pp. 74–80, p. 76.

21. José Enrique Rodó, 'Sobre América Latina' [1906], in ibid., p. 167.

22. Rodó, *El mirador*, p. 161.

23. Ardao, *Rodó*, pp. 17–18. Ardao stretches his argument beyond what is plausible, making over-much of Rodó's one mention in *Ariel* of the development of US trusts to impute to him an understanding of US political economy that is not demonstrated anywhere else in his work (p. 35).

24. Rodó, *El mirador*, p. 30.

25. Rodó, *Ariel*, p. 72.

26. Liah Greenfeld, *Nationalism: Five Roads to Modernity*, Harvard University Press, Cambridge, MA and London 1992, p. 228 and p. 234.

27. Reyes, *Vocación de América*, p. 250.

28. A typical example is Carlos Octavio Bunge, *Nuestra América (ensayo de psicología social)*, Editora Valerio Abeledo, Buenos Aires 1905.

29. Greenfeld, *Nationalism*, p. 256.

30. See, for example, José Martí, 'El hombre antiguo de América y sus artes primitivas' [1884], in *OE*, vol. II, pp. 372–5.

31. Rodó, *Ariel*, pp. 71–2. See full quotation on p. 177 above.

32. Rubén Darío, 'Edgar Allan Poe', *Los raros*, Editorial Mundo Latino, Madrid 1918, pp. 17–29, p. 20.

33. Rubén Darío, 'El triunfo de Calibán', in *Rubén Darío: el modernismo y otros ensayos*, Alianza Editorial, Madrid 1989, pp. 161–5, p. 161. José Agustín Balseiro argues that the idea of identifying the United States with Caliban was in fact originally Darío's, and was appropriated by Rodó without acknowledgement. Balseiro, *Seis estudios sobre Rubén Darío*, Editorial Gredos, Madrid 1967, pp. 117–43. Darío's article was published in a Buenos Aires newspaper, *El Tiempo*, but there is no proof that Rodó read it; the most likely immediate influence on him was Paul Groussac, who gave a speech in Buenos Aires denouncing the 'Caliban-

esque' Yanqui spirit, parts of which were reproduced in *La Razón* of Montevideo in May 1898. Rodríguez Monegal, 'Prólogo', in Rodó, *OC*, pp. 191–202, pp. 193–4.

34. Rufino Blanco-Fombona, 'La evolución política y social de Hispano-América' [1911], in *Obras selectas*, Ediciones Edimé, Madrid and Caracas 1958, p. 352.
35. Rufino Blanco-Fombona, 'La América de origen inglés contra la América de origen español' and '¿Lucha de clases, o más bien lucha de razas?' in *Obras selectas*, pp. 1,138–41 and pp. 1,161–5.
36. José María Vargas Vila, *Ante los bárbaros (Los Estados Unidos y la guerra)*, Imprenta de José Anglada, Barcelona, 2nd edn, 1918, p. 141.
37. José Vasconcelos, *Indología: una interpretación de la cultura Ibero-Americana*, Agencia Mundial de Librería, Paris 1927, p. xxiii.
38. See José Vasconcelos, *Raza cósmica, Indología* and (with Manuel Gamio), *Aspects of Mexican Civilization*, University of Chicago Press, Chicago, IL 1926.
39. See, for example, Vargas Vila, *Ante los bárbaros*, p. 156.
40. Emilio Roig de Leuchsenring, *Tradición antimperialista de nuestra historia*, Editorial de Ciencias Sociales, Havana 1977, p. 23.
41. Juan José Hernández Arregui, *¿Qué es el ser nacional? (La conciencia histórica hispanoamericana)*, Editorial Hachea, Buenos Aires 1963, p. 133.
42. Abel, in Abel and Torrents, *José Martí*, pp. 129 and 131.
43. Martí's famous observation was, 'I lived inside the monster, and I have seen its entrails – and my sling is the sling of David'. José Martí, 'Carta a Manuel Mercado' [18 May 1895], *OE*, vol. III, pp. 576–9, p. 576. On Martí's attitude towards the United States, see Gordon K. Lewis, *Main Currents in Caribbean Thought*, Johns Hopkins University Press, Baltimore and London 1983, p. 299. For Cuban Marxist views of Martí, see Centro de Estudios Martianos, *Siete enfoques marxistas sobre José Martí*, Editora Política, Havana 1985.
44. Lewis, *Main Currents in Caribbean Thought*, p. 302.
45. José Martí, 'Nuestra América' [1891], *OE*, vol. II, pp. 523 and 524.
46. Ibid., p. 522.
47. Ibid., p. 525.
48. Ibid.
49. Ibid.
50. José Martí, 'Discurso en honor de Simón Bolívar' [1893], in *OE*, vol. II, pp. 288–95, p. 291.
51. José Martí, 'The Washington Pan-American Congress' [1889], in Philip S. Foner (ed.), *Inside the Monster by José Marti: Writings on the United States and American Imperialism*, trans. Elinor Randall, Monthly Review Press, New York and London 1975, pp. 339–67.
52. José Martí, 'The Truth about the United States' [1894], in Foner, *Inside the Monster*, pp. 49–54, p. 49.
53. Ibid., p. 54.
54. See José Martí, 'A Terrible Drama: The Funeral of the Haymarket Martyrs'; 'The First Voting of Women in Kansas'; 'Jesse James, the Great Bandit'; 'The Chinese in the United States' and many other articles, in Foner, *Inside the Monster*.
55. Christopher Abel, in Abel and Torrents, *José Martí*, p. 196.
56. José Martí, 'El tercer año de PRC: el alma de la Revolución y el deber de Cuba

en América' [1894], in Emilio Roig de Leuchsenring, ed., *Ideario cubano I. José Martí*, Municipio de La Habana, Havana 1936, pp. 130–3, p. 133. Martí also suggested that Cuban and Puerto Rican independence were necessary in order to safeguard 'the dignity of the North American republic' (p. 133), believing that the new imperialist policies were undermining what he saw as the founding values (liberty and democracy) of the United States.

57. José Martí, 'El tratado comercial entre los Estados Unidos y México' [1883], in *OE*, vol. I, pp. 336–41. This treaty was negotiated at the behest of the US government, which was anxious to press home its advantage over the corrupt and weak government of Porfirio Díaz's hand-picked successor, General Manuel González (1880–84). González had overseen the passage of a series of laws to benefit foreign investors in Mexico, but was not actually keen on the trade treaty – partly because it interrupted his plans for an economic rapprochement with Europe, and partly because of the short-term loss of customs' revenue it entailed. Although the Mexican Congress did sanction the agreement in 1883, a few months later Mexico granted Most Favoured Nation status to Germany, thereby effectively cancelling out the advantages the US had gained. Ironically, as it turned out, the US-Mexican Trade Treaty was in the end refused ratification by the US Senate, which succumbed to lobbying from US farmers concerned about Mexican competition in agriculture. Friedrich Katz, 'Mexico: Restored Republic and Porfiriato, 1867–1910', in Leslie Bethell, ed., *Cambridge History of Latin America*, vol. V, Cambridge University Press, Cambridge 1986, pp. 3–78, pp. 26–7.

58. Martí, 'The Washington Pan-American Congress', p. 340.

59. José Martí, 'La Conferencia Monetaria de las Repúblicas de América' [1891] in Roig de Leuchsenring, *Ideario*, pp. 89–97, p. 92.

60. Martí, 'Nuestra América', p. 526.

61. Martí, 'La Conferencia Monetaria', p. 92.

62. Martí, 'Nuestra América', p. 526.

63. Martí, 'The Truth', p. 49.

64. Ibid.

65. José Martí, 'Vindicación de Cuba' [1889], in *OE*, vol. II, pp. 336–42, p. 337.

66. Ibid.

67. Ibid., p. 340.

68. José Martí, 'Madre América' [1889], in *OE*, vol. II, pp. 495–503, p. 502.

69. Martí, 'Nuestra América', p. 520.

70. Martí, 'The Truth', pp. 53–4.

71. José Martí, 'Manifiesto de Montecristi' [1895], in *OE*, vol. II, pp. 475–83, p. 477.

72. José Martí, 'The False Myth of Latin Inferiority' [1883], in Martí, *On Education*, pp. 63–5, p. 63.

73. Martí, 'Madre América', p. 496.

74. Terán, 'El primer antiimperialismo', p. 8.

75. For an analysis of the Argentine cultural nationalists, see Chapter 4.

76. Ugarte, 'El peligro yanqui' [1901], cited in Noberto Galasso, *Manuel Ugarte: un argentino 'maldito'*, Ediciones del Pensamiento Nacional, Buenos Aires 1981, p. 24.

77. Ugarte, *El porvenir de la América Latina*, F. Sempere y Co., Editores, Valencia 1911, pp. 84–5.

78. Ugarte, 'El peligro yanqui', p. 24.
79. Ibid., p. 25.
80. Galasso, *Manuel Ugarte*, p. 71.
81. Manuel Ugarte, *El destino de un continente* [1923], Ediciones de la Patria Grande, Buenos Aires 1962, p. 315.
82. Ibid., p. 18.
83. Ibid., p. 19.
84. Ibid., pp. 15 and 24.
85. Ibid., p. 18.
86. Ugarte, *El porvenir*, p. 126. Cipriano Castro (1899–1908) was prepared to grant concessions to foreign businesses but proved unable to maintain the stability they sought for their operations. It was largely the Anglo-German-Italian blockade of Venezuela in 1902–03 that led to President Theodore Roosevelt's 'Corollary' to the Monroe Doctrine (1905), stipulating that the United States would assume the right to 'an international police power' in order to discipline 'persistent wrong-doing' on the part of Latin American governments. The United States aided one attempt to overthrow Castro, the 'Liberating Revolution' of 1903, maintained a naval presence off the coast of Venezuela in 1908, when Vice-President Gómez took advantage of Castro's absence in Europe to seize power, and helped to ensure that Castro did not attempt to return to his native land. See Malcolm Deas, 'Ecuador, Colombia and Venezuela', in Leslie Bethell, ed., *Cambridge History of Latin America*, vol. V, pp. 641–82, pp. 676–8.
87. Ugarte, *El destino*, pp. 213–14.
88. Ibid., p. 26.
89. Ugarte, *El porvenir*, p. 127.
90. Ugarte, *El destino*, pp. 215 and 276.
91. Ibid., p. 276.
92. John Gallagher and Ronald Robinson, 'The Imperialism of Free Trade', *Economic History Review*, no. 6 (1953), pp. 1–15. The idea was developed much more fully by Robinson in his article two decades later: 'Non-European foundations of European imperialism: sketch for a theory of collaboration', in Roger Owen and Bob Sutcliffe, eds, *Studies in the Theory of Imperialism*, Longman, London 1972, pp. 118–40.
93. Ugarte, *El destino*, p. 167.
94. Ugarte, *El porvenir*, p. 95.
95. Ibid., p. 138.
96. Ibid., p. 115.
97. Ibid., p. 113.
98. Ibid., pp. 147–9.
99. Ibid., p. 151.
100. Ibid., pp. 152 and 159–70.
101. Ibid., p. 167.
102. Ibid., p. 163.
103. Ibid., p. 169.
104. Ibid., p. 170.
105. During the many years that he spent in Paris, Ugarte mixed regularly with the leading European intellectuals of his time, including Miguel de Unamuno,

Maxim Gorky, Henri Barbusse and Upton Sinclair, and contributed to many of the most prestigious European reviews.

106. Galasso, *Manuel Ugarte*, pp. 99–100.
107. Ugarte, cited in ibid., p. 24.
108. Ugarte, *El porvenir*, p. xii.
109. Ibid., p. 188.
110. Galasso, *Manuel Ugarte*, pp. 31–6.
111. Ugarte, cited in ibid., p. 46.
112. Ugarte, *El porvenir*, p. 308.
113. *La Vanguardia*, cited in Jorge Abelardo Ramos, *Manuel Ugarte y la revolución latinoamericana*, Ediciones Coyoacán, Buenos Aires, 2nd edn, 1961, p. 32 (my emphasis).
114. See Richard J. Walter, *The Socialist Party of Argentina 1890–1930*, University of Texas Press, Austin 1977, p. 69.
115. Ugarte, cited in Galasso, *Manuel Ugarte*, p. 113.
116. Ugarte, *El porvenir*, p. vi.
117. Ibid., p. 67.
118. Ibid. p. xv.
119. Ibid., p. 94.
120. Ibid., p. 179.
121. Ibid., p. xiii.
122. Ugarte, *El destino*, p. 309.
123. Ugarte, *El porvenir*, p. 83.
124. Ibid., p. 310.
125. Víctor Raúl Haya de la Torre, *El antimperialismo y el Apra*, Ediciones Ercilla, Santiago 1936.
126. Mella, '¿Qué es el ARPA?', pp. 370–403.
127. Publisher's introduction, Haya de la Torre, *El antimperialismo*, p. 7.
128. Haya de la Torre, *El antimperialismo*, p. 34.
129. Ibid., p. 53.
130. Ibid., p. 21.
131. Ibid., p. 29.
132. Ibid., pp. 51–2.
133. Ibid., p. 36.
134. Ibid., p. 29.
135. Ibid., p. 104 (original emphasis).
136. Ibid., p. 37.
137. Ibid., pp. 38–9.
138. Ibid., p. 46. Profintern, the Red International of Labour Unions, was founded in Moscow in July 1921 but was effectively made redundant by the adoption of Popular Front, alliance-building policies in 1935.
139. Ibid., pp. 69–70.
140. Ibid., p. 69.
141. José Carlos Mariátegui, 'Punto de vista anti-imperialista' [Thesis presented to the First Latin American Communist Conference, May 1929], in *Ideología y política*, pp. 87–95, p. 90.
142. Ibid., pp. 92–3.
143. Ibid., p. 87.

144. Ibid., p. 89.
145. José Carlos Mariátegui, 'La unidad de la América indo-española' [1924], in *Temas de nuestra América*, vol. 12 of *Obras completas*, Empresa Editora Amauta, Lima 1960, pp. 13–17.
146. Ibid., p. 17.
147. José Carlos Mariátegui, 'Un congreso de escritores hispano-americanos' [1925], in *Temas de nuestra América*, pp. 17–21, p. 20.
148. José Carlos Mariátegui, 'El Ibero-americanismo y pan-americanismo' [1925], in *Temas de nuestra América*, pp. 26–30, p. 28.
149. José Carlos Mariátegui, 'El destino de norteamérica' [1927], in *Defensa del marxismo*, vol. 5 of *Obras completas*, Empresa Editora Amauta, Lima, 4th edn, 1969.
150. See, for example, Mariátegui's 'El imperialismo yanqui en Nicaragua' (1927) and 'Las elecciones en Estados Unidos y Nicaragua' (1928) in *Temas de nuestra América*, pp. 144–7 and pp. 147–50.
151. Mariátegui, 'Punto de vista anti-imperialista', p. 91.
152. José Carlos Mariátegui, 'Aniversario y balance' [*Amauta* editorial, September 1928], in *Ideología y política*, pp. 246–50, p. 248.
153. Ibid.
154. Ibid.
155. Mariátegui, 'Punto de vista anti-imperialista', p. 91.
156. Mariátegui, 'Aniversario y balance', p. 248.
157. Mariátegui, 'El Ibero-americanismo y pan-americanismo' [1925], in *Temas de nuestra América*, pp. 26–30, p. 29.
158. Charles Gates Dawes (1865–1951) was a US financier and statesman, most famous for the Dawes Plan for German reparations payments after the First World War. John Pierpont Morgan (1837–1913) was a US financier.
159. Mariátegui, 'El Ibero-americanismo', p. 29.
160. José Carlos Mariátegui, '¿Existe ya un pensamiento característicamente hispano-americano?', in *Temas de nuestra América*, pp. 22–6, p. 24.
161. Flores Galindo, *La agonía*, p. 66.
162. Mariátegui, '¿Existe ya un pensamiento?', p. 25.
163. Ibid., p. 24.
164. Mariátegui, 'Aniversario y balance', p. 249.
165. Mariátegui, 'El problema de las razas', p. 29.
166. Mariátegui, 'Aniversario y balance', p. 248.
167. David Rock, 'Argentina, 1930–1946', in Leslie Bethell, ed., *Argentina since Independence*, Cambridge University Press, Cambridge 1993, pp. 173–241, p. 205.
168. See Hipólito Yrigoyen, *Pueblo y gobierno*, vol. XII, no. II, *Política emancipadora; reforma patrimonial*, Editorial Raigal, Buenos Aires, 2nd edn, 1956, for presidential messages and congressional debates leading up to the founding of YPF.
169. See, for example, Terán, 'El primer antimperialismo', p. 8.
170. Ugarte, *El porvenir*, p. 131.
171. Manuel Ugarte, 'La amenaza europea', in *El porvenir*, pp. 133–8.
172. Galasso, *Manuel Ugarte*, pp. 88–90.
173. 'Programa', *La Patria*, 1916, in María de la Nieves Pinillos, ed., *Manuel Ugarte*, Ediciones de Cultura Hispánica, Madrid 1989, pp. 95–7, p. 96.

174. See Arturo Jauretche, *FORJA y la década infame*, A. Peña Lillo Editor, Buenos Aires 1973, p. 8.

175. Rojas, *Blasón de plata*, p. 230. On Gálvez, see above, Chapter 4, note 194.

176. A subsidiary of Standard Oil of New Jersey named the West India Oil Company (WICO) had been operating in Argentina since 1911, when it took over a refinery. By the end of the First World War, WICO had a virtual monopoly over Argentina's kerosene and gasoline markets. The company became the leading target of oil nationalism – both official and non-official – during the 1920s. See Carl Solberg, *Oil and Nationalism in Argentina: A History*, Stanford University Press, Stanford, CA 1979.

177. José Ingenieros, 'América Latina y el imperialismo' [1922], in *La universidad del porvenir y América Latina y el imperialismo*, Editorial Inquietud, Buenos Aires 1956, pp. 31–47, pp. 37 and 45.

178. Ibid., p. 46.

179. Jauretche, *FORJA*, p. 34.

180. Ibid., p. 35.

181. Ibid., p. 55.

182. Raúl Scalabrini Ortiz, *Política británica en el río de la Plata*, Editorial Plus Ultra, Buenos Aires, 5th edn, 1971.

183. Ibid., pp. 254 and 314.

184. Ibid., p. 46.

185. Tulio Halperín Donghi, 'El revisionismo histórico argentino como visión decadentista de la historia argentina', *Punto de Vista*, no. 23 (April 1985), pp. 9–17, p. 13.

186. See especially Scalabrini Ortiz's article 'Pueblo y soberanía. Principios básicos de un orden revolucionario' [1946], in Raúl Scalabrini Ortiz, *Yrigoyen y Perón*, Editorial Plus Ultra, Buenos Aires 1972, pp. 127–38.

187. Raúl Scalabrini Ortiz, *El hombre que está solo y espera*, Editorial Gleizer, Buenos Aires 1931.

188. Ibid., p. 13.

189. Ibid., p. 37.

190. Ibid., pp. 15–16.

191. Juan José Hernández Arregui, *Imperialismo y cultura*, Ediciones Hachea, Buenos Aires 1964, p. 116.

192. Scalabrini Ortiz, *El hombre que está solo*, p. 159.

193. Raúl Scalabrini Ortiz, 'Palabras de esperanza para la nueva generacion' [1947], in his *Yrigoyen y Perón*, pp. 139–51, p. 140.

194. Scalabrini Ortiz, *Política británica*, p. 12.

195. Ibid., p. 9.

196. Ibid., p. 30.

197. Ibid., p. 31.

198. Ibid., p. 39.

199. Ibid., p. 44.

200. Ibid., p. 38.

201. Ibid., p. 44.

202. Eva Perón, *Historia del peronismo*, p. 40.

203. Harold F. Peterson, *Argentina and the United States 1810–1960*, State University of New York Press, New York 1964, p. 347.

204. Ibid., p. 342.

205. Scalabrini Ortiz, *El hombre que está solo*, p. 166. Scalabrini Ortiz's full skit on what he saw as the fashionable *porteño* attitude towards the men of the United States ran as follows: 'The North Americans, under Ford's direction, are going to build a gigantic factory to produce standard men. At any rate, in the United States, individuals are not interested in social contact. They are inferior to women and they don't know their own strength. Waldo Frank wants to catechize them. Waldo Frank is a dreamer, whose mistake was to have been born at all. He is a *porteño*. He is magnificent! It's such a shame! A man like him would have suited us so well. And there they won't appreciate him at all.' Ibid., p. 161.

206. See Scalabrini Ortiz's articles in the *revista Qué* (Buenos Aires), 1956–58.

207. Jauretche, *FORJA*, p. 63.

208. Raúl Scalabrini Ortiz, *Historia de los ferrocarriles argentinos*, Editorial Reconquista, Buenos Aires 1940, p. 11 (all quotations in this paragraph thus far).

209. Ibid., pp. 12 and 14.

210. Ibid., p. 15.

211. For a selection of early anti-imperialist works, see Salvador Cisneros Betancourt *et al.*, *Antimperialismo y república*, Editorial de Ciencias Sociales, Instituto Cubano del Libro, Havana 1970. The main figures among these early anti-imperialists in Cuba were independence war veteran General Enrique Collazo (1848–1921), who published *Los americanos en Cuba* [1905], Editorial de Ciencias Sociales, Havana 1972, and *Cuba intervenida*, Imprenta Cubana, Havana 1910; César Gandarilla, a journalist from Oriente province and author of *Contra el yanqui*, Rambla, Bouza y Cía, Havana 1913; and Juan Gualberto Gómez, another veteran of 1895–98. For his speeches and writings, see Gualberto Gómez, *Antimperialismo y república*, Instituto Cubano del Libro, Havana 1975.

212. Juan Gualberto Gómez, 'Respuesta al gobernador militar Wood', in Cisneros Betancourt *et al.*, *Antimperialismo*, pp. 3–21.

213. Ann Wright, 'Intellectuals of an Unheroic Period of Cuban History, 1913–1923: The "*Cuba Contemporánea*" Group', *Bulletin of Latin American Research*, 7:1, 1988, pp. 109–22.

214. Ibid., p. 115.

215. See, for example, 'Manifiesto de la liga antimperialista de las Américas' [1925], which opens with 'Demanda para la evacuación de Panamá por tropas americanas'; in Mella, *Documentos y artículos*, pp. 197–9.

216. See Julio Antonio Mella, 'Imperialismo, tiranía, soviet' [1 June 1925], in *Documentos y artículos*, pp. 188–91.

217. Julio Antonio Mella, 'La política yanqui y la América Latina' [23 August 1924], in *Documentos y artículos*, pp. 106–9, p. 107.

218. Julio Antonio Mella, 'Cuba: un pueblo que jamás ha sido libre', in *Documentos y artículos*, pp. 174–83, p. 181.

219. Julio Antonio Mella, 'La conferencia panamericana es una emboscada contra los pueblos de América Latina' [31 December 1927 and 7 January 1928], in *Documentos y artículos*, pp. 345–9.

220. Emilio Roig de Leuchsenring, *La ocupación de la República Dominicana por los Estados Unidos y el derecho de las pequeñas nacionalidades de América*, Imprenta El Siglo XX, Havana 1919.

221. Carmen Almodóvar Muñoz, *Antología crítica de la historiografía cubana (período neocolonial)*, Editorial Pueblo y Educación, Havana 1989, p. 357.

222. Emilio Roig de Leuchsenring, *Nacionalismo e internacionalismo de Martí, con motivo de un grave error de política internacional cometido por nuestra Cancillería*, Imprenta El Siglo XX, Havana 1927.

223. Emilio Roig de Leuchsenring, *Historia de la Enmienda Platt: una interpretación de la realidad cubana* [1935], Editorial de Ciencias Sociales, Instituto Cubano del Libro, 3rd edn, 1973, pp. 303–33.

224. Louis Pérez, 'Cuba *c.* 1930–1959' in Leslie Bethell, ed., *Cambridge History of Latin America*, vol. VII, Cambridge University Press, Cambridge 1990, pp. 419–55, p. 438.

225. Examples of such works by Emilio Roig de Leuchsenring include: *Ideario Cubano II. Máximo Gómez*, Municipio de La Habana, Havana 1936; *Martí en España*, Cultural, s.a., Havana 1938; *La Habana: apuntes históricos*, Municipio de La Habana, Havana 1939; *13 conclusiones fundamentales sobre la guerra libertadora cubana de 1895*, El Colegio de México, Centro de Estudios Sociales, Mexico City 1945; and *Martí: síntesis de su vida*, no publisher given, Havana 1953.

226. Emilio Roig de Leuchsenring's short book produced for the centenary of Martí's birth in 1953, *Martí, antimperialista*, 2nd edn, Ministerio de Estado, Havana 1961, is an *oficialista*, laudatory account.

227. Emilio Roig de Leuchsenring, *Los Estados Unidos contra Cuba Libre* [1959], Editorial Oriente, 2 vols, Santiago 1982.

228. Almodóvar Muñoz, *Antología crítica*, p. 365.

229. Ibid., p. 364.

230. Emilio Roig de Leuchsenring, *Cuba no debe su independencia a los Estados Unidos*, Ediciones La Tertulia, Havana 1960, p. 153.

231. Emilio Roig de Leuchsenring, *La colonia superviva: Cuba a los veintidós años de república*, Imprenta El Siglo XX, Havana 1925, p. 18.

232. Ibid., p. 22.

233. Ibid., p. 19.

234. Ibid., pp. 19–20.

235. Ibid., p. 22.

236. *Washington Post* editorial, 23 March 1925, in Roig de Leuchsenring, *La colonia*, p. 29.

237. Roberto Fernández Retamar, 'Calibán' [1971], in his *Para el perfil definitivo del hombre*, Editorial Letras Cubanas, Havana 1985, pp. 219–89, pp. 232–3.

238. For details, see Chapter 1.

239. Fernández Retamar, 'Calibán', p. 219.

240. Ibid., p. 242.

241. Ibid., p. 238.

242. Ibid., p. 275.

243. Ibid., p. 270.

244. See, for example, Hernández Arregui, *Imperialismo y cultura*, p. 35.

245. See, for example, David Healy, *Drive to Hegemony: The United States in the Caribbean, 1898–1917*, University of Wisconsin Press, Madison 1988, pp. 278–86.

246. Manuel Scorza, cited in Martin, *Journeys*, p. 197.

247. Alberto van Klaveren, 'Europe and Latin America in the 1990s', in Abraham F. Lowenthal and Gregory F. Treverton, *Latin America in a New World*, Westview

Press, Boulder and Oxford 1994, pp. 81–104, p. 101. The book referred to is Alvaro Tirado Mejía, *América Latina se ha quedado sola*, Fundación Santillana para Iberoamérica, Bogotá 1989.

Chapter 6

1. Roger Bartra, *The Cage of Melancholy: Identity and Metamorphosis in the Mexican Character* [1987], trans. Christopher J. Hall, Rutgers University Press, New Brunswick, NJ 1992, p. 175.
2. At key moments in the formation of most nations, advocates of the national idea have assigned a crucial role to history. In England, often regarded as the first nation, it was under 'Good Queen Bess' (1558–1603) that national feeling was initially invoked not only in the drama and poetry that is now seen as the pinnacle of quintessentially English culture, but also in historical studies. The Society of Antiquaries was established, and Camden, Holinshed and Warner, among others, were encouraged to write their histories of England. In early-eighteenth-century Russia, Peter the Great (1682–1725), whose promotion of the concept of 'fatherland' helped to pave the way for the later development of Russian national feeling, commissioned histories of his own and previous reigns. In Germany, the consolidation of a cohort of professionals devoted to historical study was particularly important in developing a sense of national consciousness from 1830 to unification in 1871. Even in the United States of America, where the national myth is founded on a commitment to the future rather than the past, the writing of history came to be seen as important, especially in the aftermath of the Civil War and in the face of the challenges posed by large-scale immigration in the late nineteenth century. It is worth noting that the major cultural influence in nineteenth-century Spanish America, France, itself came relatively late (after defeat in the Franco-Prussian War of 1870–71) to an awareness of the importance of establishing a historical profession. See Greenfeld, *Nationalism*, especially pp. 67 and 197. On the United States, see Peter Novick, *That Noble Dream: The 'Objectivity Question' and the American Historical Profession*, Cambridge University Press, Cambridge and New York 1988.
3. On Europe and the United States, see John Kenyon, *The History Men*, Weidenfeld and Nicolson, London, 2nd edn, 1993, especially Chapter 5.
4. In Argentina, *Sur* was established in 1931; in Chile, there was the *Revista Chilena* (1917–30) and *Atenea* (1924–); in Cuba, *Bohemia* (1908–), the *Revista Bimestre Cubana* (1910–), the *Revista de Avance* and *Cuba Contemporánea* (1913–27); in Mexico, *Contemporáneos* (1928–31); and, in Peru, the *Mercurio Peruano* (1918–31) and Mariátegui's *Amauta* (1926–30). This is to name only the best-known. At a regional level, the most influential cultural review of the 1920s in Spanish America was undoubtedly the *Revista de Occidente* (1923–36), which was edited by Ortega y Gasset and published in Madrid, although many Spanish Americans were regular contributors.
5. Halperín Donghi, *El espejo de la historia*, p. 10.
6. The Argentine Marxist thinker José Aricó claimed that it was during his exile

in Mexico in the 1970s that he became fully acquainted with historical research techniques. Juan Carlos Portantiero, 'Creador de empresas imposibles', *La Ciudad Futura*, no. 30/31 (December 1991–February 1992), p. 34. On the influence of the Spaniards, see Javier Malagón Barcello, 'El historiador español exiliado en México', *Historia mexicana* vol. XXII, no. 1, 1972, pp. 98–111. A highly critical insider account of the state of the Mexican historical profession was published in 1992: see UNAM, *El historiador frente a la historia: Corrientes historiográficas actuales*, Instituto de Investigaciones Históricas, Mexico City 1992.

7. José Joaquín Brunner, *Informe sobre la educación superior en Chile*, FLACSO, Santiago 1986, p. 277.

8. Andrés Bello, 'Modo de estudiar la historia' [1848], in *Obras completas*, vol. XIX, Ediciones del Ministerio de Educación, Caracas 1957, pp. 243–52, p. 246.

9. Harold Davis, *Latin American Social Thought*, University Press of Washington, DC 1963, p. 192. See also Leopoldo Zea, *Dos etapas del pensamiento en Hispanoamérica*, El Colegio de México, Mexico City 1949.

10. Novick contends that nineteenth-century US historians misinterpreted Ranke by emphasizing his empiricism at the expense of his belief that the historian's task was to penetrate to the essences of the past. US historians' veneration of the 'objective' fact dovetailed, argues Novick, with their ideological tasks of overcoming partisanship and promoting social optimism. See *That Noble Dream*, especially pp. 72–85.

11. Davis, *Latin American Social Thought*, p. 192.

12. For example, in Chile, Domingo Amunátegui Solar began a compilation of the documents for Chilean history to 1845, which was later completed and published in thirty-seven volumes under the aegis of Valentín Letelier (1882–1919). By comparison, in Germany the first national collection of historical documents, *Monumenta Germaniae Historica*, appeared from 1826; in France the *Documents inédits relatif à l'histoire de France* appeared from 1835. Boyd Shafer *et al.*, *Historical Study in the West*, Meredith Corporation, New York 1968, p. 18.

13. The first comprehensive history of Argentina with aspirations to professional status was published from 1936 to 1942 under the auspices of the National Academy of History, in twelve volumes edited by Ricardo Levene: *Historia de la nación argentina (desde los orígenes hasta la organización definitiva en 1862)*, Editorial El Ateneo, Buenos Aires. This work was unusual in the comparative breadth of its subject matter and in its willingness to address relatively recent events; Levene devoted two volumes to the histories of Argentine provinces and brought Argentina's history up to the electoral reform law of 1912. Nevertheless, it was still basically little more than a relatively well-documented version of official *mitrista* history, with minimal acknowledgement of alternative interpretations. In Chile, Diego Barros Arana (1830–1907) published a sixteen-volume *Historia general de Chile* from 1884 to 1902. Later, Francisco Encina's *Historia de Chile desde la prehistoria hasta 1891*, 1940*ff.*, came to be considered the definitive work of national history. In Cuba, Ramiro Guerra y Sánchez's edited compendium, *Historia de la nación cubana*, Editorial Histórico de la nación cubana, Havana, 10 vols, 1952*ff.*, was very much in the positivist tradition, despite its appearance half a century later. The leading Mexican positivist, Justo Sierra (1848–1912), wrote a highly influential synthesis of Mexican history, *Evolución política del pueblo mexicano*, in 1900–02. No strictly positivist history of Peru was

produced: indeed, there was no major national history at all until Jorge
Basadre's *Historia de la República del Perú* began publication in 1939 (it totalled
sixteen volumes by 1968). Basadre's work was largely positivist in methodology,
but it also testified to other influences, notably the *Annales* school, in its
inclusion of cultural and social issues. In comparison, George Bancroft
(1800–91) worked on his ten-volume *History of the United States* from 1834 to
1875.

14. Victoria Ocampo, *Testimonios: quinta serie (1950–1957)*, Editorial Sur, Buenos
Aires 1957, p. 28.

15. Ezéquiel Martínez Estrada, *X-Ray of the Pampa*, [*Radiografía de la pampa*, 1933],
trans. Alain Swietlicki, University of Texas, Austin and London 1971,
pp. 379–81.

16. Ugarte, *El porvenir*, pp. 124–5.

17. See Arnaldo Córdova, *La ideología de la Revolución Mexicana*, Ediciones Era,
Mexico City 1973, p. 87. See also Alan Knight, 'The Peculiarities of Mexican
History: Mexico Compared to Latin America, 1821–1992', *Journal of Latin
American Studies*, 24 (supplement), 1992, pp. 99–144, p. 104.

18. On Gamio, see Chapter 4. The Mexican government began to sponsor a series
of Congresses of History from 1933 onwards. For the purposes of these events,
history was broadly defined to include archaeology, anthropology, ethnography
and history of art.

19. Aurora Loyo analyses both Jaime Torres Bodet, ed., *México y la cultura*, Secretaría de Educación Pública, Mexico City 1946; and various authors, *La cultura*,
(part IV of various authors, *México: 50 años de revolución*, Fondo de Cultura
Económica, Mexico City 1963) mainly from a cultural perspective rather than
in terms of the relationship between history and culture. Her article was very
helpful in stimulating my own ideas on the topic, however. See Aurora Loyo,
'Balances optimistas sobre la cultura en México: la visión de los intelectuales
"consagrados", 1946–62', *Historias* (Mexico City), no. 21 (October 1988–March
1989), pp. 149–63.

20. Jaime Torres Bodet, cited in Loyo, 'Balances optimistas', p. 152. Original
emphasis.

21. Ibid., p. 153.

22. Hugo Díaz Thomé, 'El mexicano y su historia', *Historia mexicana*, vol. II (June
1952–June 1953), no. 2 (6), pp. 248–58, p. 249.

23. Wigberto Jiménez Moreno, 'Cincuenta años de historia mexicana', *Historia
mexicana*, vol. I (July 1951–June 1952), no. 3, pp. 449–55, p. 449, my emphasis.

24. Emilio Uranga, 'Optimismo y pesimismo del mexicano', *Historia mexicana*, vol.
I (1951–52), no. 3, pp. 395–410.

25. Uranga, 'Optimismo', p. 399. See also Leopoldo Zea, *El positivismo en México*,
[1943], also published as *Positivism in Mexico*, trans. Josephine H. Schutte,
University of Texas Press, Austin 1974.

26. Silvio Závala, 'Síntesis de la historia del pueblo mexicano', in *Aproximaciones a
la historia de México*, no. 12 in the series 'México y lo mexicano', Editorial
Porrúa y Obregón, Mexico City 1953, pp. 9–45.

27. For a perceptive review of Mexican historiography, see Josefina Zoraída Váz-
quez, 'Textos de historia al servicio del nacionalismo', in Michael Riekenberg,
ed., *Latinoamérica: enseñanza de la historia, libros de textos y conciencia histórica*,

Alianza Editorial, Buenos Aires 1991, pp. 36–53. There was an interesting albeit brief early precursor of the post-revolutionary approach in the first major history of Mexican independence, which was written by a participant in events, Carlos María de Bustamante. His *Cuadro histórico de la revolución de la América mexicana* (1821–27) claimed that the Aztec empire was the basis of the new Mexican nation. In harking back to the pre-Columbian era, Bustamante continued the tradition of many of the eighteenth-century Jesuits exiled from New Spain, adding on the exploits of independence heroes. See Ernest Lemoine, *Bustamante y su 'apologética historia' de la revolución de* 1810, UNAM, Mexico City 1984. However, in the first major history of Mexico as a nation, published from 1849 to 1852, the conservative Lucas Alamán (1792–1853) argued that Mexican history began with the conquest and became national only when the country became an independent republic. Liberal historians, for example José María Luis Mora (1794–1850) and Lorenzo de Závala (1788–1836), had different views from conservatives about the colonial period but they concurred in rejecting Bustamante's interpretation and identifying independence as the founding moment of the Mexican nation. As Charles Hale has pointed out, the differences between liberals and conservatives in nineteenth-century Mexico can easily be exaggerated, particularly regarding the 1830s: 'Spanish traditions were important for the liberals, just as they were for the conservatives.' The differences lay in which aspects of the colonial heritage were emphasized. Charles Hale, 'José María Luis Mora and the Structure of Mexican Liberalism', *Hispanic American Historical Review*, vol. 45:2 (May 1965), pp. 196–227, p. 211.

28. Závala, 'Síntesis', quotations at pp. 12, 15, 18, 39, 35, 37, 43 and 44 respectively.
29. Díaz Thomé, 'El mexicano', p. 258.
30. Luis Villoro, 'La cultura mexicana de 1910 a 1960', *Historia mexicana*, vol. X (July 1960–June 1961), no. 2 (38), pp. 196–219, p. 217.
31. Leopoldo Zea, *Conciencia y posibilidad del mexicano*, in the series 'México y lo mexicano', Editorial Porrúa y Obregón, Mexico City 1952, p. 11.
32. Emilio Uranga, 'Optimismo', pp. 395–410. This work was later published in Zea's series, 'México y lo mexicano'.
33. Ibid., p. 405.
34. See Chapter 2.
35. Závala, 'Síntesis', p. 44.
36. See Stephen R. Niblo, *War, Diplomacy, and Development: The United States and Mexico 1938–1954*, Scholarly Resources, Wilmington, DE 1995.
37. Zea, *Conciencia y posibilidad*, pp. 32–3.
38. Ibid., p. 30.
39. Ibid., p. 33.
40. Silvio Závala, 'El mexicano en sus contactos con el exterior', *Aproximaciones*, pp. 47–66. No exact date is given for this essay, which must have been written in 1950 or 1951.
41. Ibid., p. 47.
42. Ibid.
43. Ibid., p. 52.
44. Ibid., p. 53.
45. Ibid., p. 58.

46. Ibid., p. 65.
47. Alberto Flores Galindo, 'La imagen y el espejo: la historiografía peruana 1910–1986', *Márgenes*, vol. II, no. 4 (December 1988), pp. 55–83; Magdalena Chocano, 'Ucronía y frustración en la conciencia histórica peruana', *Márgenes*, vol. I, no. 2 (October 1987), pp. 43–60, p. 45.
48. Jorge Basadre, 'Ucronías', in *Meditaciones sobre el destino histórico del Perú*, Editorial Huscarán, Lima 1947, pp. 135–41, p. 139.
49. Manuel González Prada, 'Perú y Chile', in *Pájinas libres* (*sic*), Ediciones Peisa, Lima 1976, pp. 69–80, especially p. 76.
50. José de la Riva Agüero, *La historia en el Perú*, Imprenta Nacional de Federico Barrionuevo, Lima 1910, p. 553.
51. This was the first interpretative synthesis of Peruvian history, excepting in school textbooks. Flores Galindo, 'La imagen', p. 57.
52. Ibid., p. 58.
53. Leading examples were Guillermo Lohmann and José Agustín de la Puente.
54. Manuel Burga, 'Desconocidos inventores de tradiciones', *Márgenes*, vol. I, no. 1 (March 1987), pp. 174–82, p. 182.
55. Ibid., p. 181.
56. Ibid.
57. Flores Galindo, 'La imagen', p. 61.
58. Ibid., p. 65.
59. Chocano, 'Ucronía', p. 55.
60. Hernando de Soto *et al.*, *El otro sendero: la revolución informal* [1986] (Instituto Libertad y Democracia, Lima, 6th edn, 1987) is typical of this trend, as is José Guillermo Nugent's work inspired by 'rational choice' theory. See J. G. Nugent, 'La construcción de la vida en el Perú como identidad histórica moderna', *Páginas* (Lima), no. 100 (December 1989).
61. Flores Galindo, 'La imagen', p. 69.
62. For surveys of Argentine historiography, see Joseph R. Barager, 'The Historiography of the Río de la Plata Area Since 1830', *Hispanic American Historical Review*, XXXIX:4 (November 1959), pp. 588–642; and Tulio Halperín Donghi, 'Un cuarto de siglo de historiografía argentina (1960–1985)', *Desarrollo económico* (Buenos Aires), 25:100 (January–March 1985), pp. 487–520.
63. Alberdi, cited in Arturo Jauretche, *Política nacional y revisionismo histórico*, Editorial A. Peña Lillo, Buenos Aires 1959, p. 5.
64. Nicolás Shumway, *The Invention of Argentina*, University of California Press, Berkeley and Oxford 1991, pp. 214–96.
65. Academia Nacional de la Historia, 'Fijación y caracter inalterable de los símbolos patrios', note and draft bill sent to the Ministry of Justice and Public Instruction, August 1942, reproduced in Ricardo Levene, *La cultura histórica y el sentimiento de la nacionalidad*, Espasa-Calpe Argentina, Buenos Aires 1942, pp. 38–44.
66. An earlier attempt at revisionism had been made in 1905, when historians of what became known as the Nueva Escuela Histórica (New School of History) claimed that they were making a fresh start in Argentine historiography. These historians, led by Ricardo Levene, were convinced above all of the virtues of scientific method, the application of which, they believed, would resolve all historical problems. Halperín Donghi argues that the main limitation of the

New School of History stemmed from this insistence on methodological rigour as the sole criterion for the study of history. Working on the premiss that a change of method was sufficient, they ended up by sustaining rather than revising the standard liberal interpretations, in relation to which their approach was 'at once polemical and parasitical'. Halperín Donghi, 'Un cuarto de siglo', p. 489.

67. Jauretche, *Política nacional*, p. 7.
68. For an analysis of the emergence of both types of nationalism, see Alberto Spektorowski, 'The Ideological Origins of Right and Left Nationalism in Argentina, 1930–43', *Journal of Contemporary History*, 29 (1994), pp. 155–84.
69. Tulio Halperín Donghi, 'El revisionismo histórico argentino como visión decadentista de la historia argentina', *Punto de Vista*, no. 23 (April 1985), pp. 9–17, p. 12.
70. Halperín Donghi, 'El revisionismo', p. 13.
71. Alberto Mondragón, 'El revisionismo histórico argentino: síntesis crítica de su historiografía', in Jauretche, *Política nacional*, pp. 67–79, p. 67.
72. See Hennessy, 'Argentines, Anglo-Argentines and others', p. 32. The rewriting of Rosas began with Carlos Ibarguren's book, *Juan Manuel de Rosas, su vida, su tiempo, su drama*, Librería la Facultad, Buenos Aires 1933. See also Manuel Gálvez, *Vida de Don Juan Manuel de Rosas* [1940], Editorial Tor, Buenos Aires, 5th edn, 1965.
73. Sigal, *Intelectuales y poder*, p. 28.
74. Jauretche, cited in ibid., p. 216.
75. Arturo Jauretche, *Los profetas del odio y la yapa* [1957], A. Peña Lillo Editor, Buenos Aires, 8th edn, 1984, p. 149. See also pp. 157–64 and 283–306. The first edition of this book sold 25,000 copies in two months.
76. The most extensive study of this generation is William H. Katra, *Contorno: Literary Engagement in Post-Peronist Argentina*, Associated University Presses, London and Toronto 1988.
77. David Viñas *et al.*, *Contorno: selección*, Centro Editor de América Latina, Buenos Aires 1981, p. iv.
78. *Situation* denoted the existential context that, according to Sartre, the individual had the potential to create for himself by exercising his capacity for freedom in relation to that part of himself determined by socio-economic conditions.
79. See Chapter 2.
80. Jorge Luis Borges, 'Una efusión de Martínez Estrada', *Sur*, no. 242 (September–October 1956), pp. 52–3.
81. Katra, *Contorno*, p. 74.
82. Ibid., pp. 35–6.
83. Ibid., p. 91.
84. Aricó, *La cola*, p. 52.
85. Terán, *Nuestros años sesentas*, p. 63.
86. Arthur P. Whitaker and David C. Jordan, *Nationalism in Contemporary Latin America*, Free Press, New York, and Collier-Macmillan, London 1966, p. 70.
87. Aricó, *La cola*, p. 174.
88. Echeverría wrote: 'Only collective reason is sovereign, not collective will'. See

his *Dogma Socialista* [1837], Librería La Facultad de Juan Roldán, Buenos Aires 1915, p. 185.

89. Juan José Sebreli, 'Celeste y colorado', *Sur*, no. 217–18 (November–December 1952), pp. 70–80, pp. 71–2.

90. Ibid., p. 78.

91. Editorial: 'Peronismo . . . ¿y lo otro?', *Contorno*, no. 7–8 (July 1956), in Viñas *et al.*, *Contorno*, pp. 144–7, p. 147.

92. Ibid., p. 146.

93. *Por la reconstrucción nacional*, special issue of *Sur*, no. 237 (November–December 1955).

94. Oscar Masotta, '*Sur* o el antiperonismo colonialista', *Contorno*, no. 7–8, in Viñas *et al.*, *Contorno*, pp. 148–64, pp. 154–5.

95. Ibid., p. 156.

96. Sigal, *Intelectuales y poder*, p. 183.

97. Leon Rozitchner, 'Experiencia proletaria y experiencia burguesa', in *Contorno*, no. 7–8, July 1956, pp. 3–4, cited in Carlos S. Fayt, *Naturaleza del peronismo*, Editores Viracocha SA, Buenos Aires 1967, p. 193.

98. Emilio Rodríguez Monegal, cited in Katra, *Contorno*, p. 27.

99. Terán, *Nuestros años sesentas*, pp. 54–5.

100. Katra, *Contorno*, p. 92. See Martínez Estrada, *X-Ray of the Pampa*, an analysis of the Argentine psyche that suspended historical time; and Eduardo Mallea, *Historia de una pasión argentina* [1940], Editorial Espasa-Calpe, Madrid, 6th edn, 1969, which was a meditation on Argentina's loss of spiritual direction.

101. Beatriz Sarlo, 'Intelectuales: ¿escisión o mimesis?', *Punto de Vista*, vol. VII, no. 25 (December 1985), pp. 1–6, p. 2.

102. Sigal, *Intelectuales y poder*, p. 29, n. 8. Sigal's book drew on 140 interviews with members of the Argentine intelligentsia of the 1960s.

103. Arturo Jauretche, cited in Norberto Galasso, ed., *Las polémicas de Jauretche* [1981], Los Nacionales Editores, Buenos Aires, 5th edn, 1983, p. 13.

104. Jauretche, article in *Dinámis*, June 1971, cited in Galasso, *Las polémicas*, p. 19.

105. Ibid., p. 23.

106. Félix Luna, *El 45: Crónica de un año decisivo* [1969], Editorial Sudamericano, Buenos Aires, 3rd edn, 1971.

107. Félix Luna, editorial, *Todo es Historia*, no. 60, cited in Galasso, *Las polémicas*, p. 28.

108. The phrase 'politics of history' came from Jauretche's own essay 'Política nacional y revisionismo histórico' (1959). Jauretche, 'Revisionismo y ecuanimidad', *Dinámis*, no. 44 (May 1972), cited in Galasso, *Las polémicas*, pp. 29–33.

109. Sigal, *Intelectuales y poder*, p. 30.

110. Allen Woll, *A Functional Past: The Uses of History in Nineteenth-century Chile*, Louisiana State University Press, Baton Rouge and London 1982, p. 191.

111. For example, Diego Barros Arana (also a diplomat and educator), Benjamín Vicuña Mackenna (a senator), José Victorino Lastarria (a diplomat), Miguel Luis Amunátegui (a presidential candidate) and his brother Gregorio Víctor, Andrés Bello (an educator), Ramón Sotomayor Valdés (a diplomat) and Crescente Errázuriz. Ibid., p. 1.

112. Cristián Gazmuri, 'La idea de decadencia nacional y el pensamiento político conservador chileno en el siglo XX', *Estudios Sociales*, 28–9 (2–3), 1981,

pp. 33–54, p. 48. My account of conservative historiography in Chile is largely drawn from this article.

113. Alberto Edwards, *Bosquejo histórico de los partidos políticos chilenos* [1903], Editorial del Pacífico, Santiago 1976.

114. Gazmuri, 'La idea de decadencia', p. 34.

115. The tradition was continued from the 1930s into the 1960s by the devout Catholic Jaime Eyzaguirre, whose ideal society was the Spain of Philip II and who saw anything that detracted from it as symptomatic of decline. See, for example, Jaime Eyzaguirre, *Fisonomía histórica de Chile* [1948], Editorial Universitaria, Santiago 1973. The most recent comprehensive version of *decadentismo* is Gonzalo Vial's *Historia de Chile 1891–1973*, Editorial Santillana, Santiago, vol. I, 1981 and vol. II, 1983. Vial served as a minister in Pinochet's government.

116. Luis Galdames, *A History of Chile*, trans. and ed. Isaac Joslin Cox, University of North Carolina Press, Chapel Hill 1941; see also Gazmuri, 'La idea de decadencia', pp. 46–7.

117. Galdames, *A History of Chile*, pp. 361 and 364.

118. Ibid., p. 369.

119. Ibid., p. 438.

120. Alberto Edwards Vives, *Páginas históricas*, Editorial Difusión Chilena, Santiago 1945, p. 8.

121. Alberto Edwards Vives, *La fronda aristocrática: historia política de Chile*, Editorial Pacífico, Santiago 1928.

122. Góngora, *Ensayo histórico*, p. 16.

123. Edwards was appointed head of the newly created Department of Geography in the Ministry of the Interior in August 1927. He had previously been Director of the Office of Statistics, from 1916 until 1926, when he became Minister of the Interior for a few months. He served as Minister of Education from October 1928 until April 1931. Ricardo Donoso, *Francisco A. Encina: simulador*, Editorial Ricardo Neupert, Santiago, 2 vols, vol. 1, 1969, p. 179.

124. Guillermo Feliú Cruz, *Francisco A. Encina, historiador*, Editorial Nascimento, Santiago 1967, p. 3.

125. Donoso, *Encina*, p. 11.

126. Encina, *Nuestra inferioridad económica, sus causas, sus consecuencias*, Editorial Universitaria, Santiago 1955, p. 16.

127. Feliú Cruz, *Encina*, p. 107.

128. Encina, *Nuestra inferioridad*, p. 212.

129. Ibid., p. 68.

130. Ibid.

131. Ibid., p. 6.

132. Ibid., pp. 6 and 29.

133. Ibid., pp. 108–9 and 112.

134. Ibid., p. 153.

135. Ibid., pp. 158 and 160.

136. Ibid., p. 203.

137. Gazmuri, 'La idea de decadencia', pp. 42–4.

138. Donoso accused Encina of plagiarism, not only of Barros Arana, but also of other Chilean historians and Clarence Haring. *Encina*, p. 13. Donoso's two-volume denunciation of Encina is exaggerated in parts, but his comparisons of

passages from Barros Arana and Encina leave little room for doubt about how much the latter was indebted to his predecessor.

139. Feliú Cruz, *Encina*, p. 11.

140. Francisco Encina, 'Prólogo a la primera edicion' [1938], *Historia de Chile*, vol. I, Editorial Nascimento, Santiago, 4th edn, 1955, p. v.

141. Francisco Encina, *Portales*, 2 vols [1934], Editorial Nascimento, Santiago 1964, vol. I, p. 223.

142. Ibid., pp. 266 and 295.

143. Bernardo Subercaseaux, 'Diego Portales: singularidad histórica e interpretación retórica' [1978], in *Historia, literatura y sociedad: ensayos de hermeneútica cultural*, Ediciones Documentas, Santiago 1991, pp. 11–40, p. 38. For a striking example of the phenomenon, see Augusto Pinochet, *Clase magistral . . . con motivo de la inauguración del año académico de la Universidad de Chile*, Santiago 6 April 1979.

144. Nicolás Palacios, *Raza chilena: libro escrito por un chileno i para los chilenos*, Imprenta i Litografía alemana, Valparaíso 1904.

145. Alberto Cabero, *Chile y los chilenos*, Editorial Nascimento, Santiago de Chile 1926.

146. In a collection of essays published during the Popular Unity government and clearly out of sympathy with it, one contributor called upon Chilean intellectuals to '[outline] the characteristic traits of Chileans and Chileanity [which] could serve as a basis to work out the best structures for the development of the national soul'. Enrique Campos Menéndez, 'Chile today: concern and hope', in Pablo Baraona *et al.*, *Chile: A Critical Survey*, trans. Fernando Vial Correa *et al.*, Institute of General Studies, Santiago 1972. See also Hernán Godoy Urzúa, *El carácter chileno* [1976], Editorial Universitaria, Santiago, 3rd edn, 1991.

147. Ariel Peralta Pizarro, *El mito de Chile*, Editorial Universitaria, Santiago 1971.

148. Ibid., p. 27.

149. Ibid., p. 221.

150. Ibid., pp. 222 and 226–7.

151. Ibid., p. 230.

152. A leading example of the former was Jacobo de la Pezuela, *Historia de la Isla de Cuba*, 4 vols, Madrid 1868–78; and of the latter, José Antonio Saco, *Historia de la esclavitud*, 3 vols, Barcelona and Paris 1875–79.

153. Robert Freeman Smith, 'Twentieth-century Cuban Historiography', *Hispanic American Historical Review*, XLIV:1 (February 1964), pp. 44–73, p. 52.

154. Manuel Moreno Fraginals, *Misiones cubanas en los archivos europeos*, Instituto Panamericano de Geografía e Historia, Mexico 1951.

155. Louis A. Pérez, Jr, 'In the Service of the Revolution: Two Decades of Cuban Historiography, 1959–79', *Hispanic American Historical Review*, 60:1 (February 1980), pp. 79–89, p. 81.

156. Louis A. Pérez, Jr, 'Scholarship and the State: Notes on *A History of the Cuban Republic*', *Hispanic American Historical Review*, 54:4 (November 1974), pp. 682–90.

157. Charles E. Chapman, *A History of the Cuban Republic: A Study in Hispanic American Politics*, Macmillan Co., New York 1927.

158. Joaquín Llaverías, *Historia de los archivos de Cuba*, Archivo Nacional de Cuba, Havana, 2nd edn, 1949, especially pp. 317–24.

159. Emilio Roig de Leuchsenring, 'La cubanidad en los congresos nacionales de historia', in Sociedad Cubana de Estudios Históricos e Internacionales, *Historia y cubanidad*, Havana 1943, pp. 7–19, p. 10.

160. Ibid., p. 9.

161. Ibid., p. 19.

162. 'Acta final', in Sociedad Cubana de Estudios Históricos, *Historia y cubanidad*, p. 39.

163. Freeman Smith, 'Twentieth-century Cuban Historiography', p. 49.

164. Ibid.

165. Duvon C. Corbitt, 'Cuban Revisionist Interpretations of Cuba's Struggle for Independence', *Hispanic American Historical Review*, vol. XLIII, no. 3, August 1963, pp. 395–404, p. 403.

166. Pérez, 'In the Service', pp. 82–3.

167. Halperín Donghi, 'Nueva narrativa y ciencias sociales hispanoamericanas en la década del sesenta', *El espejo de la historia*, pp. 277–94, p. 294.

168. Aricó, *La cola*, p. 74.

169. José Joaquín Brunner, 'La intelligentsia: escenarios institucionales y universos ideológicos', *Proposiciones* (Santiago), no. 18 (1990), pp. 180–91, p. 181.

170. Carpentier, *El reino de este mundo*, Editorial Universitaria, Chile 1967, p. 16.

171. Ibid.

172. Roberto González Echevarría, *Alejo Carpentier: The Pilgrim at Home*, Cornell University Press, Ithaca and London 1977, pp. 107 and 123.

173. Ibid., p. 125.

174. Ibid., p. 130.

175. Halperín Donghi, 'Nueva narrativa', pp. 283–5.

176. José Donoso, *The Boom in Spanish American Literature: A Personal History* [1972], trans. Gregory Kolovakos, Columbia University Press, New York 1977, p. 39.

177. Carlos Fuentes, *La región más transparente*, Ediciones Cátedra, Madrid 1982, pp. 196–7.

178. Halperín Donghi, 'Nueva narrativa', p. 281.

179. Eduardo Galeano, 'Apuntes sobre la memoria y sobre el fuego' [1989], in *El descubrimiento de América*, pp. 149–61, p. 150.

180. In Argentina, the first major publication by professional historians was the Colección Historia Argentina, edited by Tulio Halperín Donghi, the first volume of which appeared in 1972 (Alberto Rex González and José A. Pérez, *Argentina indígena: vísperas de la conquista*, Editorial Paidós, Buenos Aires 1972). Daniel Cosío Villegas oversaw a nine-volume *Historia moderna de México* published from 1955 to 1970.

181. Doris Sommer, 'Irresistible Romance: The Foundational Fictions of Latin America', in Homi K. Bhabha, ed., *Nation and Narration*, Routledge, London and New York 1990, pp. 71–98, p. 74.

182. González Echevarría, *Voice of the Masters*, p. 84.

183. Carlos Fuentes, *La nueva novela hispanoamericana*, Editorial Joaquín Mortiz, Mexico City 1969, p. 58.

184. Fuentes, *The Buried Mirror*, p. 313.

185. Carlos Fuentes, 'More than a Civilising Epic', *Guardian*, 12 October 1992.

320 NOTES TO PAGES 242-8

186. David Brading, *The First America: The Spanish Monarchy, Creole Patriots and the Liberal State, 1492–1867*, Cambridge University Press, Cambridge 1991.
187. Fuentes, 'More than a Civilising Epic'.
188. Mike González, 'Not So Much a Conquest After All?', in *Travesía*, vol. I, no. 2 (1992), pp. 171–6.
189. Fuentes, 'More than a Civilising Epic'.
190. She wrote, '. . . in both attitudes there is a degree of failing to recognize the reality of past or present which hinders the possibility of understanding, as if Peru and its history were such difficult and threatening subjects that it became necessary to embark on a detour of negative definitions, to establish a distance rather than looking for the most precise point of contact.' Chocano, 'Ucronía', p. 54.
191. E. H. Carr, *What is History?* [1961], Penguin Books, Harmondsworth 1987, p. 173.
192. Ernest Renan, 'What is a Nation?' [1882], trans. Martin Thom, in Bhabha, *Nation and Narration*, pp. 8–22, p. 11.
193. Benedict Anderson, *Imagined Communities: Reflections on the Origins and Spread of Nationalism*, Verso, London and New York, revised edn, 1991, pp. 199–201.
194. Tulio Halperín Donghi, 'Prologue to the 13th Edition', *The Contemporary History of Latin America*, trans. John Charles Chasteen, Macmillan, Basingstoke 1993, p. xii.

Conclusion

1. Castañeda, *Utopia Unarmed*, p. 289.
2. John King, *Magical Reels: A History of Cinema in Latin America*, Verso, London 1990, Chapters 6 and 7.
3. Sarah Radcliffe and Sallie Westwood, *Remaking the Nation: Place, Identity and Politics in Latin America*, Routledge, London and New York 1996, p. 14.
4. Hobsbawm and Ranger, *Invention of Tradition*.
5. Castañeda, *Utopia Unarmed*, p. 282, n. 28.
6. Jürgen Habermas, *The Structural Transformation of the Public Sphere: An Inquiry into a Category of Bourgeois Society*, trans. Thomas Burger with Frederick Lawrence, Polity Press, Cambridge 1992, p. xvii.
7. Hilda Sabato, 'Citizenship, Political Participation and the Formation of the Public Sphere in Buenos Aires, 1850s–1880s', *Past and Present*, no. 136 (August 1992), pp. 139–63.
8. Lewis A. Coser, *Men of Ideas: A Sociologist's View*, Free Press, New York, and Collier Macmillan, London 1965, p. 137.
9. In his essay, 'Mi raza' (1893), Martí contended that for either blacks or whites to identify themselves in terms of their race was to provoke racism in the other, and that 'Cuban is more than white, more than mulatto, more than black'. *OE*, vol. III, pp. 217–19, pp. 217–18. See also 'Discurso en conmemoración del 10 de octubre' [1887] in *OE*, vol. II, pp. 227–38; 'Vindicación de Cuba' [1889], 'Con todos y para el bien de todos' [1891], and 'Persona y patria' [1893], *OE*, vol. III, pp. 203–7.

10. See various articles in Fernando Ortiz, *Orbita*, selection and prologue by Julio Le Riverend, UNEAC, Havana 1973.

11. Fernando Ortiz, 'Los factores humanos de la cubanidad' [1940], in *Orbita*, pp. 149–57, p. 154.

12. Ibid., p. 156.

13. Ibid., p. 157.

14. Mallon, *Peasant and Nation*, p. 311.

15. Claudio Lomnitz-Adler, *Exits from the Labyrinth: Culture and Ideology in the Mexican National Space*, University of California Press, Berkeley 1992, p. 255.

16. Mariátegui, *Siete ensayos*, p. 329.

17. Vasconcelos, *La raza cósmica*, p. 204.

18. Hobsbawm, 'Nationalism', p. 317. As early as the 1920s, about 40 per cent of generals on active service were immigrants' sons, which suggests that the military was a major vehicle for the social advancement of second-generation immigrants. Robert A. Potash, *The Army and Politics in Argentina, 1945–62*, Athlone Press, London 1980, p. 5.

19. See Edward Milenky, *Argentina's Foreign Policies*, Westview Press, Boulder, CO 1978, for an interpretation that emphasizes how these two types of nationalism have alternated in influencing foreign policy, to the detriment of its effectiveness. See also Carlos Escudé, 'Argentine Territorial Nationalism', *Journal of Latin American Studies*, 20:1 (May 1988), pp. 139–65.

20. Carlos Moore, *Castro, the Blacks, and Africa*, Center for Afro-American Studies, University of California, Los Angeles 1988. Moore argues that Castro used Martí's phrase 'Cuban is more than white, more than mulatto, more than black' in order to justify a strategy of evading the race issue (pp. 26–7).

21. Mallon, *Peasant and Nation*, p. 311.

22. Ibid., p. 19.

23. Whitaker and Jordan, *Nationalism*, p. 106.

24. José Aricó, 'Mariátegui: el descubrimiento de la realidad', *Debates*, no. 1 (October–November 1985), pp. 9–11, p. 9.

25. Ibid.

26. Daniel Pécaut, *Entre le Peuple et la Nation: Les intellectuels et la politique au Brésil*, Éditions de la Maison des sciences de l'homme, Paris 1989, p. ix.

27. Ibid., p. 14.

28. Richard Morse, 'The Multiverse', pp. 15–24.

29. Pécaut, *Entre le Peuple*, p. ix.

30. For a highly critical account of the influence of Freyre's work, see Michael George Hanchard, *Orpheus and Power: The Movimento Negro of Rio de Janeiro and São Paulo, Brazil, 1945–1988*, Princeton University Press, NJ 1994, especially pp. 45–56, quotation p. 8. For a refutation of the myth of 'racial democracy', see Florestan Fernandes, *The Negro in Brazilian Society*, Columbia University Press, New York 1969.

31. Pécaut, *Entre le Peuple*, p. 59.

32. Ibid., p. 62.

33. Roger Bastide, cited in Castañeda, *Utopia Unarmed*, p. 281.

34. Beatriz Sarlo, 'El intelectual socialista', *La Ciudad Futura*, no. 30/31, December 1991–February 1992, p. 28.

35. Allan Stoekl, *Agonies of the Intellectual: Commitment, Subjectivity and the Performative*

in the Twentieth-century French Tradition, University of Nebraska Press, Lincoln and London 1992, p. 2.

36. Michel Foucault, *Power/Knowledge: Selected Interviews and Writings, 1972–77*, ed. Colin Gordon, Harvester Press, Brighton 1980.

37. José Joaquín Brunner, 'Preguntas a José Joaquín Brunner', *Revista de Crítica Cultural* (Santiago), vol. I, no. 1 (May 1990), pp. 20–5, p. 22.

38. See José Joaquín Brunner, '¿Pueden los intelectuales sentir pasión o tener interés en la democracia?, *Documento de trabajo*, no. 303, FLACSO, Santiago de Chile July 1986.

39. Brunner, 'Preguntas', p. 20.

40. Ibid.

41. Sergio Zermeño, 'Intellectuals and the State in the "Lost Decade"', in Harvey, *Mexico: Dilemmas of Transition*, p. 282.

42. Ibid., p. 297, n. 6.

43. Ibid., p. 285.

44. *Mexico and NAFTA Report* (London), 2 December 1993, p. 8. See also Gabriel Zaid, 'Razones para la exención', in *Vuelta* (Mexico City), vol. 17, no. 196 (March 1993), pp. 43–7.

45. Mauricio Schoijet, 'La ciencia en México', *Nueva Sociedad* (Caracas), no. 107, May–June 1990, pp. 138–44, p. 139.

46. Octavio Rodríguez Araujo, 'Neoliberalismo, crisis y universidades en México', *Nueva Sociedad*, no. 107, pp. 145–53, p. 150.

47. Ibid., p. 151.

48. Oscar Shuberoff, rector of UBA, in 'La crisis del sistema universitario argentino', *La Ciudad Futura*, April 1992, pp. 12–15, p. 12.

Select Bibliography

Primary Texts by Spanish American Intellectuals

José María Arguedas, *Formación de una cultura nacional indoamericana*, Siglo XXI, Mexico City 1975.

Víctor Andrés Belaúnde, *La realidad nacional* [1930], publisher unidentified, Lima, 3rd edn, 1964.

Mario Benedetti, *El escritor latinoamericano y la revolución posible*, Editorial Nueva Imagen, Buenos Aires 1987.

Rufino Blanco-Fombona, 'La evolución política y social de Hispano-América' [1911], in his *Obras selectas*, Ediciones Edimé, Madrid and Caracas 1958.

Alberto Cabero, *Chile y los chilenos*, Editorial Nascimento, Santiago 1926.

Salvador Cisneros Betancourt *et al.*, *Antimperialismo y república*, Editorial de Ciencias Sociales, Instituto Cubano del Libro, Havana 1970.

Daniel Cosío Villegas, *Memorias*, Editorial Joaquín Mortiz, Mexico City 1976.

Rubén Darío, *Obras completas*, ed. Sanmiguel Raimúndez and Emilio Gasco Contell, Editorial Afrodísio Aguado, Madrid 1950–55, 20 vols.

——*Autobiografía* [1912], Editorial Universitaria, Buenos Aires 1968.

——*Historia de mis libros* [1913], Editorial Nueva Nicaragua, Managua 1988.

——*Escritos inéditos de Rubén Darío recogidos de periódicos de Buenos Aires y anotados por E. K. Mapes*, Instituto de las Españas, New York 1938.

——*Escritos dispersos de Rubén Darío*, ed. Pedro Luis Barcia, 2 vols, Universidad Nacional de La Plata, La Plata 1968 and 1977.

José Donoso, *The Boom in Spanish American Literature: A Personal History* (*Historia personal del 'boom'*, 1972), trans. Gregory Kolovakos, Columbia University Press, New York 1977.

Alberto Edwards Vives, *La fronda aristocrática: historia política de Chile*, Editorial Pacífico, Santiago 1928.

Francisco Encina, *Nuestra inferioridad económica, sus causas, sus consecuencias* [1912], Editorial Universitaria, Santiago 1955.

Roberto Fernández Retamar, 'Calibán' [1971], in his *Para el perfil definitivo del hombre*, Editorial Letras Cubanas, Havana 1985.

Carlos Fuentes, *La nueva novela hispanoamericana*, Editorial Joaquín Mortiz, Mexico City 1969.

——*Myself with Others: Selected Essays*, Pan Books, London 1989.

——*The Buried Mirror: Reflections on Spain and the New World*, André Deutsch, London 1992.

Eduardo Galeano, *El descubrimiento de América que todavía no fue y otros ensayos*, Alfadil Ediciones, Caracas 1991.

Rómulo Gallegos, *Una posición en la vida*, Ediciones Humanismo, Mexico 1954.

Manuel Gálvez, *El diario de Gabriel Quiroga: opiniones sobre la vida argentina*, Arnoldo Moen, Editores, Buenos Aires 1910.

——*El solar de la raza* [1913], Editorial La Facultad, Buenos Aires, 5th edn, 1930.

——*Recuerdos de la vida literaria, vol. I: Amigos y maestros de mi juventud* [1944], Librería Hachette, Buenos Aires 1961.

Manuel Gamio, *Forjando patria* [1916], Editorial Porrúa, Mexico City 1982.

——'The Indian Basis of Mexican Civilization', in José Vasconcelos and Manuel Gamio, *Aspects of Mexican Civilization*, University of Chicago Press, Chicago, IL 1926.

Víctor Raúl Haya de la Torre, *El antimperialismo y el Apra*, Ediciones Ercilla, Santiago 1936.

José Ingenieros, 'América Latina y el imperialismo' [1922], in *La universidad del porvenir y América Latina y el imperialismo*, Editorial Inquietud, Buenos Aires 1956.

Arturo Jauretche, *Los profetas del odio y la yapa* [1957], A. Peña Lillo Editor, Buenos Aires, 8th edn, 1984.

——*Política nacional y revisionismo histórico*, A. Peña Lillo Editor, Buenos Aires 1959.

——*FORJA y la década infame*, A. Peña Lillo Editor, Buenos Aires 1973.

——*Las polémicas de Jauretche* [1981], ed. Norberto Galasso, Los Nacionales Editores, Buenos Aires, 5th edn, 1983.

Leopoldo Lugones, *Obras en prosa*, Editorial Aguilar, Mexico City 1962, especially 'El payador' [1916].

Eduardo Mallea, *History of an Argentine Passion* [*Historia de una pasión argentina*, 1940], trans. Myron I. Lichtblau, Latin American Literary Review Press, Pittsburgh 1983.

José Carlos Mariátegui, *Obras completas*, 20 vols, Biblioteca Amauta, Lima 1959–70.

——*Seven Interpretive Essays on Peruvian Reality* [*Siete ensayos de interpretación de la realidad peruana*, 1928], trans. Margory Urquidi, University of Texas Press, Austin and London 1971.

——*Correspondencia 1915–1930*, ed. Antonio Melis, 2 vols, Biblioteca
   Amauta, Lima 1984.
José Martí, *Obras escogidas*, Centro de Estudios Martianos, Editora Política,
   Havana, 3 vols, 1978–81.
——*Inside the Monster: Writings on the United States and American Imperialism*,
   ed. Philip S. Foner, trans. Elinor Randall, Monthly Review Press, New
   York and London 1975.
——*Our America: Writings on Latin America and the Struggle for Independence*,
   ed. Philip S. Foner, trans. Elinor Randall, Juan Onís and Roslyn Held
   Forner, Monthly Review Press, New York 1977.
——*José Martí on Education: Articles on Educational Theory and Pedagogy*, ed.
   Philip S. Foner, trans. Elinor Randall, Monthly Review Press, New York
   1979.
Ezéquiel Martínez Estrada, *X-Ray of the Pampa* [*Radiografía de la pampa*,
   1933], trans. Alain Swietlicki, University of Texas Press, Austin and
   London 1971.
Julio Antonio Mella, *Documentos y artículos*, Editorial de Ciencias Sociales,
   Instituto Cubano del Libro, Havana 1975.
Pablo Neruda, *Memoirs* [*Confieso que he vivido: memorias*, 1974], trans. Hardie
   St Martin, Penguin, Harmondsworth 1977.
Fernando Ortiz, *Orbita*, Selection and prologue by Julio Le Riverend,
   UNEAC, Havana 1973.
Nicolás Palacios, *Raza chilena: libro escrito por un chileno i para los chilenos*,
   Imprenta i Litografía alemana, Valparaíso 1904.
Octavio Paz, *The Labyrinth of Solitude: Life and Thought in Mexico* [*El laberinto
   de la soledad*, 1950], trans. Lysander Kemp, Penguin, Harmondsworth
   1985.
——*Alternating Current* [*Corriente alterna*, 1967], trans. Helen R. Lane,
   Wildwood House, London 1974.
——*The Other Mexico: Critique of the Pyramid* [*Posdata*, 1970], trans. Lysander
   Kemp, Grove Press, New York 1972.
——*El ogro filantrópico: historia y política 1971–1978*, Editorial Seix Barral,
   Barcelona 1979.
——*Tiempo nublado*, Editorial Seix Barral, Barcelona 1983.
Samuel Ramos, *Obras completas*, UNAM, Mexico City, 3 vols 1975–77.
——*El perfil del hombre y la cultura en México*, Editorial Pedro Robredo,
   Mexico City 1934. Translated as *Profile of Man and Culture in Mexico*, trans.
   Peter G. Earle, Texan Pan-American Series, Austin, Texas 1962.
Alfonso Reyes, *Vocación de América (Antología)*, Fondo de Cultura
   Económica, Mexico City 1989.
José Enrique Rodó, *Obras completas*, ed. Emir Rodríguez Monegal, Editorial
   Aguilar, Madrid 1957.
——*Ariel* (1900), ed. Gordon Brotherston, Cambridge University Press,

Cambridge 1967. Translated as *Ariel*, trans. Margaret Sayers Peden, with a prologue by Carlos Fuentes, University of Texas Press, Austin 1988.

Emilio Roig de Leuchsenring, *La ocupación de la República Dominicana por los Estados Unidos y el derecho de las pequeñas nacionalidades de América*, Imprenta El Siglo XX, Havana 1919.

——*La colonia superviva: Cuba a los veintidós años de república*, Imprenta El Siglo XX, Havana 1925.

——*Historia de la Enmienda Platt: una interpretación de la realidad cubana* [1935], Editorial de Ciencias Sociales, Instituto Cubano del Libro, Havana, 3rd edn, 1973.

——*Cuba no debe su independencia a los Estados Unidos* [1949], Ediciones La Tertulia, Havana 1960.

——*Martí, anti-imperialist* [*Martí, antimperialista*, 1953], trans. María Juana Cazabón, Instituto del Libro, Havana 1967.

——*Los Estados Unidos contra Cuba Libre* [1959], Editorial Oriente, Santiago, 2 vols 1982.

——*Tradición antimperialista de nuestra historia*, Editorial de Ciencias Sociales, Havana 1977.

Ricardo Rojas, *Cosmópolis*, Garnier Hermanos Libreros-Editores, Paris 1908.

——*La restauración nacionalista: crítica de la Educación Argentina y Bases para una Reforma en el estudio de las Humanidades Modernas* [1909], A. Peña Lillo Editor, Buenos Aires 1971.

——*Blasón de plata*, Martín-García Editores, Buenos Aires 1912.

——*La argentinidad: ensayo histórico sobre nuestra conciencia nacional en la gesta de emancipación 1810–1816*, Editorial La Facultad de Juan Roldán, Buenos Aires 1916.

——*Eurindia: ensayo de estética sobre las culturas americanas* [1924], Editorial Losada, Buenos Aires 1951.

Domingo Faustino Sarmiento, *A Sarmiento Anthology*, trans. S. E. Grummon, ed. A. W. Bunkley, Kennikat Press, Princeton, NJ 1948; reissue, Port Washington, NY 1972.

Raúl Scalabrini Ortiz, *El hombre que está solo y espera*, Editorial Gleizer, Buenos Aires 1931.

——*Política británica en el río de la Plata* [1939], Editorial Plus Ultra, Buenos Aires, 5th edn, 1971.

——*Historia de los ferrocarriles argentinos*, Editorial Reconquista, Buenos Aires 1940.

——*Los ferrocarriles deben ser del pueblo argentino*, Editorial Reconquista, Buenos Aires 1946.

——*Yrigoyen y Perón*, Editorial Plus Ultra, Buenos Aires 1972.

Manuel Ugarte, *El porvenir de la América Latina*, F. Sempere y Co. Editores, Valencia 1911.

——*El destino de un continente* [1923], Ediciones de la Patria Grande, Buenos Aires 1962.

César Vallejo, *Contra el secreto profesional*, Mosca Azul Editores, Lima 1973.

——*The Mayakovsky Case*, trans. R. Schaaf, Curbstone Press, Willimantic, CT 1982.

——*Autopsy on Surrealism*, trans. R. Schaaf, Curbstone Press, Willimantic, CT 1986.

——*La cultura peruana: crónicas*, ed. Enrique Ballón Aguirre, Mosca Azul Editores, Lima 1987.

Mario Vargas Llosa, *José María Arguedas: entre sapos y halcones*, Ediciones cultura hispánica del Centro Iberoamericano de Cooperación, Madrid 1978.

——*Contra viento y marea*, Seix Barral, Barcelona, 2 vols, 1986.

——*A Writer's Reality*, Faber and Faber, London 1991.

——*A Fish in the Water: A Memoir* [*El pez en el agua*, 1993], trans. Helen Lane, Faber and Faber, London 1994.

José María Vargas Vila, *Ante los bárbaros: los Estados Unidos y la guerra*, Imprenta de José Anglada, Barcelona, 2nd edn, 1918.

José Vasconcelos, *La raza cósmica: misión de la raza iberoamericana* [1925], Espasa-Calpe Mexicana, Mexico City, 3rd edn, 1966. Translated in *The Cosmic Race: A Bilingual Edition*, trans. Didier T. Jaén, Johns Hopkins University Press, Baltimore and London, 2nd edn, 1997.

——'The Latin American Basis of Mexican Civilization', in José Vasconcelos and Manuel Gamio, *Aspects of Mexican Civilization*, University of Chicago Press, Chicago, IL 1926.

——*Indología: una interpretación de la cultura Ibero-Americana*, Agencia Mundial de Librería, Paris 1927.

——*Memorias*, Fondo de Cultura Económica, Mexico City, 2 vols, 1982. Translated as *A Mexican Ulysses: An Autobiography*, trans. W. R. Crawford, Greenwood Press, Westport, CO 1963.

David Viñas *et al.*, *Contorno: selección*, Centro Editor de América Latina, Buenos Aires 1981.

Silvio Závala, *Aproximaciones a la Historia de México*, series 'México y lo mexicano', no. 12, Editorial Porrúa y Obregón, Mexico City 1953.

Leopoldo Zea, *Conciencia y posibilidad del mexicano*, series 'México y lo mexicano', Editorial Porrúa y Obregón, Mexico City 1952.

Secondary Works

1. On nationalism and national identity in Spanish America

Victor Alba, *Nationalists without Nations: The Oligarchy versus the People in Latin America*, Praeger, New York 1968.

Benedict Anderson, *Imagined Communities: Reflections on the Origins and Spread of Nationalism*, Verso, London and New York 1983 and revised edn, 1991.

Jules Benjamin, 'The *Machadato* and Cuban Nationalism, 1928–1932', *Hispanic American Historical Review*, 55:1 (February 1975), pp. 66–91.

David Brading, *The Origins of Mexican Nationalism*, Cambridge University Press, Cambridge 1985.

Simon Collier, 'Nationality, Nationalism, and Supranationalism in the Writings of Simón Bolívar', *Hispanic American Historical Review*, 63:1, 1983, pp. 37–64.

Eric J. Hobsbawm, 'Nationalism and Nationality in Latin America', in Bouda Etemad, Jean Baton and Thomas David, eds, *Pour une histoire économique et sociale internationale: mélanges offerts à Paul Bairoch*, Éditions Passé Présent, Geneva 1995, pp. 313–23.

John Lynch, *The Spanish American Revolutions, 1808–1826*, W. W. Norton, New York 1973, and 2nd edn 1986.

Florencia Mallon, *Peasant and Nation: The Making of Postcolonial Mexico and Peru*, University of California Press, Berkeley and London 1995.

Gerhard Masur, *Nationalism in Latin America: Diversity and Unity*, Macmillan, New York 1966.

Anthony Pagden, 'Identity Formation in Spanish America', in Nicholas Canny and Anthony Pagden, eds, *Colonial Identity in the Atlantic World, 1500–1800*, Princeton University Press, Princeton 1988, pp. 51–93.

Fredrick B. Pike, 'The Problem of Identity and National Destiny in Peru and Argentina', in Fredrick B. Pike, ed., *Latin American History: Select Problems*, Harcourt, Brace and World, New York 1969, pp. 173–222.

Sarah Radcliffe and Sallie Westwood, *Remaking the Nation: Place, Identity and Politics in Latin America*, Routledge, London and New York 1996.

Hilda Sabato, 'Citizenship, Political Participation and the Formation of the Public Sphere in Buenos Aires, 1850s–1880s', *Past and Present*, no. 136 (August 1992), pp. 139–63.

Hugh Seton-Watson, *Nations and States: An Enquiry into the Origins of Nations and the Politics of Nationalism*, Westview Press, Boulder, CO 1977, Chapter 5.

Doris Sommer, *Foundational Fictions: The National Romances of Latin America*, University of California Press, Berkeley 1991.

Robert Swansborough, *The Embattled Colossus: Economic Nationalism and United States Investors in Latin America*, University Press of Florida, Gainesville 1976.

Mary Kay Vaughan, *Cultural Politics in Revolution: Teachers, Peasants, and Schools in Mexico, 1930–1940*, University of Arizona Press, Tucson 1997.

Claudio Veliz, 'Centralism and Nationalism in Latin America', in Howard J. Wiarda, ed., *Politics and Social Change in Latin America: The Distinct Tradition*, University of Massachusetts Press, 1974.

Arthur P. Whitaker, *Nationalism in Latin America, Past and Present*, University of Florida Press, Gainesville 1962.

2. *On intellectuals in Spanish America*

Christopher Abel and Nissa Torrents, eds, *José Martí: Revolutionary Democrat*, Athlone Press, London 1986.

Jorge Abelardo Ramos, *Manuel Ugarte y la revolución latinoamericana*, Ediciones Coyoacán, Buenos Aires, 2nd edn, 1961.

Orlando Albornoz, *Education and Society in Latin America*, St Antony's/ Macmillan, Basingstoke 1993.

Carlos Altamirano and Beatriz Sarlo, *Literatura/Sociedad*, Librería Hachette, Buenos Aires 1983.

Raquel Ángel, ed., *Rebeldes y domesticados: los intelectuales frente al poder*, Ediciones El Cielo por Asalto, Buenos Aires 1992.

Manuel Aquézolo Castro, ed., *La polémica del indigenismo*, Mosca Azul Editores, Lima 1976.

Ruth E. Arboleyda and Luis Vásquez León, *Mariátegui y el indigenismo revolucionario peruano*, Instituto Nacional de Antropología e Historia, Mexico City 1979.

José Aricó, *La cola del diablo: itinerario de Gramsci en América Latina*, Puntosur, Buenos Aires 1988.

Alicia Barrios and José Joaquín Brunner, *La sociología en Chile: instituciones y practicantes*, FLACSO, Santiago 1988.

Roger Bartra, *The Cage of Melancholy: Identity and Metamorphosis in the Mexican Character* [*La jaula de la melancolía*, 1987], trans. Christopher Hall, Rutgers University Press, New Brunswick, NJ 1992.

Mario Benedetti, *Genio y figura de José Enrique Rodó*, Editorial Universitaria de Buenos Aires, 1966.

John Beverley, Michael Aronna and José Oviedo, eds, *The Postmodernism Debate in Latin America*, Duke University Press, Durham, USA 1995.

José Joaquín Blanco, *Se llamaba Vasconcelos: una evocación crítica*, Fondo de Cultura Económica, Mexico City 1977.

José Joaquín Brunner, *Los intelectuales: esbozos y antecedentes para la constitución del campo de estudios*, Documento de trabajo, no. 135, 2 vols, FLACSO, Santiago March 1982.

——*América Latina: cultura y modernidad*, Editorial Grijalbo, Mexico City 1992.

Roderic A. Camp, *Intellectuals and the State in Twentieth-century Mexico*, University of Texas Press, Austin 1985.

Roderic A. Camp, Charles A. Hale and Josefina Zoraída Vásquez, eds, *Los intelectuales y el poder en México*, El Colegio de México/UCLA Latin American Center Publications, Mexico City 1991.

Eduardo José Cárdenas and Carlos Manuel Payá, *El primer nacionalismo argentino en Manuel Gálvez y Ricardo Rojas*, Editorial A. Peña Lillo, Buenos Aires 1978.

Gabriel Careaga, *Los intelectuales y la política en México*, Editorial Extemporáneos, Mexico City 1971.

Lourdes Casal, *El caso Padilla: literatura y revolución en Cuba*, Ediciones Universal, Miami 1971.

Jorge Castañeda, *Utopia Unarmed: The Latin American Left after the Cold War* [*La utopía desarmada*], Knopf, New York 1993.

Jesús Chavarría, *José Carlos Mariátegui and the Rise of Modern Peru, 1890–1930*, University of New Mexico Press, Albuquerque 1979.

James D. Cockcroft, *Intellectual Precursors of the Mexican Revolution, 1900–1913*, University of Texas Press, Austin and London 1968.

Jorge Cornejo Pilar, *Intelectuales, artistas y Estado en en Perú del siglo XX*, Cuadernos de Historia, no. XVII, Universidad de Lima, 1993.

Harold Davis, *Latin American Social Thought*, University Press of Washington, DC, 1961.

Gabriella de Beer, *José Vasconcelos and His World*, Las Americas Publishing Company, New York 1966.

José Deustua and José Luis Renique, *Intelectuales, indigenismo y descentralismo en el Perú, 1897–1931*, Centro de Estudios Rurales Andinos 'Bartolomé de Las Casas', Cuzco 1984.

Claude Fell, *José Vasconcelos: los años del águila (1920–1925)*, UNAM, Mexico City 1989.

Alberto Flores Galindo, *La agonía de Mariátegui*, Editorial Revolución, Madrid 1991.

Will Fowler, ed., *Ideologues and Ideologies in Latin America*, Greenwood Press, Westport, CO and London 1997.

Jean Franco, *The Modern Culture of Latin America: Society and the Artist*, Pall Mall Press, London 1967.

Norberto Galasso, *Vida de Scalabrini Ortiz*, Ediciones del Mar Dulce, Buenos Aires 1970.

——*Manuel Ugarte: un argentino 'maldito'*, Ediciones del Pensamiento Nacional, Buenos Aires 1981.

Néstor García Canclini, *Hybrid Cultures: Strategies for Entering and Leaving Modernity* [*Culturas híbridas: estrategias para entrar y salir de la modernidad,* 1992], trans. Christopher L. Chiappari and Silvia L. López, University of Minnesota Press, Minneapolis 1995.

Roberto González Echevarría, *The Voice of the Masters: Writing and Authority in Modern Latin American Literature,* University of Texas Press, Austin 1985.

Ángeles González Gamio, *Manuel Gamio: una lucha sin final,* UNAM, Mexico City 1987.

GRAL Institut d'Études Mexicaines-Perpignan, *Intellectuels et état au Mexique au xxe siècle,* Éditions du CNRS, Paris 1979.

——*Champs de pouvoir et de savoir au Mexique,* Éditions du CNRS, Paris 1982.

María Guerra and Ezéquiel Maldonado, eds, *El compromiso del intelectual,* Editorial Nuestro Tiempo, Mexico 1979.

Tulio Halperín Donghi, *Historia de la Universidad de Buenos Aires,* Eudeba, Buenos Aires 1962.

Alastair Hennessy, ed., *Intellectuals in the Twentieth-century Caribbean,* vol. II, *Unity in Variety: The Hispanic and Francophone Caribbean,* Warwick University Caribbean Studies, Macmillan, London and Basingstoke 1992.

Pedro Henríquez Ureña, *A Concise History of Latin American Culture* [*Historia de la cultura en la América Hispánica,* Fondo de Cultura Económica, Mexico City 1947], trans. Gilbert Chase, Pall Mall Press, London 1966.

Juan José Hernández Arregui, *La formación de la conciencia nacional 1930–1960,* Ediciones Hachea, Buenos Aires 1960.

——*Imperialismo y cultura,* Ediciones Hachea, Buenos Aires 1964.

Iván Jaksić and Sol Serrano, 'In the Service of the Nation: The Establishment and Consolidation of the University of Chile, 1842–79', *Hispanic American Historical Review,* 70:1 (February 1990), pp. 139–71.

Noé Jitrik, *Leopoldo Lugones, mito nacional,* Editorial Palestra, Buenos Aires 1960.

William H. Katra, *Contorno: Literary Engagement in Post-Peronist Argentina,* Associated University Presses, London and Toronto 1988.

John King, *Sur: A Study of the Argentine Literary Journal and Its Role in the Development of a Culture, 1931–1970,* Cambridge University Press, Cambridge 1986.

Enrique Krauze, *Caudillos culturales en la Revolución mexicana,* Editorial Siglo XXI, Mexico City 1985.

Daniel C. Levy, *University and Government in Mexico: Autonomy in an Authoritarian System,* Praeger, New York 1980.

——*Higher Education and the State in Latin America: Private Challenges to Public Dominance,* University of Chicago Press, Chicago and London 1986.

Gordon K. Lewis, *Main Currents in Caribbean Thought,* Johns Hopkins University Press, Baltimore and London 1983.

Myron Lichtblau, *Manuel Gálvez*, Twayne Publishers, New York 1972.

Claudio Lomnitz-Adler, *Exits from the Labyrinth: Culture and Ideology in the Mexican National Space*, University of California Press, Berkeley 1992.

Joseph Maier and Richard W. Weatherhead, eds, *The Latin American University*, University of New Mexico Press, Albuquerque 1979 (includes translation of José Luis Romero's article on university reform).

Carlos Mangone and Jorge A. Warley, *Universidad y peronismo (1946–1955)*, Centro Editor de América Latina, Buenos Aires 1984.

Juan Marsal, ed., *El intelectual latinoamericano: un simposio sobre sociología de los intelectuales*, Editorial del Instituto, Buenos Aires 1970.

Jesús Méndez, 'Argentine Intellectuals in the Twentieth Century, 1900–1943', PhD thesis, University of Texas at Austin, 1980.

Doris Meyer, ed., *Lives on the Line: The Testimony of Contemporary Latin American Authors*, University of California Press, Berkeley and Los Angeles 1988.

Richard Morse, 'The Multiverse of Latin American Identity, *c.*1920–*c.*1970', in Leslie Bethell, ed., *Cambridge History of Latin America*, vol. X, *Latin America since 1930: Ideas, Culture and Society*, Cambridge University Press, Cambridge 1995, pp. 1–127. *New World Soundings: Culture and Ideology in the Americas*, Johns Hopkins University Press, Baltimore and London, 1989.

Julio Ortega, *Cultura y modernización en la Lima del 900*, Centro de Estudios para el Desarrollo y la Participación, Lima 1986.

Louis A. Pérez, *José Martí in the United States: The Florida Experience*, Arizona State University Press, Tempe 1995.

Víctor Pérez Petit, *Rodó: su vida – su obra* [1918], Claudio García, Montevideo 1967.

James Petras and Morris Morley, 'The Metamorphosis of Latin America's Intellectuals', in their *US Hegemony under Siege*, Verso, London 1990, pp. 147–56.

Mariano Picón-Salas, *A Cultural History of Spanish America from Conquest to Independence* [1944], trans. Irving Leonard, University of California Press, Berkeley 1962.

Juan Carlos Portantiero, *Estudiantes y política en América Latina 1918–1938*, Siglo Veintiuno, Mexico and Argentina, 2nd edn, 1987.

Jeffrey M. Puryear, *Thinking Politics: Intellectuals and Democracy in Chile, 1973–1988*, Johns Hopkins University Press, Baltimore and London 1994.

Ángel Rama, *La ciudad letrada*, Ediciones del Norte, Hanover, NH 1984. Translated as *The Lettered City*, trans. and ed. John Charles Chasteen, Duke University Press, Durham, USA, and London 1990.

Julio Ramos, *Desencuentros de la modernidad en América Latina: literatura y política en el siglo XX*, Fondo de Cultura Económica, Mexico City 1989.

José Luis Romero, *Latinoamérica: las ciudades y las ideas*, Siglo XXI, Buenos Aires and Mexico City, 4th edn, 1986.

Beatriz Sarlo, *Una modernidad periférica: Buenos Aires 1920 y 1930*, Ediciones Nueva Vision, Buenos Aires 1988.

——*Escenas de la vida posmoderna: intelectuales, arte y videocultura en la Argentina*, Editora Espasa Calpe/Ariel, Buenos Aires 1994.

Henry C. Schmidt, *The Roots of Lo Mexicano: Self and Society in Mexican Thought, 1900–1934*, Texas A&M University Press, College Station and London 1978.

Ofelia Schutte, *Cultural Identity and Social Liberation in Latin American Thought*, State University of New York Press, Albany 1993.

Nicolás Shumway, *The Invention of Argentina*, University of California Press, Berkeley and Oxford 1991.

Silvia Sigal, *Intelectuales y poder en la década del sesenta*, Puntosur Editores, Buenos Aires 1991.

Jesús Silva Herzog, *Una historia de la Universidad de México y sus problemas*, Siglo Veintiuno, Mexico City 1974.

John Skirius, *José Vasconcelos y la cruzada de 1929*, Siglo XXI, Mexico City 1978.

Martin Stabb, *In Quest of Identity*, University of North Carolina Press, 1967.

——*The Dissenting Voice: The New Essay of Spanish America, 1960–1985*, University of Texas Press, Austin 1994.

William Stokes, 'The Drag of the "Pensadores"', in J. W. Higgins and Helmut Schoeck, eds, *Foreign Aid Re-examined*, Public Affairs Press, Washington, DC 1958.

Bernardo Subercaseaux, *Fin de siglo: la época de Balmaceda. Modernización y cultura en Chile*, Editorial Aconcagua, Santiago 1988.

——*Historia, literatura, sociedad: ensayos de hermeneútica cultural*, Ediciones documentas, Santiago 1991.

Volodia Teitelboim, *Neruda: An Intimate Biography*, trans. Beverly J. DeLong-Tonelli, University of Texas Press, Austin 1991.

Oscar Terán, *Nuestros años sesentas: la formación de la nueva izquierda intelectual en la Argentina 1956–1966*, Editores Puntosur, Buenos Aires 1991.

Vicky Unruh, *Latin American Vanguards: The Art of Contentious Encounters*, University of California Press, Berkeley 1994.

Harry E. Vanden, *National Marxism in Latin America: José Carlos Mariátegui's Thought and Politics*, Lynne Rienner, Boulder, CO 1986.

Hugo Verani, ed., *Las vanguardias literarias en Hispanoamérica: manifiestos, proclamas y otros escritos*, Fondo de Cultura Económica, Mexico City, 2nd edn, 1990.

David Viñas, *Apogeo de la oligarquía: literatura argentina y realidad política*, Ediciones Siglo Veinte, Buenos Aires 1975.

Fernando Vizcaino, *Biografía política de Octavio Paz o La razón ardiente*, Editorial Algazara, Málaga 1993.

Richard J. Walter, *Student Politics in Argentina: The University Reform and Its Effects, 1918–1964*, Basic Books, New York and London 1968.

Judith A. Weiss, *Casa de las Américas: An Intellectual Review in the Cuban Revolution*, Estudios de Hispanofila, Chapel Hill, NC 1977.

Ann Wright, 'Intellectuals of an Unheroic Period of Cuban History, 1913–1923: The *Cuba Contemporánea* Group', *Bulletin of Latin American Research*, 7:1 (1988), pp. 109–22.

George Yúdice, Jean Franco and Juan Flores, eds, *On Edge: The Crisis of Contemporary Latin American Culture*, University of Minnesota Press, Minneapolis and London 1992.

Saúl Yurkievich, *A través de la trama: sobre vanguardias literarias y otras concomitancias*, Muchnik, Barcelona 1984.

——*Identidad cultural de Iberoamérica en su literatura*, Alhambra, Madrid 1986.

Gabriel Zaid, *De los libros al poder*, Editorial Grijalbo, Mexico City 1988.

Iris M. Zavala, *Colonialism and Culture: Hispanic Modernisms and the Social Imaginary*, Indiana University Press, Bloomington and Indianapolis 1992.

Leopoldo Zea, *The Latin American Mind* [*Dos etapas del pensamiento en Hispanoamérica*, 1949], trans. James H. Abbott and Lowell Dunham, University of Oklahoma Press, Norman 1963.

Sergio Zermeño, 'Intellectuals and the State in the "Lost Decade"', in Neil Harvey, ed., *Mexico: Dilemmas of Transition*, British Academic Press for the Institute of Latin American Studies, University of London, London and New York 1993, pp. 279–98.

Alberto Zum Felde, *Proceso intelectual del Uruguay y crítica de su literatura*, Editorial Claridad, Montevideo 1941.

Index